Security and De

D1418747

shown below.

Security and Development in Global Politics

A Critical Comparison

JOANNA SPEAR AND PAUL D. WILLIAMS, EDITORS

Georgetown University Press
Washington, DC

Georgetown University Press, Washington, D.C. www.press.georgetown.edu
© 2012 by Georgetown University Press. All rights reserved. No part of this book may be reproduced or utilized in any form or by any means, electronic or mechanical, including photocopying and recording, or by any information storage and retrieval system, without permission in writing from the publisher.

Library of Congress Cataloging-in-Publication Data
Security and development in global politics : a critical comparison / Joanna Spear and
    Paul D. Williams, editors.
        p. cm.
    Includes bibliographical references and index.
    ISBN 978-1-58901-886-0 (pbk. : alk. paper)
    1. Security, International. 2. Economic development. I. Spear, Joanna, 1961–
II. Williams, Paul, 1975–
JZ5588.S42845 2012
338.9—dc23
                                                                            2011035690

♾ This book is printed on acid-free paper meeting the requirements of the American National Standard for Permanence in Paper for Printed Library Materials.

19 18 17 16 15 14 13 12   9 8 7 6 5 4 3 2
First printing

Printed in the United States of America

This volume is dedicated to the memory of Dr. Caroline Thomas, author of the pioneering work on security and development, In Search of Security *(1987).*

Caroline was an initial contributor to our project but ill health prohibited her full participation and eventually stole her away from our discipline.

A great researcher, a clever and inspiring teacher, an incisive examiner, an administrator with sound political instincts and a penchant for "cutting to the chase," she is much missed.

CONTENTS

Acknowledgments ix

List of Illustrations xi

Introduction 1
Joanna Spear and Paul D. Williams

1   Conceptualizing the Security–Development Relationship:
    An Overview of the Debate 7
    Joanna Spear and Paul D. Williams

PART I: AID

2   Aid: A Security Perspective 37
    Bernard Harborne

3   Aid: A Development Perspective 57
    Daniel Morrow

    Aid: Editors' Comments 73
    Joanna Spear and Paul D. Williams

PART II: HUMANITARIAN ASSISTANCE

4   Humanitarian Assistance: A Security Perspective 77
    Robert Maletta with Joanna Spear

5   Humanitarian Assistance: A Development Perspective 97
    Sabina Dewan

    Humanitarian Assistance: Editors' Comments 111
    Joanna Spear and Paul D. Williams

PART III: GOVERNANCE

6   Governance: A Security Perspective 115
    Terrence Lyons

7   Governance: A Development Perspective 131
    Alasdair Bowie

    Governance: Editors' Comments 149
    Joanna Spear and Paul D. Williams

PART IV: HEALTH

8   Health: A Security Perspective   153
George C. Fidas

9   Health: A Development Perspective   171
Julie E. Fischer

Health: Editors' Comments   189
Joanna Spear and Paul D. Williams

PART V: POVERTY

10 Poverty: A Security Perspective   193
Paul D. Williams

11 Poverty: A Development Perspective   209
Inder Sud

Poverty: Editors' Comments   225
Joanna Spear and Paul D. Williams

PART VI: TRADE AND RESOURCES

12 Trade and Resources: A Security Perspective   229
Joanna Spear

13 Trade and Resources: A Development Perspective   247
Raymond Gilpin

Trade and Resources: Editors' Comments   267
Joanna Spear and Paul D. Williams

PART VII: DEMOGRAPHY

14 Demography: A Security Perspective   271
Jack A. Goldstone

15 Demography: A Development Perspective   291
Richard P. Cincotta

Demography: Editors' Comments   311
Joanna Spear and Paul D. Williams

16 Conclusion: The Comparative Conversations between
Security and Development   313
Joanna Spear and Paul D. Williams

Contributors   319

Index   323

ACKNOWLEDGMENTS

We are particularly grateful to the Cumming family for providing the funding for this project on security and development. It is not often in life that anyone gets offered a sum of money to do something important and interesting, and we thank the Cumming family for giving us that opportunity.

We were lucky enough—thanks to the Cumming family—to be able to hold three workshops for this security and development project. These were terrific opportunities to bring together academics and practitioners. The first workshop, in October 2007, was a joint endeavor between the Elliott School at George Washington University and the British Economic and Social Research Council's "New Security Challenges" Program; we thank Stuart Croft for his collaboration to bring over some of the leading British thinkers on these issues. We would also like to thank Lee Ann Fujii for her critical review of the existing literature; this was a helpful springboard for all of our work. The second and third workshops were focused on the chapters for the book, and we would like to thank Beth Cole of the United States Institute of Peace, Karin von Hippel, and Sean Roberts of the International Development Program at the Elliott School for acting as discussants in the third workshop. We are also grateful to David Gow for his help in the early stages of this project.

During the long process from idea to finished volume, we have received valuable help from our program assistants. Dan Trapp helped with the first workshop, and Kaitlin Potter and John Townsend helped with the later two; John also assisted in reading draft chapters. We thank them all.

ILLUSTRATIONS

Figures

5.1 The Political Spectrum of Humanitarians and Their Attitudes Toward Traditional Operating Principles   100

13.1 Trade Tariff Restrictiveness Index   258

14.1 Percent of Population under Fifteen Years Old, 2009   277

15.1 The Demographic Transition Showing Idealized Death Rate and Birth Rate Transitions and Relative Changes in Population That Result   293

15.2 The Successional Sequence of Population Age Structures Experienced by Japan, 1935–2025   295

15.3 The Positions of the Populations of the World's Countries along the Path of the Age-Structural Transition   296

15.4 The Income–Fertility Trajectories of Four East Asian and Four Latin American States   298

Tables

1.1 Conceptualizing the Security–Development Relationship   21

11.1 Numbers and Proportions of Absolute Poor in Developing Countries   211

13.1 Global Trade and Economic Growth   253

13.2 Export Concentration Index   262

14.1 The World's Largest Countries   273

14.2 The Fastest Growing Countries, 2005–2010   274

14.3 Aging and Labor Force Change in Major European and Other Countries, 2009–2050   279

16.1 Conceptualizing the Security–Development Relationship   314

INTRODUCTION

Joanna Spear and Paul D. Williams

Security and development matter; they often involve issues of life and death, and they determine the allocation of truly staggering amounts of the world's resources. Underdevelopment and insecurity are dominating the lives of billions of people. As we complete this book, approximately 1 billion people are undernourished, and roughly one in three human beings exist on less than two dollars a day. At the same time, more than seventy armed conflicts continue to rage, most of them in some of the world's least developed countries.[1]

With statistics like these, it is not surprising that security and development have been so central to the theory and practice of international affairs. Concern is not only stimulated by a humanitarian interest in the fate of others; there are often strong motivations of self-interest at work, such as stopping civil wars before they spread their many problems beyond their country's borders and preventing "ungoverned spaces" from becoming havens for terrorism. In a more positive sense, however, underdevelopment abroad is also a missed opportunity for trade—and therefore further development—at home. Despite these connections, the issue of how security and development relate to each other is a relatively recent preoccupation, one spurred by policymakers trying to deliver solutions to some of the world's most "wicked problems."[2]

Although currently attracting significant attention from policymakers and analysts alike, the relationship between security and development in global politics is still not well understood in either theory or practice. This book intends to improve that understanding by tracking the course of the debate so far and providing a "comparative conversation" between experts within the arenas of security and development. We do this by exploring a set of seven core international issues from the perspectives of experts in both security and development in order to assess the extent to which there really is a "nexus" between these two concepts, and, crucially, whether that nexus should be encouraged or resisted.

In the debate so far, claims about a nexus between the two arenas have revolved around issues relating to unconventional armed conflict (i.e., insurgencies), so-called failed states, and—particularly outside of the United States—the concept of "human security." Even in these issue areas, where the links between security and development seem real and desirable, we are skeptical of the claims of an almost automatic nexus. This becomes more apparent if the relationship between the two arenas is considered across a wider set of issues than armed conflicts and counterinsurgency responses. The following chapters thus examine security and development perspectives on seven core issues: aid, humanitarian assistance, governance, health, poverty, trade and resources, and demography. We start by considering the core issues for which claims have regularly been made for a security–development nexus but then consider others where the relationship has received much less attention. By mapping the security–development relationships across a more comprehensive set of issues, the implications of combining the two arenas become clearer.

ARENAS AND CONTESTATION

Throughout this volume we deliberately refer to security and development as "arenas." This is to signal an important but often forgotten starting point for debate, namely, that there is no sense of common agreement *within* the arenas of security and development, let alone between them. We also want to avoid any implication that there is a monolithic group of actors within each arena, or that there is agreement over core issues, methods, and policies. Indeed, one common feature of both arenas is the increasing diversity of actors, issues, and approaches. Viewing security and development as arenas helps illuminate the various contours of contestation within each of them; there are disagreements between theorists, between theorists and practitioners, and between practitioners.

More specifically, we think that security and development are best understood as arenas of thought and practice obliquely structured around a core set of questions that produce a range of different answers. Among the fundamental questions that underlie this volume are the following: What does security/development mean? What referent object(s) should security/development prioritize: people? groups? states? regions? or the whole planet? What counts as a security/development issue? What principles should guide security/development policies? How might security/development be promoted in practical terms?

THE FOCUS AND CONTRIBUTION OF THIS BOOK

One interesting point of commonality across most of the existing studies on security and development is the extent to which their conceptualization of the relationship centers on the issue of armed conflict and the so-called "failed state" agenda. This has often generated a policy-led demand that the two arenas be combined in order to deal with the practical problems that the world's governments and organizations are grappling with. In contrast, our volume does not limit the security–development relationship to a conflict context but also extends the analysis to other issue areas such as health, poverty, and demography. Indeed, we feel that concentrating on activities in war zones and the failed state agenda provides only a partial account of the security–development relationship and misses some important points as a result.

The volume's examination of security and development issues beyond the focus on armed conflict leads us to offer a more nuanced answer to the question of whether the two arenas should be combined. In many situations the consequence of combination is that development loses out to security concerns; this is, in our opinion, a significant problem. We are therefore measured in our conclusions about the appropriate relationship and about what we see as the potential for effective synergies.

CONTRIBUTORS

Our intention through this volume is not only to discuss the two substantive arenas of security and development but also to encourage dialogue between academics/analysts and policymakers/practitioners. With this in mind, we brought together experts from different parts of the two arenas. Some of us are practitioners either in international institutions or in nongovernmental organizations (NGO), some of us teach and research, and some of us work on policy issues in think tanks. Most of us are currently based in Washington, DC (although three of us are British), and we have all done significant fieldwork as academics, practitioners, or both. We were drawn together by acknowledgment of the huge security and development challenges that are facing the world and by a desire to better understand how these two important arenas look at core issues and how this understanding can inform and improve policymaking.

CONCEPTUAL SCHEME AND METHODOLOGY

Our book employs a unique conceptual scheme designed to illuminate comparisons and contrasts between the ways that the security and development arenas look at and act upon a core set of issues. Our methodology involves some deliberate matchmaking; bringing together people who work on the same core issue but who do so from the distinct perspective of either security or development. For each of our core issues we have a chapter written by a development expert and a chapter from a security expert. Each pair of chapters is followed by short editors' commentaries that highlight the commonalities and contrasts between them. Together, these provide the reader with a clear overview of the points of divergence and convergence of the two arenas on the issue in question.

Contributors were given a deceptively simple task: to explain what their arena has been preoccupied with in relation to that particular issue. Our aim in asking this question was to elicit a true sense of what the security and development arenas have been focused on. We deliberately did not give our paired authors an agenda to consider, as we felt this would artificially impose a congruity where one might not exist—although this means that the paired chapters sometimes discuss quite different issues. Nor did we determine what level of analysis they should work at, which means that there is variation in this respect as well. We see the existence of such differences as interesting and analytically illuminating rather than as a problem because we wanted to tease out both similarities and contrasts in order to make a more systematic contribution to the growing literature on the security–development relationship. This structure enables us to identify where the security and development arenas converge and diverge, to look for synergies, and to identify ways in which the arenas may be working against (as well as with) each other. As a consequence, this structure illuminates both perils and opportunities in bringing security and development together.

The first chapter in this volume, by Spear and Williams, seeks first to make explicit key conceptual characteristics and political functions of security and development. It then reviews the existing literature on security and development, considering not just academic studies but also work by practitioners and relevant work emerging across the full gamut of the two arenas.

The next two chapters consider our first core issue area, aid. In the chapter written from a security perspective, Harborne considers the recent policy convergence between aid and security but is skeptical of the extent to which this has been successful in practice. In the chapter discussing aid from a development perspective, Morrow regards aid as having *always* been dominated by security concerns and priorities. He focuses on the current priority, the link between aid and statebuilding.

The second set of chapters is focused on the core issue of humanitarian assistance. There is some congruence between the security and development arenas on the issue but also different points of emphasis and attention. In the chapter from a security perspective, Maletta and Spear examine how the security arena has increasingly used humanitarian assistance for instrumental purposes. They note in particular the tensions in the triangular relationship between the goals—and between the communities conducting—statebuilding, counterinsurgency, and humanitarianism. The chapter concludes with a case study of Somalia that shows how the United Nations has pursued a political–security agenda through its use of humanitarian assistance for statebuilding. Dewan's chapter, written from a development perspective, considers the "relief-to-development" continuum. Whereas these were once distinct phases, they are increasingly melding together due to situations on the ground and the actors involved who conduct both humanitarian assistance and long-term development.

Our third set of chapters considers the core issue of governance. Here, despite the fact that both arenas have common concerns about failed states, there are significantly different agendas. In the chapter from a security perspective, Lyons focuses on the way in which mechanisms of governance have played crucial roles in the periods before, during, and after contemporary civil wars. He places particular emphasis on the way in which the security arena has sought to use the mechanism of democratic elections to end conflicts and enable withdrawal of foreign forces. By contrast, Bowie's chapter, written from a development perspective, sees the most important dimension of governance as the establishment and maintenance of institutions that can authoritatively allocate resources.

The fourth set of chapters is focused on health. While the two chapters agree on the nature and definition of contemporary health challenges and the need to pay greater attention to them, they have very different views on the best way to generate such attention. In the chapter written from a security perspective, Fidas is positive about the way that health challenges have been securitized, considering that the issues deserve the attention and resources that such securitization brings. Not surprisingly, Fischer's chapter, written from a development perspective, is concerned about the consequences of securitization and the shift in the level of caring away from the individual to primarily considering national and regional (security) dimensions of health.

The next set of chapters considers the key issue of poverty; here there are significantly different agendas between the two arenas. In the chapter from a security perspective, Williams considers the debate over different approaches to defining poverty before going on to examine the ways in which poverty has been perceived as posing a threat to security at the individual, state, and global levels. He emphasizes the extent to which thinking of poverty in terms of marginalization and exclusion has had more important ramifications in the security arena than a focus on economic measures. Sud's chapter, from a development perspective, also discusses the preoccupation with definitions of poverty but illustrates the extent to which the development arena's major focus has remained on the effort to stimulate and sustain economic growth.

The penultimate set of chapters is concerned with the issues of trade and resources. Here there is significance divergence between the agendas of the security and development arenas. In the chapter from a security perspective, Spear focuses on three dimensions of trade and resource issues that preoccupy the security arena: combatants who fund their activities through trade in resources, malevolent transnational actors who profit from the trade system, and US concerns with the way that China is using trade to promote its geostrategic influence. Gilpin's chapter, from a development perspective, displays a completely different focus: how to make trade function most effectively—and without distortions—in order to enable economic development.

The final set of chapters considers demography. Here the two chapters demonstrate a high degree of agreement over data but real differences over what matters. For Goldstone, working from a security perspective, the key issues are the ways in which global demographic trends will magnify some of the transnational problems that the security arena is already dealing with, such as disease spread, humanitarian disasters, and illicit trafficking in goods and people. Whereas Goldstone focuses on six distinct demographic trends, Cincotta, working from a development perspective, identifies a new, focused development agenda concerning "demographic cresting" whereby states (primarily in the West but also China) will contain growing numbers of old people who will not produce resources but will consume them. These graying populations will decrease economic growth and prosperity.

In the concluding chapter, Spear and Williams return to the question of the relationship between the security and development arenas. They conclude that the relationship is best described not as a nexus but as "selectively co-constitutive," meaning that there are points of both divergence and convergence that defy easy labels but that reflect the many actors, processes, and issues in each arena.

Notes

1. These figures come from "The State of Food Insecurity in the World," *Food and Agriculture Organization of the United Nations*, www.fao.org/publications/sofi/en/; *The World Development Report 2008* (Washington, DC: World Bank, 2008); and the Uppsala Conflict Data Program, *Department of Peace and Conflict Research*, accessed January 18, 2011, www.pcr.uu.se/research/ucdp/.

2. This term refers to complex, interrelated problems involving multiple stakeholders that are difficult to define, defy optimal solutions, and are resistant to linear methods because each attempt to create a solution changes the problem. Horst Rittel and Melvin Webber, "Dilemmas in a General Theory of Planning," *Policy Sciences* 4 (1973): 155–59.

Chapter 1

CONCEPTUALIZING THE SECURITY–DEVELOPMENT RELATIONSHIP: AN OVERVIEW OF THE DEBATE

Joanna Spear and Paul D. Williams

The "nexus" between security and development has become a hot topic for policy-makers and analysts keen to solve the problems associated with "failed," "fragile," and "at risk" states; postconflict reconstruction and peacebuilding; and waging effective counterinsurgency campaigns. The 2006 US National Security Strategy, for example, argued that "development reinforces diplomacy and defense, reducing long-term threats to our national security by helping to build stable, prosperous, and peaceful societies."[1] In the 2010 version, development was conceived as "a strategic, economic, and moral imperative" in US national security.[2] In similar fashion, the United Kingdom's first-ever National Security Strategy stated that "it is wrong to talk of a choice between security and economic development, or security and good governance."[3] At the African Union, heads of state and government declared that one of the principles underlying their proposed Common African Defence and Security Policy was "the fundamental link and symbiotic relationship that exists between security, stability, human security, development and cooperation."[4] At the United Nations (UN), Secretary-General Kofi Annan concluded that "in an increasingly interconnected world, progress in the areas of development, security and human rights must go hand in hand. There will be no development without security and no security without development. And both development and security also depend on respect for human rights and the rule of law."[5] This policy concern with bringing the two arenas together is also found in the writing on human security, which encompasses concepts that were traditionally development concerns, such as poverty and access to food and water. Thus, the relationship between security and development is a priority for policymakers in a number of ways.

These approaches, and many others like them from around the world, assume that fusing security and development is desirable and will produce positive outcomes. This book challenges these easy assumptions by examining the varied and complex relationships between the arenas of security and development in the core areas of aid, humanitarian assistance, governance, health, poverty, trade and resources, and demographics. The purpose of this chapter is twofold: first, to highlight some of the significant characteristics and political functions of the concepts of security and development, and second, to provide an overview of the different strands of literature that have explored the security–development relationship.

KEY CHARACTERISTICS OF TWO CONTESTED CONCEPTS

As concepts, security and development display several important characteristics; as political practices, they serve a range of functions for a variety of different actors. This section briefly elaborates on these functions and characteristics because, although often forgotten or ignored, they are the essential context, and they help explain the content of much of the existing literature on the so-called security–development nexus.

Functions: Political Values

Security and development are important political values. That is, they play significant roles in determining who gets what, when, and how (to borrow Harold Lasswell's famous definition of politics).[6] But as values they also have an aspirational quality that goes beyond mere physical survival. To be secure or developed, people need to feel that they are able to fulfill their cherished values. These may be hard to define and may differ across individuals and groups, but the attempt to promote them preoccupies a great deal of every society's political processes. They may also be in conflict with those values held by other individuals or groups; hence, much of the conceptual and practical debate is about how to resolve competing security and development agendas.

Functions: Justificatory Devices

As political values, security and development are both regularly used to legitimize action and are deployed instrumentally as justificatory devices. In the security realm, for example, the aftermath of the 9/11 attacks saw many countries place constraints upon civil liberties and justify them in the name of national security. Similarly, the push for further liberalization of world trade through the current round of World Trade Organization negotiations has been justified as a stimulus to economic development for all when it will clearly generate new winners and losers. The two values are also used to justify spending.

Functions: Allocation of Resources

Both security and development represent political choices; money spent on one cannot be spent elsewhere. Moreover, within each arena numerous issues compete for attention and funding, with different issues gaining prominence at different times. These concerns are reflected in the flows of international development assistance. In geographic terms, after the Cold War, much of the aid that had routinely flowed to Africa and Asia was diverted into the transition states of the former Soviet bloc. Moreover, in thematic terms, as the development agenda grew to encompass a wider range of issues (governance, education, migration, security sector reform, etc.) so the competition between issues to secure funding intensified, just as official development assistance levels were declining.

Although in most states the security "pie" is generally much larger, such zero-sum thinking has also prevailed at times. For example, in the last five years a debate has occurred within the Pentagon over what types of weapons systems to procure, advanced fighter aircraft such as the F-22 (vital for fighting a major war against a peer competitor) or additional armored land systems for use in environments such as Afghanistan and Iraq. After several years of internal sparring, the Department of Defense decided against the extremely impressive—but extremely expensive—F-22.[7]

A concern evident in the development arena is that increasing convergence with the security arena will lead to development resources remaining static or diminishing as security actors gain a greater slice of the budget.[8] This applies especially in countries where there is a deep reluctance to cut national security budgets but where politicians view cutting back on development aid as a soft target. Indeed, in many parts of the world there is generally much less dispute over military budgets and other clearly security-related spending than there is over monies for international development assistance. This is ironic given that it is difficult to draw a causal connection between monies spent on troops and weapons and security outcomes. This mindset is partly attributable to the way in which security is perceived as a necessity whereas enhancing the development of foreigners is often regarded as more of a political choice or even luxury. Simply put, security is about "us" but development is about "them." This perception appears particularly entrenched within successive US administrations, which continue to spend as much on defense as the rest of the world combined yet have often been among the least generous donors within the Organisation for Economic Co-operation and Development (OECD) in terms of the percentage of gross national income (GNI) devoted to official development assistance.[9]

Functions: The Theory–Praxis Relationship

Security and development are not merely intellectual pursuits; these salient issues affect real people, often in matters of life and death. This has encouraged a tendency within both arenas to generate fast conversions of theory into practice (and vice versa). Thus, while the academic discipline might be in the early stages of debating a new theory or idea, the policy community may already be trying to implement it. Similarly, academics who observe novel practices and techniques in the field are quick to try and refine theories accordingly. This is one of the reasons for contestation in both arenas—academia critiquing ideas that have already been turned into policy by practitioners. In the security arena, for example, although the idea that "democracies do not fight one another" has a long lineage going back to Immanuel Kant, it received renewed attention when written about by Michael Doyle in the 1980s.[10] The idea was subsequently taken up by the Clinton administration even as security and democracy specialists were picking apart the very roots of the idea.[11] In development, the case of postwar theory creation is illustrative of another aspect of the theory–praxis relationship. In the aftermath of World War II, the swift success of the US-funded Marshall Plan in rebuilding European economies caught the attention of a number of economists who wished to bring that success to development in other regions. Many of these early development economists worked in policy institutions such as the United Nations and World Bank and sought to replicate the success of the Marshall Plan.[12] This, then, was a case of theory following practice and influencing further practice. Unfortunately, the model proved harder to replicate elsewhere than they had anticipated, which led to others positing different theories on how to spur and sustain development.

Characteristics: Essentially Contested Concepts

Security and development are good examples of what social scientists call "essentially contested concepts."[13] Like other important concepts such as justice, freedom, and peace, the ideological element within them generates unsolvable debates over their specific meaning and application because it "renders empirical evidence irrelevant as a means of resolving the dispute."[14] Essentially contested concepts are thus understood to delineate an area of concern rather than a particular condition. They can be defined precisely only in relation to specific cases. This explains why security and development are often defined in general, negative terms as being about the alleviation of threat and the alleviation of need, respectively. But what these concepts mean in more positive terms is contingent: the concepts can be defined only with reference to real people and places at particular points in history. Blanket statements about the relationship between these two arenas and the consequences of combining them can thus be dangerously misleading.

Characteristics: Stovepipes and Tunnel Vision

Part of the problem with the contemporary debate about the security–development relationship is that these fundamental points about contestation and contingency are often forgotten. Those in the development arena understand the disputes in their own arena but not those of the security arena, and vice versa. Although security and development experts sometimes use the same vocabulary, work on the same issues, and increasingly work in the same geographical spaces, they often continue to speak past each other because each often assumes that the other arena is unproblematic; that the other is working with clearly understood agents, priorities, referents, causal relationships, and effective bureaucracies; and that the other has a track record of practical success. Indeed, specialists in each area sometimes see the other as possessing new and improved tools to adapt to tackle the problems that they face without necessarily understanding the difficulties that need to be overcome or understanding the mixed records of each approach. On close inspection, security and development experts often begin from different starting points, see different worlds and different problems, want different sorts of outcomes, and, hence, use different approaches and tools to overcome challenges. Unless these differences are understood, faced, and in some sense dealt with, policies cannot possibly achieve what is expected of them and may have unexpected (and undesirable) consequences.

Characteristics: Derivative and Relative Concepts

Security and development are also what social scientists refer to as derivative and relative concepts. To say that security and development are derivative concepts means that "different attitudes and behaviour associated with [them] are traceable to different political theories."[15] In other words, how one thinks about security and development depends on the assumptions one holds about human nature and about the significant units, structures, and processes that characterize world politics. Policy debates about security and development therefore represent an "epiphenomenon of political theory"—although this rarely gets explicitly acknowledged.[16] Describing security and development as relative concepts means that it is not clear what absolute security or total development would look like or if such conditions would be desirable even if they were possible. Security and development are matters of degree. The tendency is thus to view them in relational terms, that is, relative to the circumstances of other actors.

Characteristics: (Mis)Perception

As contested, derivative, and relative concepts, perceptions—beliefs, images, and intentions—are crucial to defining and understanding both security and development because different people and societies pursue diverse values, have different tolerances of danger (i.e., resiliency), and possess unequal abilities to cope with development challenges. For example, in the case of development, what one group perceives it needs to cope with adverse circumstances may vary substantially from another group. This sometimes manifests in a debate over what constitutes poverty and whether it should be thought of in absolute or relative terms (see chapters 10 and 11 in this volume). In the security arena we see remarkably different levels of tolerance for risk, dictated by peoples' lived experiences. For those living cozy lives in the West, it is hard to imagine how people continue to function when subject to regular bombings (Pakistan or Israel), constant civil war (Somalia or Colombia), or extreme levels of gun violence (Juarez, Mexico). In these cases, people continue to function to the best of their abilities, having incorporated these high risks into their perceptual frameworks and rendered them in some way manageable.

Characteristics: Sovereignty's Shadow

In an international society composed of independent states, it is not surprising that the contemporary theory and practice of security and development have been heavily influenced by the concept of sovereignty, which has set many of the "rules of the game" within which actors in both arenas function. In terms of security, sovereignty grants legal equality and independence to the world's states and gives them the right to establish a legitimate monopoly over the means of violence within their territory. It has also led to a powerful strain of thinking within international relations that threats to security come from outside the state, whereas there is a realm of order and stability inside its borders, although this is an idea disputed by anthropologists and sociologists. In terms of development, sovereignty gives states the right to establish the relevant policies and practices free from outside interference. For example, after Cyclone Nargis hit Burma/Myanmar in May 2008, the Junta was able to obstruct attempts by NGOs and other states to provide relief to the victims on the grounds that any forcible delivery of aid would represent an unacceptable breach of Burmese sovereignty.

Sovereignty's importance encouraged analysts and especially practitioners to approach security and development as ideas that operated primarily at the state level. Consequently, it was states that were conceived as the central referent objects and governments that were supposed to act as the key agents, designing and implementing policies to achieve these goals or to set the balance between them. However, this focus on the state as the level of analysis and arena for action has been challenged both theoretically and practically. Theoretically, as is discussed below, analysts have questioned whether states should form either the primary referent object or agent for development and security policies.[17] In policy terms, many contemporary security threats do not respect borders (drugs, bugs, thugs), and the utility of working at a state level has been severely challenged by the processes of globalization and rising transnational threats, which have intensified dramatically since the 1980s.[18] The shift in development circles has been from growth maximization for state- and institution-building toward poverty-reduction strategies and attempts to empower individuals and groups within civil society.[19] Thus, in both the security and development arenas, greater emphasis has been placed on working directly with individuals and nonstate actors and thinking about challenges across multiple levels of analysis. These policy developments are also helping to push the two arenas toward paradigm shifts.

Characteristics: Contestation and Paradigm Shift

Historically, it is possible to trace how scholarship and political practice in both arenas have been dominated by particular assumptions and approaches at different times. At least in the Western literature and practice, the security and development arenas have evolved in similar ways through a number of phases—or what Thomas Kuhn called "paradigms"—where one approach to thinking and practice dominated for a period but was then challenged and modified or replaced in "paradigm shift."[20] In each case, the dominant theories and ideas were reflections of their time and the preoccupations of the hour.[21] During the Cold War both the security and development arenas were in the grip of statist paradigms—that is, ideas that saw the state as the key referent object—but now these are being challenged.

In the contemporary period the arenas of security and development are both in what Kuhn called "a state of crisis," in which old paradigms do not fit all the data and reality; a new paradigm has been formed, but it is not accepted by all and there is a battle between the old and new paradigms. The battles are fought with both empirical data and theoretical argument. The usual expectation is that "crisis" is followed by "paradigm shift" (although Kuhn never actually used that term). The battle in security is between the traditional statist paradigm that makes the security of the state the priority and a new paradigm, human security, which prioritizes the individual and acknowledges a wider range of threats than just armed conflict. These contrasting approaches thus have different referent objects (states or individuals) and work at different levels of analysis. In development the paradigm shift was initiated by the failure of some theories and their practice to create sustainable economic growth. As with security, this has led to a shift in the referent object and level of analysis away from the state. Two alternative approaches subsequently emerged, one focusing on markets as the referent object and the other on individuals. Neoliberalism saw the market as the way to ensure development and focused on privatization and liberalization of the economy as the route to economic growth. However, as Gerd Junne noted, "functioning markets suppose functioning states."[22] Given the fragility and dysfunction of many states, the market approach to development has not delivered in all circumstances. Consequently, we have seen a trend back toward attempting to improve the performance of the state through good governance in order to facilitate market activity (an example of paradigm modification). Another alternative to the statist development paradigm makes the individual the referent object (for example, through poverty-reduction strategies and microfinance initiatives that work from the bottom upward). There are in development, therefore, two alternative approaches to the statist paradigm vying for dominance.

Characteristics: The Expansion of Security Studies

Particularly since the end of the Cold War, the academic discipline of security studies has diversified to encompass a wide range of new theoretical perspectives and issues. This expansion reflects a broadening and deepening of the security agenda derived from a combination of developments related to the disposition of material power in world politics, innovations in knowledge and technology, significant events, the prevailing construction of academic and political debates, and the changing configurations of wealth and institutional dynamics within the discipline.[23] By deepening, analysts refer to the different referent objects of security that are now considered important both above and below the traditional focus on the state (e.g., human beings, social groups, ethnic groups, regions, civilizations, planet earth). By broadening, analysts mean a focus on sectoral issue areas beyond the use of military force (e.g., economic security, environmental security, societal security, cyber security). This expansion of both the referents and the sectors in security studies has been the subject of heated debate between the old and new paradigms.[24]

This expansion of security studies spurred several significant developments. In policy terms, arguably the main innovation was the growing call for "human security" to be given a central place in academia and in the foreign policies of states and international organizations.[25] The catalytic document was the UN Development Programme's (UNDP) 1994 *Human Development Report*, which sought to engineer a paradigm shift away from states and onto people and the problems they face. The UNDP's conception of "human security" encompassed two main aspects: "safety from such chronic threats as hunger, disease and repression" and "protection from sudden and hurtful disruptions in the pattern of daily life—whether in homes, in jobs or in communities." These are often summarized (following Maslow) as being about freedom from fear and freedom from want.[26] In more detailed terms, the UNDP identified seven dimensions of human security:

- Economic security: Requires either an assured basic income or some publicly financed safety net.

- Food security: All people at all times have both physical and economic access to basic food.
- Health security: Requires access to effective health care systems.
- Environmental security: Human beings require a healthy physical environment.
- Personal security: Security from physical violence.
- Community security: Most people derive their security from membership of groups that can provide a reassuring set of values.
- Political security: Refers to people's right to live in a society that honors their basic human rights.[27]

While this idea has been influential in a range of international organizations, it has also been subject to significant criticism.[28] Arguably, the most important point that has emerged concerns the most appropriate referent object of security. Despite popular political fashions that frame the debate as a decision to prioritize either states or individuals, it is important to remember that the relationship between individuals and collectivities has always been at the heart of security studies and should remain so.[29] Hence, while a preoccupation with state security has certainly been part of the problem, ignoring the important roles played by some states or other forms of political collectivities would also be problematic.

In conceptual terms, however, the major development—at least across much of Europe—was the notion of "securitization." Developed during the early 1990s by Ole Wæver, securitization captured the idea that security issues or threats do not simply exist objectively "out there" but are constructed discursively by powerful actors. Security issues were constructed through "speech acts" wherein "the utterance *itself is* the act. By saying it, something is done (as in betting, giving a promise, naming a ship)."[30] The successful securitization of an issue, however, required a two-stage process. In the first stage, the actor in question had "to present an issue as urgent and existential, as so important that it should not be exposed to the normal haggling of politics but should be dealt with decisively by top leaders prior to other issues."[31] This would usually require breaking existing rules or adopting some kind of emergency remedial action. In the second stage, a relevant audience had to agree to this move and accept as legitimate the countermeasures proposed to meet the threat at hand. Securitization only occurs if the initial securitizing move is accepted by the relevant audience.

This approach has been subjected to a wide range of critiques.[32] For our purposes, however, it is enough to note that the concept of securitization allows us to see how different phenomena—external invasions, environmental degradation, climate change, infectious pandemics, genocide, and so on—can get framed as "national security" issues. For Wæver, the central political problem was that securitization brought with it certain modes of thought and action. Specifically, it meant issues tended to get framed in militaristic and "us versus them" terms that might be unhelpful for overcoming challenges in a variety of areas. As a result, the practical goal should be to "desecuritize" issues by taking them out of the realm of security and bringing them back into the usual haggling associated with what Wæver and his colleagues called "normal politics."[33]

In the world of policy, as Robin Luckham observed, this expansion of the concept of security has led to security practitioners becoming engrossed in development issues.[34] Not only has this raised difficult practical challenges for the militaries in question, it has also generated a chorus of opposition among development experts who warn that when lines between military activities and development initiatives are blurred, the lives of development workers are endangered.

As the operations in Afghanistan and Iraq have shown, the lack of civilian capacity and the dangers for civilians of working in the field has meant that military forces (or militarized contractors) have shouldered the majority of the activity that would usually be called "development work." Although the aim of the leading governments has been to increase the percentage of civilians involved in such operations, this has proved to be challenging. In the meantime, the militaries have been learning to set up markets, build and run schools, dig wells, and so on, in order to try and complete their mission (see the chapters by Harborne; Maletta and Spear; and Dewan). In some circles this has generated unease about the consequences for readiness, the loss of core fighting skills, and the weakening of claims for expensive defense systems, all of which could result from this "developmentalization" of the military. This was exemplified by Condoleezza Rice's view that US armed forces should not be engaged in social work abroad, or as she put it with reference to the Balkans, "We don't need to have the 82nd Airborne escorting kids to kindergarten."[35]

Characteristics: Core Problems and Convergent Agendas

In both the security and development arenas, contemporary scholars and practitioners continue to struggle with some long-running problems. For security specialists, the central fear remains the same—armed conflict—but the problem set has shifted from a preoccupation with major interstate war to a growing concern about intrastate war and transnational threats such as violent organized crime groups. To those trying to overthrow the statist security paradigm, the concern is to ensure that a wider range of threats are considered. For those in the field of development, the primary problem remains the same: underdevelopment. So does the central puzzle: how to stimulate development. The answers to this problem and the techniques deployed, however, have shifted over time and continue to alter. One of the most interesting evolutions in development thinking is the various phases of seeing the state either as a facilitator of development or as the central impediment to it.[36]

Particularly after the 9/11 terrorist attacks on the United States, there has been significant convergence around the problem of so-called fragile and failed states.[37] For both security and development specialists, states that failed to exercise juridical and empirical sovereignty—the ability to control the means of violence within their territory and to exercise legitimate authority in order to provide some degree of welfare to their citizens—became a core problem that required both sets of expertise. However, as Gerd Junne has pointed out, even when focused on the same issue, the security and development arenas see different dimensions of the problem; for security, it is the risk of terrorists operating from the failed state; for development, it is the state's inability to provide for all citizens.[38] With the common focus on failed and failing states, security and development specialists became concerned with what were traditionally considered the core issues of the other. Thus, those in the security arena now worry about underdevelopment as a potential driver of terrorism and conflict, and those in the development arena recognize the need for a secure state and an absence of warfare as a platform for sustainable development and have tactical worries about securing the delivery of assistance in areas of conflict. Despite these convergences, however, as we argue through this volume, much in the security and development arenas remains focused on distinct issues and approaches.

Characteristics: Timelines

One clear point of contrast between the security and development arenas concerns the timelines they routinely deal with. In the development arena, after an initial flush of enthusiasm that development was going to be easily achieved elsewhere as it had been in Europe, there has been a considerable downgrading of expectations of success. In the more sober contemporary assessments of the chances for development, it is expected to be a long process, often taking two generations (i.e., up to fifty years). For the security arena, timelines are much more immediate; it has to be achieved soon, before the enemy can bring a weapons system online, or to ensure that an enemy cannot preempt you.

The challenge of different timelines becomes apparent when examining the convergent agendas, noted earlier. In Afghanistan and Iraq, militaries have taken on projects that can be swiftly completed with an expectation that they will have lasting development value. They have often been disappointed. In the same theaters, policymakers have been disappointed that more traditional development work (being done by development actors) is not leading to the swift payoffs for which they had hoped. Development actors in Afghanistan and Iraq are frustrated that they are being expected to achieve development outcomes—which usually take decades to achieve—in double-quick time. The incompatibility of timelines is a major source of tension in dealing with the challenges posed by failed and failing states.

Characteristics: Expertise

The significance of the issues at stake is reflected in the way expertise and professional credentials are deployed in the security and development arenas. Both have established "barriers to entry" for nonexperts and both jealously guard whose opinion should be taken seriously. One dimension of this issue is geopolitical; that is, the concepts of security and development have been most heavily influenced by academics and practitioners in the global "North" and then often practiced in the "South," usually with little, narrow, or no consultation with local actors. Other widely debated dimensions include the roles of gender, class, race, ethnocentrism, and even anthropomorphism in the construction of knowledge about security and development. Thus, the "legitimate" voices in these debates have always been somewhat limited—although there are periodic assaults on the elitism that comes with this.[39] Whose voices get heard also connects to the dominance of certain paradigms; as there are now more voices in both arenas, the traditional statist paradigms are under greater assault.

One way in which new actors have influenced theory and practice is by changing the dominant discourse or discourses surrounding particular issues. For example, when landmines were seen only as a security issue (a means to hold territory and repel invasion), there was a very narrow group of people—really just the military—who were considered legitimate voices on the issue. However, when landmines were also defined as a medical and development issue (initially by Vietnam Veterans of America, an NGO composed of former military and therefore in some senses a legitimate actor), this opened the door to new voices, such as victims of mines, medical professionals, and so on. Working with sympathetic governments—and some military players who doubted the necessity and efficacy of landmines—these new voices influenced the agenda and led to lasting change through the Ottawa Convention.[40] In the development arena, some of the new voices are actually coming from the military, not just as an implementing agent but also as a source of development funding. Other new voices include new nonstate donors such as the Gates Foundation, and new state donors such as China and India who do not necessarily approach development in the same way as others already in the arena. In these cases money has been the key to making them a legitimate part of the discourse!

Some actors who had traditionally worked on one type of issue have become increasingly engaged in new areas and developed novel skill sets. The European Union, for example, began developing its role in crisis management and peacebuilding.[41] But this opening up went only so far, for the voices in this new wider debate still tended to be "elites" (albeit a wider range of elites than during the Cold War years), came primarily from the "North," and often still sought to impose solutions on the "South."[42] In some senses, therefore, there has been a "democratization" of the two arenas, with actors outside the usual states and international organizations making valuable contributions in understanding, assessing, policymaking, and implementing. This addition of new actors has also had an effect on the existing statist security and development paradigms and helped to bring in new approaches and challenges to old ways of thinking.

Characteristics: Measurement and Results

Another characteristic of both arenas is the extent to which they are measurement cultures wherein academics and practitioners try to gauge the levels of security and development. It has been common to measure security, for instance, in terms of possession of armed forces and weapons.[43] During the Cold War this measurement was carried out in quasi-scientific terms, completing "net assessments" and comparing nuclear throw-weights and numbers of troops, tanks, and bombers. However, the military capacity that a state possesses is only one dimension of power and tells us very little about intentions. Nor is it always a reliable guide when looking at security outcomes; witness, for example, the asymmetric attacks of 9/11 or the failure of the (strong) Israeli state against (apparently weak) nonstate groups such as Hezbollah in Lebanon in 2006. Another example of the measurement culture is the growing number of institutions engaged in developing indices to measure levels of state failure, fragility, and weakness.[44]

Measurement has also been a core feature of the theory and practice of development.[45] Part of the impulse here is to see that the resources being invested are producing the desired results.[46] In development, there are also cases where the quantitative measures used are not a good guide to outcomes. For example, aid to a state or region does not automatically translate into equal development outcomes—far from it, in fact. One recent African participant in this debate over aid effectiveness attracted significant media attention when she asserted that "in the past fifty years, more than $1 trillion in development-related aid has been transferred from rich countries to Africa. Has this assistance improved the lives of Africans? No. In fact, across the continent, the recipients of this aid are not better off as a result of it, but worse—much worse."[47] The response to this attack from some prominent development experts was little short of incandescent anger.[48] At the level of practice, concerns about the ability of aid to actually deliver development produced the search for and implementation of new approaches at the micro level (e.g., microfinance schemes), the state level (e.g., the US government's Millennium Challenge Corporation, which works with states that are potential development "winners"), and at the structural level (e.g., attempts at further World Trade Organization progress in creating a freer trading system).

We are now seeing a concerted global attempt to measure progress in development, and thus encourage more action, through the Millennium Development Goals (MDG)—eight goals to be achieved by 2015 in relation to poverty and hunger, education, gender equality, child health, maternal health, HIV/AIDS, environmental sustainability, and global partnerships. These MDGs were set through the UN system and represent the most ambitious attempt yet seen to measure—and spur—progress. But the goals are not uncontroversial. Not only are they silent on the security dimensions of global politics (i.e., here the security–development nexus is conspicuous only for its absence) but, to the disappointment of those who advocate a "rights-based approach to development," the MDGs also ignore issues such as justice, torture, genocide prevention, and so on.[49]

At the operational level, where security and development come together, the measurement discourse replicates whichever field's experts are involved. Thus, in the case of the US military's Commander's Emergency Response Program (CERP), funds for urgent humanitarian relief and reconstruction in Iraq and Afghanistan, a Governmental Accountability Office (GAO) report noted five years after the program was started that "no performance metrics exist for CERP. . . . Without performance measures or indicators, MNC-I and DOD do not have the necessary data to assess the results or outcomes of the CERP projects."[50] By contrast, projects funded by the US Agency for International Development (USAID) in the same countries have been subjected to their standard processes of measurement and evaluation, which means they have been much less nimble but more is known about their efficacy.

One ploy used by development advocates to get around this obvious disparity in interrogation is to try to define their problem as a threat to security both to access greater resources and to escape the worst of the measurement culture. As was discussed earlier, however, the tactic of "securitizing" development issues to gain funding can have negative consequences.

To summarize, security and development have a number of comparable and contrasting functions and characteristics that are of vital importance. They are rarely explicitly discussed in the literature to be examined in the next section, but they are important underlying conditions to be borne in mind.

THE EXISTING LITERATURE

In large part because of its importance for policy, much of the research, writing, and reflection on the relationships between security and development has been conducted by those engaged in making or implementing policy, and academia has largely played catch-up. In this literature review we consider a wide range of sources because we are dealing with broad arenas of contestation here, and good work has emerged from places beyond academia. To capture the diversity of approaches within each arena and gain a sense of the many voices now engaged in this debate, we group the existing literature into four categories reflecting their primary intent: theoretical and conceptual studies, policy-focused studies, practical and operational studies, and advocacy studies. Of course, some works are hybrids, reflecting different types of intent. For example, the journal *Conflict, Security and Development* has been particularly effective as an outlet for policy-focused lessons learned and more conceptual work. In such cases we have categorized work by the primary purpose as we have discerned it.

Theoretical and Conceptual Studies
A huge amount of literature exists covering specific aspects of either security or development (a lot of which is discussed in subsequent chapters of this book). In comparison, there have been far fewer attempts to explicitly conceptualize the relationship between security and development. One of the earliest was Caroline Thomas's *In Search of Security: The Third World in International Relations*. Published in 1987, it is a rare call to conceptualize security in broad terms to include food security, secure trading systems, monetary security, and health security, with a particular emphasis on the way the organization of international capitalism affected the options open to people and states.[51] Thomas also blurs the distinction between the internal and external dimensions of security and in some respects inverts the traditional hierarchy that had tended to prioritize the latter. Her book is also pioneering in the referent object it adopted; it focuses on the people of the developing world and seeks to address the needs of the poor and excluded, rather than their states. In this sense it is a forerunner of the human security

approach and frames development and security issues as covering much the same terrain.

In the twenty-first century an influential but contrasting perspective on the security–development relationship is Mark Duffield's, *Global Governance and the New Wars: The Merging of Development and Security*. Duffield, a former head of Oxfam in Sudan turned academic, argues that during the post–Cold War era the problem of underdevelopment in the global South had been increasingly securitized as a source of instability, which could affect the global North.[52] As a result, and drawing from his experiences in Sudan, Duffield describes the multiple ways in which the development industry was engaging—and, to an extent, steering—the states of the developing world as well as overseeing their transformation to fit the dominant liberal economic model. Development, for Duffield, had thus become a project to support the peace and stability of the North.[53]

This issue also lies at the heart of the debates over the so-called liberal peace agenda. Some analysts view security and development interventions into developing world countries as an acceptable and necessary part of liberal internationalism.[54] Others explicitly reject this assumption, arguing that the ethnocentrism and global power dynamics that have shaped the dominant (Western) tools of analysis have operated at "a level of abstraction far removed from the lived experiences of those facing the challenges of conflict and development."[55] One strand of this critique depicts aid as a form of triage designed to keep the people of the developing world *in* the developing world and staunch overwhelming migrations to the developed world.[56] In this view, the development industry (donor states and NGOs) was designed to help those people who lack social insurance from a welfare state to become self-sufficient so they would not burden the developed world: development had thus become an instrumental tool of powerful actors in the security community.

The wide-ranging volume *Peace, Security and Development in an Era of Globalization*, edited by Gelijn Molier and Eva Nieuwenhuys, conceives of development as an essential element of an "integrated security approach" for dealing with regime change and postconflict reconstruction.[57] In this approach development is seen as an essential instrument of security (similar to Duffield), but the book takes a more benign view of the intentions and outcomes of the security–development relationship. Nevertheless, the hierarchy and dominance of security concerns is clear.

Other volumes that address the security–development relationship have cast their analytical net widely, addressing issues ranging from human rights and aid to conflict prevention and the economics of war, but have ultimately failed to adjudicate on how the different issues relate to one another.[58] This has left readers with a confusing range of perspectives and little idea of whether they should all be treated with an equal degree of validity. It is possible that security and development challenges should be treated as sui generis, but it would be useful to have criteria by which such a conclusion might be reached. Others have zeroed in on one particularly important issue. For Tschirgi, Lund, and Mancini, this is the failed state agenda and the three big challenges of poverty, the environment, and demographics.[59] Once again, however, their book's detailed empirical studies only

Table 1.1 Conceptualizing the Security–Development Relationship

Type of Relationship	Description
Zero-sum	Security and development are framed in either–or terms where allocating resources to one detracts from the potential to achieve the other; e.g., the guns-versus-butter debate.
Positive-sum	Security and development are understood as mutually reinforcing; the provision of one increases the likelihood of achieving the other.
Distinct	Security and development are both viewed as important goals but are understood as distinct enterprises best pursued using different methods.
Synonymous	Security and development are basically about the same thing: ensuring that the referent object can pursue its cherished values effectively.
Sequential	Security and development are conceived as preconditions for the other; e.g., development can only progress in a secure environment, or genuine national security requires a certain level of economic development.
Hierarchical	Security priorities are said to structure the choice of development projects undertaken. For some, this has produced a situation where the development industry has become a project to support the peace and stability of the North.
Selectively co-constitutive	Security and development are interconnected but in complex and not necessarily similar ways; e.g., only in certain contexts or with respect to particular issues.
Sui generis	Security and development issues are always entirely context dependent; hence, it is impossible to draw meaningful conceptual generalizations across different times and places.

traces how the security–development relationship plays out in particular countries that have experienced armed conflict, and traces how powerful governments might respond. Less effort is devoted to making more general claims.

The existing academic literature has therefore not provided anything like a systematic account of the possible ways of conceptualizing the security–development relationship. Indeed, Björn Hettne recently argued that if viewed from a macrohistorical perspective, "it is abundantly clear that the 'nexus' between development and security is anything but static or one-dimensional."[60] This is a useful reminder that there is no single answer to the question "how are security and development related?" because both arenas are inevitably contested and different contexts inevitably generate distinct dynamics. Nevertheless, as table 1.1 shows, it is possible to sketch the different ways in which the security–development relationship has been conceptualized in the relevant literature.

Of these conceptualizations, we favor the "selectively co-constitutive" approach as an analytical point of departure; there are times when the arenas can and do come together, but there are other times when this is a false conjoining for instrumental purposes, and it has negative consequences for one or both arenas. There are also situations in which the security and development arenas are focused on completely different issues and approaches, and this needs to be acknowledged; hence our preference for the idea of a "selective co-constitutive" relationship between the arenas.

Policy-Focused Studies

Policy-focused studies are one of the richest veins for work on aspects of the relationship between security and development (although not for conceptualizing that relationship). Analysts and policymakers in a variety of countries, international organizations, NGOs, civil society groups, and even firms are all trying to perfect policies on a range of security and development issues.

A lot of the early policy-relevant work on security and development was done by Europeans and Canadians. It was often produced in think tanks or university settings, but much of it was sponsored and supported by government funds. Prominent outlets for such work include the Human Security Report; the Conflict Security and Development Group at King's College London; FAFO's "New Security Programme" in Norway; the Swedish Stockholm Initiative on Disarmament Demobilisation and Reintegration (DDR); the Conflict Research Unit within the Clingendael Institute sponsored by the Netherlands Ministry of Foreign Affairs; the Berghof Research Center for Constructive Conflict Management in Germany; and the International Peace Academy (now Institute) project on the security–development nexus.[61]

The United States, after a slower start, has become increasingly engaged with these issues, in large part because the interventions in Afghanistan (2001) and Iraq (2003) have resulted in the United States doing exactly those sorts of activities—ironically, activities that the federal government funds but never does at home where education, health, welfare, and so on are all implemented at the state level. In this case, problems have driven policy; as an issue arises, the policy community seeks to deal with it.

Because the US policymaking system (which encompasses more than just the government but also think tanks, lobbies, NGOs, and public interest groups) is so big and well resourced, grappling with these policy challenges has produced an array of writings on aspects of security and development. In the US system, the two years preceding a presidential election is a time when people vie for attention—for themselves and their ideas—in the hope of impressing candidates and eventually transferring themselves and their work into the government. The 2008 presidential election was an example of that process par excellence, with many people seeking to advance their professional agendas. Consequently, those works on security and development produced by people who joined the Obama administration and are now making policies in these areas are of particular interest.

Two examples are books edited by Lael Brainard, who now works at the US Department of the Treasury, and Derek Chollet, who now works in the State Department's Policy Planning Office.[62] Brainard's edited work, *Security by Other Means*, for instance, advocates innovative approaches to reforming US foreign assistance, including integrating security and conflict prevention concerns into the dispensing of foreign aid. In the run-up to the election, much attention turned to the fate of US foreign aid and the organization of the government for more effective work on security and development (i.e., interagency reform debate).[63] The context for this was that the USAID had suffered from what three former agency heads described in a bid for more resources as "20 years of accumulated neglect by both Republicans and Democrats in the executive and legislative branches."[64] Not only have the US government's development capabilities been downsized, and much of its business contracted out, it has also been fragmented—leading to a damaging incoherence across the "myriad agencies" involved.[65] Despite these concerns, it took the Obama administration eleven months to nominate a new head for the USAID, a worrying sign given all the rhetoric about prioritizing development.[66]

Another strand of literature appeared in the wake of US attempts to "fix" the policy problems it encountered in Iraq and Afghanistan.[67] Some of these works were written by former participants in decision making who sought to rebuild their reputations and lay blame for problems on the US bureaucracy.[68] Others were penned by disillusioned professionals, for example, the work of the former USAID Iraq mission director James Stephenson, who focused his book on the failure to capitalize on the so-called golden hour of the early reconstruction phase in Iraq.[69]

Policy work on security and development issues also emerges from international institutions. One of the earliest and most widely cited examples was the UNDP's 1994 *Human Development Report*, discussed earlier. While this report views human security as having important links with human development, they were not the same: human development is about widening the range of people's choices, whereas human security is about being able to exercise these choices freely and safely. This perspective has become known as the human security approach and is a particularly important lens for considering the relationship between security and development. It is used in a number of the chapters in this volume and is returned to in the conclusion.

Popular criticisms of the human security approach include the idea that it overly extends and therefore dilutes the usefulness of the concept of security and that its focus on individuals underplays the importance of groups and communities and debates about international inequality between states.[70] One of the most radical criticisms suggests that, to date, the practical implementation of the human security approach represents little more than a sophisticated form of damage insulation by the world's most powerful governments by attempting to institute just enough self-reliance among underdeveloped communities to prevent the residents from leaving their homelands and traveling to richer parts of the world.[71]

Following the UNDP's pioneering work on security and development, a number of other international institutions came to address the relationship. The rising cost of violent conflict led the World Bank and the OECD's Development Assistance Committee (DAC) to pay more attention to the links between the two areas.[72] Indeed, the World Bank's president, Robert Zoellick, has championed a new approach to respond to the challenges of fragile states by securing development. According to Zoellick, this would involve a certain order of sequencing as well as

looking beyond the analytics of development—to a different framework of building security, legitimacy, governance and economy. This is not security as usual, or
development as usual. Nor is it about what we have come to think of as peacebuilding or peacekeeping. This is about *Securing Development*—bringing security and development together first to smooth the transition from conflict to peace and then
to embed stability so that development can take hold over a decade and beyond.
Only by securing development can we put down roots deep enough to break the
cycle of fragility and violence.[73]

In a new area of emphasis for the World Bank, the 2011 World Development Report is focused on "conflict, security and development."[74]

The European Union also began to place the security–development relationship at the heart of its foreign and security policies. The *European Security Strategy*,
for instance, declares up front that "security is the first condition for development"—suggesting that it sees the two in a sequential relationship.[75] But it was
not only Western organizations that drew connections between security and development. In Africa, for example, these connections were always more evident,
and a large number of documents emphasizing the links were produced by various international commissions and panels.[76] For our purposes, one of the most
interesting is the Solemn Declaration on a Common African Defence and Security
Policy of 2004. Formulated by members of the African Union, this emphasized the
"fundamental links" and "symbiotic relationship" that existed between development issues and what it called a "newer, multi-dimensional notion of security."

One common theme across all these organizations was that delivering on
such new agendas would require major institutional reorganization and changes
within their respective bureaucratic cultures. In relation to development goals, for
instance, the UN Secretary-General's High-Level Panel lamented that

> International institutions and States have not organized themselves to address the
> problems of development in a coherent, integrated way, and instead continue to
> treat poverty, infectious disease and environmental degradation as stand-alone
> threats. The fragmented sectoral approaches of international institutions mirror
> the fragmented sectoral approaches of Governments: for example, finance minis-
> tries tend to work only with the international financial institutions, development
> ministers only with development programmes, ministers of agriculture only with
> food programmes and environment ministers only with environmental agencies.[77]

In the security realm, US secretary of defense Robert Gates recently highlighted
some of the huge problems in his government's structure and suggested that the
relationship between the Pentagon, the State Department, and USAID needed to
see a significant redistribution of resources away from the former and into the latter institutions.[78] Although it took several years to finalize, the official State Department answer to how the Obama administration would harness its civilian power
in unison with the military came in the form of a new Quadrennial Diplomacy
and Development Review.[79]

Practical and Operational Studies

Practical and operational studies encompass the vast array of writings looking at particular aspects of security and development practices in order to perfect them. There exist extensive literatures on practices such as disarmament, demobilization, and reintegration; security sector reform; running elections; transitioning command economies into market economies; building health services from scratch; dealing with traumatized populations; tackling HIV/AIDS, and so on. This literature is far too voluminous to summarize here, but the Human Security Gateway's research and information database is useful in bringing together relevant documents, reports, NGO outputs, and academic writings on all relevant issues in security and development.[80] These literatures implicitly assume that the relationships between security and development inherent in each of these activities can be improved (if not perfected), and combine this with a pragmatic approach that something has to be done about these issues.

One technical area of the security–development relationship that has generated considerable debate is the problem encountered in the field when distinct organizational cultures collide and energy is wasted in bureaucratic competition, mutual misunderstanding, and competing agendas. This is true within governments and international institutions, and between governmental and nongovernmental actors. Several studies have assessed these problems and proposed solutions, particularly about how to improve the performance of provincial reconstruction teams in Afghanistan and Iraq.[81]

A particular subset of practical and operational studies are the "lessons learned" documents produced by bureaucracies on the basis of their field experience.[82] There have been some really important and successful lessons learned experiences, for example, the UNHCR study on Kosovo, the Rwanda Steering Committee (as a response to learning about the problem of UN coherence), and the Brahimi Report, all of which had significant effects on subsequent international behavior.[83] In practice, however, lessons learned processes have not always borne fruit.[84] There are many reasons why large institutions are rarely good at learning, let alone consistently implementing lessons. While the ad hoc and reactive approaches to most security and development challenges do not help the process, anthropologists have long argued that the only real learning that takes place is by the author or authors of the report in question.[85]

In the context of the operations in Afghanistan and Iraq, the US military established various means of capturing and disseminating lessons learned—some of which pertain to the relationship between security and development in counterinsurgency operations, including those contained in the new manual (discussed later).[86] Other militaries have developed similar mechanisms.[87] Not surprisingly, the evidence suggests that these militaries still tend to focus more on perfecting combat than on improving their performance on development. Journalistic works have also recounted the ignominious record of the early days of postwar reconstruction in Iraq and to a lesser extent Afghanistan.[88] Although not systematic accounts of practice on the ground, or of lessons learned, they are revealing of the (classic) problems encountered, ranging from lack of realistic planning and expectations, interagency dysfunction and a tremendous failure to initially understand—or listen—to local needs for reconstruction and development.

Advocacy Studies

The groups most commonly associated with advocacy on security and development issues are NGOs such as Oxfam, Save the Children, and the International Crisis Group. Often these groups stand outside the formal policymaking process (and in some tension with it), which shapes their tactics for gaining attention for their issue. They provide authoritative reports and data from the field, brief policymakers on issues, provide testimony to parliaments and legislatures, lobby lawmakers, and attract media attention through expert knowledge or through staging "events" (for example, Bono's extensive charity work and George Clooney's activism on Sudan). When access to the corridors of power is unavailable, NGOs have used memberships to pressure lawmakers to enact particular policies. Strategies that involve developing and deploying expert knowledge have also added to the literatures on security and development. Oxfam, for example, has a respected journal, *Development in Practice*, that for two decades has disseminated information from its researchers as well as acting as a hub for the work of other practitioners and policymakers.[89] As NGOs have become increasingly engaged with security issues in the world's conflict zones, the knowledge gained by their field staff has filtered into these accounts.

It is worth briefly noting that individual parts of the UN system also advocate for development (and on occasion security) policies. Like NGOs they provide expert knowledge and have long used celebrities as figureheads for campaigns, for example, Angelina Jolie's work as a Goodwill Ambassador for the UN High Commission for Refugees (UNHCR).

Advocacy is not something only practiced outside of governments, however. In large bureaucracies with complex and competing agendas, a group of "policy entrepreneurs" may have to work hard to get a particular issue accepted and prioritized.[90] Sometimes this only occurs after a period of sustained advocacy. In the security and development arenas a good example of this process concerns the US government and the types of military policies it has pursued in Iraq and Afghanistan and the role of development in supporting them. In particular, there was an extensive advocacy campaign launched within the Pentagon and across the government to move US military strategies in the two countries to counterinsurgency (or COIN, as it is known).

Part of the reason why the COIN approach required sustained advocacy is that, at the outset of the war in Iraq, the Bush administration had no expectation that the United States would need to fight insurgents; rather, the administration expected the war to be a "cakewalk," in the words of Defense Science Board member Kenneth Adelman. US officials assumed that their troops would be welcomed, in Vice President Dick Cheney's words, "as liberators."[91] Another factor was that the US military was still primarily trained, organized, and equipped for war with a peer competitor rather than insurgent militias. Nevertheless, various policy entrepreneurs within the US Department of Defense—for example, Gen. David Petraeus, Lt. Col. John Nagl, and peers in other militaries supportive of them—advocated for the move to a COIN strategy. As the insurgencies in Iraq and Afghanistan became bolder and more problematic, these events empowered the COIN advocates within the US government. A sign of their success was the creation of the new US Army and Marine Corps *Counterinsurgency Field Manual*.[92] The advocacy campaign met resistance from various quarters, for example, from development specialists who did not wish to see development used in an instrumental fashion and from the parts of the uniformed military that would not have a major role in COIN (i.e., the air force, although it has subsequently tried to carve out a role to secure the resources that role would bring).[93] Although the COIN advocates seem to have "won" the battle for now, there are already some rearguard actions within the Department of Defense to reorient strategy back to more traditional military concerns. This will achieve greater momentum if the COIN campaign in Afghanistan is unsuccessful.

CONCLUSION

Although talk of a "nexus" between security and development has become fashionable in policy and academic circles, there is no single or simple relationship between these two arenas. As this chapter has pointed out, this is partly because of the social functions security and development play as inherently political values, as justificatory devices, as trump cards in the allocation of resources, and as crucial ingredients in debates over how theory should relate to practice. Moreover, these arenas exhibit a variety of similar and contrasting characteristics. On the one hand, security and development are both essentially contested as well as derivative and relative concepts, their practical meaning hinges on perceptions and misperceptions, both suffer from problems of tunnel vision, both deploy notions of expertise to fend off criticisms and challenges, and both have been constrained by the powerful forces of sovereignty in contemporary world politics.

Both arenas are also in phases of a "paradigm shift" with traditional statist paradigms being challenged by both international developments and new voices in their respective arenas. While both arenas have grappled with some long-standing core problems, they have also increasingly encroached on each other's traditional terrain, although it is fair to say that security studies have been the most expansionist. On the other hand, however, they have exhibited rather different ideas about the appropriate timelines necessary to produce results. And while they have both been keen to devise metrics for measuring those results, the resources allocated to the development arena have usually come under the most scrutiny. It is on this fluid conceptual and practical terrain that the contemporary debates about security, development, and the relationship between them have unfolded. The following chapters discuss how these debates have taken shape with regard to the important issues of aid, humanitarian assistance, trade and resources, poverty, governance, health, and demography.

Notes

For their comments on much earlier drafts of this chapter, we would like to thank Alex Bellamy, Michael Brown, Neil Cooper, Stuart Croft, Ciarán Devane, Lee Ann Fujii, David Gow, Bernard Harborne, Dan Morrow, Zoe Nielsen, Sean Roberts, Karin von Hippel, and our anonymous reviewers.

1. *The National Security Strategy of the United States of America* (Washington, DC: The White House, March 2006), 33.

2. *The National Security Strategy of the United States of America* (Washington, DC: The White House, May 2010), 15.

3. *The National Security Strategy of the United Kingdom: Security in an Interdependent World* (London: TSO, Cm 7291, March 2008), para. 3.56.

4. *Solemn Declaration on a Common African Defence and Security Policy*, signed by African Union members at Sirte, Libya, February 28, 2004, 7. www.africa-union.org/News _Events/2ND%20EX%20ASSEMBLY/Declaration%20on%20a%20Comm.Af%20Def%20 Sec.pdf.

5. Report of the UN Secretary-General, *In Larger Freedom: Towards Security, Development and Human Rights for All* (UN doc. A/59/2005, March 21, 2005), Annex, para. 2.

6. Harold D. Lasswell, *Politics: Who Gets What, When, How* (New York: McGraw-Hill, 1936).

7. "F-22 Raptor: Procurement and Events (updated)," *Defense Industry Daily*, December 13, 2009, accessed January 4, 2010, www.defenseindustrydaily.com/f22-raptor-procurement-events-updated-02908/.

8. Ruth Jacoby, "Policymaking for Peace and Prosperity," in *Security and Development: Investing in Peace and Prosperity*, ed. Robert Picciotto and Rachel Weaving (Abingdon: Routledge, 2006), 4.

9. On how successive US administrations have kept the US Agency for International Development (USAID) famished, see J. Brian Atwood, M. Peter McPherson, and Andrew Natsios, "Arrested Development," *Foreign Affairs* 87, no. 6 (2008): 123–32. To cite just one important indicator, while in 1980 USAID had 4,058 permanent American employees, by 2008 the number was just 2,200.

10. Michael W. Doyle, "Kant, Liberal Legacies, and Foreign Affairs," *Philosophy and Public Affairs*, 12, no. 3 (1983): 205–35.

11. See Michael E. Brown, Sean Lynn-Jones, and Steven Miller, eds., *Debating the Democratic Peace* (Cambridge, MA: MIT Press, 1996).

12. James M. Cypher and James L. Dietz, "Developmentalist Theories of Economic Development," in *The Process of Economic Development*, 2nd ed., 140–67 (Abingdon: Routledge, 2004).

13. W. B. Gallie, "Essentially Contested Concepts" in *The Importance of Language*, ed. Max Black, 121–46 (Englewood Cliffs, NJ: Prentice Hall, 1962).

14. Richard Little, quoted in Barry Buzan, *People, States and Fear*, 2nd ed. (Hemel Hempstead: Harvester Wheatsheaf, 1991), 7.

15. Ken Booth, *Theory of World Security* (Cambridge: Cambridge University Press, 2007), 150.

16. Ibid.

17. See ibid.; and Anthony Payne and Nicola Phillips, *Development* (Cambridge: Polity, 2010).

18. For an overview, see David Held, Anthony G. McGrew, David Goldblatt, and Jonathan Perraton, *Global Transformations* (Oxford: Polity, 1999).

19. Robert Picciotto, "Overview: Investing in Peace and Prosperity," in *Security and Development: Investing in Peace and Prosperity*, ed. Robert Picciotto and Rachel Weaving (Abingdon: Routledge, 2006), 7. For a critique that concludes that the orthodox development approaches

of the World Bank and International Monetary Fund have actually disempowered ordinary people in Africa by facilitating the construction of "exclusionary democracies," see Rita Abrahamsen, *Disciplining Democracy* (London: Zed, 2000).

20. Thomas Kuhn, *The Structure of Scientific Revolutions* (Chicago: University of Chicago Press, 1968).

21. See, for example, Barry Buzan and Lene Hansen, *The Evolution of International Security Studies* (Cambridge: Cambridge University Press, 2009); Bill McSweeney, *Security, Identity and Interests* (Cambridge: Cambridge University Press, 1999), part 1; Payne and Phillips, *Development*; and Vanessa Pupavac, "International Development Policies and Global Security" in *Global Security and International Political Economy*, ed. Pinar Bilgin et al., 250–82 (UNESCO: EoLSS Publishers, 2011). Available at www.eolss.net/.

22. Gerd Junne, "Integrating Development Studies in Peace and Security Studies," in *Peace, Security and Development in an Era of Globalization*, ed. Gelijn Molier and Eva Nieuwenhuys (Dordrecht: Martinus Nijhoff Publishers, 2009), 55.

23. Buzan and Hansen, *Evolution of International Security Studies*, 39–65.

24. For some analysts, the key problem with the expanding agenda was that such a broad focus diluted the traditional focus of security away from armed conflict and the use of force, thus significantly reducing the concept's analytical utility. See, for example, Stephen M. Walt, "The Renaissance of Security Studies," *International Studies Quarterly* 35, no. 2 (1991): 211–39. Others were concerned that bringing the "security" (read: military) mindset and organizational dynamics to bear on complex nonmilitary problems would do more harm than good. See, for example, Daniel Deudney, "The Case against Linking Environmental Degradation and National Security," *Millennium* 19, no. 3 (1990): 461–76. For others, the broadening and deepening had not gone far enough or succeeded in altering the traditional patterns of thought and action that had dominated the academic and policy communities. See, for example, Ken Booth, "Security and Self: Reflections of a Fallen Realist," in *Critical Security Studies: Concepts and Cases*, ed. Keith Krause and Michael C. Williams, 83–119 (London: UCL Press, 1997).

25. See, for example, Neil MacFarlane and Yuen Foong Khong, *Human Security and the UN* (Bloomington: Indiana University Press, 2006); and *Human Security Now* (New York: Commission on Human Security, 2003).

26. Abraham Maslow, *Motivation and Personality* (New York: Harper & Row, 1970).

27. United Nations Development Programme, *Human Development Report 1994: New Dimensions of Human Security* (1994), ch. 2; 25–33. http://hdr.undp.org/en/reports/global/hdr1994/.

28. See, for example, Roland Paris, "Human Security: Paradigm Shift or Hot Air?" *International Security* 26, no. 2 (2001): 87–102; and the special section "What Is Human Security?" in *Security Dialogue*, 35, no. 3 (2004).

29. See Emma Rothschild, "What Is Security?" *Daedalus* 124, no. 3 (1995): 53–98.

30. Ole Wæver, "Securitization and Desecuritization," in *On Security*, ed. Ronnie D. Lipschutz (New York: Columbia University Press, 1995), 55.

31. Barry Buzan, Ole Wæver, and Jaap de Wilde, *Security: A New Framework for Analysis* (Boulder, CO: Lynne Rienner, 1998), 29.

32. Examples include Pinar Bilgin, Ken Booth, and Richard Wyn Jones, "Security Studies: The Next Stage?" *Nação e Defesa* 84, no. 2 (1998): 131–57; McSweeney, *Security, Identity, and Interests*; Lene Hansen, "The Little Mermaid's Silent Security Dilemma and the Absence of Gender in the Copenhagen School," *Millennium* 29, no. 2 (2000): 285–306; Michael C. Williams, "Words, Images, Enemies: Securitization and International Politics," *International Studies Quarterly* 47, no. 4 (2003): 511–31; and Claire Wilkinson, "The Copenhagen School on Tour in Kyrgyzstan: Is Securitization Theory Useable outside Europe?" *Security Dialogue* 38, no. 1 (2007): 5–25.

33. Buzan, Wæver, and de Wilde, *Security*.

34. Robin Luckham, "The International Community and State Reconstruction in War-Torn Societies," in *Security and Development: Investing in Peace and Prosperity*, ed. Robert Picciotto and Rachel Weaving (Abingdon: Routledge, 2006), 288.

35. Quoted in Michael R. Gordon, "The 2000 Campaign: The Military," *New York Times*, October 21, 2000.

36. Derrick W. Brinkerhoff, "The State and International Development Management: Shifting Tides, Changing Boundaries, and Future Directions," *Public Administration Review* 68, no. 6 (2008): 985–1001; and Anil Hira, "State of the State: Does the State Have a Role in Development?" in *Introduction to International Development*, ed. Paul A. Haslam, Jessica Schafer, and Pierre Baudet, 123–34 (Oxford: Oxford University Press, 2009).

37. Picciotto, "Overview," 24. For an important critique of this terminology, see Charles T. Call, "The Fallacy of the 'Failed State,'" *Third World Quarterly* 29, no. 8 (2008): 1491–1507.

38. Junne, "Integrating Development Studies," 65.

39. In relation to security, see, for example, Booth, "Security and Self"; and Tarak Barkawi and Mark Laffey, "The Postcolonial Moment in Security Studies," *Review of International Studies*, 32, no. 2 (2006): 329–52. In relation to development, see, for example, Arturo Escobar, *Encountering Development: The Making and Unmaking of the Third World* (Princeton NJ: Princeton University Press, 1994); David Mosse, *Cultivating Development* (London: Pluto, 2005); and William Easterly, *The White Man's Burden* (New York: Penguin, 2006).

40. The Convention on the Prohibition of the Use, Stockpiling, Production and Transfer of Anti-Personnel Landmines and on Their Destruction, September 18, 1997, accessed January 4, 2009, www.un.org/Depts/mine/UNDocs/ban_trty.htm. For an account of the change in the discourse see Richard Price, "Reversing the Gun Sights: Transnational Civil Society Targets Landmines," *International Organization*, 52, no. 3 (1998): 613–44.

41. Joanna Spear, "The Emergence of a European 'Strategic Personality' and the Implications for the Transatlantic Relationship," *Arms Control Today* 33, no. 9 (2003): 13–18.

42. Roger MacGinty and Andrew Williams, *Conflict and Development* (Abingdon, UK: Routledge, 2009), ch. 3.

43. See, for example, the International Institute for Strategic Studies' annual publication, *The Military Balance*, accessed July 26, 2011, www.iiss.org/publications/military-balance/.

44. See, for example, the indices compiled by The Fund for Peace and *Foreign Policy* magazine, accessed July 26, 2011, www.fundforpeace.org, and www.foreignpolicy.com/failed states; and the Brookings Institution's "Index of State Weakness in the Developing World," www.brookings.edu/reports/2008/02_weak_states_index.aspx. For an alternative attempt to measure the levels of peace rather than insecurity, see Vision of Humanity's "Global Peace Index," at www.visionofhumanity.org/index.php.

45. The UN Development Programme's annual Human Development Index is a good example, accessed July 26, 2011, http://hdr.undp.org/en/statistics/.

46. See, for example, "DAC Evaluation Quality Standards (for test phase application), OECD-DAC, DAC Evaluation Network, March 2006, accessed September 8, 2009, www.oecd.org/dataoecd/30/62/36596604.pdf.

47. Dambisa Moyo, *Dead Aid* (New York: Farrar, Straus & Giroux, 2009). For more nuanced analyses, see William Easterly, *The Elusive Quest for Growth* (Cambridge, Mass.: The MIT Press, 2001); and Roger Riddell, *Does Foreign Aid Really Work?* (Oxford: Oxford University Press, 2007).

48. See Jeffrey Sachs, "Aid Ironies," *The Huffington Post*, May 24, 2009, accessed June 4, 2009, www.huffingtonpost.com/jeffrey-sachs/aid-ironies_b_207181.html. See also William Wallis, "Opposition Builds to Zambian Economist Who Challenges the Liberal Aid Establishment," *Financial Times* (US), May 23–24, 2009, 1 and 4.

49. See Ellen Dorsey and Paul Nelson, eds., *New Rights Advocacy*, 2nd ed. (Washington, DC: Georgetown University Press, 2008).

50. GAO, *Military Operations: Actions Needed to Better Guide Project Selection for Commander's Emergency Response Program and Improve Oversight in Iraq* (GAO08-736R May 2, 2008).

51. Caroline Thomas, *In Search of Security: The Third World in International Relations* (Boulder, CO: Lynne Rienner, 1987).

52. It is important to remember that this is nothing new; recall that a significant part of the rationale for Western development aid in the Cold War years—for example, the Marshall Plan—was to end poverty, which was thought to lead to communism.

53. Mark Duffield, *Global Governance and the New Wars: The Merging of Development and Security* (London: Zed Books, 2001).

54. See, for example, Robert Picciotto and Rachel Weaving, eds., *Security and Development: Investing in Peace and Prosperity* (Abingdon: Routledge, 2006), first published as a special issue of the journal *Conflict, Security and Development*; and Neclâ Tschirgi, Michael S. Lund, and Francesco Mancini, eds., *Security and Development: Searching for Connections* (Boulder, CO: Lynne Rienner, 2010).

55. MacGinty and Williams, *Conflict and Development*, 3.

56. Mark Duffield, *Development, Security and Unending War: Governing the World of Peoples* (Cambridge: Polity, 2007).

57. Gelijn Molier and Eva Nieuwenhuys, eds., *Peace, Security and Development in an Era of Globalization: The Integrated Security Approach Viewed from a Multidisciplinary Perspective* (Dordrecht: Martinus Nijhoff Publishers, 2009).

58. Picciotto and Weaving, *Security and Development*. Similar points could be made about Stephan Klingebiel, ed. *New Interfaces between Security and Development: Changing Concepts and Approaches* (Bonn: German Development Institute, 2006).

59. Tschirgi, Lund, and Mancini, *Security and Development*.

60. Björn Hettne, "Development and Security: Origins and the Future," *Security Dialogue*, 41, no. 1 (2010), 47. See also Maria Stern and Joakim Öjendal, "Mapping the Security Development Nexus: Conflict, Complexity, Cacophony, Convergence?" *Security Dialogue* 41, no. 1 (2010): 5–29.

61. See the Human Security Report at www.humansecurityreport.info/; the Human Security Gateway at www.humansecuritygateway.com/; King's College London's Conflict, Security and Development group at www.securityanddevelopment.org/, accessed July 26, 2011; FAFO at www.fafo.no/nsp/index.htm; the Stockholm Initiative on DDR (SIDDR) at www.sweden.gov.se/sb/d/4890; the Clingendael Institute at www.clingendael.nl; *The Berghof Handbook for Conflict Transformation* at www.berghof-handbook.net/std_page.php?LANG=e&id=3; International Peace Institute, "Security-Development Nexus: Research Findings and Policy Implications," February 14, 2006, at www.ipinst.org/publication/policy-papers/detail/131-security-development-nexus-research-findings-and-policy-implications-security-development-nexus-program-report.html. (Unless otherwise noted, all websites accessed April 12, 2010.)

62. Lael Brainard and Derek Chollet, eds., *Too Poor for Peace? Global Poverty, Conflict, and Security in the 21st Century* (Washington, DC: Brookings Institution, 2007); and Lael Brainard, ed., *Security by Other Means* (Washington, DC: CSIS and the Brookings Institution, 2007).

63. For example, Report to Congressional Requesters, "Foreign Aid Reform" (US Government Accountability Office, GAO-09-192, April 2009), accessed January 27, 2010, www.gao.gov/new.items/d09192.pdf. For an overview of the interagency reform debate, see Catherine Dale, Nina Serafino, and Pat Towell, *Organizing the US Government for National Security* (Washington, DC: Congressional Research Service Report RL 34455, December 2008).

64. Atwood, McPherson, and Natsios, "Arrested Development," 123.

65. Ibid.

66. "Testimony of Dr. Rajiv Shah, Administrator Designate, U.S. Agency of International Development, before the Senate Committee on Foreign Relations, December 1, 2009," accessed July 26, 2011, www.usaid.gov/press/speeches/2009/ty091201.html.

67. Jacquelyn Williams-Bridgers, "Afghanistan and Pakistan: Oversight of US Interagency Efforts," Testimony before the Subcommittee on National Security and Foreign Affairs, Committee on Oversight and Government Reform, Government Accountability Office, US House of Representatives. September 9, 2009, accessed January 7, 2010, www.docstoc.com/docs /19527577/Afghanistan-and-Pakistan-Oversight-of-US-Interagency-Efforts-September-9 -2009-GAO-Report.

68. For example, Douglas Feith, *War and Decision: Inside the Pentagon at the Dawn of the War on Terrorism* (New York: HarperCollins, 2008); Richard Perle, "Ambushed on the Potomac," *National Interest* (January–February 2009); Kenneth M. Pollack, *The Threatening Storm: The Case for Invading Iraq* (New York: Council on Foreign Relations, 2002); and Kenneth M. Pollack, "Next Stop Baghdad?" *Foreign Affairs* 81, no. 2 (2002): 32–47. In these works by Pollack, he made the case for war, but in later works he has written about why the intelligence was faulty. See Kenneth M. Pollack, "Spies, Lies and Weapons: What Went Wrong," *The Atlantic* (January–February 2004).

69. James Stephenson, *Losing the Golden Hour: An Insider's View of Iraq's Reconstruction* (Washington, DC: Potomac Books, 2007).

70. See, for example, Roland Paris, "Paradigm Shift or Hot Air?" *International Security* 26, no. 2 (2001): 87–102.

71. Mark Duffield, "The Liberal Way of Development and the Development-Security Impasse," *Security Dialogue* 41, no. 1 (2010): 54–77.

72. Paul Collier, V. L. Elliott, Havard Hegre, Anke Hoeffler, Marta Reynal-Querol, and Nicholas Sambinas, *Breaking the Conflict Trap: Civil War and Development Policy* (Washington, DC: World Bank, 2003); and OECD, "The Security and Development Nexus: Challenges for Aid," (DCD/DAC(2004)9/REV2), www.oecd.org/dataoecd/40/59/31526546.pdf.

73. Robert Zoellick, "Fragile States: Securing Development," *Survival* 50, no. 6 (2008–9), 69.

74. Worldbank.org, *Conflict and Development: Overcoming Conflict and Fragility*, http:// blogs.worldbank.org/conflict/world-development-report-2011.

75. Council of the European Union, "EU Security Strategy: A Secure Europe in a Better World" (Brussels: December 2003), www.consilium.europa.eu/uedocs/cmsUpload/78367.pdf.

76. For an overview of these initiatives, see Ian Taylor, *NEPAD: Towards Africa's Development or Another False Start?* (Boulder, CO: Lynne Rienner, 2005), ch. 1.

77. High-Level Panel on Threats, Challenges, and Change, *A More Secure World* (2004), 26. www.un.org/secureworld/report2.pdf.

78. Robert Gates, Landon Lecture, Kansas State University, November 26, 2007, US Department of Defense website, www.defenselink.mil/speeches/speech.aspx?speechid=1199.

79. *Leading through Civilian Power: The First Quadrennial Diplomacy and Development Review* (Washington, DC: Department of State/USAID, December 2010). Available at www.state .gov/s/dmr/qddr/#.

80. See the Human Security Gateway's research and information database at www .humansecuritygateway.com/.

81. See, for example, Daniel L. Byman, "Uncertain Partners: NGOs and the Military," *Survival*, 43, no. 2 (2001): 97–114; Alan Doss, "Eyewitness: Crisis, Contention and Coherence—Reflections from the Field," *International Peacekeeping* 15, no. 4 (2008): 570–81; Michael J. McNerney, "Stabilization and Reconstruction in Afghanistan: Are PRTs a Model or a Muddle?" *Parameters* (Winter 2005–6): 32–46; and Touko Piiparien, "A Clash of Mindsets? An Insider's Account of Provincial Reconstruction Teams," *International Peacekeeping* 14, no. 1 (2007): 143–57.

82. See, for example, the OECD Development Co-operation Directorate, DAC Network on Governance, "Synthesis of Lessons Learned of Donor Practices of Fighting Corruption" (June 23, 2003), http://unpan1.un.org/intradoc/groups/public/documents/UNTC/UNPAN 016841.pdf.

83. Astri Suhrke, Michael Barutciski, Peta Sandison, and Rick Garlock, *The Kosovo Refugee Crisis: An Independent Evaluation of UNHCR's Emergency Preparedness and Response* (2000), UN High Commissioner for Refugees Evaluation and Policy Analysis Unit, accessed April 12, 2010, http://repository.forcedmigration.org/show_metadata.jsp?pid=fmo:3644; Office of the UN Resident Coordinator for Rwanda, "'One UN' Steering Committee in Rwanda: Terms of Reference," n.d., accessed April 12, 2010, www.undg.org/docs/7208/ToR%20One%20UN%20 Steering%20Committee%20in%20Rwanda.pdf.; and "Report of the Panel on United Nations Peace Operations" (UN doc. A/55/305-S/2000/809, August 21, 2000), accessed July 26, 2011, www.un.org/peace/reports/peace_operations/docs/full_report.htm.

84. See, for example, Lise Morje Howard, *UN Peacekeeping in Civil Wars* (Cambridge: Cambridge University Press, 2008).

85. See Rob van den Berg and Philip Quarles van Ufford, "Disjuncture and Marginality: Towards a New Approach to Development Practice" in *The Aid Effect*, ed. David Mosse and David Lewis, 196–212 (Ann Arbor, MI: Pluto Press, 2005).

86. United States Army Combined Arms Center, "The Center for Army Lessons Learned," http://usacac.army.mil/cac2/call/index.asp; and James M. Dubik, "Accelerating Combat Power in Afghanistan," Best Practices in Counterinsurgency Report No. 2 (Washington, DC: Institute for the Study of War, December 2009), accessed January 16, 2011. www .understandingwar.org/files/AccelCombatPower.pdf.

87. For example, the Australian Army has a Centre for Army Lessons, www.defence.gov .au/army/cal/. The Canadian Army Lessons Learned Centre has been active more than a decade, http://armyapp.dnd.ca/allc-clra/default_e.asp.

88. See, for example, James Fallows, "Blind into Baghdad," *Atlantic* (January–February 2004), www.theatlantic.com/magazine/archive/2004/01/blind-into-baghdad/2860/; Rajiv Chandrasekaran, *Imperial Life In the Emerald City* (New York: Vintage, 2006); George Packer, *The Assassins' Gate: America in Iraq* (New York: Farrar, Straus and Giroux 2005); Thomas E. Ricks, *Fiasco: The American Military Adventure in Iraq* (New York: Penguin, 2006); and Ahmed Rashid, *Descent into Chaos: The US and the Disaster in Pakistan, Afghanistan, and Central Asia* (New York: Penguin, 2009).

89. See *Development in Practice*, www.developmentinpractice.org/.

90. See James M. Goldgeier, *Not Whether but When: The US Decision to Enlarge NATO* (Washington, DC: Brookings Institution, 1999).

91. Kenneth Adelman, quoted in *The Washington Post*, February 13, 2002; Vice President Dick Cheney on *Meet the Press*, March 16, 2003.

92. US Army and Marine Corps, *Counterinsurgency Manual* (Chicago: Chicago University Press, 2007).

93. Kenneth Beebe, "The Air Force's Missing Doctrine: How the US Air Force Ignores Counterinsurgency," *Air and Space Power Journal* (Spring 2006), accessed January 7, 2010, www.airpower.au.af.mil/airchronicles/apj/apj06/spr06/beebe.html; and "COIN Air Force on Its Way," *Defense Tech*, July 23, 2009, accessed January 7, 2010, http://defensetech.org/2009 /07/23/coin-air-force-on-its-way/.

Part I

AID

Chapter 2

AID

A Security Perspective

Bernard Harborne

In late August 2008 the renegade general Laurent Nkunda and his five-thousand-strong militia launched several successful attacks against twenty-five-thousand troops of the Congolese army deployed in eastern Democratic Republic of Congo (DRC). This started another round of the low-intensity war in the subregion. In a few days some two hundred thousand people were uprooted, adding to the toll of 1 million displaced persons in north and south Kivu provinces. Further rape, violence, death, and recrimination followed. Clearly, the Goma peace engagement of January 2008, which had attempted to reconcile the labyrinthine interests in eastern Congo, had failed. Diplomatic hand-wringing ensued, with European foreign ministers visiting Goma unwilling to commit additional troops to a beleaguered UN peacekeeping mission there. A number of peace summits were convened, and on December 22 the UN Security Council passed Resolution 1856 condemning the violence, reaffirming commitment to the failed Goma process, and approving the appointments of former Nigerian and Tanzanian presidents Olusegun Obasanjo and Benjamin Mkapa, respectively, as chief mediators.

A few days earlier, bureaucrats of a different sort were hand-wringing in Washington, DC, as the major donors with the Bretton Woods institutions tried to find ways in which they could help the DRC government out of a very deep fiscal hole. The emerging global financial crisis was having its most significant impact upon the African continent in the already beleaguered DRC. World copper, cobalt, and oil prices had dropped dramatically. As a result, some two hundred thousand mine workers lost their livelihoods in Katanga. Economic growth was projected to decline from 10 percent in 2008 to less than 2.7 percent in 2009. Export revenue projections for 2009 were revised down by about $1.9 billion, equivalent to 14.6 percent of gross domestic product. The current account deficit was expected to widen to about 15 percent of gross domestic product in 2009 (from 5 percent in 2008). In sum, the state apparatus of DRC, already fragile, was facing complete financial meltdown. The government could not survive financially without further life support from its international partners.

What was interesting about these two responses to "another African crisis" was the absence of connections between security and development aid objectives. In the high-level deliberations at the end of 2008 at the UN and within the international financial institutions (IFIs), there was little or no discussion of the parlous state of Congo's finances and their relationship to the war. The fact that the earlier donor commitments of some $1.5 billion, backing the first Goma accord of January

2008, had failed to consolidate peace was also passed over. As it turned out, two neighbors and erstwhile enemies, DRC and Rwanda, signed a deal (without international involvement) and launched joint military operations in January 2009 that addressed their respective security threats.

This case is but one example of how the combined efforts of external aid and security interventions (in this instance through UN peacekeeping) failed to protect local populations in danger. As is shown in the following, while there is an increasing emphasis on the convergence of security and aid agendas, responses to the eastern Congo crisis highlighted the inability of two of the principal global governance institutions, the UN and the World Bank, to incorporate and integrate these two concerns. Each was treated in separation from the other, despite all the evidence of their inextricable linkages.[1]

This anecdote poses the question: is the emerging orthodoxy, the so-called security–development "nexus," having any impact in protecting such populations? The focus of this chapter is on the way in which aid policy and instruments coincide with security approaches to manage conflict and violence. It challenges the notion that we have an increasingly happy marriage between security and aid in policy and practice. In reality, we have development aid working for security objectives of aid-donor countries rather than security working for the development objectives of developing countries such as the Congo. It is argued that the security–development nexus gained most currency in the aftermath of 9/11, and that the reconfiguration of aid and security instruments was made particularly by traditional donor governments to contend with terrorism and their own security interests, rather than as part of a more generous look at sustainable and peaceful development.

On paper at least, security and development are no longer uncomfortable bedfellows.[2] Further, in development circles, there is common agreement that violence is one of the main impediments to many countries reaching their development targets, such as halving poverty, enshrined in the Millennium Development Goals (MDGs).[3] Inside the military, there is growing recognition that external aid, particularly in the form of job creation and setting up of basic infrastructure, is critical to security objectives.[4] In turn, there have been great efforts to ensure congruence of decision making around security and aid, particularly with advocacy for the 3-D agenda (defense, diplomacy, and development) within some governments. The so-called whole-of-government approach has been a shoehorn effort to enhance the ways in which these things are done.

While this chapter recognizes these changes, an analysis of current outcomes at the strategic–macro and operational levels suggests that this nexus remains a matter for policy papers rather than having real impact upon the lives of poor and marginalized peoples. To substantiate this argument the chapter reviews recent trends in development aid and security and the attempts at convergence. It examines various aspects of development and security interventions in practice and investigates the connections that do or do not exist to test the assumption behind the security–development agenda. Such an investigation includes looking at the current critique of this nexus, and particularly the claims that national security interests are overriding development priorities.

TRENDS IN FOREIGN AID

For the purposes of this analysis, aid is categorized as external finance for recovery and reconstruction to repair and rehabilitate infrastructure and services devastated by naturally triggered disaster or armed conflict, and for development to boost long-term investment and growth and reduce poverty.[5] Several trends are notable in the level of aid, its composition, purpose, and the degree of fragmentation.

International aid is on the increase; aid flows grew from $67 billion in 2002 to $134 billion in 2008.[6] However, much of this increase was due to large flows of debt relief, particularly for Iraq and Nigeria. Moreover, core development aid is increasing at a slower rate than overall aid (defined by the main donor countries as official development assistance, ODA), and ODA has declined in real terms since 2005.[7] ODA from traditional donors fell from $122.3 billion in 2008 to $119.6 billion in 2009 but is expected to rise again to $126 billion in 2010.[8]

The composition of ODA is also changing. Currently, most ODA originates from twenty-two countries in the Organisation for Economic Co-operation and Development (OECD), the traditional donors who comprise the OECD Development Assistance Committee (DAC). First, within governments, there are notable changes, most significantly with defense departments and ministries taking on developmental roles. The global numbers are difficult to estimate. One analysis of the US government states that ODA managed by the Pentagon has jumped from 3.5 percent in 1998 to 22 percent in 2005.[9] The other new players are the so-called non-DAC donors. These include governments such as the "BRIC" countries—Brazil, Russia, India, China—which provided an estimated $9.5 billion in 2009 (a rise of 63 percent from 2008) as well as private donors, such as the Gates Foundation, which provided in total some $14.6 billion in 2006.[10] While donor tracking is not yet able to account for where most of this non-DAC aid goes, the majority of DAC ODA is concentrated on a core set of recipient countries. Indeed, Afghanistan and Iraq account for nearly half of the recent increase in ODA, a trend that will be discussed later in the chapter.[11]

These aid numbers should also be compared to other financial flows. Foreign direct investment is projected to be $400 billion for developing countries in 2009 (down from $580 billion in 2008), and remittances are estimated at $300 billion per year.[12] Nevertheless, these combined figures pale when compared with those for military spending, which are estimated to be more than $1,100 billion per annum and rising (2004 projections, of which $500 billion is non-US government spending).[13]

Aid has gone through a number of reinventions since World War II in its attempt to assist poorer countries, from the "big push" in the immediate postcolonial period, financing large-scale infrastructure, to the ideological use of aid in the Cold War, to the "structural adjustment" era of the 1980s.[14] More recent iterations of the "development enterprise" have had to address global challenges such as climate change, food and other commodity price shocks, postconflict reconstruction, toxic waste, depletion of the oceans, and now the financial crisis. While the causal relationship between aid finance and development remains contested, aid is now also being called upon to address an increasing array of the world's problems, including conflict and insecurity.

As aid has increased, there has been a dramatic fragmentation of effort (more donors, more projects, more activities) leading to concerns about its overall efficacy and rationale. Over the last decade or so four policy steps have been taken to redress these concerns. First, donors have become more selective based on the premise that aid only works in good policy environments; "good" countries are hence preferred to "bad" ones (see Morrow's chapter for more on this point).[15] Second, donors have rallied their efforts behind a common set of objectives most recently articulated in the MDGs—commitments made by heads of state to reduce extreme poverty and to meet a set of time-bound targets—with a deadline of 2015. Third, some donors have moved away from financing projects to give direct budget support to poor governments.[16] About 20 percent of ODA is given in this way (an increase from 8 percent in 2001).[17] Finally, donors, particularly those from the traditional DAC club, have committed themselves to greater coordination of effort. This has been enshrined in the Declarations in Paris (March 2005) and Accra (September 2008). These seek donor harmonization in alignment with national recovery or development strategies formulated by host governments, such as the Poverty Reduction Strategy Paper (the PRSP).[18]

In sum, two major trends are emerging in aid financing: first, an effort by traditional, largely European and North American donors to mitigate the dysfunctional aspects of aid associated with fragmentation and lack of coordination in an effort to make overall aid something more than its multifarious parts; second, some new donors are bringing their own views about sovereignty, good governance and democracy, and the ways in which aid is used to further certain objectives. These new actors often work outside orthodox norms and standards that can lead to potential conflicts over approach.[19] The role of China in development in Sudan, the DRC, and Zimbabwe is a case in point.[20]

SECURITY TRENDS

The end of the Cold War brought about a sea change in military thinking with the demise of the USSR and the emergence of an array of newly significant challenges. Global military spending declined (from $1.3 trillion in 1986 to $840 billion in 1994), and costly nuclear arsenals and conventional forces were partially dismantled.[21] A rapid decline in industrial interstate war began to impact upon military thinking and, in turn, the policies and budgets that drove the defense ministries of the developed world. While the overall number of conflicts and related battle deaths diminished in the 1990s, a number of commentators highlighted the mutating nature of armed conflict.[22] Wars increasingly took on a "post-Westphalian" character, with many more intrastate wars configured around global commercial networks and the breakdown of state structures.

During this period we can see first an attempt by developed states, particularly NATO allies, to perfect third-generation or maneuver warfare. The use of aerial bombing as a favored means to deal with recalcitrant states, notably Iraq and

Serbia, indicated the priority put on airpower and rapid reaction forces as the fastest means to destroy an enemy's command, control, and logistics and ultimately the enemy's will to fight.[23]

The second trend, and a major precursor to the security–development nexus in the twenty-first century, was the increasing alliance between military adventurism and so-called humanitarian purpose, for example in Somalia (1992), Kosovo (1999), and Sierra Leone (2000). Governments were using military instruments where aid had failed. And where aid was useful, the military were increasingly the providers of that aid or worked side by side with its providers. The United States' more assertive international role was curtailed after the disastrous involvement in Somalia, including the "Blackhawk down" incident and the subsequent issuing of Presidential Decision Directive 25.[24] US involvement in peacekeeping operations became more limited, save for protecting strategic interests. This underlined two further trends: Western militaries rarely sent their manpower to nonstrategic but dangerous parts of the world, such as Africa, leading to a peacekeeping apartheid; and advanced technology was seen as critical in projecting lethal force while taking Western foot soldiers out of harm's way.

It was also in Africa that the third and fourth concerns emerged as indications of ways in which development objectives had an effect on the security discourse. The third concern was the Rwandan genocide in which some eight hundred thousand persons were killed over a period of three months in 1994. The failure of international actors, particularly the European and North American military powers, to prevent or stop the genocide resulted in much soul-searching.[25] These inquiries covered a range of security issues from how outside actors could prevent conflict or gross human rights abuse from occurring in the first place to how military forces could be used for humanitarian purposes at their onset (i.e., protecting of populations in danger and being a force for good). Fourth, at this time there was also an increasing concern about the rise in deaths relating to HIV/AIDS, particularly in Africa. The relationship between this disease and national security was recognized by a wide range of actors, including the US government and the UN Security Council.[26]

POLICY CONVERGENCE BETWEEN AID AND SECURITY

In contrast to the Clinton years, the post-9/11 era saw the United States play a more assertive military role, especially in Afghanistan and Iraq, and there was a concomitant defense spending increase. This coincided with a notable move to see development and poverty reduction, and hence foreign aid, as part of the terrorism solution (see Williams's chapter in this volume). As the World Bank president put it, "the war against terrorism will be won by eliminating poverty."[27]

Al-Qaeda's use of Afghanistan as a global launch pad placed great emphasis on so-called failed and failing states. Development aid was useful because it was thought to provide a critical instrument for engineering the behavior of both states and individuals. At the geopolitical level, aid was critical in preventing or shoring up failed states; at the more micro level, aid was vital in winning hearts and minds in counterinsurgency efforts. Civil–military relations therefore underwent another shift during this period with the military playing an active role as a provider of aid in a variety of war zones.

In the formulation of national security and defense doctrine, aid was seen as an increasingly significant component.[28] It was particularly important within counterinsurgency doctrine and what has been termed fourth generation warfare: "the use of all available networks—political, economic, social and military—to convince the enemy's political decision makers that their strategic goals are either unachievable or too costly for the perceived benefit."[29] No longer preoccupied with conventional interstate warfare, military planners had to call upon the experiences of pacification in Vietnam, Northern Ireland, and Bosnia where the fighting was done "amongst the people."[30]

In the policy arena, the security–development nexus was highlighted in a number of groundbreaking reports in the early twenty-first century that called for a greater convergence between security, development, and foreign assistance.[31] Particularly post-9/11, donors confronted the issues of how development assistance could be used to meet security objectives and, in turn, how could they organize themselves more effectively to address contemporary multidimensional challenges. As the USAID administrator observed, development had taken "its place alongside defense and diplomacy as one of the three essential components of American foreign policy."[32] This so-called 3D agenda in Washington reverberated elsewhere with conflict and security issues now commonplace in literature discussing foreign aid whether, from universities, government departments, think tanks, or international organizations (see chapter 1 in this volume).

Next we need to analyze what this policy change has meant in practice; is it a cacophony or a convergence?[33] First, some overriding concerns should be noted. In particular, leaving aside the respective merits for military intervention, the pursuit of security objectives in some instances has had dire developmental consequences. The deterioration in socioeconomic indicators in Iraq, Afghanistan, and Somalia—front line states in the so-called war on terror—give little evidence of synergy; rather, they provide evidence that security objectives have triumphed and undermined development ones. The chapter now considers the main ways in which the new security–aid paradigm has been incorporated institutionally, financially, and operationally by donor governments and multilaterals.

THE INTERNATIONAL ARCHITECTURE

As development actors have confronted security challenges, steps have been taken to reconfigure institutional arrangements to better coordinate public policy and strategic thinking. Some bilateral donors have adopted whole-of-government approaches to certain crises and armed conflicts. Notably, the United Kingdom and the United States established institutional mechanisms to allow diplomats, defense personnel, and development practitioners to work together.[34] Others, such as Canada and the Netherlands, followed. This has had some interesting results, particularly in trying to get different organizational cultures (e.g., military and development practitioners) to think about complex crises in common. To date, most of that energy has been focused on those countries where donors are militarily involved, such as Iraq and Afghanistan.

Likewise, it has led to some innovative thinking around complex development challenges such as security sector reform (SSR).[35] Acceptance of the objectives behind SSR have led to a relaxation of the definition of ODA (i.e., aid for the promotion of economic development and welfare) to allow aid spending on some aspects of the security sector, albeit still excluding direct support to foreign militaries.[36]

There has also been a push at the multilateral level to strengthen coherence in dealing with crisis states. The UN system and the World Bank have adopted guidelines to mitigate the worst aspects of poor coordination. These have been enshrined in two instruments, the Post-Conflict Needs Assessment and the Transitional Results Matrices.[37] In turn, these have been expanded to include a framework agreement among the UN, European Commission, and the World Bank on how the three key multilateral institutions operate in such settings.[38] Now, as good practice, the UN and World Bank jointly lead—with other donors and counterpart host governments—an exercise of assessing needs and setting of prioritized plans of action including all security, relief, and developmental aspects. Such needs assessments have been used in Haiti, East Timor, Sudan, and Somalia.

Donors have also gone further in using the multilateral system to pool finances in an attempt to ensure greater aid discipline. Multidonor trust funds (MDTF) are increasingly used to "improve resource efficiency and effectiveness by reducing transaction costs and . . . managing the high risk levels inherent in post-crisis environments."[39] In some instances, such as Afghanistan, MDTFs have included security components, such as the payment of police salaries. However, although they represent an important platform for coordinated use of aid, they remain small compared to overall aid flows. For example, the Afghanistan MDTF disbursed about $100 million per year compared to total flows of up $3 billion per year; the Iraq MDTF was some $1.5 billion compared to overall commitments of $25.6 billion.[40]

Similarly to policy rhetoric, however, these institutional changes have not resulted in real changes; development practitioners may be at the table, but development outcomes are not prioritized.[41] A number of evaluations have highlighted that coordination at the ministerial level does not necessarily result in more coordinated and effective programming to address peace and security issues on the ground.[42]

AID FINANCING

There is a concern that aid, particularly development assistance, is reverting to a "cold war mentality" insofar as objectives of genuine human development and self-sufficiency are being outweighed by national security interests.[43] In turn, there is evidence that suggests that aid used in this way can be more of an impediment to peace and security than a help.

One difficulty in untangling the confluence of security and development financing is that even the DAC donors do not have a common way of reporting on foreign security assistance spending.[44] In the last brief on financing to fragile and conflict-affected states, the OECD noted that ODA funding of security activities had increased from 2007 to 2008 by 61 percent (from $947 million to $1.5 billion), about half of which was for SSR.[45] This remains a small proportion of overall financing for such states, which stands at about $33 billion a year. Another study estimated about $33.3 billion was spent by donors in 2007 on "security specific aid" including conflict prevention, security sector, counterterrorist, and peacekeeping activity.[46] But counting is not easy. Take an aid project supporting irrigation in the Andes: is this a genuine development activity or a measure aimed at undermining the Shining Path rebels? It is hard to tell. USAID is the sole donor that actively traces annual spending, and GTZ (the German development cooperation) makes occasional special allocations.[47]

Another way of counting aid is by recipient country. Donors and public policy actors use a range of criteria for defining certain (usually "failing" or "fragile") states, including national income and governance indicators.[48] What is clear from the OECD data is that development funding for fragile and conflict-affected states is increasing, from $26.8 billion in 2006 to $37.2 billion in 2007, representing some 38.4 percent of ODA.[49] These funds went to 48 fragile and conflict-affected states.[50] However, more than half of this ODA went to just five countries: Iraq (23 percent), Afghanistan (10 percent), Ethiopia, Pakistan, and Sudan.[51] ODA to fragile and conflict-affected states remains highly concentrated; 51 percent of 2008 ODA for the 43 fragile states went to only six countries, of which Afghanistan and Iraq have accounted for 34 percent of all increases in ODA since 2000.[52] A World Bank study in 2005 put these kinds of distortions into perspective when analyzing over a three-year period the per capita postconflict aid receipts, which ranged from $508 in Iraq to $21 in the DRC.[53]

The concern is that, although overall aid for fragile and conflict-affected states is increasing, a few favored countries are particularly benefiting from ODA, and these distortions in allocation suggest that transnational "terrorism is replacing poverty as the main *raison d'être* for development co-operation." [54] Reflecting this distortion is the increasing shift of aid financing from multilateral donors to bilateral giving, as the latter donors wish to retain greater flexibility in pursuing more political ends (about 75 percent of ODA in 2005 was provided by bilaterals compared to 60 percent in the mid-1990s).[55]

FINANCING POSTCONFLICT RECOVERY

A particular subset of recipient countries are those emerging from armed conflict. The general evidence so far is that in these contexts international aid can have a positive effect in consolidating peace, especially if there is also an effective peace-keeping operation.[56] Extensive econometric research suggests that low national income levels are one of the key risks to the onset of organized violence. The research also posits that "there is a 39% risk that a peace will collapse within the first five years and a 32% risk that it will collapse in the next five years."[57] Countries going through a war-to-peace transition are therefore vulnerable to recidivism, and external financial support can mitigate conflict risks in low-income countries as "the effect of aid . . . is super-effective in raising growth in post-conflict situations—about twice as effective as normal."[58]

However, some point to the damaging effects of such large influxes of aid, technical assistance, and development agency "power" in such settings.[59] The difficulty in entering into the for-or-against "postconflict assistance" arguments is that there are few alternative comparisons: very few countries emerging from war in the modern era have not undergone some kind of UN–World Bank and other donor operation. Those few, such as Vietnam or the self-declared state of Somaliland, are excellent examples of what can be achieved, including substantial stability, with little or no international support.[60] Their number, however, is unfortunately too low to illustrate definitively another kind of approach to peacebuilding.

Another key challenge is that "postconflict" is often a misnomer. Foreign aid is increasingly being used to start reconstruction efforts in highly nonpermissive hostile environments: aid is therefore simply unable to meet the expectations of peace consolidation while the conflict is unresolved. A most obvious example is that of the Occupied Palestinian Territories. West Bank and Gaza received aid totaling around $8 billion between 1994 and 2004, volumes "almost unparalleled in international peacebuilding and statebuilding."[61] Despite "the highest sustained rate of per capita disbursements to an aid recipient in the world since the Second World War" the asymmetric conflict between Israel and Palestine continues, and key issues at the heart of that conflict, including the right of refugee return, the capital, land, and contiguity of state boundaries, remain unresolved.[62] Aid flows are clearly not a panacea. Security—and therefore political settlement of conflict—has to be sustained before other efforts such as economic reform and growth can take place.[63]

Further, there are certain misgivings about the role that aid plays in the political economy of war-to-peace transitions. The exponents of greed being a driver of war and aid as driver for peace seem to forget that greed can continue. Whether aid is more likely to fuel conflict than put out its flames is, however, difficult to prove. More work has been done in terms of the relationship between humanitarian aid and war than the contribution of development aid. Peter Uvin's excoriating critique certainly suggests that the "development enterprise" played a role in underpinning the structural fault lines that resulted in the Rwandan genocide.[64] It is important to note that while it would be overplaying the role of aid to suggest it can lead to war, it can certainly help consolidate elite structures and subregional, linguistic, or ethnic disparities that are not conducive to long-term peace.[65] The converse is also true: aid withdrawn in the late 1980s at the end of the Cold War certainly assisted state fragmentation and civil war, with Somalia and Liberia being good examples.

Hence, it is arguable that postconflict financing is very much power-based development. Aid agencies respond to political elites in recipient countries; they are not answerable to whole populations. Aid therefore consolidates power rather than reshapes it, and the emphasis upon speed of project delivery is more to satisfy recipient governments than actual postwar needs of the local populations.[66]

Further, delivery of large allocations of aid in the form of direct budget support or debt relief contributions can significantly alter the balance of power within governments, on occasion favoring those who have achieved power through violent means.[67] Some commentators go so far to note that aid and debt relief in substantive proportions have sustained a state's ability for violent predation on neighbors, for example, Uganda in the DRC.[68]

Regarding the role of aid in postconflict settings, several conclusions can be reached. First, aid instruments are often not adequately evaluated to determine their contribution to peace; in contrast to the efforts made to better measure development outcomes, there are no uniform standards to measure contributions to peace outcomes. Second, aid is increasingly being called upon to resolve conflicts it cannot hope to resolve. Third, sequencing also presents a dilemma to all policymakers; without sustained efforts toward stabilization, other reforms are not possible. However, what are the means to sustain security and stabilization other than through economic recovery, job creation, and reinforcement of social cohesion?—which are all tasks for development actors.[69]

ANALYTICAL APPROACHES

One way in which aid agencies have tried to incorporate security perspectives is by adopting increasingly sophisticated techniques to better understand context. This is not easy. As a rule, such aid actors do not have the kinds of technology, resources, or time available to intelligence agencies to work out the players and dynamics underpinning any given conflict. In turn, some development agencies, prohibited by their rules from intervening in the politics of any given country, shy away from overt analysis of current events.[70] Despite these challenges, along with NGOs, key donors have developed analytical tools generically called conflict assessments.[71] These have been used to increase knowledge of conflict factors to improve country programming.

A recent evaluation of such assessments pointed out the advantages of joint analysis in encouraging coordinated responses as well as the challenges in incorporating constructive buy-in from local stakeholders, including host governments.[72] However, the evaluation skirted the principal weakness of such analyses: the precise recommendations made are rarely acted upon. Aid agencies are therefore taking the right steps toward a better understanding of security, but they do not take the essential step of attempting to address the issues raised. For example, a country social assessment of Kenya in 2006, undertaken by the World Bank, unraveled many of the socioeconomic dynamics, including issues around horizontal inequality and youth and group violence.[73] The general conclusion was that Kenya was undergoing a fragile transition and that violence was part of the quotidian reality. When violence broke out around the elections of December 2007, many of the key donor agencies were seemingly caught by surprise. The early warning signs were there, but were they acted upon? Since Kenya was a significant recipient of aid, could donors have done more to try to address the underlying fissures in the fragile polity before they boiled over during the contested elections?

Another example is the work undertaken on the foreign armed groups in the DRC, notably the Forces Démocratiques pour la Libération du Rwanda (FDLR), which is associated with the Interahamwe groups responsible for the 1994 genocide in Rwanda. The continued presence of the FDLR in the DRC is commonly agreed to be one of the key residual reasons for the continued conflict in the subregion. The FDLR is a complex set of military forces comprising some seven thousand combatants with bases in Katanga and the north and south Kivu provinces, and with a political command living in parts of northern Europe and America. Throughout 2006 and early 2007 a series of studies were undertaken on the FDLR to better understand their size, force projection, motivations, objectives, command, and control. This work was undertaken by a small group of Congolese and international researchers. The resulting report was probably the most in-depth study of the rebel group to date that set out clear recommendations on how to go about dismantling the force.[74] Few of these were taken up by international actors, no common strategy was forged, and, ironically, as mentioned at the start of the chapter, it was the former belligerents, the governments of Rwanda and DRC, that took matters into their own hands in January 2009. It is too early to say whether these joint actions will be successful, but the failure of international actors to address this issue for the last fifteen years is a crucial outstanding problem.

Knowledge of political context is therefore critical in designing appropriate aid responses.[75] The problem seems to be that despite the kind of analysis on security issues being produced, the right people are not reading them, such analysis presents the kinds of political obstacles and difficulties that bureaucrats are often unwilling to contend with, and there is little accountability if such analysis is missed.

OPERATIONAL RESPONSES

There is nothing new in development projects being used to further security objectives; aid was used by the US military as part of "village pacification" during the Vietnam War.[76] The question now for development practitioners is whose security interests are served by the use of aid in this way?

Development aid is certainly being used to counter the supply side of terrorist action. For example, at the global level, the IFIs were involved with key bilateral donors in tackling the funding of terrorist groups. The Financial Action Task Force, established in 2002, came up with forty recommendations to address money laundering and terrorist financing.[77] While these steps went a long way in securitizing the international financial system, early measures against alleged transfer companies had potentially hazardous developmental consequences upon marginal populations. For example, the closure of the Al-Barakat money transfer system severely reduced the $1 billion annual remittance lifeline to Somalia.[78]

Other counterterrorism measures financed by aid have included infrastructure projects (airports and ports) as well as police, intelligence, and defense service reform. Considerable effort has been undertaken by the United States in forging common security and development approaches, for example, in Africa, to assist countries in adopting stronger counterterror measures, including the Trans-Sahara

Counterterrorism Partnership, established in 2006, and the Combined Joint Task Force for the Horn of Africa. A review of these operations, costing more than $100 million each, suggests that there was a serious misalignment of approaches, and whereas there was "widely shared recognition that US counter-terrorism efforts should be 80% civilian and 20% military . . . the actual proportion has often been the reverse."[79]

Armed conflict settings represent another interesting intersection of counterterrorism, counterinsurgency, and conflict-reducing measures. Development aid is increasingly being called upon to reduce violence in the heart of ongoing hostilities to buy time for peace in the immediate aftermath. There is little difference at times between aid operations used for counterinsurgency or those used for demobilization and reintegration of ex-combatants.[80] Analysis of results remains sparse, but there are indications that aid used in this way is not very effective.

Attention has been given to US strategies in Iraq and Afghanistan and in particular the use of the Provincial Reconstruction Teams (PRTs) to undertake development in the respective theaters. However, there was little baseline data to allow assessment of the impact of projects, and to date there has been little sign of improvement in the rule of law and governance indicators.[81] In sum, it is difficult to say that development aid assisted in the stabilization of populations.

Another type of aid program used for security purposes is the disarmament, demobilization, and reintegration (DDR) of ex-combatants. DDR has become the default option for underpinning peace agreements, particularly where there is a lack of overall security. As the UN secretary-general suggested, "the process of DDR has repeatedly proved vital to stability in a post-conflict situation."[82] DDR processes are seen as the principal means to break the command and control of former belligerents who are encouraged to participate in political as opposed to violent arenas. A recent survey of DDR indicated that there have been some sixty documented programs since the late 1980s.[83] In terms of numbers of ex-combatants, they have ranged from 864 demobilized ex-combatants in 2003 in the Solomon Islands to 150,000 in Ethiopia by the end of 2005. In terms of finance, they have ranged from aid allocations of $30 million in Djibouti to more than $558 million in the Great Lakes regional program, with a total yearly average of $630 million spent on DDR in the mid-2000s.[84] A number of evaluations undertaken in the 1990s suggested that these programs had made significant contributions to peacebuilding, primarily downsizing militaries and motivating factional elites to form power-sharing governments.[85]

Yet in the 2000s, questions began to be raised about DDR programs. In Sierra Leone, for instance, one study found "no evidence that UN operations were instrumental in facilitating DDR at the individual level and we did find some adverse affects. Non-participants in DDR do just as well as those who entered the formal demobilization program."[86] The disarmament and demobilization process may work, but reintegration has not. Such misgivings were reinforced in Liberia where some 1,000–2,000 fighters at most were estimated to have participated in the fighting in Monrovia leading up to the demise of the Charles Taylor government in early 2003. In December 2003, the UN launched a DDR program, and twelve months later some 104,000 "ex-combatants" had been processed. What this demonstrated to policymakers was that (1) numbers of rebel forces are extremely difficult to calculate; (2) policies relating to women and children had widened the door to DDR programs so that they were increasingly seen as the only welfare program of note in postconflict settings; and (3) DDR was thus open to the kinds of manipulation in which anyone could enter the process claiming to be an ex-combatant. This in turn reinforced elites associated with violence by allowing for a system of kickbacks from program beneficiaries.

DDR is by no means a panacea and is not the only solution to dealing with the problems associated with state consolidation of the means of violence. However, the success or failure of these kinds of operations points to the crux of the development–security sequencing dilemma. Every successful DDR operation has been on the back of a successful political agreement between military commanders. Development funds to finance the elaborate process of putting former combatants back into civilian life are only useful once a security framework is in place. Without such a framework, incentives packaged in an aid project, such as cash payments or the promise of short-term employment, are no real competition to the possible economic motivations associated with organized violence, such as extortion and resource rents.

CONCLUSIONS AND WAYS FORWARD

In considering the security dimension of aid, we can see two interrelated dynamics at play. First, development finance, as during the Cold War, is being manipulated to support the national security interests of donor governments. Some critiques go so far as to suggest that aid is used as a tool for containment and control in unruly and unmanageable parts of the globe.[87] While this probably places too much significance on the contribution of aid to the history and progress of these parts of the world, the conflation around "fragile" states as a new paradigm to contend with security issues is certainly a concern. Is aid being channeled to fragile states because this is where a billion of the poorest of humanity reside, or, as the evidence suggests, are certain fragile states being favored for national security reasons? The other concern is that despite all the rhetoric, the security–development nexus, as far as it pertains to trying to understand and appropriately respond to protecting populations in danger, remains very much a paper tiger. Some say that it is now such a norm in bureaucratic-speak that it has become an antipolicy; decision makers are evading responsibility for making effective interventions.[88]

What promise is there for those war-affected communities in eastern Congo or elsewhere in the future? Attempts were made to ensure greater coherence at the strategic level with the creation of the UN Peacebuilding Commission in June 2006. This was designed as "a dedicated institutional mechanism to address the special needs of countries emerging from conflict towards recovery, reintegration and reconstruction and to assist them in laying the foundation for sustainable development."[89] Views of the commission and its attendant peacebuilding fund have thus far been mixed.[90] There is no doubt that the commission has brought a degree of coordination and critical supplementary financing (not bound by ODA restrictions) for peacebuilding, particularly in the case countries: Sierra Leone, Burundi, Central African Republic, and Guinea-Bissau. This is a young institution that member states have curtailed in remit and scope, such as nixing the initial intention for it to play a monitoring and prevention role for the UN system. What this and the recent UN secretary-general's report on peacebuilding suggest is that successful attempts at reform of the international architecture are still some way off.[91] For example, the UN report demands greater IFI–UN collaboration, despite this being one of the key intentions behind the creation of the UN Peacebuilding Commission itself three years earlier.

Despite tinkering at the edges, the international architecture of the twenty-first century has not been able to contend with the challenges it faces. However, two pointers suggest optimism for change at the global level over the next two decades. First is the emergence of the nontraditional diplomatic and aid powers as personified in the BRIC countries. These countries will have an enormous impact upon global governance arrangements and propel a realignment of the post–World War II architecture. The second is the increasing significance of socioeconomic issues in thinking about security. Issues such as climate change and sustainable energy are having a fundamental impact on military thinking. Yet the old statist paradigm remains in the ascendancy in terms of primarily serving national interests, usually through the projection of the military apparatus as a solution. However, due to a number of failed military adventures and the growing recognition of the interrelated challenges of climate change, natural resource management, and increasing marginalization, one hopes that collective approaches to achieve sustainable security are realized to be more effective than simply increasing military expenditures and protecting national self-interest.[92]

At the more operational level, there are also reasons to be optimistic. Innovations and adaptations of older models of delivery indicate a more sophisticated approach to the interaction of development and security instruments. Starting with the granular, one of the challenges with peacebuilding is both understanding context and measuring impact. Analysis of poverty has traditionally been done at the level of the household; measuring insecurity has been far less precise by way of newspaper reporting or recording battle deaths, for example. Moves to link such analysis at the individual household level will support a much better analysis of insecurity, integrate the views of survivors, and allow a more robust assessment of progress by external actors.[93]

From analysis to operations, there are sweeping changes occurring to development approaches to building infrastructure, local governance, and job creation—particularly coming out of Latin America—which are having a profound impact on development thinking around the issue of violence prevention. Very practical, people-centered, and equitable approaches to municipal regeneration and infrastructure by the mayor of Bogota, Colombia, for example, had dramatic effects in terms of reducing homicide and street crime.[94]

In the battle zones there are also some positive innovations. The use of technology is beginning to allow for greater accountability in aid provision. Mobile phones were used for cash payments to more than 130,000 ex-combatants in the DRC, a country bereft of financial infrastructure in rural areas. Phones have also been used by the World Food Program for food voucher systems for Iraqi refugees as well as in Haiti. This level of precision promises much greater chances of ensuring the confidence and credibility of programming among beneficiary communities. Recent evidence from Afghanistan suggests low credence has been given to the use of aid (for food, schools, health posts, etc.) in counterinsurgency campaigns, resulting in little positive security impact; in fact, the manipulation of aid can cause further instability and conflict.[95] Yet, when aid is programmed to ensure community ownership and decision making, then other evidence suggests this can have a significant impact upon social cohesion and stability.[96] Ultimately, tackling organized violence needs first a political–security framework in order to address the protagonists, preferably through mediation, not force. Then development aid can be used in ways to consolidate such political processes. Given that so much of this occurs at the local level, well beyond the capital city, international actors should more rigorously examine the ways in which security and aid are provided to communities. Strangely enough, the much-maligned PRTs are an example of how this could work. The key here is the presence of a legitimate peacekeeping force, working in tandem with those actors supporting community recovery and job creation that could make the security–development nexus a reality. It is at these local levels that international reform should start.

Notes

The views expressed here are the author's alone and do not represent the views of the World Bank.

1. See, for example, various UN and Global Witness reports. For example, see the final report of the UN Panel of Experts on the Illegal Exploitation of Natural Resources and Other Forms of Wealth of the DRC, October 23, 2003, UN Report S/2003/1027, http://daccess-dds-ny .un.org/doc/UNDOC/GEN/N03/567/36/IMG/N0356736.pdf?OpenElement; and "Faced with a Gun, What Can You Do ?" War and the Militarization of Mining in Eastern Congo, *Global Witness*, July 2009, www.globalwitness.org/library/global-witness-report-faced-gun -what-can-you-do.

2. Among others, Brussels European Council, "European Security Strategy: A Secure Europe in a Better World" (Brussels: Brussels European Council, December 12–13, 2003); OECD, "The Security Development Nexus: Challenges for Aid" (Paris: OECD, April 2004); Report of the UN Secretary-General, "In Larger Freedom: Towards Security, Development and Human Rights for All" (UN doc. A/59/2005, March 21, 2005); and Department for International Development, "Fighting Poverty to Build a Safer World: A Strategy for Security and Development" (London: DFID, 2005).

3. See the World Development Report, *Conflict Security and Development* (Washington, DC: World Bank, 2011).

4. See, for example, *US Counter-Insurgency Field Manual* (Chicago, IL: University of Chicago Press, 2006).

5. Adapted from Dimitri Demekas, J. McHugh, and T. Kosma, "The Economics of Post-Conflict Aid" (Washington, DC: IMF Working Paper, 02/198, 2002).

6. OECD, "Development Aid at Its Highest Ever in 2008," OECD press release, March 30, 2009.

7. World Bank, "Global Monitoring Report" (Washington, DC: World Bank, 2008).

8. World Bank, "Global Monitoring Report" (Washington, DC: World Bank, 2010).

9. Mark Malan, *US Civil-Military Imbalance for Global Engagement* (Washington, DC: Refugees International, July 2008).

10. Other donors include, among others, Saudi Arabia, Venezuela, Malaysia, and Thailand. See World Bank, "Global Monitoring Report" (2008 and 2010).

11. World Bank, "Global Monitoring Report" (2008).

12. World Bank, "Global Development Finance Report" (Washington, DC: World Bank, June 2008); and IFAD, "Sending Money Home: Worldwide Remittance Flows to Developing Countries" (April 2008), www.ifad.org/remittances/maps/index.htm.

13. SIPRI, *Military Expenditure: SIPRI Yearbook 2008* (Oxford: Oxford University Press, 2008).

14. Michael Kremer and Edward Miguel, "The Illusion of Sustainability" in *Reinventing Foreign Aid*, ed. William Easterly (Boston: MIT Press, 2008).

15. Craig Burnside and David Dollar, "Aid, Policies and Growth," *American Economic Review* 90, no. 4 (2000): 847–68. For example, the Millennium Challenge Corporation was established by the US government in 2004 on these principles.

16. Nilsson Maria, *Effects of Budget Support: A Discussion of Early Evidence* (Sweden: Sida, 2004).

17. World Bank, *Aid Architecture: An Overview of the Main Trends in Official Development Assistance Flows* (Washington, DC: World Bank, February 2007).

18. The PRSP sets out national government priority development objectives as the main framework for donor collaboration and now a condition for debt relief. See World Bank, *Partners in Transforming Development* (Washington, DC: World Bank, 2000).

19. See, for example, David Hale, "The Rise of China and India: Implications for African Growth and Security," in *African Security, Commodities and Development* (London: RUSI, Whitehall Report 4-06, 2006).

20. Ngaire Woods, "Whose Aid? Whose Influence? China, Emerging Donors and the Silent Revolution in Development Assistance," *International Affairs* 84, no. 6 (2008): 1205–21.

21. Carl Conetta and Charles Knight, "Post-Cold War US Military Expenditure in the Context of World Spending Trends" (Washington, DC: Project on Defense Alternatives Briefing Memo, January 1997).

22. "Human Security Brief 2007," *Human Security Centre*, www.humansecuritybrief.info/; Mary Kaldor, *New and Old Wars* (Oxford: Blackwell, 1999); and Mark Duffield *Global Governance and the New Wars* (London: Zed Books, 2001).

23. Thomas Hammes, *The Sling and the Stone: On War in the 21st Century* (Minneapolis: Zenith Press, 2006).

24. John L. Hirsch and Robert B. Oakley, *Somalia and Operation Restore Hope: Reflections on Peacemaking and Peacekeeping* (Washington, DC: USIP Press, 1995). Presidential Decision Directive 25 established a "vital national interest" by which to decide whether US forces should be involved in multilateral peacekeeping activities. See White House press release, "President Clinton Signs PDD Establishing 'US Policy on Reforming Multilateral Peace Operations,'" May 5, 1994. www.fas.org/irp/offdocs/pdd25.htm.

25. Linda Melvern, *Conspiracy to Murder: The Rwandan Genocide*, rev. ed. (London: Verso, 2006).

26. Timothy Docking, "AIDS and Violent Conflict in Africa" (Washington, DC: USIP Special Report, October 2001); and "Examining Implications of HIV/AIDS for UN Peacekeeping Operations" (UN S/PRST/16, 2001).

27. Larry Elliott, "The West Knows Now There Is No Wall to Hide Behind," *Guardian*, November 12, 2001, www.guardian.co.uk/business/2001/nov/13/warinafghanistan2001.globalisation.

28. See "The National Security Strategy of the United States of America" (Washington, DC: The White House, September 2002), www.au.af.mil/au/awc/awcgate/nss/nss_sep2002.pdf.

29. Hammes, *The Sling and the Stone*, 208.

30. Rupert Smith, *The Utility of Force* (New York: Vintage, 2008).

31. International Commission on Intervention and State Sovereignty, *The Responsibility to Protect* (Ottawa: IDRC, December 2001), www.iciss.ca/report2-en.asp; UN, *A More Secure World: Our Shared Responsibility*, Report of the High-Level Panel on Threats, Challenges and Change (New York: UN, 2004), www.un.org/secureworld/report2.pdf; and UN General Assembly, "In Larger Freedom: Towards Development, Security and Human Rights for All," Report of the UN Secretary-General, 59th session, www.un.org/largerfreedom /contents.htm.

32. USAID, *Foreign Aid in the National Interest: Promoting Freedom, Security and Opportunity* (Washington, DC: Heritage Foundation, 2002), www.usaid.gov/fani/Full_Report—Foreign _Aid_in_the_National_Interest.pdf.

33. Maria Stern and Joakim Ojendal, "Mapping the Security Development Nexus: Conflict, Complexity, Cacophony, Convergence?" *Security Dialogue* 41, no. 1 (2010): 5–29.

34. Foreign and Commonwealth Office, *The Global Conflict Prevention Pool: A Joint UK Government Approach to Reducing Conflict* (London: Department for International Development, 2004); and "Office for the Coordinator for Reconstruction and Stabilization," *US State Department*, www.state.gov/s/crs/.

35. See, for example, *OECD DAC Handbook on Security Sector Reform* (Paris: OECD, 2007), www.oecd.org/dataoecd/43/25/38406485.pdf.

36. DAC, *DAC Statistical Reporting Directives* (Paris: OECD, April 2007).

37. UN Development Group and World Bank, "Post-Conflict Needs Assessments," www .undg.org/index.cfm?P=144.

38. World Bank, *UN–World Bank Partnership Framework for Crisis and Post-Crisis Situations* (Washington, DC: World Bank, October 2008).

39. Scanteam and World Bank, "Review of Post-Crisis Multi-Donor Trust Funds" (Norad: Oslo, February 2007), available at Norad website, www.norad.no/en/Tools+and+publications /Publications/Publication+Page?key=109604.

40. Ibid.

41. Nicholas Waddell, "The Ties that Bind: DFID and the Emerging Security and Development Agenda," *Conflict, Security and Development* 6, no. 4 (2006): 531–55.

42. See, for example, Dan Smith, *Toward a Strategic Framework for Peacebuilding: Getting Their Act Together* (Oslo: PRIO Joint Utstein Study of Peacebuilding, 2004); and N. Ball, P. Biesheuval, and F. Olanisakin, "Security and Justice Sector Reform Programming in Africa" (London: DFID Evaluation Working Paper, 2007).

43. Duffield, *Global Governance*; and Ngaire Woods, "The Shifting Politics of Foreign Aid," *International Affairs* 81, no. 2 (2005): 393–409.

44. Michael Brzoska, "Extending ODA or Creating a New Reporting Instrument for Security Related Expenditures for Development," *Development Policy Review* 26, no. 2 (2008): 131–50.

45. OECD, "Ensuring Fragile States Are Not Left Behind" (OECD, February 2010), www .oecd.org/dataoecd/38/33/44822042.pdf.

46. Brzoska, "Extending ODA."

47. Jakob Ibsen and Timo Kivimaki, "Existing Development Cooperation in the Field of Terrorism Prevention," in *Development Cooperation as an Instrument of Prevention of Terrorism* (Copenhagen: DANIDA, August 2003).

48. See, for example, Monty Marshall and Benjamin Cole, "Global Report on Conflict Governance and State Fragility 2008," *Foreign Policy Bulletin*, Center for Systemic Peace, www .systemicpeace.org/Global%20Report%202008.pdf.

49. DAC, *Monitoring Resource Flows to Fragile States: 2007 Report* (Paris: OECD, 2007), www.oecd.org/dataoecd/4/21/41680220.pdf.

50. In addition to this figure, these states often hosted UN peacekeeping operations, which by the mid-2000s were costing between $5 billion and $8 billion per year.

51. DAC, *Monitoring Resource Flows.*

52. "Ensuring Fragile States Are Not Left Behind, Summary Report," February 2010, OECD/ DAC, www.oecd.org/dataoecd/12/55/45659170.pdf.

53. World Bank, Africa conflict data per capita postconflict aid over a three-year average: $21 DRC, $31 Burundi, $129 Afghanistan; $211 Bosnia; $270 East Timor; and $508 Iraq.

54. Jo Beall, Thomas Goodfellow, and James Putzel, "On the Discourse of Terrorism, Security and Development," *Journal of International Development* 18, no. 1 (2006): 51–67.

55. IDA, "Operational Approaches and Financing in Fragile States" (Washington, DC: IDA, June 2007), http://siteresources.worldbank.org/IDA/Resources/IDA15FragileStates.pdf.

56. Human Security Report Project, "Human Security Brief, 2007," Simon Fraser University, Vancouver, Canada, www.hsrgroup.org/human-security-reports/2007/overview.aspx; and Michael Doyle and Nicholas Sambanis, *Making War and Building Peace* (Princeton, NJ: Princeton University Press, 2006).

57. Paul Collier and Anke Hoeffler, "Conflicts," *Global Crises, Global Solutions*, ed. Bjorn Lomborg (Cambridge: Cambridge University Press, 2004), 146.

58. Paul Collier, *Development and Conflict* (Oxford: Centre for the Study of African Economies, October 2004), 8.

59. Naomi Klein *The Shock Doctrine* (New York: Metropolitan Books, 2007).

60. H.V. Luong, ed., *Post-War Vietnam* (Lanham, MD: Rowman and Littlefield, 2003); and Mark Bradbury, *Becoming Somaliland* (Oxford: James Currey, 2008).

61. Rex Brynen, "Palestine: Building Neither Peace nor State" in *Building States to Build Peace*, ed. Charles T. Call (Boulder, CO: Lynne Rienner, 2008).

62. World Bank, *Four Years—Intifada, Closures and Palestinian Economic Crisis: An Assessment* (Washington, DC: World Bank, 2004), http://siteresources.worldbank.org/INTWEST BANKGAZA/Resources/wbgaza-4yrassessment.pdf.

63. Derick W. Brinkerhoff, ed., *Governance in Post-Conflict Societies* (Abingdon, UK: Routledge, 2007).

64. Peter Uvin, *Aiding Violence: The Development Enterprise in Rwanda* (Hartford, CT: Kumarian Press, 1998).

65. See, for example, Jonathan Goodhand, "Violent Conflict, Poverty and Chronic Poverty" (INTRAC, May 2001), www.chronicpoverty.org/uploads/publication_files/WP06_Good hand.pdf; and Frances Stewart, "Development and Security," CRISE Working Paper 3 (Oxford, CRISE, 2004).

66. James Boyce, "Beyond Good Intentions: External Assistance and Peacebuilding," in *Good Intentions*, ed. Shep Forman and Stewart Patrick, 367–82 (Boulder, CO: Lynne Rienner, 2000).

67. Tony Addison and Mansoob Murshed, *Debt Relief and Civil War*, Discussion Paper 2001/57 (Helsinki: UN University World Institute for Development Economics Research, August 2001).

68. William Reno, "Uganda's Politics of War and Debt Relief," *Review of International Political Economy* 9, no. 3 (2001): 415–35.

69. James Dobbins, John G. McGinn, Keith Crane, Seth G. Jones, Rollie Lal, Andrew Rathmell, Rachel Swanger, and Anga Timilsina, *America's Role in Nation-Building: From Germany to Iraq* (New York: Rand, 2003).

70. International Bank of Reconstruction and Development, World Bank Group, Articles of Agreement, Article IV Section 10, http://siteresources.worldbank.org/EXTABOUTUS /Resources/ibrd-articlesofagreement.pdf.

71. USAID, "Conducting a Conflict Assessment: A Framework for Analysis and Program Development" (Washington, DC: USAID, August 17, 2004); DFID, *Conducting Conflict Analysis: Guidance Notes* (London: DFID, January 2002); Per Wam and Shonali Sardesai, *Conflict Analysis Framework* (Washington, DC: World Bank, 2005).

72. World Bank, "Effective Conflict Analysis Exercises: Overcoming Organizational Challenges," Report No. 36446-GLB (Washington, DC: World Bank, June 21, 2006), http://site resources.worldbank.org/INTCPR/214578-1111741001753/21045309/Effective_Conflict _Analysis_Exercises_Report_2006.pdf.

73. World Bank, "Country Social Assessment, Kenya, 2006" (Washington, DC: World Bank, 2006).

74. Hans Romkema, "Opportunities and Constraints for the Disarmament and Repatriation of Foreign Armed Groups in the DRC: The cases of the FDLR, FNL and ADF/ NALU" (Washington, DC: MDRP Secretariat, World Bank, June 2007), www.mdrp.org/PDFs/MDRP _DRC_COFS_Study.pdf

75. DAC, "Principles for Good International Engagement in Fragile States and Situations" (Paris: OECD, 2007).

76. Jeffrey Record and Andrew Terrill, *Iraq and Vietnam* (Carlisle, PA: Strategic Studies Institute, May 2004).

77. FATF/OECD, "FATF 40 Recommendations" (Paris: FATF/OECD, October 2003), www .fatf-gafi.org/dataoecd/7/40/34849567.PDF.

78. Abdulsalam Omar and Gina El Koury, "Regulation and Supervision in a Vacuum: The Story of the Somali Remittance Sector," *Small Enterprise Development*, 15, no. 1 (2004): 44–52.

79. CSIS, "Integrating 21st Century Development and Security Assistance" (Washington, DC: CSIS, January 2008), 6, http://csis.org/files/media/csis/pubs/080118-andrews-integrating 21stcentury.pdf.

80. Joanna Spear, "Counterinsurgency," in *Security Studies: An Introduction*, ed. Paul D. Williams (Abingdon, UK: Routledge, 2008), 402–3. For a discussion of how aid is used in COIN, see David Kilcullen, *The Accidental Guerilla* (Oxford: Oxford University Press, 2009).

81. See, for example, CSIS, "Integrating 21st Century Development"; and Anthony Cordesman, "The Iraq War and Lessons for Counterinsurgency" (Washington, DC: CSIS March, 2006).

82. Report of the Secretary-General, "The Role of UN Peacekeeping in Disarmament Demobilization and Reintegration" (UN: S/2000/101, February 11, 2000), para. 3.

83. See Robert Muggah, ed., *Security and Post Conflict Reconstruction* (London: Routledge, 2009); and Nicole Ball, "Review of the International Financing Arrangements for DDR" (Sweden: Stockholm Initiative for DDR, 2006).

84. Multi-Country Demobilization and Reintegration Program, MDRP (2002–9), www .mdrp.org.

85. World Bank, "DDR: Seven Case Studies" (Washington, DC: World Bank, 1993); and N. Colleta, Marcus Kostner, and Ingo Wiederhofer, "Case Studies in War-to-Peace Transitions: The Demobilization and Reinitgration of Ex-Combatants in Ethopia, Namibia and Uganda," World Bank Discussion Paper No. 331 (Washington, DC: World Bank, 1996).

86. Jeremy Weinstein and McCartan Humphreys, "Disentangling the Determinants of Successful Demobilization and Reintegration" (Washington, DC: Centre for Global Development, 2005).

87. Mark Duffield, *Development, Security and Unending War* (Cambridge: Polity, 2007).

88. David Chandler, "The Security Development Nexus and the Rise of Anti-Foreign Policy," *Journal of International Relations and Development*, 10 (2007): 362–86.

89. UN General Assembly, *2005 World Summit Outcome* (UN: A/60/L.1, October 24, 2005), para. 97, http://daccess-dds-ny.un.org/doc/UNDOC/GEN/N05/487/60/PDF/N0548760 .pdf?OpenElement.

90. Mats Berdal, "The UN Peacebuilding Commission" in *Whose Peace? Critical Perspectives on the Political Economy of Peacebuilding*, ed. Michael Pugh, Neil Cooper, and Mandy Turner (Basingstoke, UK: Macmillan, 2008).

91. UN, "Report of the Secretary-General on Peacebuilding in the Immediate Aftermath of Conflict" (UN A/63/881-S/2009/304, June 11, 2009), www.un.org/ga/search/view_doc.asp?symbol=A/63/881.

92. Chris Abbott, Paul Rogers, and John Sloboda, "Global Responses to Global Threats" (Oxford: Oxford Research Group, June 2006); and Gayle E. Smith, *In Search of Sustainable Security* (Washington, DC: Center for American Progress, June 2008).

93. Rachael Diprose, "Safety and Security," CRISE Working Paper No. 52 (Oxford: CRISE, April 2008).

94. World Bank Conference, "Violence Prevention: A Critical Dimension of Development," Washington, DC, April 6–7, 2009, http://web.worldbank.org/WBSITE/EXTERNAL/TOPICS/EXTSOCIALDEVELOPMENT/0,,contentMDK:22142384~menuPK:2644098~pagePK:64020865~piPK:51164185~theSitePK:244363,00.html.

95. Andrew Wilder, *Winning Hearts and Minds: Understanding the Relationship between Aid and Security* (Boston: Tufts University, 2008); and Andrew Wilder, "A Weapons System Based on Wishful Thinking," *Boston Globe*, September 16, 2009.

96. James Fearon, Macartan Humphreys, and Jeremy M. Weinstein, "Can Development Aid Contribute to Social Cohesion after Civil War, Evidence from a Field Experiment in Post-Conflict Liberia." Paper presented at the American Economic Association Annual Meeting, January 2009, San Francisco. www.indiana.edu/~workshop/colloquia/materials/papers/fearon_paper.pdf.

Chapter 3

AID

A Development Perspective

Daniel Morrow

From its origins after World War II, official development assistance (ODA) was motivated in large measure by the security interests of the aid-providing governments.[1] Aid from the bilateral agencies of most Western governments and Japan—and from the multilateral institutions that these governments controlled—was considered an instrument for resisting the expansion of Soviet and Chinese influence.[2] In theory, this could be achieved directly by bolstering the resources of anticommunist regimes and indirectly by accelerating economic development and thereby weakening the appeal of communism within recipient states. As expressed by Carol Lancaster, "Without the Cold War, aid would likely not exist today—or if it did, it would be much smaller than the $100 billion in aid provided by all governments in 2004. Aid is, in short, a child of hardheaded, diplomatic realism."[3]

Particularly since the end of the Cold War, the concept of security has changed and expanded (see chapter 1). Within the "statist" paradigm, it is widely argued that the long-term security of high-income states can be enhanced by increasing the number and strength of democratic regimes among low- and middle-income states, by decreasing the incidence of violent conflicts within low-income states that might trigger regional conflicts, and by strengthening the economy and governance within fragile or failed states that might otherwise become havens for terrorists and international criminals. Since the early 1990s, a human security paradigm of security has gained ground: security means reduced risk or severity of disruption of the well-being of individuals due to income shocks, disease, natural disaster, or other threats.[4] And there has been much discussion of the possible interactions between state-centric and human-centric concepts of security—in particular, the ways and extent to which the stability and capacities of states are affected by the security of individuals.[5]

After the rationale for ODA as an instrument to resist expansion of communist influence evaporated, the global volume of ODA declined—from about $58 billion in 1991–92 to $52 billion in 1996–97 (net disbursements in 2006 dollars).[6] However, since the mid-1990s, these new and broader concepts of security have provided new rationales for aid, and, partly in response to these new security-related objectives, the total volume of ODA has increased significantly—to $69 billion in 2003, an average of $105 billion for 2005–7, and almost $120 billion in 2008.

In response to state-centric security objectives, substantial aid has been provided to support the growth of market economies and democracy, especially among the "transition economies" in Eastern Europe and Central Asia, and to support economic development within countries that have recently suffered violent conflict, other fragile states at risk of falling into such conflict, and "failed states." The latter goal has become increasingly important following the 9/11 terrorist attacks on the United States and the consequent wars in Afghanistan and Iraq.[7] Aid to "fragile and conflict-affected states," as defined by the Organisation for Economic Co-operation and Development (OECD) and its Development Assistance Committee (DAC), grew from about $15 billion in 2000 to about $37 billion in 2007. Most of that increased aid went to Iraq and Afghanistan, and in 2007 just five countries—Iraq, Afghanistan, Ethiopia, Pakistan, and Sudan—accounted for about half of the ODA destined for the forty-eight fragile and conflict-affected states.[8] Aid volumes to other fragile and conflict-affected states have varied from year to year depending on their circumstances.[9]

Aid agencies have also increased their attention to human security. This has been part of a renewed focus on poverty reduction—defined multidimensionally to include reduced vulnerability to hunger, disease, loss of employment, natural disaster, and other potential shocks to well-being (see the chapters by Williams and Sud in this volume). This has involved expanded programs for disease control, health services, social safety nets, social protection, and preparation for and mitigation of natural disasters. The volume of ODA devoted to such objectives has almost certainly grown substantially over the past twenty years—although data for aid focused on human security objectives are not readily available.[10] Two entirely new official institutions—the Global Fund to Fight AIDs, Tuberculosis and Malaria and the US President's Emergency Plan for AIDS Relief—were created specifically for the purpose of reducing the insecurity caused by these diseases. In addition, there has been a huge increase in private development assistance, especially directed toward reducing the risks and impacts of infectious diseases.

Given these trends, there is now a broad, rich agenda for research about the linkages between development assistance and security. Among those who want to maximize the impact of ODA on economic growth and poverty reduction (which probably includes most of the staff in development agencies), a key question is whether the use of ODA to pursue state security might skew the allocation of aid resources in favor of countries in which aid providers have a more direct security interest without adequate regard to how well those recipient governments can use aid effectively for economic development.[11] Among those who are most concerned about mitigating various sorts of security threats, a key question is how to allocate limited aid resources among these various threats.

This chapter addresses a related but different and equally important question: under what circumstances and through what means can aid be used effectively to improve security-related development outcomes? With respect to aid's potential contribution to human security, the question about its effectiveness is the central question. With respect to aid's potential contribution to state security, this chapter considers only the first link in the presumed causal chain—that is, the link from aid to economic development. The next link is that economic development leads to improved political stability to greater security for the aid providers. It is the first link in this chain that has traditionally been the primary concern of the professional staff within both bilateral and multilateral development agencies, even when they recognize that other actors within their political "authorizing environment" are largely concerned about the subsequent links. The other two links in this presumed causal chain are equally important and controversial but beyond the scope of this chapter.

THE PROBLEM OF ACHIEVING AID EFFECTIVENESS: LESSONS OF EXPERIENCE

To address the question of whether aid can effectively contribute to economic development and thereby to security-related objectives, it is important to understand the track record of aid and past impediments to aid effectiveness. In the broadest terms, that track record indicates that it is quite feasible for aid donors to achieve rather narrowly defined objectives of discrete "projects," but that in many countries these successful projects have not added up to broad and sustainable development. Indeed, over the past decades, voluminous ex post facto evaluations of aid-financed projects—which have been the primary modality for aid delivery—suggest that about two-thirds of these projects have satisfactorily achieved their stated developmental objectives.[12]

With respect to impacts on overall development, however, these evaluations are unreliable and potentially misleading for three reasons.[13] First, such evaluations typically are conducted just after the support by the external aid agencies has ended and therefore do not capture how well the benefits of the aid were sustained over time. There is considerable evidence that aid-financed projects are often not sustainable—primarily due to lack of interest or capacity within the recipient country—and that the medium- to long-term impacts of aid projects are therefore often negligible.[14] Second, aid agencies seldom evaluate to what extent the aid-financed activities have had any unintended, negative effects on the capacities of the institutions of the recipient government beyond the boundaries of the aid project. Other evidence strongly indicates that, among countries receiving large amounts of aid, the plethora of aid-financed projects implemented by myriad uncoordinated donors often have undermined the capacity and perhaps the authority of the recipient government's own institutions.[15] The government's capacity is undermined in two ways: aid agencies set up their own project implementation units outside of the government's bureaucracy—bypassing the government and often poaching the best nationals to staff these units; and the aid-financed activities impose high transaction costs on government officials, diverting their attention from nonaid activities. Third, to some extent, aid agencies have financed projects that the recipient governments would have done anyway, so some part of the aid funds indirectly financed other unidentified, unevaluated, and possibly nondevelopmental activity chosen by the government. For example, an aid agency might nominally finance new road construction that the government had intended to do anyway, but given the fungibility of money, the aid in fact makes possible increased military spending.[16] These three problems—lack of sustainability, unintended negative impacts on the government's overall institutional capacity, and fungibility—have plagued development assistance. Although some aid-financed projects have undoubtedly contributed to overall, sustainable development, many have failed to do so because of some combination of these three problems.

Another common problem of development assistance deserves mention—the limited effectiveness of policy conditionality. In the early 1980s, aid providers became increasingly convinced that whether or not their discrete projects were successful was less important than whether or not they could persuade or compel recipient governments to pursue better national economic policies. The primary means for inducing better national economic policies became aid "conditionality," that is, making some aid disbursements conditional on agreed policy reforms. However, by the late 1990s, aid providers determined that such conditionality usually did not work to induce governments to undertake and sustain policy reforms that they did not "own."[17] In many cases governments did not have the political or institutional capacities to implement such reforms. Often aid agencies did not have sufficient incentive to enforce their conditions. And so, by about 2000, most aid agencies had largely abandoned their attempts to force governments to implement policies that did not have sufficient political support within the recipient country.

RECENT EFFORTS TO IMPROVE AID EFFECTIVENESS

Based on these experiences, a dominant view has emerged among bilateral and multilateral aid agencies over the past decade about what ought to be done to increase the likelihood that aid will effectively contribute to broad and sustainable development. Although these ideas found expression in various ways in earlier decades and again strongly in the late 1990s, they have recently been articulated most fully and clearly in the Paris Declaration on Aid Effectiveness in 2005.[18] This declaration was prepared under the auspices of the Development Assistance Committee (DAC) of the Organisation for Economic Co-operation and Development (OECD) and endorsed by almost all aid-providing and most aid-receiving governments.[19]

The main tenet of the Paris Declaration is that aid is likely to be effective only if it is solidly grounded in the principles of "country ownership," "alignment," and "harmonization."[20] These principles imply that recipient countries should put forward their own national development strategies and programs, and—to the extent that aid providers consider these strategies and program viable—donors should align aid with them and should use harmonized processes that reduce the transaction costs of aid as well as the negative impacts of aid on national institutions.

Full application of the Paris Declaration principles would have two major consequences. First, aid should be allocated primarily to those recipient governments that have been able to put forward coherent and credible development programs and have demonstrated their capacities to implement them. This implies that aid providers would exercise "country selectivity" in favor of the most capable governments. Second, aid should increasingly be provided through some form of "budget support" rather than through discrete projects managed by the aid providers. In other words, aid providers should finance a share of a recipient government's budgeted programs and rely on that government's own bureaucracy and "country systems" for implementation, financial accountability, and monitoring and evaluation. Such an approach to aid should, in theory, overcome the historical impediments to aid effectiveness: country ownership would ensure the implementation and sustainability of desired investments and policy reforms; the use of national institutions would exercise and strengthen their capacities and authority; and attention to the overall public sector budget would avoid fungibility (that is, aid would not be redirected). However, this approach to aid would *not* eliminate the need for aid agencies to acquire sufficient knowledge of a recipient country's economy, politics, and institutions in order to make reasonable judgments about the viability of the country-owned strategy and programs and about the recipient government's capacity for implementation.

Recent attempts at implementation of these principles have taken several forms. Most importantly, the Poverty Reduction Strategy initiative, launched by the World Bank and IMF in 2000 and quickly adopted by most other aid agencies, requires low-income countries to put forward country-owned development strategies, and aid providers are expected to align themselves with these strategies, relying increasingly on country institutions and systems for implementation.[21] This initiative is still being pursued with varying degrees of seriousness by most low-income countries and their aid providers. Also, the first major new US bilateral aid initiative in more than forty years—the Millennium Challenge Corporation (MCC), which started in 2004—partially reflects the principles of the Paris Declaration. The basic idea of the MCC is to allocate funds only to well-performing countries that have met specific criteria for "ruling justly, investing in people and promoting economic freedom." In principle, the selected countries are expected to propose their own programs for MCC financing and to take primary responsibility for implementation. As another example, the Global Fund to Fight AIDS, Tuberculosis and Malaria relies on programs conceived and then implemented by organizations within the recipient countries.

It is clear that successful application of the Paris Declaration principles is fraught with difficulties and contradictions. Among other obstacles, responding to country-owned initiatives and relying on the recipient's own institutions run counter to powerful internal incentives of the aid providers. It would reduce their control, visibility, and potentially the required size of their own bureaucracies and budgets, and strict country selectivity might limit the total amount that the aid agencies disburse.[22] Considering these incentives among the donor agencies, it should be expected that implementation of the Paris Declaration principles would be slow and halfhearted.

Nevertheless, there is partial evidence that, in some cases, the approach to development assistance advocated by the Paris Declaration is being pursued and *might* lead to greater aid effectiveness. At the OECD/DAC conference in Accra, Ghana, in September 2008, aid providers and recipients largely reconfirmed their commitment to the Paris Declaration principles as the most promising approach for overcoming the long-standing problems of aid effectiveness. Survey results presented at the Accra conference indicate that implementation of these principles is improving—albeit only slowly and only within a small subset of countries with better economic governance, such as Ghana, Tanzania, Rwanda, and Vietnam.[23] Many aid agencies and recipient governments have also been experimenting with budget support as the best modality for aid, and some of these experiments seem promising.[24]

MAKING DEVELOPMENT ASSISTANCE MORE EFFECTIVE IN ADDRESSING SECURITY CONCERNS

Assuming that low levels of development constitute a threat to state security or human security, security could be enhanced by increasing the effectiveness of development assistance. As just discussed, historical and more recent experience with development assistance indicates that such effectiveness is most likely to be achieved through application of the principles of the Paris Declaration. But are these principles equally applicable and promising across the full range of security-related concerns?

Almost certainly, application of the Paris Declaration principles would increase the effectiveness of development assistance in promoting human security within middle-income and well-governed low-income countries. The human security–related activities of aid agencies can be grouped broadly under the headings of "social protection" and "preparation for and mitigation of natural disasters." Social protection refers to diverse public actions taken in response to levels of vulnerability, risk, and deprivation that are deemed socially unacceptable within a given polity or society. Preparation for and mitigation of the impact of natural disasters (as distinct from ex post facto relief) involve a host of activities from creating national disaster relief institutions to creating insurance markets to enforcing better building codes.

A priori, there are compelling reasons to believe that application of the Paris Declaration principles would be essential for the effectiveness of aid in many domains related to human security. First, with respect to social protection, the issues involved are likely to be politically contentious within aid-recipient countries because they deal with redefining the responsibilities of the state to its citizens. In this regard, social protection as a means to improve human security requires "state-building" in the broad sense of renegotiating the social contract. Second, appropriate social protection policies must be designed with full understanding of the local society and culture. In particular, it is necessary to be aware of the traditional, nongovernmental arrangements by which individuals, families, and communities cope with risk and then to design public actions that do not unintentionally undermine them. Third, implementation of any social protection or many sorts of natural disaster preparation and mitigation programs involves developing substantial and sustainable institutional capacities, which takes time and sustained political support.[25] Even after appropriate institutions are put in place, large-scale implementation of these programs takes time.

These broad characteristics of most social protection and natural disaster mitigation activities imply that the principles of the Paris Declaration are likely to be especially relevant and necessary for successful development assistance in these areas.[26] Policies and programs need to be "home-grown" in order to ensure that they are based on sustainable political support and well attuned to local society and culture.[27] Such country ownership is essential to bring about the creation and strengthening of the institutions required for implementation. This cannot be done within the normal time frame for aid-financed projects, although such projects might serve as an experiment or demonstration activity.

THE CHALLENGE OF AID TO FRAGILE STATES

But are the Paris Declaration principles for aid effectiveness relevant in the set of countries that are now the focus of state security concerns—postconflict, fragile, or failed states? Almost by definition, these countries—referred to generically as fragile states—do not have the political and institutional capacities to design and implement their own development strategies and programs. The problem, as expressed by DAC, is "What can donor agencies do in situations where this partnership model [embodied by the Paris Declaration principles], and in particular the role played by the government, does not seem likely to lead to effective use of aid?"[28]

That question has been the subject of much debate among aid agencies over the past decade. Initially, there was a strong movement toward the view that, in most if not all fragile countries, aid agencies would need to bypass national governments—at least temporarily—and provide basic services more directly through projects implemented by NGOs and perhaps local government institutions with substantial engagement by the aid agencies themselves. The 2001 OECD/DAC document on "Poor Performers: Basic Approaches for Supporting Development in Difficult Partnerships" expressed the view that

> it is important to support the poor in countries with severe governance problems . . . and [aid] agencies need pragmatically to focus on shorter-term progress while at the same time taking steps to build longer-term capacity. . . . Where it is not possible to engage with the central government, it may be feasible in some cases to work with sub-national government structures, as well as with civil society, to provide short-term support for poverty reduction and to support agents of change.[29]

Similarly, the World Bank's 2002 Task Force for Low-Income Countries under Stress (the Bank's term for fragile states at that time) advocated that the Bank often should bypass the government and promote "independent service authorities" to deliver basic services. Statements from various aid agencies recognized in theory the desire to balance the goals of short-term impact and long-term capacity development. As expressed in the 2005 US Agency for International's (USAID) Fragile States Strategy, "Because those living in fragile states cope with instability and uncertainty . . . short-term measures are critical to meeting their immediate needs and promoting an environment of security. At the same time, the urgent need for short-term measures should also be considered in the context of longer-term efforts required to advance stability, reform, and institutional capacity."[30]

Much recent experience indicates that aid agencies have usually not been able to find the right balance or to move steadily from bypassing to building up government institutions. Instead, in many of the fragile states in which donors have been active, largely ignoring the Paris Declaration principles, they have relied heavily on the traditional approach of many donor-driven, project-based activities—designed to provide basic services and move aid money fast while postponing or even short-circuiting national institution-building. In most cases, even if individual projects seem successful during the period of donor engagement, these approaches will likely fail to generate sustainable development for the same reasons that aid in general has so often failed over decades. Attempting to substitute for the weak leadership of nationals and bypassing the government institutions in an effort to quickly implement investments and provide basic services have not helped in most cases to lay foundations for achieving the ultimate goal of state-building. Indeed, these practices have probably undercut that goal.[31]

Consider the case of Afghanistan following the initial defeat of the Taliban in 2002. Ashraf Ghani, the minister of finance during 2003–5, has noted that aid agencies and aid-financed NGOs proliferated rapidly to take on roles that substitute for state functions, such as building and managing schools, clinics, and food distribution, through a series of structures that ran parallel to the government. He concluded that these "quick-impact projects" not only were rather ineffective in delivering basic services but also unintentionally undermined state-building. Based on that experience, he argues that "the aid system as currently configured tends to undermine rather than support state institutions . . . and has been an exercise in the perpetuation of dependence."[32] Because of the immense fragmentation of the aid system, donors undermine the national budget as a central instrument of policy and, "instead of becoming catalysts for orderly policy management, donors become instruments of division and chaos."[33] The Afghan deputy minister of finance at the time put it this way: "Capacity . . . in the public sector . . . can only be increased if donors direct their assistance toward government organizations rather than to third-party organizations. Otherwise, a culture of substitution will prevent needed institutional development in the public sector and lead to a loss of its professional-grade workers."[34]

The US experience in Iraq during 2003–8 demonstrated the importance of the Paris Declaration principles for successful development assistance in a fragile state even when there is only one large aid provider. According to the report of the US special inspector general for Iraq reconstruction, the traditional approach of donor-managed projects, which the United States pursued for several years, usually failed to generate sustainable benefits, and outcomes began to improve only when the United States started to involve Iraqi institutions in project planning and execution and started to help build capacity among those institutions. Based on this experience, the report concluded that "developing the capacity of people and systems is as important as bricks and mortar reconstruction" and "host country buy-in is essential to reconstruction's long-term success."[35] In reviewing the experiences in Afghanistan, Iraq, and elsewhere, Francis Fukuyama concluded that "foreign donors are primarily interested, understandably, in providing immediate humanitarian relief and services to the long-suffering local population. They typically do so, however, in ways that undermine the authority of and strip the capacity from the newly forming indigenous government."[36]

On the positive side, there have been some fragile states in which aid agencies have experimented—with apparently modest success—with new modalities involving at least partial application of the Paris Declaration principles. As described by Leader and Colenso, there is a spectrum of potential aid modalities between, at one end, entirely "projectized" aid with little or no country ownership or alignment and, at the other end, full "budget support" for a country-owned strategy to which all aid donors are aligned using common processes.[37] For example, in Timor-Leste, the government and its donors, led by the World Bank and the UN, prepared a transition results matrix that served initially as an instrument for government-led priority setting and donor coordination, and donors financed these government priorities through a common trust fund.[38] The National Solidarity Program in Afghanistan also served effectively for a while as a means for donors to finance local community development without undermining the authority of the central government. Manor also describes some cases of successful aid efforts in fragile states—typically relying on local, not central government, institutions.[39]

Based on many negative and some positive experiences, by 2007, the dominant view emerged within the OECD DAC that the Paris Declaration principles remain relevant even to the circumstances of fragile states, although their application must be adapted to the specific country circumstances and may take a variety of forms. Its "Principles for Good International Engagement in Fragile States and Situations" are explicitly intended "to complement the partnership commitments set out in the Paris Declaration on Aid Effectiveness." The document deserves to be quoted at length:

- "A focus on state-building . . . is equally, if not more important, than poverty reduction as a framework for engagement."
- State-building is "a primarily endogenous development" and "successful state-building will almost always be the product of domestic action, though it can be significantly enabled by well-targeted, responsive international assistance."
- "Where the state leadership has a credible strategy for fostering the social contract, a state-building approach would strongly emphasize forging a joint, multi-donor strategy with the government and then providing direct support to the state budget."
- "Where possible, international actors should seek to avoid activities which undermine national institution-building, such as developing parallel systems without thought to transition mechanisms and long-term capacity development. It is important to identify functioning systems within existing local institutions, and work to strengthen these."

- Acknowledging that this would unavoidably favor longer-term processes over shorter-term service delivery, it also stressed that "international engagement may need to be of longer-duration than in other low-income countries."[40]

But what about assistance to fragile states with noxious authoritarian governments or other circumstances in which aid agencies do not want to enhance the legitimacy of the existing government? A related OECD DAC report on aid to fragile states recommends that in such cases "diplomatic/political engagement, not development assistance, should be the primary mode of bilateral and multilateral engagement."[41] In other words, development assistance should be largely withdrawn rather than provided in circumstances that cannot contribute to state-building within the framework of a tolerable government.

Some analysts have accepted the need for better application of the Paris Declaration principles in fragile states but seem to think that this can be achieved rather easily. For example, Patrick suggests that the United States can help end the pattern of substituting for the state, thereby undermining its effectiveness simply by reducing the proportion of aid that is tied to the procurement of US-sourced goods and services.[42] While this would be a useful step forward, it would not be enough to transform the donor's impact from undermining to supporting state capacities. Unfortunately, despite the widespread agreement in theoretical terms within the donor community, application of the Paris Declaration principles among fragile states will require significant and difficult changes in the policies and behaviors of both recipient governments and most aid agencies.

Among the recipient governments, in order to move beyond rather shallow application of the principles, a particularly challenging requirement is the creation and operation of a tolerable public sector system of financial accountability. This is a complex, technocratic task involving systems for budgeting, procuring, and auditing that can limit corruption and thus provide sufficient assurance to aid donors that their funds will be spent broadly as intended. Through technical assistance, aid donors can help governments to create and run such systems. But the key requirement is political will within the government, and that might be in short supply because many governments in fragile states depend on various sorts of clientelism for maintaining political support and such patronage-based systems are necessarily weakened by decent financial accountability.[43] Even where the political will exists, the process of creating systems of financial accountability takes time, and even the best systems cannot prevent all corruption and other misuse of funds.[44]

Other obstacles to the application of the Paris Declaration principles arise from the internal incentives within aid agencies.[45] These obstacles are manifest in all circumstances but are especially acute in the context of fragile states. First, aid agencies often find it very difficult to truly respect the need for country ownership and responsibility because this would reduce their control over the use of funds and involve various risks associated with that loss of control, including the risks of some level of corruption in the use of donor funds. For example, discussing the US failures in Iraq, Fukuyama wrote: "The [Coalition Provisional Authority] . . . did not want to give up control over the political process, a mindset that fails to recognize the importance of local ownership."[46] As expressed by the National Academy of Public Administration in its report on the failures of aid to Haiti since 1990, "Donors often think that they can simultaneously control development, while eliciting strong country buy-in. They cannot. The very notion of country ownership necessitates a lessening role for donors, and increasingly more responsibility for Governments. Donors must accept the risk."[47] But aid agencies—and the managers within them—are usually risk adverse.

Second, most aid agencies are best prepared and staffed for focusing on physical reconstruction and service delivery and not on the less concrete tasks associated with institution-building. In the former activities they can employ not only their own staffs but also their cadres of foreign consultants and contractors, and they are on familiar ground on which their technical expertise is relevant and their insufficient knowledge of local institutions and society is less important. In its 2006 evaluation of the World Bank's work in fragile states, the Bank's independent evaluation group (IEG) highlighted unsuitable staff skills as one reason for the Bank's poor results in many countries.[48]

Third, aid agencies have often been unable to discipline themselves—individually or collectively—to set priorities consistent with the limited capacities of the governments of fragile states. In its 2002 guidelines for working in fragile states, the World Bank prescribed a focus on a very limited set of "zero-generation reforms," but the 2006 IEG review found that the Bank compliance with that guideline was "low."[49] In Afghanistan, for example, donors collectively generated 120 pieces of draft legislation for the parliament—clearly beyond the capacity of the new institution.[50] This reflected the internal incentives within aid agencies for each set of experts to gain a seat at the table and the lack of any effective mechanism among donors for selectivity and prioritization.

In summary, it seems increasingly clear that aid effectiveness even in most fragile states requires substantial adherence to the principles of country ownership, alignment, and harmonization as articulated in the Paris Declaration. Doing so will require the aid donors to overcome the problems just noted—and, although there are indications that some aid agencies are attempting to do so, this will be difficult.[51] Any serious attempt to do so would have two important implications. First, the donors and the government must give priority attention to building up the country's state institutions and, in particular, its systems for financial accountability—but without insisting that these institutions meet standards that are only realistic in much more developed countries. This requires technical assistance from the donors but not a great deal of money. Second, as these institutions are being built up, the donors should refrain from attempting to disburse much money either through these nascent institutions or even through nongovernmental channels. Rapidly expanding the volume of aid resources to fragile states is likely to be counterproductive to the long-term task of institution-building because it would likely create excessive temptations for corruption and would draw the best national staff into donor projects rather than the national institutions.[52]

Such a "go slow" approach that is focused on state-building and initially limits the volume of aid would be consistent with the recommendations of several prominent analysts. Fukuyama advocates that aid agencies should seek a "light footprint" in fragile states.[53] Collier advises that, although substantial technical assistance can be very helpful once a government has the political will to reform, the volume of other aid for postconflict countries should be limited in the initial years until the capacities of the government can be developed sufficiently to absorb more aid.[54] Indeed, based on his analysis, "money early in reform is actually counterproductive."

Applying the Paris Declaration principles by concentrating on state-building and limiting aid volumes until that capacity expands is the most promising approach, but it is certainly not a panacea.[55] A recent report by OECD DAC on monitoring implementation of these principles within six fragile states indicates at best "moderate" success, noting in particular that "country consultations drew attention to many examples of harm, mainly where international presence leads to the weakening of state capacity and/or legitimacy."[56] Even in relatively favorable country circumstances and even with better behavior by aid agencies, aid might contribute to state-building and development in fragile states only slowly. Aid is a weak instrument, and it must be recognized as such. It must be applied with patience, persistence, and a high tolerance for setbacks or even failure. It is counterproductive to imagine that aid agencies can do directly and quickly what the recipient government must learn, by painful trial and error, to do for itself.

CONCLUSION

There are undoubtedly many links between development and security and the state security and human security interests of high-income countries and the international community as a whole. Having traced such linkages, the question becomes, by what policy instruments can development—or any specific dimension of development—be advanced to improve security? Aid is often the first instrument to be considered—despite the fact that the track record of such assistance is highly variable and there is usually acute awareness of its limitations.

The frustrating lessons of experience with development assistance over decades have led to broad agreement about the principles that ought to be followed to increase the likelihood that such aid will be able to achieve its objectives. These principles of country ownership, alignment, and harmonization, as articulated and elaborated most fully in the Paris Declaration on Aid Effectiveness, are abstract and might be dismissed as useless jargon and slogans. However, there are operational applications of these principles that have been formulated and, in many cases, are being attempted by some aid agencies and recipient governments. Despite the difficulties and impediments to their operational applications, these principles remain the most promising approach to achieving some—even if modest—degree of aid effectiveness. They are relevant not only for much of the aid intended to improve human security and for aid to relatively well-governed countries, but also for aid to fragile states. The challenge is to push through the reforms in the practices of aid agencies that are required to apply these principles more consistently and to adapt their application to the specific requirements of country and sector circumstances.

Notes

1. Official development assistance (ODA) refers to assistance from official sources, that is, financed by governments directly or through multilateral agencies. In this chapter the term "aid" refers only to ODA that is nominally intended for development purposes, not military or strictly humanitarian assistance from official sources and not assistance for any purposes from nonofficial sources.

2. Aid has also been an instrument for pursuing other foreign policy and security objectives. For example, former colonial powers such as the United Kingdom and France have used aid to maintain influence with the governments of former colonies. Since the Camp David Accords in 1979, the United States has used substantial bilateral aid to Israel and Egypt to reinforce adherence to that treaty. Of course, the relevance of foreign policy objectives varied among aid agencies, and some agencies were motivated more strongly by developmental than foreign policy objectives. See Carol Lancaster, *Foreign Aid: Diplomacy, Development, Domestic Politics* (Chicago: University of Chicago Press, 2007).

3. Ibid., 25.

4. The seminal document on the concept of human security was the UN Development Programme's "Human Development Report 1994: New Dimensions of Human Security." For a good summary of the concept and its evolution, see the Commission on Human Security, *Human Security Now* (New York: UN, 2003).

5. For a recent example that defines "sustainable security" in terms of three elements—national security, human security, and collective security, see Gayle Smith, *In Search of Sustainable Security* (Washington, DC: Center for American Progress, 2008).

6. ODA statistics here are from the OECD/DAC database at www.oecd.org/dac/stats/data.

7. On the extent to which the aid allocations of major aid providers—the United States, Japan, the United Kingdom, and the EU—have shifted toward state-centric security concerns, see Ngaire Woods, "The Shifting Politics of Foreign Aid," *International Affairs* 81, no. 2 (2005): 393–409.

8. OECD, "Ensuring Fragile States Are Not Left Behind: Summary Report" (Paris: OECD March 2009), www.oecd.org/dataoecd/14/57/43293283.pdf.

9. For the argument that most fragile states have been "under-aided" and that their aid flows have been much more volatile than those to other low-income countries, see Mark McGillivray, "Aid Allocation and Fragile States," Discussion Paper No. 2006/01 (Helsinki: UN University–World Institute for Development Economics Research).

10. The share of ODA devoted to the DAC category of "social and administrative infrastructure" increased from 25 percent in 1986–87 to 37 percent in 2006–7, but not all activities in this category should be regarded as directed at human-centric security objectives.

11. For example, see Woods, "Shifting Politics of Foreign Aid."

12. For a review of this ex post facto project evaluation data, see Roger C. Riddell, *Does Foreign Aid Really Work?* (Oxford: Oxford University Press, 2007). Econometric studies about to what extent ODA as a whole has contributed positively to economic growth are inconclusive due to serious methodological problems. In particular, it is very problematic to correct for the possibility of reverse causation—meaning that aid flows are intentionally given disproportionately to countries that are growing slowly and therefore presumably need more assistance—and to account for the substantial time lags for different types of aid. For a review of the econometric literature on aid effectiveness, see David Roodman, "Macro Aid Effectiveness Research: A Guide for the Perplexed," Working Paper Number 134 (Center for Global Development, December 10, 2007), www.cgdev.org/content/publications/detail/15003.

13. Because project evaluations are usually done by the aid agency itself, it is also likely that many of the evaluations are biased toward favorable conclusions.

14. See, for example, Riddell, *Does Foreign Aid Really Work?*, especially 253–54.

15. On these negative affects of aid on national institutions, see, for example, Deborah Brautigam and Stephen Knack, "Foreign Aid, Institutions, and Governance in Sub-Saharan Africa," *Economic Development and Cultural Change* 52, no. 2 (2004): 255–85; Stephen Knack and Aminur Rahman, "Donor Fragmentation and Bureaucratic Quality in Aid Recipients," Development Research Group, Policy Research Working Paper 3186 (Washington, DC: World Bank, 2004); and Todd Moss, Gunilla Pettersson, and Nicolas van de Walle, "An Aid-Institutions Paradox? A Review Essay on Aid Dependency and State Building in Sub-Saharan Africa," Working Paper 74 (Washington, DC: Center for Global Development, 2006).

16. For example, Collier estimates that around 40 percent of Africa's military spending has been inadvertently financed by aid. Paul Collier, *The Bottom Billion* (Oxford: Oxford University Press, 2007), 103.

17. For example, see Paul Collier, "The Failure of Conditionality," in *Perspectives on Aid and Development* (Policy Essay No. 22), ed. Catherine Gwin and Joan Nelson (Washington, DC: Overseas Development Council, 1997); and Stephen Browne, *Aid and Influence: Do Donors Help or Hinder?* (London: Earthscan, 2006), ch. 4.

18. See OECD, "Paris Declaration on Aid Effectiveness: Ownership, Harmonization, Alignment, Results and Mutual Accountability," Statement by High Level Forum, Paris, February 28–March 3, 2005, accessed August 22, 2011, www.adb.org/media/articles/2005/7033 _international_community_aid/paris_declaration.pdf. Very similar ideas had been put forward earlier by the OECD (in 1996 and 1997) and in the World Bank's concept of a comprehensive development framework. In 2000 these core concepts were made more operational among the entire international development community through the Poverty Reduction Strategy Paper (PRSP) initiative. The importance of many elements of the Paris Declaration had been well recognized in many of the early documents about foreign aid, as summarized in Riddell, *Does Foreign Aid Really Work?*, ch. 2.

19. The DAC includes representatives of all of the OECD members who provide official development assistance; it has long been the forum for reviewing aid and recommending good practices.

20. The Paris Declaration also emphasizes the principles of "mutual accountability" and "managing for results." These are not discussed here merely for the sake of brevity.

21. For an early and independent description of the PRSP initiative, see "Poverty Reduction Strategy Papers (PRSPs): A Rough Guide," *Bretton Woods Project*, April 2003, www .brettonwoodsproject.org/topic/adjustment/PRSP%20rough%20guide/PRSP%20rough%20 guide.pdf.

22. On the tensions between the Paris Declaration principles and the internal incentives of aid agencies, see Andrew Rogerson, "Aid Harmonization and Alignment: Bridging the Gaps between Reality and the Paris Reform Agenda," *Development Policy Review* 23, no. 5 (2005): 531–52; and Paolo de Renzio with David Booth, Andrew Rogerson, and Zaza Curran, "Incentives for Harmonization and Alignment in Aid Agencies," ODI Working Paper No. 248 (London: ODI, 2005), www.odi.org.uk/resources/download/1374.pdf.

23. See OECD, "2008 Survey on Monitoring the Paris Declaration: Making Aid More Effective by 2010" (Paris: OECD, 2008), www.oecd.org/dataoecd/58/41/41202121.pdf; and Bernard Wood, Dorte Kabell, Nansozi Muwanga, and Francisco Sagasti, "Evaluation of the Implementation of the Paris Declaration: Phase One, Synthesis Report" (Copenhagen: Ministry of Foreign Affairs of Denmark, July 2008), www.oecd.org/dataoecd/19/9/40888983.pdf. For a full discussion of the case of Rwanda, see Rachel Hayman, "From Rome to Accra via Kigali: 'Aid Effectiveness' in Rwanda," *Development Policy Review* 27, no. 5 (2009): 581–99.

24. See Stefan Koeberle, Zoran Stavreski, and Jan Walliser, eds., *Budget Support as Effective Aid?: Recent Experiences and Emerging Lessons* (Washington, DC: World Bank, 2006).

25. In many countries, there are likely to be some large, discrete natural disaster mitigation activities—such as construction of levees—that in fact are well suited to traditional aid-financed projects.

26. There is one important security-related domain, however, in which the Paris Declaration principles may not be as relevant—infectious disease control. When the eradication of a disease through targeted, global programs of limited duration is a feasible objective, then "vertical" programs designed and implemented largely by external agencies can be—and have been—effective. The best example is the historic campaign to eradicate smallpox. However, even for programs of infectious disease control, effectiveness is likely to be greatly enhanced by country ownership of programs and donor alignment and harmonization. See Ruth Levine and the What Works Working Group with Molley Kinder, *Millions Saved: Proven Successes in Global Health* (Washington, DC: Center for Global Development, 2004).

27. On the importance of designing social protection programs that are appropriate to specific country contexts, see Ugo Gentilini, "Social Protection in the 'Real World,'" *Development Policy Review* 27, no. 2 (2009): 147–66.

28. See OECD DAC, *Poor Performers: Basic Approaches for Supporting Development in Difficult Partnerships,* November 27, 2001, 3, www.oecd.org/dataoecd/26/56/21684456.pdf.

29. Ibid., 4.

30. USAID, "Fragile States Strategy," PD-ACA-999 (Washington, DC: USAID, January 2005), 6, www.usaid.gov/policy/2005_fragile_states_strategy.pdf.

31. For a good summary of this argument, see Francis Fukuyama, *State-Building: Governance and World Order in the 21st Century* (Ithaca, NY: Cornell University Press, 2004); and Monica François and Inder Sud, "Promoting Stability and Development in Fragile and Failed States," *Development Policy Review* 24, no. 2 (2006): 141–60.

32. Ashraf Ghani and Clare Lockhart, *Fixing Failed States* (Oxford: Oxford University Press, 2008), 98–99. For a discussion of the Afghanistan experience, see Clare Lockhart, "Prepared Testimony to the Senate Foreign Relations Committee," September 17, 2009, accessed August 22, 2011, http://foreign.senate.gov/imo/media/doc/LockhartTestimony 090917a1.pdf.

33. Ghani and Lockhart, *Fixing Failed States*, 109. Some donors' efforts—in particular, the Afghanistan Reconstruction Trust Fund, managed jointly by the Asian Development Bank, the Islamic Development Bank, the UN Development Program, and the World Bank—have attempted to avoid these problems by directing funds through the national budget and building the capacity of central government institutions. See "Afghanistan Reconstruction Trust Fund," *World Bank*, www.worldbank.org/artf.

34. Koeberle, Stavreski, and Walliser, *Budget Support as Effective Aid?*, 376.

35. Special Inspector General for Iraq Reconstruction, *Hard Lessons: The Iraq Reconstruction Experience* (Washington, DC: US Government Printing Office, 2009), 329–33.

36. Francis Fukuyama, "Conclusion," in *Nation-Building: Beyond Afghanistan and Iraq*, ed. Francis Fukuyama (Baltimore, MD: Johns Hopkins University Press, 2006), 241.

37. Nicholas Leader and Peter Colenso, "Aid Instruments in Fragile States," PRDE Working Paper 5 (London: DFID, 2005).

38. Despite the apparent utility of the transition results matrix, aid initiatives in Timor-Leste have been plagued by many of the same problems noted elsewhere and cannot be regarded as very successful overall.

39. James Manor, ed., *Aid That Works: Successful Development in Fragile States* (Washington, DC: World Bank, 2007).

40. OECD, "Principles for Good International Engagement in Fragile States and Situations" (Paris: OECD DCD-DAC, April 2007), 8, www.oecd.org/dataoecd/61/45/38368714.pdf.

41. OECD, "Concepts and Dilemmas of State Building in Fragile Situations: From Fragility to Resilience," 2008. www.oecd.org/dataoecd/59/51/41100930.pdf, 9.

42. Stewart Patrick, "US Policy toward Fragile States" in *The White House and the World*, ed. Nancy Birdsall (Washington, DC: Center for Global Development, 2008), 336.

43. On the tensions between the political imperatives of governments in fragile states and the donors' desire for technocratic systems of financial accountability, see Nicolas van de Walle, *Overcoming Stagnation in Aid-Dependent Countries* (Washington, DC: Center for Global Development, 2005).

44. Any misuse of funds directed through the country's budget must be judged relative to the misuse of funds (that is, the failure of funds to reach intended beneficiaries) that occurs in typical aid projects that depend heavily on subcontracting to foreign consulting firms that have high administrative and security-related costs.

45. For a discussion of issues of donor agency incentives, see OECD, *Improving Incentives in Donor Agencies: Good Practice and Self-Assessment Tool* (Paris: OECD, 2009).

46. Fukuyama, "Conclusion," 238.

47. National Academy of Public Administration, "Why Foreign Aid to Haiti Failed," Academy International Affairs Working Paper Series (2006), 31, www.napawash.org/publications -reports/why-foreign-aid-to-haiti-failed/. In that same spirit, that report recommended increasing reliance on budget support even in the circumstances of Haiti.

48. World Bank Independent Evaluation Department, *Engaging with Fragile States* (Washington, DC: World Bank, 2006), xxx, www.worldbank.org/ieg/licus/download.html.

49. Ibid., xxv.

50. Ibid., xxix.

51. For example, see "Why We Need to Work More Effectively in Fragile States" (London: DFID, n.d.), accessed August 22, 2011, www.jica.go.jp/cdstudy/library/pdf/20071101_11.pdf; World Bank, "Good Practice Note for Development Policy Lending" (Washington, DC: World Bank, Operations Policy and Country Services, June 2005), http://siteresources.worldbank.org /PROJECTS/Resources/DPOsinfragilestates-June7.pdf.

52. It must be recognized that "fragile states" are a very diverse set of countries, and there may be some in which the capacity of national institutions to absorb large amounts of aid has already been established.

53. Fukuyama, "Conclusion," 242–43.

54. Collier, *Bottom Billion*, 111–20.

55. For a discussion of the limited applicability of the Paris Declaration principles in various situations, see OECD, "Evaluation of the Implementation of the Paris Declaration: Thematic Study. The Applicability of the Paris Declaration in Fragile and Conflict-Affected Situations" (Paris: OECD, Oxford Policy Management and the IDL Group, 2008), www.oecd .org/dac/evaluationnetwork.0

56. OECD, "Monitoring the Principles for Good International Engagement in Fragile States and Situations" (Paris: OECD DAC, 2009), www.oecd.org/dataoecd/33/24 /46233053.pdf.

AID

Editors' Comments

Joanna Spear and Paul D. Williams

Both the security and the development arenas define aid in a similar manner: as assistance (either direct or through multilateral agencies) to rehabilitate infrastructure and services degraded by natural disasters or armed conflict or to promote development by reducing poverty and boosting long-term investment and economic growth, or both. There is also broad support for increasing levels of aid for both development and security purposes—as long as it is deployed effectively.

Both perspectives warn of aid's significant limitations, particularly in achieving the second goal where the power of aid to cause particular outcomes is often in dispute. In conflict zones, aid is generally not central to war economies, especially not in theaters rich in natural resources. Nor is it clear how aid can be used to build stable peace. In underdeveloped territories, aid alone is clearly unable to create "good" governments and sustained equitable growth in countries where local political dynamics push in other directions. Nevertheless, both perspectives recognize important niche roles for aid whether in counterterrorism and disarmament, demobilization, and reintegration programs or in local development initiatives.

A further point of agreement is that aid agendas—who gets assistance and why—tend to be subservient to the security concerns of the great powers. Indeed, both perspectives suggest that the recent increase in aid owes much to its "securitization," most notably via the US-led "global war on terror." However, as non-OECD donors such as China, Saudi Arabia, and various types of nonstate actors play increasingly important roles as donors, they will pose a significant challenge to the established (OECD) rules of the aid game.

Harborne and Morrow seem to be in broad agreement about the central challenges facing donors, three of which stand out. First, there remain problems of coordination both within the bureaucracies of individual states and organizations as well as in attempts to design a global institutional architecture. This is exacerbated by the lack of international agreement over the strategic objectives of aid. A second related problem concerns evaluation and the criteria that should be used to assess whether aid has been used effectively. Neither field has produced a consensus in either theory or practice.

The third problem is that the roles aid is supposed to play have not always been clearly conceptualized within the broader promotion of security and development. Harborne notes that despite much talk of merging security and development agendas, official harnessing of aid to security objectives has failed many people who are trapped in the world's conflict zones. Despite all the rhetoric, he concludes that the security–development nexus thus remains very much a paper tiger. In development, however, a greater degree of consensus has emerged around the OECD's Paris Declaration on Aid Effectiveness (2005) and its three core principles of country ownership, alignment, and harmonization. Nevertheless, aid agencies continue to struggle with the traditional problems of unsustainability, unintended negative impacts on the recipient's institutional capacity, and fungibility as well as newer problems arising from the decisions of some donors to provide direct budget support to recipient states (ironically a central tenet of the Paris Declaration). For Morrow, the Paris principles remain basically sound even when applied in the challenging circumstances of "fragile states." "The challenge," as he puts it, "is to push through the reforms in the practices of aid agencies that are required to apply these principles more consistently and to adapt their application to the specific requirements of country and sector circumstances."

Finally, it is clear that both perspectives recognize that these challenges are particularly acute when aid is delivered to war zones and in authoritarian states. In such settings diplomacy must lead since aid alone can provide neither security nor genuinely national and sustainable development.

Part II

HUMANITARIAN ASSISTANCE

Chapter 4

HUMANITARIAN ASSISTANCE
A Security Perspective

Robert Maletta with Joanna Spear

This chapter begins by charting the ways in which the security studies field has come to focus on humanitarian assistance as a useful tool of policy. This trend of using assistance instrumentally has become doctrine in the United States with the promulgation of the "3Ds": defense, development, and diplomacy, which are to be used in an integrated fashion to maximize the impact of US foreign and security policy. It is also reflected in the "whole of government" approaches adopted by a number of Western governments keen to improve their impact in conflict environments.[1]

One important form of assistance is humanitarian aid, where resources—money, food, water, tents, and so on—are given to a community in need. Humanitarian assistance is a wider concept, though, encompassing the provision of transport and personnel (rescue teams, medical teams, engineers, and so on), debt forgiveness, and other forms of help that do not involve transfers of resources to the stricken community. The two have different consequences and implications in situations of humanitarian emergency; in particular, humanitarian aid can be misappropriated or become a "conflict good" that is fought over. By contrast, humanitarian assistance is not usually misused in these ways because overseas personnel usually remain in control of those physical resources (though sometimes vehicles get stolen or offices looted) and people, but humanitarian assistance can have important political consequences in terms of local balances of power and local perception of humanitarians. Because humanitarian assistance can be nonmaterial (e.g., time, energy), there are increasingly large numbers of actors willing and able to provide such assistance, which has resulted in a proliferation of humanitarian assistance actors and activities.

The tradition of humanitarianism codified in the Geneva Conventions and international humanitarian laws emphasizes compassion in the face of human suffering. The humanitarian imperative is to save lives, alleviate suffering, and preserve dignity. In its ideal form, humanitarianism is carried out without ulterior motive. The traditional humanitarian actors—nongovernmental organizations (NGO) and international organizations—rely on being seen as neutral, impartial, and independent by all parties and therefore able to occupy a "humanitarian space" in often violent settings. However, while these actors have sought to cleave to their core values, the tool they use, humanitarian assistance, has also increasingly been deployed by a range of other actors (e.g., international organizations, states, militaries, rebels, NGOs) who clearly have ulterior motives. Moreover, there have emerged a raft of new NGOs who are willing to work with (and even be co-opted by) state humanitarian agendas. The consequence of this has been a blurring of the identities of the traditional humanitarians with those of more overtly political organizations using the same humanitarian assistance tool. To traditional humanitarians, the unwelcome consequences of this have been local communities doubting their neutrality, impartiality, and independence, and being physically endangered by this identification with these politicized actors.

An obvious connection between the security field and humanitarian assistance is that assistance is often provided and aid delivered by militaries (or, in certain cases, by rebels) as the events necessitating the assistance—famines, natural disasters, war, and so on—mean that the militaries (or rebels) are one of the few actors able to function in such an environment. However, while this is ideal for a short duration, many crises now drag on for months and years, so the military can begin to regard its humanitarian mission as a nonkinetic means of gathering intelligence and maintaining a strategic presence in an area.

In addition, Western militaries increasingly have their own aid budgets, so they are not just a delivery vehicle and assistance provider but aid donors in their own right. This raises all sorts of familiar issues about the "securitization" of foreign aid as well as about what could be called the "developmentalization" of the military.

This chapter first looks at some of the classic ways in which humanitarian assistance has been deployed. It then focuses on some of the new and positive ways humanitarian aid is used specifically in terms of "disaster diplomacy," where the provision of humanitarian aid has positive geostrategic consequences. The next two sections assess the role of rebels and military forces in delivering aid and increasingly funding humanitarian activities. The chapter concludes with an in-depth case study of NGOs in Somalia trying to deliver humanitarian aid in a situation where that aid and those actors have been unwillingly "securitized."

HUMANITARIAN ASSISTANCE AS A POLITICAL TOOL

Despite the rhetoric that humanitarian assistance was and is apolitical, there is significant evidence that it has always been used in political ways. For example, Drury, Olson, and Van Belle's study of US foreign disaster assistance (which might be expected to be the least politicized form of humanitarian aid) between 1964 and 1995 concluded that "our analysis puts to rest the notion that US foreign disaster assistance is purely objective and nonpolitical. It is not even close. . . . Indeed, our results paint a picture of high US foreign policy decision makers as realists at heart, seeing disasters as opportunities to enhance security."[2] During the Cold War, humanitarian assistance was a classic "soft power" tool in the ideological struggle between the superpowers. For example, the Western allies' delivery of humanitarian aid through the 1948–49 airlift, after Berlin was closed off by the Soviet Union, had important strategic and psychological effects. The Soviet Union used the tool around the world too.[3] Illustrating the conjoining of humanitarian and strategic goals, the United States provided humanitarian aid to camps in Pakistan housing refugees from the Afghan civil war, but these camps were also bases for the *mujahideen* forces who were launching attacks across the border against the Soviet forces occupying Afghanistan.[4] Similarly, the United States helped fund refugee camps in Thailand for rebels fighting the Cambodian government.[5]

While the two ideological blocks consistently used humanitarian assistance for political purposes, there were also NGOs seeking to provide such assistance in a nonpolitical way. During the Cold War the activities of the United Nations were severely limited by a strict interpretation of sovereignty. NGOs stepped into the void to deal with the consequences of various crises and internal conflicts. "Typically, new NGOs or NGO consortia, often church based, emerged in relation to controversial cross-border or cross-line type programmes. The illicit nature of these activities reinforced an earlier tradition that humanitarian relief must be neutral. That is, to eschew politics and only provide externally monitored, basic relief items."[6] One of the earliest examples of humanitarian NGOs becoming involved—despite the disapproval of states—was the 1968 famine in Biafra, Nigeria.[7] Subsequently, NGOs became active in Bangladesh, Ethiopia, the West African Sahel, and Cambodia.[8] In these various humanitarian engagements the NGOs perceived themselves to be—and were generally seen as—politically neutral. Nevertheless, the decision to engage is in essence a political one. NGOs chose to become active in humanitarian situations, even where state sovereignty was contested, based on the principles of neutrality, impartiality, and humanitarian need. Another example of activism is in Afghanistan, where by 1990 more than two hundred NGOs had played a role in alleviating the crisis. As Helga Baitenmann notes, "as in other war environments, the 'humanitarian' work performed by these NGOs became, in many cases and to varying degrees, politicised."[9]

The phrase "military humanitarianism" was coined in the 1990s to describe instances where relief operations were guarded by military forces. Examples included the protection of aid to Kurds in the north of Iraq after 1991, Somalia in the early 1990s, and Bosnia in the mid-1990s. Military humanitarianism was an erosion of the division between the military and humanitarian actors, and not the only one. For example, many NGOs were forced to hire private security firms or local actors to protect their humanitarian missions. In places such as Somalia in the late 1980s and early 1990s, it became common for NGOs to employ the young men to protect the aid and their personnel.[10] In essence, the NGOs paid protection money.

After the Cold War there was a shift in thinking (within the UN system and at the national level) about sovereignty and the role of the state. Unconditional respect for state sovereignty eroded with demands that "states must be able to demonstrate their commitment to uphold international law and to adhere to basic principles of economic and political behavior."[11] Failure of the state could now be seen as justifying intervention. The UN and other organizations became involved in various forms of multilateral intervention that would not have been considered during the Cold War. This coincided with the rise of the "human security" approach (see chapter 1), which justified much more intervention—on the basis of human need—but was also a useful pretext for things that states wanted to do anyway.

Despite states and organizations now being empowered to intervene within states, the number and activism of NGOs still grew dramatically, in part due to the privatization of aid delivery. Foreign assistance was one of the fields where many Western governments chose to provide money to NGOs and corporations to deliver humanitarian aid and undertake development, retaining only a managerial role in the process. This created a range of NGOs that are reliant upon governments for funding but still try to retain the aura of independence.

In the aftermath of the Cold War, humanitarian assistance ceased to be the major preserve of the superpowers, and other states, organizations, philanthropists, and nonstate groups began to participate.[12] The overall levels of government money devoted to foreign development assistance declined significantly (see the chapter by Morrow). In parallel, however, the level of humanitarian assistance increased steeply. Between 1990 and 2000 the volume of official humanitarian assistance rose significantly from $2 billion to $5.9 billion.[13] The increase was need-driven; the emergence in the early 1990s of what are called "complex humanitarian emergencies" (CHE) required the deployment of a range of policy tools, including humanitarian assistance. These CHE are often long-lasting and difficult to solve, making it less likely that development can begin and more likely that humanitarian assistance will be needed for a significant time. The case study of Somalia, following, is an excellent example of a situation where the assistance is for humanitarian relief rather than development. Mark Duffield remarked in 1994 that "in the post–Cold War era humanitarian aid is the North's principal means of political crisis management in the now marginal South."[14] This is a radical critique of aid (both developmental and humanitarian), which he has continued to develop.[15]

After 9/11, this convergence between security and humanitarian assistance was to undergo another evolution—and a step too far for many NGOs—when governments saw the role of humanitarians as vital in combating extremism. This was most clearly articulated by the US administration and the military in the planning stage of the Afghanistan war in the weeks following 9/11. In the bluntest terms, humanitarians were to serve as "force multipliers," and their actions were to be coordinated and controlled to ensure winning "hearts and minds" and gaining strategic benefit.[16] American NGOs were given notice that they must support US security objectives in this post–9/11 world or they would risk losing their funding.[17] NGOs feared that this identification with the "global war on terrorism" (GWOT) would completely erase the (already blurry) line between humanitarian and political intervention, and would increase the risks faced by aid workers. Within the UN system, UN humanitarian offices stand in an analogous relationship to the political agenda and face much the same risks of being politicized as NGOs.

On a different note, the security community has identified another strategic application of humanitarian aid: "disaster diplomacy." Recognition of the positive role that humanitarian aid could play in improving relations between states first came in 1999 with the "disaster diplomacy" between Turkey and Greece when each was struck by an earthquake. The two states provided each other with emergency rescue teams, doctors, and medicines—and, especially in response to the severe Turkish earthquake, significant supplies of food, tents, money, and so on. The aid came from the government, national and local organizations, and individuals. As James Ker-Lindsey has pointed out, the effects of the diplomacy should not be overstated because a political rapprochement was already under way, though it had not been popular in either state. "Disaster diplomacy" achieved a vast improvement in public perceptions of the other state, creating a completely new atmosphere and pressure for progress between them. There has subsequently developed a security studies literature that charts instances of "disaster diplomacy" and considers why and how it plays a role in conflict mitigation.[18]

With an interest in harnessing the potential for positive "disaster diplomacy," the United States has been increasing its strategic use of humanitarian assistance. The prime example of this was the US response to the Indian Ocean tsunami of December 26, 2004. Initially the United States was slow to respond to the crisis and was heavily criticized. However, by January 6, 2005, Secretary of State Colin Powell had offered US aid, explaining that the aid was to be viewed as part of the GWOT as "it dries up those pools of dissatisfaction that might give rise to terrorist activity. That supports not only our national security interest but the national security interests of the countries involved."[19] He also identified a public diplomacy angle: "We'd be doing it regardless of religion, but I think it does give the Muslim world and the rest of the world an opportunity to see American generosity, American values in action."[20] There was a similar US military role in providing humanitarian aid to Pakistani Kashmir after the earthquake in 2005. Although in both cases the assistance was appreciated at the time, it has not had a lasting impact upon US diplomatic and security relations with the Muslim world. Similarly, single acts of humanitarianism by the US military cannot achieve lasting public diplomacy outcomes and other actions by the United States easily mitigate the positive effects of humanitarian assistance.[21] As Andrew Wilder concluded, "There was little evidence of any significant 'hearts and minds' or security benefits as a result of the US's generous support for the earthquake response. This is certainly not to suggest that US assistance was ineffective. US assistance was extremely effective in promoting the humanitarian objective of saving lives and alleviating suffering."[22] Thus, assistance failed to achieve its instrumental goals but did fulfill its traditional humanitarian objectives.

In contrast to the positive findings associated with humanitarian aid and disaster diplomacy discussed earlier, there is a growing security literature suggesting that disasters (particularly fast-moving ones) are positively associated with the onset of internal conflicts.[23] This is at least in part due to the scarcity of resources and disasters exacerbating existing tensions. Nevertheless, the peace achieved in Aceh in the aftermath of the Asian tsunami would seem to be one counterexample to this.

REBELS AND HUMANITARIAN ASSISTANCE

Rebels and extremist groups have also used humanitarian assistance. This section looks at the roles of rebels in both giving and receiving assistance. In terms of giving humanitarian assistance, rebels have had successes. That the Liberation Tigers of Tamil Eelam (LTTE), for example, were initially partners in distributing aid in Sri Lanka in the aftermath of the 2004 tsunami—and did so more efficiently than the Sri Lankan military—gave them added legitimacy as political actors in the country. After the Kashmir earthquake in 2005, Pakistani extremist groups were involved in humanitarian assistance activities, having "fashioned an uneasy truce with American soldiers ferrying relief supplies to the 3.2 million people left homeless by the quake."[24] The coexistence during that time legitimized their role and the efficient operations of groups such as Jammat-ud-Dawa (a successor to the banned group Lashkar-e-Taiba) showed up the—much larger—forces of the Pakistan military.[25] Possibly the most impressive example of an extremist group's role in providing and delivering humanitarian assistance comes from Lebanon, where Hezbollah was the first to provide substantial aid to the Southern Lebanese affected by the 2006 war with Israel. There developed a humanitarian aid "alms race" between Hezbollah (backed by Iran) and the Lebanese government (backed by the United States). Hezbollah won.[26] Hezbollah distributed $12,000 cash to those made homeless and promised to build new homes within three years. It also brought in work crews, craftsmen, and architects to work on rebuilding.[27]

In terms of receiving humanitarian assistance, there are situations where civilians are manipulated and turned into refugees for the express purpose of attracting humanitarian aid. Ben Barber gives the examples of the LTTE in Sri Lanka in the 1990s and the holding "hostage" of Rwandan Hutu refugees in Zaire by militiamen using them as cover to attract aid and launch raids into Rwanda.[28] Humanitarian aid can allow rebels to prolong a conflict that would otherwise be terminated.[29] Moreover, there have been situations where humanitarian aid has been fought over by rebels.[30]

When humanitarian aid pours into a stricken region, it can help rebels in a number of ways: "relief can feed militants; sustain and protect the militants' supporters; contribute to the war economy; and provide legitimacy to combatants."[31] According to Dawn Brancati, disasters also have significant "effects in countries already experiencing conflict since rebels can capitalize on earthquakes to attract popular support, recruit soldiers, and finance campaigns."[32] David Shearer shows, however, that aid's effect on the political economy of conflict has sometimes been overestimated.[33] Importantly, rebels often want humanitarian aid but not assistance, because this would bring in foreigners who could observe what they were up to, try to prevent diversion of resources, and alert the international community to what was going on.

That "undesirable" actors may gain advantage from receiving humanitarian aid is increasingly factored into the decisions by donors about where, when, and under what conditions they provide humanitarian aid. This form of reactive politicization by the West can result—as it did during the Cold War—in the neglect of the neediest communities in favor of the most strategically relevant or (more worryingly) politically uncomplicated. In country, this politicization of assistance can lead to the prioritization of certain missions over others; for example, in Pakistan in 2005, NATO prioritized "the construction of secondary schools amid fears that teenage boys are most at risk from fundamentalists looking to attract recruits."

Given that many people were still without adequate shelter and supplies for the bitter winter, from a purely humanitarian perspective, schools were not a key priority.[34]

MILITARY FORCES AND HUMANITARIAN ASSISTANCE

With the moves toward fighting long-term asymmetric conflicts in Afghanistan and Iraq, the United States and its allies have been moving toward a counter-insurgency (COIN) strategy. The US Army and Marine Corps' *Counterinsurgency Field Manual* makes clear that the US military regards humanitarian assistance as a legitimate tool to use in the battle against insurgents. From the US military's perspective, for example, "there is no such thing as impartial humanitarian assistance or CMO [civil-military operations] in COIN. Whenever someone is helped, someone else is hurt, not least the insurgents. So civil and humanitarian assistance personnel often become targets. Protecting them is a matter not only of providing a close-in defense, but also of creating a secure environment by co-opting local beneficiaries of aid and their leaders."[35] In 2003 Congress, as a part of US counter-insurgency strategy, authorized funds for the Commander's Emergency Response Program (CERP) for operations in Iraq and Afghanistan. This legislation "specified that the commanders could spend the funds for urgent humanitarian relief and reconstruction projects. These projects had to immediately assist the Iraqi and Afghan peoples within a commander's area of operations."[36]

The commander has a lot of discretion with CERP funds, the reporting requirements are minimal, and they find the funds invaluable.[37] For example, Col. John Carlton recounted: "During my 15 month tour in Anbar, we spent over $80 million for CERP projects . . . literally thousands of projects. . . . The results were clearly evident on the ground. Attacks in my area went from 30–35 per day down to essentially zero. . . . Bottom line—I think we definitely followed the spirit and intent of CERP in our area and it was extremely effective."[38] Given that the US military are increasingly engaged alongside USAID in delivering humanitarian and development aid, there have been attempts to increase the militaries' understanding of how reconstruction and development should be done.[39]

ASSESSMENT

The military can play a vital role in ensuring that humanitarian assistance gets provided in a crisis. Moreover, it is also often easier for security actors to ask for—and receive—extra resources compared to civilian agencies. On the other side of the ledger, there are some clear problems with the military playing such roles. First, assistance is clearly politicized when it is supplied, delivered, and implemented by the military, and this can have a toxic effect for NGOs and international actors working in the same terrain. Second, if militaries are delivering assistance, it might have the undesirable consequence of legitimizing a rebel role in doing the same. Third, this military role adds to the lack of integration across government assistance programs and increases policy incoherence.[40] Fourth, militaries that are involved in the delivery of humanitarian aid may be more open to the idea of manipulating it to achieve desired security outcomes, viewing it instrumentally. For example, coalition forces in Afghanistan admitted to using humanitarian aid as a reward for information about the activities of the Taliban and al-Qaeda.[41] Similarly, in the Democratic Republic of Congo in November 2009, Médicins Sans Frontières alleged that they were used as "bait" to enable attacks on civilians when an agreed ceasefire for a mass vaccination campaign against measles was ignored by the DRC Army.[42]

Fifth, because the military sees humanitarian assistance as a strategic instrument, if the situation changes, they will have no compunction about terminating that aid, regardless of the consequences. Sixth, because aid is instrumental for the military, their time horizon is inevitably short, which does not match well with protracted emergencies, or with the necessary planning for a transition from humanitarian assistance to development. Seventh, in taking on a humanitarian assistance mission, a military does not cease to play a security role; they may use the mission to keep a presence in or gather intelligence on a place that they would not normally get access to. As Reuben Brigety has pointed out concerning the US military drilling wells in Northern Kenya, "with chaos inside Somalia threatening the stability of the region and enabling the rise of extremism, using US military assets to perform a humanitarian mission serves a dual purpose. It shows the face of American compassion to a skeptical population while also giving the military an eye on activity in the area."[43] This type of surveillance was certainly the fear of some hard-line Islamists in Pakistan who denounced the US and British military presence after the 2005 earthquake as "nothing more than an extension of their activities in Afghanistan and Iraq."[44] In this case, Pakistan did not allow Indian helicopters to cross the border into their Kashmir territory—fearing spying—which severely hampered the initial aid deliveries. This was all the more poignant because many communities had improvised helipads in the anticipation of aid deliveries from helicopters that never came.[45]

Brigety's example of well drilling in Kenya highlights an eighth problem with using the military to complete these humanitarian missions: soldiers have no training in designing and implementing humanitarian aid projects, but that is exactly what they are doing. They have therefore learned by trial and error, often experiencing a lot of error. This sometimes has negative consequences for local attitudes toward those forces (having a negative effect on "hearts and minds"), and toward other humanitarian actors. In the Kenya case, the military did not find drinkable water at two of the sites where they drilled, undermining faith in their reliability as partners to the locals. Another implication of this activism in humanitarian aid is that it can degrade the military's skills for its core mission, fighting.

A final point concerns the cost of using military forces to complete ongoing humanitarian missions. Using the Kenya case, Brigety notes, "During those five months, American taxpayers spent $250,000 on two wells that did not work. By contrast, an underground well dug by civilian humanitarian agencies typically costs around $10,000."[46] Using the military is therefore a very expensive means of delivering humanitarian assistance in the long term.

HUMANITARIAN ACTORS IN A SECURITIZED ENVIRONMENT: SOMALIA

This section discusses the challenges facing humanitarian agencies (international and local NGOs) and their attempts to position themselves between different warring groups and explicitly political actors in this polarized landscape. In this context, humanitarian principles and action have faced multiple challenges on a number of fronts. From an NGO perspective, any attempt to co-opt and securitize humanitarian assistance is a threat to core humanitarian values, especially in countries classified as a battlefront in the GWOT. The case of Somalia is analyzed to illustrate the challenges faced by humanitarian agencies in a country where the GWOT is being fought, a state-building project has been conducted in a context of unresolved conflict, and a massive humanitarian crisis has developed.[47] That Somalia is still mired in conflict and that insecurity is spreading in the forms of maritime piracy, transnational terrorism, and rampant criminality are a testament to the policy failures of a variety of international actors as well as the lack of unselfish national leadership.

Somalia is also an example of the dangers of applying static political and developmental frameworks in fluid social and security contexts. Humanitarian approaches that do not calibrate the almost daily changes in the program environment risk applying inappropriate interventions that can fuel competition and conflict. Somalia is a hard—and, thus far, failed—test for efforts to contain and stabilize a situation spinning out of control. This, unfortunately, is the legacy of international society's engagement with a country it does not understand and where a state-building agenda has been prioritized over the humanitarian one. Somalia is a case study of what happens when political objectives coexist within the same space as nonpolitical humanitarian activities and the two struggle for primacy.

International engagement in Somalia in the early 1990s was traumatizing for all involved—interveners, Somalis, NGOs, and the UN. In the years after the debacle of UNOSOM II (UN Operation in Somalia II), the UN ceased to play a leading and coordinating role in the international response. Multilateral engagement was done through the Somalia Aid Coordination Body (SACB) and led by donors, such as the European Commission. Within this framework, relief and development activities were aligned according to stabilization strategies that were more or less accepted by many NGOs operating within this coordination framework. Benign neglect from the world's governments allowed a degree of functionality in humanitarian aid delivery.

This arrangement was to shift, however, when the Transitional Federal Institutions, formed following a peace process in Kenya in 2004, were endorsed internationally, and the UN took over the lead role of supporting this entity. The Transitional Federal Government (TFG) of the Republic of Somalia was the fifteenth international attempt to restore national institutions to Somalia since the collapse of the Siad Barre regime in 1991. The UN was determined to reassert its lead role in the country after the failure of UNOSOM II, and the TFG would be the vehicle for this assertion. Donor funds began to flow toward the UN Development Programme (UNDP) while the UN's Office for the Coordination of Humanitarian Affairs took over the humanitarian coordination roles previously subsumed within the SACB framework. It was understood that reconstruction and development assistance would be articulated and coordinated within the framework of the reconstruction and development plan. Touted as a plan formulated through participatory processes across south and central Somalia, Puntland, and Somaliland, it was seen as a way to secure the legitimacy and viability of the TFG through the support of humanitarian, development, and political actors.

Up to 2006 humanitarian and political actors sat together at meetings to coordinate joint action within a development framework designed by the UN and donors. It was clear that these activities were geared toward empowering the government and thus (in the eyes of humanitarian NGOs and the locals) were overtly political. Any misgivings as to the mixing of relief, recovery, and development agendas were mediated by a widespread perception that this was a benign undertaking. This fiction was harder to maintain after the TFG's arrival in Mogadishu resulted in massive war crimes by all parties.

After its decade in the international shadows, Somalia's return to notoriety began in the first half of 2006, when a homegrown confederation of Shari'a courts known as the Islamic Courts Union (ICU) wrested control of Mogadishu from a conglomerate of US-backed warlords and began spreading its presence through the southern and central regions of Somalia.[48] With the temporary end of warlord control, roadblocks were dismantled, and people were able to walk the streets in relative safety. By contrast, the internationally recognized TFG remained outside the capital, unable to establish the foundation for a viable government.

In December 2006, following statements that the ICU might occupy part of the Ogaden region of Ethiopia, Ethiopian forces allied with the TFG swept through Somalia, retaking territory and arriving in Mogadishu. Attempts to establish control of Mogadishu led to bloody street battles between the aligned TFG-Ethiopian forces and a spectrum of armed opposition groups. For aid agencies, this was the beginning of a slow-motion major humanitarian disaster, and it initiated a further rethinking of how to operate in Somalia.

The dissolution of the ICU did not result in a clear military or political victory for the TFG or its backers. It was only the end of one chapter and the beginning of a new phase of conflict in the central and southern regions of Somalia. The ICU was replaced by more militant Jihadist groups in the form of Harakat al-Shabaab al-Mujahideen ("Movement of Striving Youth") and Hizbul Islam ("Party of Islam"). In 2008 al-Shabaab would be designated by Western governments a terrorist organization with ties to al-Qaeda. It was against this backdrop that the United Nations would attempt to implement its state-building activities, thus becoming a partisan player in a highly polarized conflict. This arrangement would prove to be extremely problematic for humanitarian agencies, which now had to contend with an institution that sought to coordinate or co-opt their activities in its state-building agenda.

The installation of the TFG in Mogadishu was seen by the UN and government donors as a chance to bring peace to Somalia through the reestablishment of a central government. In January 2007 the UN humanitarian and resident coordinator stated: "The international aid community must take immediate advantage of the window of opportunity that now exists in Somalia by substantially re-engaging in the capital."[49] Given that the war was not yet over, such an approach carried real risks for ostensibly neutral humanitarian agencies.

From March to May 2007 the use of heavy weaponry by warring parties in the city's densely populated neighborhoods had a devastating effect upon the people of Mogadishu. More than 400,000 people were displaced, and up to 1,300 killed. As the conflict raged on, there were reports of massive human rights violations.[50] All sides to the conflict were accused of committing war crimes.[51] Reports continued of indiscriminate fire in civilian areas, extrajudicial executions, disproportionate use of force, looting, and arbitrary arrests by all sides, often resulting in the deaths of civilians. Initially international reaction regarding the breaches of international humanitarian law and human rights law was muted until governments were forced to respond to public statements made by NGOs on the situation.[52]

Insecurity due to the expansion of jihadi groups and clashes with Ethiopian forces caused the withdrawal of virtually all international staff from major operational centers in the south and central regions of Somalia. By January 2009 more than 3 million people (about half the country's population) were in need of emergency food assistance at a time when the humanitarian presence was reduced.

Apart from the operational difficulties faced by aid agencies, this was also a test of the UN's ability to deliver on a political agenda of state-building without diminishing humanitarian space and increasing suffering. This divergence of agendas—humanitarian and political—compromised the UN's attempts at integrating humanitarian agencies under one political umbrella because it was unable to project itself as an impartial institution. The UN's role in pushing a political state-building process that was deeply unpopular with many Somalis and its attempt to co-opt NGOs to stabilize the humanitarian situation were deeply controversial. The UN was viewed by NGOs as a threat to the core humanitarian principles central to local acceptance, and several frontline humanitarian agencies requested that the UN stop politicizing the role of NGOs or else face isolation.[53] Donor funds were supporting a political agenda that some NGOs viewed as driving a massive urban conflict. At the same time, funds from donors were being channeled to aid agencies to pick up the pieces. Such dissonance led to a warning that the European Commission could be complicit in the commission of war crimes.[54] Somalis felt abandoned because governments failed to use their diplomatic leverage to make accountable those responsible for violations.[55] Many felt that they had lost whatever protection international laws afforded them as the international community was trying to establish a central government at almost any cost.

After the 9/11 attacks co-option of the humanitarian agenda in Somalia meant more than stabilization, it meant complicity in an antiterrorist agenda to get the "bad guys" at all costs. While, for Washington, the bad guys were the people responsible for the 1998 US embassy bombings in Kenya and Tanzania, for Ethiopia, the bad guys were those attempting to liberate its Ogaden region, or "Western Somalia." Most Somalis shared neither view of who the problematic actors were. Clearly, there were multiple incompatible agendas in play. Humanitarians were expected to do their part by picking up the pieces of any collateral damage and not challenging the overall security agenda. At the regional level, some political actors were uneasy about the role they were playing in supporting Somali politicians, many of whom were former warlords. Yet, wider foreign policy objectives stopped them from speaking up.

Humanitarian NGOs began to question what their role was within this evolving tragedy. As insecurity spread and the political situation became more polarized, NGOs were pressed openly by the UN and TFG to take sides. In the not-so-subtle antiterrorist rhetoric of the day, Somali NGOs and local civil society activists were challenged by local political and security authorities over whether "they were with the TFG or with the terrorists."

This conflation of a state-building process with military–antiterrorist aims was to prove a real threat to aid agencies. Warring groups increased the stakes with a dramatic escalation in the number of aid workers and civil society activists whom they targeted in the course of the next two years.[56] In addition to the risks posed by cross fire, kidnapping, roadside bombs, and arrests, assassination was an alarming new trend. This injected an element of unpredictability, making risk analysis and management extremely difficult to the point that several NGOs either withdrew or suspended their operations. Somalia became notorious as "the most dangerous place in the world for aid workers."[57]

Consequently, humanitarian NGOs scrambled for cover behind their humanitarian principles, and development agencies lowered their profile. Agencies that were normally willing to engage with political actors edged away from them for fear that it would make them targets. Meanwhile, Somalis continued to move out of Mogadishu to escape the growing lawlessness and fighting between TFG forces and armed opposition groups.

With more than 1 million people displaced and half the population needing emergency assistance, it seemed that an internationally sponsored state-building enterprise had derailed and catalyzed a humanitarian disaster. A multilateral humanitarian effort had been overtaken by counterterror concerns.[58] For now, the TFG would act as cover to further the GWOT, and in its wake would eliminate accountability and exacerbate the already dire humanitarian and human rights situation.

THINGS FALL APART: THE FAILURE OF COHERENCE IN SOMALIA

With the appointment of Ahmedou Ould-Abdallah as UN special representative for the secretary-general for Somalia in September 2007, new impetus was injected into the political process. Early in his tenure, NGOs were heartened by his dynamism and willingness to listen. Yet as the months passed it became clearer that this new engagement had its price: increased calls for the NGOs to be active members in the negotiations between the TFG and the opposition alliance. Humanitarian NGOs declined, citing the need to preserve their political neutrality and independence. This response was perceived by some diplomats as unreasonable and even obstructionist. Repeated attempts by the UN Political Office for Somalia to engage NGOs in political discussions only elicited silence.

Vindication of the NGO position was forthcoming after the first round of Djibouti reconciliation talks in June 2008. During this period Somali civil society activists and aid workers were systematically threatened and assassinated. In addition, two US cruise missile strikes against "high-value terrorists" resulted in the death or injury of al-Shabaab commanders and many civilians. Consequences were swift and profound, and in the coming months Somali aid workers were detained, interrogated, or even killed by al-Shabaab elements on suspicion of being involved in counterinsurgency activities. Hostility toward Western-based NGOs would result in the expulsion of several agencies from their regions of operations, depriving hundreds of thousands of people of life-saving assistance, such as food and health care.

While the insurgency regrouped and fought back with renewed vigor, the TFG was riven with internal disagreements resulting in the resignation of one prime minister and the appointment of a more conciliatory one, who immediately fell into disagreement with the president, who was then forced out of office. United support from international political actors dissolved as it became obvious that the TFG leadership were as much a part of the problem as the insurgency.

Meanwhile, the UN Security Council (UNSC) failed time and again to take any practical steps to put into place protection measures for Somalis, instead prioritizing protecting the political process.[59] UNSC resolutions were more symbolic expressions of concern than reflections of political will to send troops or hold accountable violators of international laws. Meanwhile, the humanitarian situation deteriorated as people moved into poorly serviced camps outside Mogadishu.

If not for the legality conferred upon it by international society and the might of the Ethiopian National Defense Force backing it, the TFG could not have existed as a viable institution. It lacked legitimacy in the eyes of many Somalis and continually violated its own transitional charter by failing to protect them.[60] International society, however, was content to feed the illusion of legitimacy. Powerful governments in the UNSC seemed satisfied as long as appointed individuals held official titles; to them, this meant an institution existed with which they could do business. This meant that warlords with nominal status could benefit from official largesse and legitimacy even if it meant that donor money supported private militias that preyed upon the civilian populace.[61] The situation was clearly unsustainable as conflict and criminality spread, but the UNSC was unwilling to address it.

Jihadist websites denounced the UN as the enemy of Islam because it supported the TFG and, by extension, the Ethiopians. UN staff were systematically targeted and killed within Somalia, and a car bomb blew up a UNDP compound in Hargeisa, the normally quiet capital of the breakaway Republic of Somaliland.

The UN faced its own internal tensions, principally between those agencies operating with a humanitarian mandate (i.e., the UNHCR, UNICEF, and WFP) and the development arm of the UNDP and the UN Political Office (UNPOS). These presented unique challenges to the UN resident and humanitarian coordinator, who tried to mediate between a political agenda and the idea of humanitarian impartiality. Any talk now of a UN integrated mission or some other multinational configuration was viewed suspiciously by many NGOs because that was how Somalis would regard it too. In 2010, attempts to implement a structurally integrated UN mission by the UN Department of Political Affairs in an attempt to achieve better coherence and coordination met with stiff resistance from the UN humanitarian agencies and NGOs.[62] They saw this as a threat to their operations due to the fear that armed opposition groups would perceive this as the co-option of humanitarian activities by the UN Political Office and its pro-TFG agenda.[63]

Coherence of action in Somalia once assumed a shared vision of peace and security and a complementarity of humanitarian and conflict management within the framework of a UN-led mission. When coherence was hijacked by the GWOT as cover for an ill-conceived counterinsurgency strategy, it became toxic to aid agencies that would otherwise have acquiesced to a larger vision of state formation for a country without a central government.

What started out as an ostensibly benign stabilization and state-building effort mutated into a nightmare for millions of Somalis. A "soft" securitization agenda meant to reinstall a central government was used as cover for the "hard" security agenda of counterterrorism. The UN and donor involvement in this lent legitimacy and generated the illusion of a shared political and humanitarian agenda. This agenda is largely discredited, and integration of humanitarian assets into a state-building effort has failed.[64] What now should the relationship be between international institutions charged with unrolling a political process and aid agencies trying to address the emergency needs of millions of Somalis?

DEFINING ROLES AND RECLAIMING LOST SPACE

As this case study has shown, without clear analysis of the conflict dynamics, policymakers are handicapped and risk fueling the conflict through support to warlords and using inappropriate template-driven interventions. This tendency and the lack of transparency in the past have undermined the confidence of Somalis in the stabilization activities of international and regional actors, leading to charges of hidden agendas. As was shown, policymaker's actions have also been significant in compromising perceptions of NGO impartiality and consequently shrinking the humanitarian space.

More transparency on the part of governments, the UN, and NGOs with regard to their mandates is needed so that they can position themselves firmly in their respective missions and minimize confusion about their roles. A clearer definition is needed of the agendas and relationships between them, and this needs to be clearly communicated to all warring parties and Somalis.

Governments must recognize that the ability of aid agencies to operate within an insecure environment is largely based upon the perceptions of communities and warring parties. Attempts by political and military actors to instrumentalize humanitarian assistance threaten the ability of aid agencies to operate by casting them as supporting political or military agendas.[65]

Ideally, governments should accept that their political engagement must prioritize the humanitarian agenda without politicizing it. Governments should start measuring the effectiveness of their policies by the impact they have on the lives of ordinary Somalis. Acknowledging this is fundamental toward rebalancing the political agenda, making it more acceptable and accountable to Somalis and more likely that humanitarian NGOs will work with them. Through engagement with NGOs in nonpolitical forums, they need to educate themselves about the operational realities faced by humanitarian actors and work around them to minimize the risks of politicizing the role of humanitarians. Unfortunately, political actors have limited influence to negotiate humanitarian access or protect humanitarian workers under the current conditions, which should lead them toward policies with modest aims.

The UN resident and humanitarian coordinator can help to regain some measure of transparency by addressing the UN's own internal tensions between its political and humanitarian operations. This should be acknowledged, and the coordination of activities and communications managed in such a way to avoid giving the impression that UN humanitarian assistance is politically "tainted." As the UN's development work is inevitably seen as political, the UN political leadership needs to understand the distinctions between these two fields of activities and respect the differences and not mix them. Overlaps in transition and relief activities need careful management to avoid politicizing those NGOs that do not want to be affiliated with UN lead coordination mechanisms or its political agenda. This will need to be sensitively handled in terms of the UNDP's involvement and the way it presents itself in proximity to humanitarians in the field. Deft diplomacy on the part of the UN resident and humanitarian coordinator will need to be exercised to mediate this UN-NGO discussion.

NGOs must also recognize their own responsibility to be transparent, accountable, and principled. This is hard to achieve with a plethora of NGOs with different aims, agendas, and modes of operation. There nevertheless needs to be a clear definition of what aid agencies are about as well as clear communication to all political actors of what they are prepared to do and not to do. This requires an acknowledgement by NGOs that "the issue is not *whether* humanitarian aid is political, but *how*."[66] It may not be fair for a humanitarian agency to claim neutrality and then complain about the way a political process is threatening its work. Indeed, engagement with political actors may be needed out of "self-defense." Therefore, political acumen on the part of NGOs will be needed to identify when to engage and what needs to be said to protect their humanitarian space.

CONCLUSION

Despite the image attached to it, humanitarian aid has a long history of being used as a political tool, whether in relation to "disaster diplomacy" or within zones of armed conflict. This is unlikely to end any time soon, not least because of the trend toward using militaries as sources and providers of humanitarian assistance. Indeed, humanitarian assistance will always have political effects, even if it does not have political intent. This was certainly the case in Somalia, where a range of NGOs and humanitarian agencies of the UN have struggled to provide aid to those most in need because of the strong political currents generated by the GWOT and the priority given to state-building within the country by international actors.

It is clear from the case of Somalia and other examples given here that humanitarian aid is increasingly being seen as a Western concept, as having instrumental motives, and is therefore to be viewed with great suspicion. Seen in this light, it is no wonder that working for a humanitarian NGO is an increasingly dangerous profession.[67] The other side of this is that it creates more space for different types of humanitarian aid donors, from rebels, to charities, to solidarity movements, to states such as China, which do not carry the same "baggage" as the traditional humanitarian aid donors. Although these too may have instrumental reasons for involvement, they are increasingly welcomed by locals as new sources of humanitarian aid.

Notes

1. Stewart Patrick and Kaysie Brown, *Greater Than the Sum of Its Parts? Assessing "Whole of Government" Approaches to Fragile States* (New York: International Peace Academy, 2007).

2. A. Cooper Drury, Richard Stuart Olson, and Douglas A. Van Belle, "The Politics of Humanitarian Aid: US Foreign Disaster Assistance, 1964–1995," *Journal of Politics* 67, no. 2 (2005): 470. See also James H. Lebovic, "National Interests and US Foreign Aid: The Carter and Reagan Years," *Journal of Peace Research*, 25 (June 1988): 115–35.

3. See Marshall I. Goldman, *Soviet Foreign Aid* (New York: Praeger, 1967).

4. The United Nations High Commission for Refugees (UNHCR) spent up to $400 million per year supporting the camps with humanitarian assistance. Cited in Sarah Kenyon Lischer, "Collateral Damage: Humanitarian Assistance as a Cause of Conflict," *International Security* 28, no. 1 (2003): 95.

5. Ben Barber, "Feeding Refugees, or War? The Dilemma of Humanitarian Aid," *Foreign Affairs* 76, no. 4 (1997): 9.

6. Mark Duffield, "Complex Emergencies and the Crisis of Developmentalism," *IDS Bulletin* 25, no. 3 (1994): 4.

7. Alex de Waal, *Famine Crimes* (Oxford: James Currey, 1997), 72–77. This led to the birth of Médicins sans Frontières as a response to the inactivity of the International Committee of the Red Cross over Biafra.

8. David Chandler, "The Road to Military Humanitarianism," *Human Rights Quarterly* 23 (2001): 681; and Mark Duffield, *Global Governance and the New Wars* (London: Zed, 2001), ch. 4.

9. Helga Baitenmann, "NGOs and the Afghan War: The Politicisation of Humanitarian Aid," *Third World Quarterly* 12, no. 1 (1990): 62.

10. Jonathan T. Dworken, "Restore Hope: Coordinating Relief Operations," *Joint Forces Quarterly*, Summer 1995, 17.

11. Joanna Macrae and Nicholas Leader, *The Politics of Coherence* (London: Humanitarian Policy Group Briefing, ODI, July 2000), 2.

12. Carol Adelman, "Global Philanthropy and Remittances: Reinventing Foreign Aid," *Brown Journal of World Affairs* 15, no. 2 (2009): 23–33.

13. Joanna Macrae, "The New Humanitarianisms: A Review of Trends in Global Humanitarian Action," Humanitarian Policy Group Report No. 11 (London: Overseas Development Institute, 2002), 11.

14. Ibid., 3.

15. Mark Duffield, *Development, Security and Unending War* (Cambridge: Polity, 2007).

16. "Remarks by Secretary of State Colin L. Powell to the National Foreign Policy Conference for Leaders of Non-Governmental Organizations," October 26, 2001, accessed August 22, 2011, http://avalon.law.yale.edu/sept11/powell_brief31.asp.

17. Andrew Natsios, "Remarks at the InterAction Forum, Closing Plenary Session," May 21, 2003, accessed August 22, 2011, www.usaid.gov/press/speeches/2003/sp030521.html.

18. See, for example, Ahmet O. Evin, "Changing Greek Perspectives on Turkey: As Assessment of the Post-Earthquake Rapprochement," *Turkish Studies* 5, no. 1 (2004): 4–20; and Ilan Kelman and Theo Koukis, eds., "Disaster Diplomacy" Special Issue *Cambridge Review of International Affairs* 14, no. 1 (2000): 214–94.

19. Paul Reynolds, "An Opportunity but No Guarantee," *BBC News*, January 5, 2005, accessed December 1, 2009, http://news.bbc.co.uk/2/hi/asia-pacific/4148977.stm.

20. Bill Van Auken, "Powell Declares Tsunami Aid Part of Global War on Terror: Imperialism in Samaritan's Clothing," *World Socialist Website*, January 6, 2005, accessed December 1, 2009, www.wsws.org/articles/2005/jan2005/powl-j061.shtml.

21. Golnaz Esfandiari, "Iran/US: Hopes of Bilateral 'Earthquake Diplomacy' Appear to be Crumbling," *Radio Free Europe Radio Liberty*, January 9, 2004, accessed July 4, 2011, www.rferl.org/content/article/1051129.html.

22. Testimony of Andrew Wilder, Research Director, Feinstein International Center, Tufts University, at a hearing on "US Aid to Pakistan: Planning and Accountability" before the House Committee on Oversight and Government Reform, Subcommittee on National Security and Foreign Affairs, December 9, 2009, accessed February 14, 2010, www.hks.harvard.edu/cchrp/sbhrap/news/Wilder_PakistanAidTestimony_12_9_09.pdf.

23. See, for example, Dawn Brancati, "Political Aftershocks: The Impact of Earthquakes on Intrastate Conflict," *Journal of Conflict Resolution* 51, no. 1 (2007): 715–43; Edward Miguel, Satyanath Shaner, and Ernest Sergenti, "Economic Shocks and Civil Conflict: An Instrumental Variables Approach," *Journal of Political Economy* 112, no. 4 (2004): 725–53; and Carol R. Ember and Melvin Ember, "Resource Unpredictability, Mistrust and War: A Cross-Cultural Study," *Journal of Conflict Resolution* 36, no. 2 (1992): 242–62.

24. John M. Glionna, "Doctor Who Treated Osama," *The Indian Express*, December 4, 2005, accessed November 11, 2009, www.indianexpress.com/storyOld.php?storyId=83238.

25. Jan McGirk, "Kashmir: The Politics of an Earthquake," October 18, 2005, *OpenDemocracy*, accessed December 1, 2009, www.opendemocracy.net/conflict-india_pakistan/jihadi_2941.jsp.

26. Jeremy M. Sharp; Kenneth Katzman; Carol Migdalovitz; Alfred Prados; Paul E. Gallis; Diane E. Rennack; John Rollins; Steven R. Bowman; Foreign Affairs, Defense, and Trade Division; and Connie Veillette, "Lebanon: The Israel-Hamas-Hezbollah Conflict," CRS Report for Congress (Washington, DC: Congressional Research Service, September 15, 2006), 14.

27. Daniel Steinvorth, "A State within A State: The Footrace to Rebuild Lebanon," *New York Times*, September 4, 2006, accessed December 1, 2009, http://query.nytimes.com/gst/fullpage.html?res=9905E1D81631F937A3575AC0A9609C8B63&sec=&spon=&pagewanted=2; Ivan Watson, "Hezbollah Takes Lead in Rebuilding Lebanon," *National Public Radio*, August 17, 2006, accessed December 1, 2009, www.npr.org/templates/story/story.php?storyId=5662485; and Dr. Karin von Hippel of CSIS, personal interview after her visit to reconstruction sites in Lebanon, November 21, 2006, Washington, DC.

28. Barber, "Feeding Refugees, or War?" 10–12.

29. Edward N. Luttwak, "Give War a Chance," *Foreign Affairs* 78, no. 4 (1999): 36–44.

30. Philippe Le Billion, *The Political Economy of War*, Humanitarian Policy Group Network Paper No. 33 (London: Overseas Development Institute, 2000); S. Neil MacFarlane, *Humanitarian Action: The Conflict Connection*, Occasional Paper No.43 (Providence, RI: Thomas J. Watson Jr. Institute for International Studies, and Tokyo: United Nations University, 2001).

31. Lischer, "Collateral Damage," 82.

32. Brancati, "Political Aftershocks," 716.

33. David Shearer, "Aiding or Abetting? Humanitarian Aid and Its Economic Role in Civil War," in *Greed and Grievance*, ed. Mats Berdal and David M. Malone, 198–203 (Boulder, CO: Lynne Rienner, 2000).

34. Dan McDougall, "Children Die as Winter Snow Sweeps Quake Valleys," *The Observer*, December 4, 2005, accessed November 9, 2009, www.guardian.co.uk/environment /2005/dec/04/pakistan.naturaldisasters.

35. The US Army and Marine Corps, *Counterinsurgency Manual* (Chicago: Chicago University Press, 2007), 300, A-47.

36. Ibid., 358, D-29.

37. Austin Bay, "Money Is Ammo in Iraq," *Strategy Page*, September 14, 2004, accessed December 1, 2009, www.strategypage.com/on_point/2004914.aspx; and Mark Martins, "No Small Change of Soldiering: The Commander's Emergency Response Program (CERP) in Iraq and Afghanistan," *The Army Lawyer*, February 1, 2004.

38. Dana Hedgpeth and Sarah Cohen, "Money as a Weapon," *Washington Post* transcript of question and answer session about CERP, August 11, 2008, accessed August 22, 2011, www .washingtonpost.com/wp-dyn/content/discussion/2008/08/10/DI2008081001774.html.

39. See, for example, Andrew S. Natsios, "The Nine Principles of Reconstruction and Development," *Parameters* 35, no. 3 (Autumn 2005): 4–20.

40. J. Brian Atwood, M. Peter McPherson, and Andrew Natsios, "Arrested Development: Making Foreign Aid a More Effective Tool," *Foreign Affairs* 87, no. 6 (2008): 126.

41. Sarah Kenyon Lischer, "Military Intervention and the Humanitarian 'Force Multiplier,'" *Global Governance* 13 (2007): 105.

42. "DR Congo Army 'Used Aid as Bait,'" *BBC News*, November 6, 2009, accessed November 6, 2009, http://news.bbc.co.uk/2/hi/8347503.stm.

43. Reuben E. Brigety II, *Humanity as a Weapon of War* (Washington, DC: Center for American Progress, June 2008), 2.

44. McDougall, "Children Die."

45. Ibid.

46. Brigety, *Humanity as a Weapon of War*, 1–2.

47. As used here, "Somalia" will only refer to the south/central regions and Puntland.

48. For details, see Ken Menkhaus, "Governance without Government in Somalia," *International Security* 31, no. 3 (2006–7): 74–106; and Ken Menkhaus, "The Crisis in Somalia: Tragedy in Five Acts," *African Affairs* 106 (2007): 357–90.

49. UN Press Release (Nairobi), "The Humanitarian Coordinator for Somalia calls for immediate re-engagement in Mogadishu," January 17, 2007, http://ochaonline.un.org/Ocha LinkClick.aspx?link=ocha&docid=34399.

50. Human Rights Watch, *Shell-Shocked: Civilians under Siege in Mogadishu*, August 12, 2007, www.hrw.org/en/node/10783/section/1.

51. See ibid.

52. The first NGO outcry was in the form of a collective letter addressing the humanitarian crisis in Mogadishu on April 11, 2007. This was immediately followed by statements from the UN resident and humanitarian coordinator and the European Commission.

53. Minutes of the meeting of the Interagency Standing Committee, July 9, 2008. Copy in author's possession.

54. "EU Given War Crime Warning over Somalia Aid," *Guardian*, April 7, 2007.

55. Author's interview with a Somali civil society activist in April 2007.

56. During 2008, thirty-six aid workers were killed, most of whom were Somali.

57. "Somalia Now World's Most Dangerous Place for Aid Workers, Says UN Official," *UN News Centre*, April 24, 2007, www.un.org/apps/news/story.asp?NewsID=22334&Cr=somalia &Cr1.

58. Cedric Barnes and Harun Hassan, *The Rise and Fall of Mogadishu's Islamic Courts* (London: Chatham House Report, April 2007).

59. See Security Council Report, *Cross-Cutting Report No. 2 Protection of Civilians*, October 14, 2008. www.securitycouncilreport.org/site/c.glKWLeMTIsG/b.4664099/k.1776/Cross Cutting_Report_No_2brProtection_of_Civiliansbr14_October_2008.htm.

60. Unfortunately, the TFG was widely viewed as a Trojan horse for Ethiopian security interests, and little was done by the transitional authorities to address these concerns in a conciliatory manner.

61. Human Rights Watch, *So Much to Fear: War Crimes and the Devastation of Somalia*, December 8, 2008, www.hrw.org/node/76419..

62. Structural integration of the UN would place political, security, development, and humanitarian activities under the political leadership of the UNPOS.

63. The way in which the UN Department of Political Affairs attempted to implement structural integration was also seen by humanitarian agencies as flawed, nontransparent, and without proper consultation.

64. Menkhaus argues that the burden of proof should fall on those advocating continuation of the same boilerplate approaches. Ken Menkhaus, "Somalia: A Country in Peril, a Policy Nightmare," ENOUGH Strategy Paper, September 2008, www.enoughproject.org/publications /somalia-country-peril-policy-nightmare.

65. Antonio Donini. Larissa Fast, Greg Hansen, Simon Harris, Larry Minear, Tasneem Mowjee, and Andrew Wilder, eds., *Humanitarian Agenda 2015 Final Report* (Medford, MA: Feinstein International Center, Tufts University, March 2008). https://wikis.uit.tufts.edu/con-fluence/display/FIC/Humanitarian+Agenda+2015+—+The+State+of+the+Humanitarian +Enterprise.

66. Macrae and Leader, *Politics of Coherence*, 1.

67. Abby Stoddard, Adele Harmer, and Victoria DiDomenico, "Providing Aid in Insecure Environments: 2009 Update," Humanitarian Policy Group Brief 34 (London: Overseas Development Institute, April 2009), especially, 2.

Chapter 5

HUMANITARIAN ASSISTANCE
A Development Perspective

Sabina Dewan

The relationship between humanitarian assistance and development assistance is complex in both theory and practice. While the two are related by their mutual aspiration of improving the human condition, they have historically been separated by their temporal and substantive scopes. In practice, the two are at times mutually reinforcing, and at other times humanitarian assistance and development assistance may be somewhat at odds with one another.

This chapter sketches the broad contours of the relationship between humanitarian assistance and development assistance. The relationship between humanitarian and development assistance has evolved in recent years in the face of protracted emergencies and burgeoning military engagement in humanitarian and development activities. There are also significant challenges in linking humanitarian and development assistance in practice, especially regarding bureaucratic funding and organization. This chapter explores these dynamics that challenge the traditional humanitarian relief–to-development continuum. Yet with smart policies on the part of both governmental and nongovernmental entities, these dilemmas can be managed over time. This chapter makes some recommendations on doing so.

HUMANITARIAN AND DEVELOPMENT ASSISTANCE: A COMPLICATED RELATIONSHIP

Humanitarian assistance focuses on immediate interventions to save the lives of people at imminent risk of harm from the consequences of natural disasters or man-made conflicts. Typically such interventions are limited to actions such as providing temporary shelter, water and sanitation, emergency food rations, and immediate health care. Development assistance, on the other hand, seeks to address the structural causes of poverty in the hopes of spurring self-sustaining economic growth that improves the material and social well-being of a population. Macroeconomic stabilization, investments in public institutions, agricultural innovation, infrastructure support, improved access to primary education, and increased capacity for health care systems are some typical developmental approaches.

In theory, there should be seamless links between humanitarian and development assistance, and the two should be mutually reinforcing. On the one hand, successful development assistance can lay the groundwork for effective and efficient dissemination of humanitarian assistance. Reliable public systems and services, for example, are vital to managing the repercussions of a natural or man-made disaster, and sound infrastructure is necessary to ensuring the timely delivery of humanitarian assistance in its aftermath.

Humanitarian assistance, on the other hand, should lead to long-term development. For instance, emergency disaster assistance should advance the long-term infrastructure development to repair the ravages of nature. Immediate food aid should be followed by agricultural support to ensure that a chronically food-insecure country can feed itself in the future. Outbreaks of highly communicable yet treatable diseases should be addressed not only with the immediate influx of expatriate medical personnel and supplies but also by enduring efforts to strengthen indigenous health care structures.

Yet the so-called relief-to-development continuum has often proved anything but smooth in practice. The devastation caused by humanitarian crises sets development back even as underdevelopment makes the delivery of humanitarian assistance more difficult. Sustaining popular and political support to make a smooth transition from humanitarian assistance to development assistance proves to be challenging once television sets are switched off and media crews move on. Differences in funding streams for humanitarian and developmental aid, variances in international political will to treat pressing humanitarian emergencies rather than enduring developmental challenges, and restraints in the mandates of organizations that perform humanitarian and developmental programs have all made bridging this gap a perpetual problem.

In addition, there have been at least three trends over the last decade that have made the relationship between humanitarian and development assistance even more problematic, particularly for the US government and American non-governmental agencies (NGO). The first has been the persistence of protracted emergencies in which saving lives often requires interventions measured in years rather than weeks or months. The second has been the evolution of the US military's humanitarian activities from immediate disaster response to longer-term activities to win the hearts and minds of local populations in the countries in which they operate. Finally, bureaucratic organization and funding levels of the US government in both humanitarian and development assistance have real operational consequences. Each of these phenomena has uniquely complicated the relationship between humanitarian and development assistance in the context of American action in the development field.

A practical example of some of these challenges occurred in 2007 when the US government launched the Haitian Stabilization Initiative (HSI). Originally planned as a development strategy for all of Haiti in the wake of a major UN peacekeeping operation, the HSI was eventually limited to $20 million applied to Cite Soleil, the most notorious of slums in Port-au-Prince. Over the course of two years, the project proved very successful in improving the lives of the people it touched. A new marketplace was built, hundreds of tons of rubbish were removed from the streets, a community radio station was established, and paved roads were introduced. US officials organized and worked with local community groups to determine the community's needs. Working in partnership with the local population, NGOs, the

UN, and the Haitian National Police, the level of crime was dramatically reduced. In many ways, it was a model development program.

Except that it was funded by money from the Department of Defense. As part of the Pentagon's 1207 program, in which defense dollars can be used for civilian assistance to support national security objectives around the world, HSI was seen as a critical tool in stabilizing a country which suffered from episodic humanitarian crises (both natural and man-made from political turmoil) and chronic underdevelopment. In 2009 when the Cite Soleil initiative of HSI was completed and deemed by the Pentagon not to be of critical strategic significance relative to other priorities around the world, the program was ended without a predetermined plan by the Defense Department, the State Department, or the US Agency for International Development (USAID) to continue its effective initiatives in a sustainable manner. In its time-sensitive success, its developmental impact, and its strategic linkages, the HSI is indicative of the promise and challenges of modern developmental operations as they relate to humanitarian philosophy and practice.[1]

The tangible improvements made in Cité Soleil helped set out the beginnings of the groundwork for a more effective delivery of humanitarian assistance. Yet the short duration of the program meant that the steps toward stability and development in the area were extremely fragile and were quickly reversed in the aftermath of the devastating earthquake that rocked Haiti in January 2010. Within a month of the crisis, the US government including the Department of Defense, the Federal Emergency Management Agency, USAID, and others reengaged in Haiti, contributing more than $394 million in earthquake response funding for the ravaged nation.[2]

USAID/Haiti directed more than $7.5 million to the HSI in Martissant, Carrefour, and Carrefour Fuilles for immediate earthquake response. The focus of this initiative ranged from removing debris and rehabilitating key infrastructure to providing financial services to microentrepreneurs and trying to create jobs.[3]

HUMANITARIAN AND DEVELOPMENT ACTORS: SIMILAR MOTIVATION AND ASPIRATION, DIFFERING ACTIONS

Humanitarian and development actors share the common desire to improve the human condition. Yet in practice the urgency that motivates humanitarian assistance leads to a different set of objectives and, consequently, behavior than development assistance. Furthermore, humanitarian actors may or may not choose to insulate their work from the political environment in which they operate. Development aimed at addressing the structural causes of poverty and spurring self-sustaining growth, however, must inevitably involve public sector engagement. By virtue of doing so, it inherently includes a political dimension.

"Humanitarianism" is usually associated with helping and protecting victims of disasters or conflicts irrespective of where they are, who they are, and why they are in need. As such, "the sanctity of human life" is usually understood as "the first principle for all humanitarians and overrides other considerations."[4] However,

Figure 5.1 The Political Spectrum of Humanitarians and Their Attitudes Toward Traditional Operating Principles

	Classicists ◄► Minimalists ◄► Maximalists ◄► Solidarists		
Engagement with political authorities	Eschew public confrontations	◄————————————►	Advocate controversial public policy
Neutrality	Avoid taking sides	◄————————————►	Take the side of the selected victims
Impartiality	Deliver aid using proportionality and nondiscrimination	◄————————————►	Skew the balance of resource allocation
Consent	Pursue as sine qua non	◄————————————►	Override sovereignty as necessary

Source: Thomas G. Weiss, "Principles, Politics and Humanitarian Action," *Ethics & International Affairs*, 13, no. 1 (1999): 11–12. Figure reprinted with permission from John Wiley & Sons, Inc.

not all self-styled humanitarian actors think about the practicalities of delivering humanitarian assistance in the same way. Thomas Weiss has provided a useful typology to understand the differences within what is often referred to as the "humanitarian community" of NGOs. These differences became particularly stark in the 1990s after what Weiss described as the "collective identity crisis among aid workers in war zones."

Weiss unpacked the operating principles adopted by different humanitarian actors and arrayed them as a spectrum along which he identified four ideal types of humanitarian engagement. At one end were the "classicists." Led by the International Committee of the Red Cross, the classicists believe that humanitarianism can and should be completely insulated from politics. The other three ideal types were different brands of what Weiss called "political humanitarians," all of whom believed that politics and humanitarianism "could not and should not be disassociated." The political humanitarians come with several agendas but all agreed on employing humanitarian action as part of some international public policy to resolve or manage conflict and set the stage for long-term development. There were the "minimalists," whose aim was to "do no harm";[5] the "maximalists," who had a more ambitious agenda of employing humanitarian action as part of a comprehensive strategy to transform conflict; and the "solidarists," who explicitly chose sides and abandoned any pretense of neutrality and impartiality. This typology is depicted in figure 5.1.

As Weiss noted, "Humanitarian action for each group from left to right of the diagram is respectively: warranted as long as it is charitable and self-contained, defined only by the needs of the victim and divorced from political objectives and conditionalities; worthwhile if efforts to relieve suffering do not make matters worse and can be sustained locally; defensible when coupled with steps to address the roots of violence and as part of a conscious and comprehensive political strategy; and justifiable when siding with the main victims."[6]

Although Weiss believed that the classicist's aspiration of apolitical humanitarianism was a chimera, the political humanitarians also faced a range of practical challenges that meant their own efforts did not always result in better policies or results. "Under the right circumstances," he concluded that "the maximalist approach could be viewed as an opportunity to address the roots of violence rather than place emergency Band-Aids, however well funded and effective, on wounds. Nonetheless, some of the more grandiose claims of maximalists should lead to extreme skepticism: there literally is no space for conflict resolution or development activities when deep insecurity prevails. In the darkest moments of civil war, only emergency relief efforts are plausible, and even these are often under siege."[7]

Weiss concedes that addressing the roots of violence is an inherently long-term proposition, a matter of promoting stability through development processes rather than mere "Band-Aids." Yet humanitarians cannot and should not try to deny political realities in which they operate. There is room for humanitarians to consider how their initiatives will affect local conflict dynamics and use whatever leverage they may possess to promote conflict transformation. Conflict transformation is a subtle process that entails playing a proactive role in changing the relationships that fuel violence.

Teaching tolerance in an effort to overcome ethnic conflict in transitional education programs in refugee camps is an example. It is, however, difficult to gauge the success of efforts by humanitarian actors in promoting conflict transformation because transforming public sentiment and attitudes is inevitably a long, complex, and difficult process requiring action on the part of several actors. Nonetheless, humanitarian actors have an opportunity to sow the seeds for conflict transformation.

Weiss therefore concedes that it is possible for humanitarian assistance to reinforce development, and, as such, there can be overlap in both aspiration and practice of both sets of actors. But, as Weiss rightly points out, the roles of humanitarian versus development actors diverge significantly in the face of severe emergencies that call for immediate interventions and immediate results.

The delineation between the roles of humanitarian and development actors nonetheless becomes ever more complicated as humanitarians increasingly find themselves operating in what have come to be known as "protracted emergencies." Such prolonged emergencies blur the temporal boundaries of activities between humanitarian and development actors, as in the case of Somalia discussed by Maletta and Spear in this volume, and in situations when they became joined by the new breed of "military humanitarians." Both of these occurrences are analyzed in the ensuing sections.

PROTRACTED EMERGENCIES AND THE DEVELOPMENT CONUNDRUM

Protracted emergencies have complicated the humanitarian to development assistance continuum. The definition of humanitarian assistance now encompasses a broad range of activities from addressing the challenges confronting displaced communities to problems associated with national disasters, failed or fragile states, armed conflict, and genocide, for example. The scope and duration of these challenges persists beyond the short-term time frame that is conventionally associated with an emergency. When the length of a humanitarian operation exceeds that no-tionally associated with an emergency, but the conditions on the ground preclude conventional development programs, then the intended beneficiaries in need are caught in between.

Addressing protracted emergencies has increasingly bedeviled American NGOs and governmental agencies over the last ten years or more, with implications for development assistance in challenging contexts. Protracted emergencies present challenges both to the humanitarian assistance communities and the development assistance communities because they create situations in which neither is poised for optimal impact. The atypically long duration of protracted emergencies can threaten the capacity or will of humanitarian agencies to maintain their services to at-risk populations. Donor support for protracted emergencies is difficult to sustain as governments' strategic priorities tend to shift with changes in the social, political, or economic climate. As harsh conditions persist and move from being acute to chronic in nature, both international donor and public interest can wane, thereby decreasing the resources available to aid agencies and forcing them to revaluate their global assistance priorities. The Pentagon's decision to end the Hai-tian Stabilization Initiative in 2009 (discussed earlier) is but one example. Similar challenges confront those operating in Democratic Republic of Congo, Sudan, and Afghanistan to name a few.

Conversely, development agencies can often find it difficult to conduct ef-fective programming in protracted emergencies, especially those associated with armed conflict. This is not least because protracted emergencies tend to coincide with political instability that precludes the type of institution-building required for addressing the structural causes of poverty and to promote self-sustaining eco-nomic growth. Often, as in Somalia, for example, violent conditions on the ground are just too dangerous to launch and sustain effective poverty alleviation programs and meet essential human needs in a consistent manner (see the Maletta and Spear chapter).

Alternatively, the introduction of traditional development interventions—such as supporting agricultural programs—can have an emergency humanitarian objective of enhancing food security and reducing aid dependency in protracted situations. Yet continued violence and displacement may make it extremely chal-lenging to do so.[8] The weakness of indigenous governmental structures during prolonged crises can hamper effective development interventions (particularly in areas such as education, health care, and infrastructure improvement) that require capable government partners.

Hence, a gap can emerge between the relative competencies of humanitar-ian and development agencies that affect the efficacy of both. The intended ben-eficiaries of humanitarian and development assistance lose out in the face of a protracted emergency that neither humanitarian nor development actors are op-timally equipped to deal with.

Humanitarian agencies have addressed this gap by reconceptualizing the tem-poral component of emergencies.[9] Indeed, the very introduction into the humani-tarian lexicon of the term "protracted emergency"—deemed oxymoronic just over a decade ago—signals the recognition that effective humanitarian response must be prepared to deliver services in both acute and chronic situations over the short and long term. Funding sources, bureaucratic structures, and organizational mandates must be prepared to work accordingly.

Development organizations must similarly adapt to this challenge. The principal question is, how should organizations pursue enduring poverty reduction programs in situations of chronic insecurity and poor governance that threaten the lives of beneficiaries even as they make durable solutions exceedingly difficult to find? Furthermore, poverty is, to a significant extent, path dependent. This means that as scores of children growing up in refugee camps miss out on opportunities for education and health, it is likely that their children will also struggle with literacy and health, thus sentencing future generations to lives with limited prospects for economic mobility. This compounds the development challenge in protracted emergencies, making it ever more pressing to devise strategies that promote economic opportunity even in adverse circumstances to break this path dependency.

Paul Collier has argued that persistent armed conflict is one of the major factors trapping some countries in a vicious cycle of endemic poverty.[10] Therefore, addressing the humanitarian consequences of armed conflict (in addition to peacebuilding measures required to achieve durable political solutions) should at least be seen as concerns of developmental practice, if not outright objectives thereto. Even as experienced development professionals and astute observers grapple with the notion of protracted emergencies and the implications for sound development practice, most agree on one thing: Using the concept of "crisis" to delineate between humanitarian operations on the one hand and developmental initiatives on the other has become increasingly problematic.[11] The passing of the baton from the humanitarians to development actors is not as clear-cut in protracted emergencies calling for the two to operate in tandem. New thinking and approaches in the field will continue to be required to improve developmental programs in the most challenging environments around the world.

Liberia serves as a good example. Between 1989 and 2003, Liberia was embroiled in armed conflicts that decimated the country's economy and infrastructure and led to the loss of more than 250,000 lives. Humanitarian aid and assistance flowed into the country from UN agencies, donor governments, and NGOs. Ellen Johnson Sirleaf—the first African woman to be elected head of state—was inaugurated as Liberia's president in 2006 and set out a different trajectory for Liberia that helped the country transition from a humanitarian crisis to a path of long-term development. With the help of NGOs and international actors, the government developed a poverty reduction strategy in 2008 that served as a framework for its recovery, reconstruction, and development efforts.

MILITARY HUMANITARIAN ASSISTANCE

In the aftermath of the September 11, 2001, terrorist attacks, one of the approaches of the United States that has generated significant controversy has been the increasing involvement of the American military in civilian assistance programs as a means of advancing US security objectives. While these concerns have largely been raised by traditional humanitarian nongovernmental actors, they also have significant implications for development practice as well.

The doctrine of the US military generally defines humanitarian assistance as any activity it undertakes in any context that aims to improve the lives of an indigenous population by addressing core human needs (such as shelter, health care, building construction, and delivery of supplies). It uses the term "disaster response" to refer to the emergency life-saving assistance it provides to civilians in the wake of calamities—either natural or man-made—such as its response to the 2004 Asian tsunami or the evacuation of civilians during the 2006 Israeli-Lebanese war. This latter definition of disaster response is more closely aligned to what civilian aid workers refer to as humanitarian assistance—neutral, impartial, independent action motivated solely by a concern for human suffering. But military involvement in humanitarian assistance that goes beyond disaster response is where the controversy lies.

Concerns in the NGO community over the so-called militarization or instrumentalization of humanitarian assistance began in earnest during Operation Enduring Freedom, the military campaign against al-Qaeda and the Taliban that began in the autumn of 2001. For the first time, US aircrews delivered air-dropped emergency food rations to Afghan civilians on the ground at the same time that they attacked enemy targets with conventional munitions. The purpose of the humanitarian airdrops was not only to forestall starvation in the Afghan populace during the winter but also to demonstrate to the world that the United States was at war only with violent al-Qaeda elements and their allies, rather than with innocent Muslim civilians. The NGO groups involved in administering humanitarian assistance in Afghanistan would largely be perceived as tending to human need even if their actions actually intended to address the roots of violence and were part of a conscious and comprehensive political strategy; here Weiss's typology for political humanitarians is particularly relevant.

Beyond the questionable efficacy of the airdrops, some NGOs protested this explicitly partisan purpose of the military's humanitarian activities in Afghanistan. They noted that humanitarian activity explicitly performed with a strategic motivation cannot by definition be considered humanitarian. Further, they feared that the military's performance of humanitarian activities (whether through airdrops or through military personnel performing projects in civilian clothes, as many civil affairs teams had done) in the same theater of operations where they were active belligerents would threaten the neutral identity of civilian aid workers and put their lives at risk from al-Qaeda and Taliban fighters who could not distinguish between the identities or motivations of US military forces and independent relief workers.

These issues were largely worked out through "Guidelines for Relations between US Armed Forces and Non-Governmental Humanitarian Organizations in Hostile or Potentially Hostile Environments" jointly negotiated by the Department of Defense and InterAction through the United States Institute of Peace in 2007.[12] Yet this problem that originated with military involvement in disaster response has migrated to military humanitarian assistance activities, albeit strategically motivated, in permissive (i.e., noncombat and nonemergency) environments, with direct implications for the civilian development community.

As the US military came to grips with the global terrorism challenge in the decade following 9/11, it came to the conclusion that it needed to follow two lines of effort: kinetic operations to kill and capture the enemy, and nonkinetic operations to counter support for the ideologies of violent extremism. The tools it adopted to address the nonkinetic line of effort were largely developmental in nature. For example, they included building schools in Ethiopia, sending Navy hospital ships to treat indigenous populations for nonemergency medical conditions in Indonesia, performing well-drilling operations in Kenya, funding democracy programs performed by USAID in Nepal, and the like.

These sorts of activities presented significant operational and philosophical challenges for civilian development professionals. Their first set of arguments was largely practical. Well-meaning military personnel were simply not as proficient or as cost-effective at developmental interventions as were their civilian counterparts. They did not spend as much time with local communities as development professionals did and thus did not intimately understand local dynamics or needs very well. Using military equipment and personnel could also be several times more expensive than civilian resources to do everything from well drilling to providing medical care. Finally, military humanitarian projects were often "one-off" in nature, without the planning or consistent engagement necessary for sustainable economic growth and long-term planning, which is the goal of all "real" development work. Since military humanitarian assistance was motivated by strategic objectives, once the strategic objective had been fulfilled, the assistance would also subside.

While these concerns had varying degrees of validity, ultimately the response from the military and some in the development community was that these concerns could be addressed through better training, planning, and experience on the part of military humanitarian actors as well as through a smoother operationalization of the relief-to-development continuum in which military humanitarian activities complimented long-term development efforts. But this is complicated by situations of protracted crisis where the lines between development and humanitarian assistance are blurred.

Despite attempts to resolve this dilemma, development actors have still not formulated an adequate response that recognizes the increasing military interest in this field yet preserves the development community's leading role in supporting sustainable antipoverty programs with all relevant parties. This is further complicated by the military's rapid response capabilities driven by greater access to funding, technology, and equipment as compared to other organizations.

BUREAUCRATIC ORGANIZATION AND FUNDING

Scholars of humanitarian practice and development assistance often have rich theoretical debates about the challenges and opportunities inherent in these fields.[13] The nuances and rigor of such dialogues, however, must often confront the cold and prosaic reality of state bureaucratic and financial arrangements. The evolution of the US government's assistance structure has contributed to the difficulty of operationalizing a seamless humanitarian to development continuum, even as the United States ranks (in absolute terms) as the largest national donor of official development assistance (ODA) in the world. This is due, in large measure, to a lack of flexible development programming in the field and insufficient numbers of staff to implement and monitor programs at the humanitarian–development nexus effectively.[14]

Even though USAID is the United States' main governmental arm for the funding and conduct of nonmilitary overseas assistance, it is still responsible for only a fraction of US ODA disbursements (38.8 percent in 2006).[15] The rest is distributed across over a dozen other federal agencies, with a whopping 21.7 percent delivered by the Defense Department in 2006 (the latest year for which figures are available).

Despite this fragmentation, there are bureaucratic reasons to suggest coherence in the relationship between humanitarian relief and development assistance. Chief among these is that the principal humanitarian and development organizations are colocated within USAID. The Office of Foreign Disaster Assistance (OFDA), located within the Democracy, Conflict, and Humanitarian Assistance bureau of USAID, is the leader in overseas humanitarian response for the US government. The OFDA has flexible funds it can apply to save lives in emergencies from earthquakes and floods to civil wars and international armed conflicts. Special "notwithstanding" authorities allow the OFDA to provide rapid assistance to countries (such as Iran and North Korea) where other US government agencies are prohibited from operating. Disaster-assistance response teams, composed of sectoral specialists in vital areas (such as shelter, water and sanitation, and health), can deploy to disaster zones around the world within hours and begin working with host governments and NGOs immediately to address urgent humanitarian needs.

Despite this robust capability nesting within USAID, the handoff between humanitarian operations and development work is not always smooth. In large measure, this is because USAID development assistance dollars cannot be spent as rapidly or as flexibly as humanitarian assistance funds. Often development assistance is heavily earmarked by congressional appropriators, thus legally requiring USAID missions in the field to spend money in particular ways (on maternal health or primary education, for example) regardless of the need for long-term institution-building or of the needs on the ground in the aftermath of a particular crisis. Without such flexibility in development portfolios to match that of humanitarian crises, achieving improved coherence between relief and development efforts will be extremely challenging.

IMPLICATIONS

The links between humanitarian and development assistance provide great potential for complementarity. Yet there remain significant tensions. The common problem among the challenges posed by protracted emergencies, military "humanitarian assistance," and the developmental mandate is the need for de-velopment actors to advance their issues under circumstances that are arguably more complex than those faced by their humanitarian counterparts, even as those circumstances are often generated by circumstances first encountered in humani-tarian operations.

The problem of sustainable poverty reduction is inherently more complicated, though no more or less important, than alleviating human suffering in the wake of natural disasters or complex emergencies. Coordinating host governmental pri-orities, directing external resources, working with local populations, and address-ing multisectoral priorities without the useful pressure of time that accompanies humanitarian action have always been inherent in the challenges of development work. Sustaining popular and political support, both technical and financial, for activities the results of which are not immediately apparent and that take time to emerge makes conducting successful development assistance even more difficult.

As humanitarian action has increasingly confronted the problems associated with protracted emergencies on the ground as well as the strategic priorities of donor governments and their militaries, so too have these factors increasingly challenged effective development. They will surely continue to do so in the com-ing decade. Accordingly, development actors—NGOs and US government agencies as well as development theory—must come to grips with this altered reality.[16] They must also draw useful lessons from their colleagues in the humanitarian assistance business. Two critical steps should be taken in this regard.

The most important thing for the developmental enterprise is to develop greater clarity on the poverty reduction imperative vis-à-vis the altered global land-scape. It is not enough to declare that poverty must be history. Particularly in the American context, a sound development strategy must take into account the real strategic priorities of the United States as well as the political constraints on the ground where development actually happens.

It is important for development actors, as principled advocates, to press the United States and other governments to focus on poverty alleviation as a goal in and of itself. Yet they should also target development programs principally to places of greatest need, especially when the priorities of the US government direct its developmental resources elsewhere. Indeed, there should be efforts to foster a global synergy between the programs of the US government and other donors on the one hand and nongovernmental development agencies on the other, with the latter focused principally on places of the greatest need. In so doing, they can make the argument to donor governments that they are actually working in partnership with fundamental strategic and moral imperatives by focusing their work in places that may be of importance though not necessarily of vital national interest.

Second, it is important for developmental actors to accept the reality that the US military—and to some extent its partner militaries—will be involved in development-related activities for the foreseeable future. US military campaigns to win the hearts and minds of the local populations in countries where they operate such as Afghanistan make this likely, as does the fact that the US military has access to much more funding than do American aid agencies.

So long as the defense establishment is convinced that nonkinetic civilian assistance operations are useful (and even necessary) means of building trust with local populations and countering violent ideologies, they will continue to engage in these activities. The challenge for development actors is to find a way to operate in this environment in a manner that does not undermine their long-term poverty reduction objectives and at the same time does not encroach upon the functions of humanitarian actors. On the contrary, development assistance should potentially support humanitarian assistance, and vice versa. A good start would be for nongovernmental development actors to establish similar rules of the road as their humanitarian colleagues have done with the military. This should be done in a way that not only draws clear boundaries between civil and military action that are intellectually sound and operationally implementable but also finds common ground and ways in which the two groups can be supportive of each other's work.

Developmental assistance has been of critical importance in lifting millions out of poverty and improving the human condition over the last sixty years. It will prove increasingly important in the coming decades as the world population grows at an unprecedented rate, as resources become increasingly scarce, and as billions of people struggle to reap the benefits of increased integration into the global economy. Similarly, development will be increasingly linked to humanitarian action—with all of the synergies and challenges that accompany it—as political, economic, and environmental pressures confront fragile countries with limited capacity to handle them. Getting the humanitarian relief–to–development continuum right in the twenty-first century requires that development actors learn the right lessons from the preceding decades and make bold and savvy choices to be effective in the future.

Notes

1. Reuben E. Brigety II and Natalie Ondiak, "Haiti's Changing Tide: A Sustainable Security Case Study" (Washington, DC: Center for American Progress, September 2009).

2. USAID/DCHA/OFDA, "Haiti—Earthquake," Fact Sheet #16, Fiscal Year 2010 (January 28, 2010), 3. www.usaid.gov/helphaiti/documents/01.28.10-USAID-DCHAHaitiEarthquakeFactSheet16.pdf.

3. Ibid., 3

4. Thomas G. Weiss, "Principles, Politics and Humanitarian Action," *Ethics and International Affairs* 13, no. 1 (1999), 11–12.

5. See Mary B. Anderson, *Do No Harm: How Aid Can Support Peace—or War* (Boulder, CO: Lynne Rienner, 1999).

6. Weiss, "Principles," 4.

7. Ibid., 19.

8. Francois Grunwald, "Responding to Long-Term Crises," *Humanitarian Exchange*, March 2001, 2.

9. Ibid.

10. Paul Collier, *The Bottom Billion* (New York: Oxford University Press, 2007), 35–37.

11. Grunwald, "Responding to Long-Term Crises."

12. See "InterAction US Civilian–Military Guidelines, July 2007," *InterAction.org*, accessed January 30, 2011, www.interaction.org/document/interaction-us-civilian-military-guidelines-July-2007.

13. See, for example, Michael Barnett and Thomas G. Weiss, eds., *Humanitarianism in Question: Politics, Power, Ethics* (Ithaca, NY: Cornell University Press, 2008); Fiona Terry, *Condemned to Repeat? The Paradox of Humanitarian Action* (Ithaca, NY: Cornell University Press, 2002); Jeffrey D. Sachs, *The End of Poverty: Economic Possibilities for Our Time* (New York: Penguin, 2005); and William Easterly, *The White Man's Burden* (New York: Penguin, 2008).

14. See J. Brian Atwood, M. Peter McPherson, and Andrew Natsios, "Arrested Development," *Foreign Affairs* 87, no. 6 (2008): 123–32.

15. OECD, "United States (2006) DAC Peer Review: Main Findings and Recommendations," accessed January 30, 2011, www.oecd.org/document/27/0,3343,en_2649_34603_37829787 _1_1_1_1,00.html.

16. See Adele Harmer and Joanna Macrae, eds., "Beyond the Continuum: The Changing Role of Aid Policy in Protracted Crisis" (London: ODI Humanitarian Policy Group Research Report, 2004), www.odi.org.uk/resources/download/236.pdf.

HUMANITARIAN ASSISTANCE
Editors' Comments

Joanna Spear and Paul D. Williams

Although the security and development arenas broadly share a definition of humanitarian assistance, their ideas about what such assistance is for and the problem that it addresses are radically different. The development community conceives the importance of humanitarian assistance purely as a way to save lives and alleviate the suffering of those most in need. Moreover, such assistance is seen as a prior step to effective poverty reduction policies and longer-term development strategies. In contrast, security analysts and practitioners have tended to view humanitarian assistance instrumentally as an element in crafting desirable security outcomes. During the Cold War humanitarian assistance was a way to score points against the Soviets; today it is used to try and curry favor with the Muslim world and enhance counterinsurgency campaigns.

The different ideas about the central purpose of humanitarian assistance reflect the fact that security and development are often focused on different levels of analysis, with development conceiving of humanitarian assistance as working primarily at the individual level of alleviating suffering and enhancing people's prospects for development. For the security arena, although there is a growing interest in improving human security, the major focus remains on the state level. In situations of intrastate armed conflict, the principal aim has been to strengthen state authority and capacity by deploying humanitarian assistance as part of effective counterinsurgency campaigns. In more peaceful settings, humanitarian assistance has been used to improve relations between states through positive public diplomacy and disaster diplomacy.

The two arenas also conceive of causality differently. Development practitioners and analysts generally see a positive causality between effective humanitarian assistance and the prospects for development in the longer term. They also entertain the idea that there can be positive causality in the other direction; if development aid has been effective, it should pave the way for effective humanitarian assistance after a disaster or in times of war. The central conclusion about causality drawn in the security arena suggests that the provision of humanitarian assistance facilitates geostrategic goals such as successful counterinsurgency, positive public diplomacy with Muslim countries, and conflict resolution through disaster diplomacy. However, the security arena is increasingly recognizing pronounced dissonance between these assumptions and the outcomes that have been produced through the instrumental use of humanitarian aid.

Security specialists have thus been on a steep learning curve, but they have started to identify and respond to the gap between the expected political benefits of using humanitarian assistance instrumentally in the context of the fight against terrorism and the actual political outcomes delivered to date, which have been disappointing. Indeed, the push-back against the militarization of foreign assistance from humanitarian nongovernmental organizations and sections of the United Nations has shown that there might be strong negative consequences of instrumentalizing humanitarian assistance.

The development arena has also identified a core problem, but it is one of policy implementation rather than causality. Specifically, the development arena is grappling with the persistent gap between humanitarian assistance and development assistance despite efforts to create good transitions from one to the other. This problem is well known, yet overcoming it has proved difficult in the face of bureaucratic, budgetary, and political hurdles.

Part III

GOVERNANCE

Chapter 6

GOVERNANCE
A Security Perspective

Terrence Lyons

Issues of governance have always been an important dimension of the theory and practice of security. Within the security studies literature, governance has usually referred to a distinct set of institutions beyond the system of national governments. In many cases these structures and mechanisms were geared toward the management and regulation of issues by multiple (public and private) authorities that were intended to produce at least a minimal degree of routine and order. Such an understanding was considered useful because as one study of contemporary European security put it, adopting a "governance" perspective could help "ascertain how the 'rules' of security develop" and how the institutions of security have been "coordinated, managed and regulated."[1] Understood in this manner, the concept of governance has been at the heart of a variety of recent debates about international security.

The 1990s discourse of rogue states, for example, linked certain types of insidious foreign policies to the aggressive "nature and motivations" of these regimes and the particular traits of their governance structures. This form of governance—beyond the regime's specific behavior—was regarded as the security threat. According to Washington, rogue states were characterized by elite corruption, the brutalizing of their own populations, a lack of respect for international law, the determination to acquire weapons of mass destruction, the sponsorship of terrorism, the rejection of "basic human values," and a "hatred" of everything for which the United States stands.[2]

A later example is the discourse about "failed" states. Here various governments and organizations pointed to the absence of government and effective governance as providing opportunities for hostile actors to use territory within such states as a base for their nefarious activities. Failed states shifted from being a danger to their own populations, as in Somalia in the early 1990s, to become major threats to international security. In the immediate aftermath of the attacks of 9/11, this line of thinking was reflected most prominently in the conclusion of the US National Security Strategy that "America is now threatened less by conquering states than we are by failing ones."[3] As a direct consequence, restoring effective governance and rebuilding state institutions was often said to be a crucial part of ending armed conflicts and the security threats posed by state failure.[4]

Naturally, the flip side of this argument about "rogue" and "failed" states was that if the wrong type of governance was a problem, then liberal governance could provide a solution by encouraging cooperation, peace, and stability within international affairs. Here, a large and ongoing debate revolved around the merits of the liberal democratic peace thesis—the idea that liberal democratic states do not wage war on one another and that liberal democracy provides the best available antidote to civil war—and the extent to which this form of governance might help humanity finally rid itself of war.[5] One variant of this debate was over the extent to which particular patterns of governance at the regional level could produce durable "security communities" where peace would become predictable and warfare between the members would become politically unthinkable.[6]

This chapter will examine the links between governance and security as they relate to civil wars. Governance is inherently about conflict, with some forms managing conflict through the orderly processes and formal institutions of "normal politics" while other forms fail to manage or escalate conflict. As William Zartman put it, "governance is conflict management."[7] Forms of governance that effectively manage conflict and prevent wide-scale violence depend upon well-understood and widely accepted rules of interaction and a set of norms and institutions that reinforce these rules.[8] In contrast, governance that does not manage conflict effectively will have rules and institutions that are under challenge.

Governance in the form of norms, expectations, and patterns of behavior shape perceptions of what is politically possible. For example, if an opposition movement has seen an authoritarian government regularly respond to peaceful marches with violent crackdowns, it is likely to develop its strategy in response to that expectation. Governance, whether authoritarian as in this example or any other type, creates the political context in which strategies are considered and adopted. Transforming governance—that is, changing the expectations and patterns of behavior—will alter political opportunities and thereby influence the likelihood of war and peace.[9]

Governance may be more or less formally articulated and may or may not be accompanied by organizational arrangements. In peaceful times governance is shaped by formal institutions (parliaments, bureaucracies, courts) and law (constitutions). The sustained violence of civil war is clear evidence of the failure of one system of governance, but the patterns of violence are themselves reflections of another type of governance. Civil wars are not periods of anarchy and political vacuum but are alternative systems of governance based on fear and predation and that reward violence.

Governance does not require a government but rather is always present where humans exist. There are no inhabited zones without governance. States that are in the throes of civil war and even those that have collapsed have processes that shape conflict dynamics, create expectations, and thus reinforce or undermine different military and political strategies. In Somalia, for example, an informal mosaic of business groups, traditional authorities, and civic groups have created "governance without government."[10]

This chapter explores the types of governance that are most prevalent before, during, and after armed conflicts, particularly civil wars. Civil wars, of course, are not the only form of conflict linked to governance. Different systems of governance shape all forms of contentious politics, from armed disputes at a less lethal level, mass political movements, authoritarian repression, and human rights abuses, to one-sided violence such as genocide. Civil wars, however, provide an important set of cases to trace patterns that link governance and security. This chapter examines governance structures related to civil war onset, prolongation, and resolution, and illustrates these using a wide range of empirical examples. Governance that blocks the aspirations of significant constituencies is central to the shift from less violent forms of contentious politics to widespread armed conflict. Civil wars last because alternative systems of governance are established that reward strategies of violence and predation and those militarized organizations that thrive in a context of fear and insecurity. The governance question is also at the core of the process to end the war and create new institutions that can demilitarize politics and sustain long-term peacebuilding.

POLITICAL BLOCKAGES AND CIVIL WAR ONSETS

Governance that fails to provide opportunities for peaceful change is at the source of most sustained armed conflicts. Clapham, for example, states that "insurgencies derive basically from blocked political aspirations."[11] In most cases, governance is organized through the institutions of a government; thus, the struggle is between the incumbent regime and an insurgent competitor. Conflicts and insecurity, therefore, are fundamentally about politics and governance as different sets of processes and institutions make violence a dominant strategy used by actors in the pursuit of their goals. In this sense even brutal wars are rational and the use of violence follows an instrumental logic. People take up arms because they see no other solutions or opportunities to achieve their aspirations. Mobilization is often facilitated by ethnicity, and resources are needed to sustain such conflicts. When governance obstructs peaceful paths to pursue political goals, then some actors are likely to perceive violence as the best means to meet their aspirations. As Cochrane says, "armed conflicts are (in the main) started and perpetuated by rational actors with different sets of political goals and interests. . . . For the most part people go to war because they think that it will work."[12]

Governance shapes political opportunity and the management of political competition. Whether the rules and organization of the government provide openings for political aspirations is critical to conflict management. Weak institutions, Fearon and Laitin argue, allow insurgencies to develop and civil wars to begin.[13] States that can provide public goods and that can effectively project political power both limit grievance and increase the costs for rebellion. State weakness (and proxies such as poverty and mountainous terrain) do not vary significantly from year to year, however, and therefore miss the political processes that are associated with civil war onset. Not all weak states have the same systems of governance and not all have seen widespread adoption of violence as a political strategy.

Strategic choice is shaped heavily by the historical legacies of previous contentious processes. Past patterns of interaction play significant roles in expectations of future interaction. Civil wars do not erupt suddenly in peaceful, well-governed societies but are the result of governance that increasingly failed to manage conflict at an earlier state of dissent. Civil wars are preceded by human rights violations, stolen elections, coup attempts, or violent demonstrations. In other words, civil wars are part of the spectrum of contentious politics and grow out of lower-level conflicts between the state and dissidents that are not managed. Civil war represents an escalation in conflict rather than an abrogation of a preexisting peace.[14] Pre–civil war behavior by both the state and dissident groups shapes later behavior. Systems of governance that violently repress dissent and encourage the use of violence by the opposition create the context for insurgent groups to mobilize and for civil war to begin. State repressiveness and forms of governance that encourage the opposition to adopt violent tactics, rather than state weakness alone, make civil war more likely.

Conflict in Liberia illustrates this point. After generations of rule by a minority regime dominated by Americo-Liberians, a tentative political opening in the late 1970s allowed a student opposition movement to develop and demonstrations to be organized. Governance shifted in 1980 with a military coup, followed by fraudulent elections in 1985, a failed coup attempt, and collective retribution by the Liberian armed forces against the ethnic groups linked to the coup attempt. The invasion by Charles Taylor's National Patriotic Front of Liberia in December 1989 and the subsequent period of extremely violent civil war was an escalation and a shift in tactics that built on earlier decades of contentious politics. In the 1970s political opportunities encouraged a student movement and riots, in the 1980s, military coups and fraudulent elections, and in the 1990s, civil war. Each of these phases of politics in Liberia was characterized by a particular system of governance that shaped the expectations of both the government and opposition and hence the strategies chosen.

Governance, therefore, is fundamental to the onset of civil war. Different forms of governance create different incentives and political opportunities that may or may not promote conflict management. Expectations are informed by an assessment of both formal and informal institutions and norms. In addition, they are often heavily path-dependent as civil wars arise out of prior patterns of repression and violence.

WARTIME GOVERNANCE AND PROTRACTED CIVIL WAR

Large-scale armed conflicts are sustained by the creation of alternative systems of governance that are based on fear and predation, and they end when new processes are put in place that lead key actors to perceive better opportunities to achieve their goals through peaceful means. Other types of violence—communal conflicts, pogroms, urban riots—may not require a high level of institutionalization and may reflect a relatively unorganized, spontaneous outpouring of grievance-driven frustration or anger.[15] Protracted civil wars, however, require institutions with highly developed capacities and structures to mobilize supporters and provision armed forces. This is true of both the government and the insurgency. Civil wars may be initiated by grievance or frustration, but to become protracted and sustained for decades requires institutions that respond to the incentives and opportunities of violence, successfully mobilize and coordinate large numbers of fighters and supporters, and overcome the collective action problem. Grievance may be the "backbone" of rebellion, but "resources become necessary to pay selective benefits to keep the rational rebel soldier supporting a rebellious movement and to offset government efforts to lure the rebel soldier away."[16] Civil wars produce "wartime governance," and this system of governance in turn reinforces strategies of violence. "Warlord politics" is often brutal and devastating for civilians but is conducted within a system of institutions and processes that provide attractive opportunities for those skilled in the strategies of violence.

Scholars studying protracted civil wars have noted that such conflicts create vested interests in continuing the struggle, thereby developing a self-reinforcing logic that perpetuates the violence.[17] As conflict expands and escalates, parties to the conflict become more militarized and polarized, which contributes to further escalation. Parties to the conflict evolve and transform themselves in response to the incentives and opportunities created by the conflict or else they disappear. Civil society organizations and other social formations of peacetime are distorted under these tremendous pressures. Some collapse while others adapt and create new forms of social life that are symbiotic with violence.[18] Institutions of war, such as the militarized organizations of the state and the insurgency, black market and humanitarian relief networks, and chauvinistic, exclusionary identity groups develop and even thrive in the context of wartime governance.

Rather than creating anarchy, war restructures economic, political, and social life in profound and specific ways. Duffield argues that war is "an axis around which social, economic, and political relations are measured and reshaped to establish new forms of agency and legitimacy."[19] War represents, according to Keen, the "creation of an alternative system of profit, power, and protection."[20] Wartime governance encourages creative institutional development as well as institutional destruction.

Protracted civil war requires insurgents who have adopted strategies that allow them to function effectively in the context of violence and fear. Insurgencies often begin with a small, dedicated group of committed fighters. The Eritrean People's Liberation Front started with eleven men; twenty-seven fighters began the National Resistance Movement in Uganda; one hundred, the National Patriotic Front for Liberia; and thirty-five, the Revolutionary United Front of Sierra Leone.[21] These earlier joiners may be motivated by ideology or commitment to social justice, but sustained insurgency requires broader social mobilization. To function for any significant length of time rebels must either elicit or compel cooperation, or at least acquiescence, from at least a portion of the population. Revenues must be collected and soldiers recruited, trained, and equipped. Of course, taxes may be coerced in the form of extortion and recruitment may be through force, depending on whether the state or insurgency is regarded as legitimate or not. Regardless, "to sustain participation," Lichbach suggests, a movement "needs organization to supply leadership, financing, ideology, communication, strategies, and tactics. In short, enduring dissident action requires dissident organization."[22]

Most insurgencies are put down by the state, often with only brief and low-level violence. Many putative rebel movements are little noted and fade quickly into history. There have been many insurgencies, but very few have been successful and either defeated the incumbent regime or even sustained their movement.[23] Few trials and challenges to organizational capacity and structure are as severe and unforgiving as war. As Clapham suggests, "warfare exposes organizations to the supreme test of prolonged conflict, often accompanied by heavy casualties, and the ultimate indicator of their effectiveness is the way in which they develop or decay over time."[24] Poorly institutionalized regimes sometimes fall rapidly to insurgents, as seen in the collapse of Hissèn Habré's regime in Chad in 1990, Mohammad Najibullah's government in Afghanistan in the face of the Taliban in 1996, and the Mobutu regime in Zaire in 1997. Insurgencies and governments that have the capacity to juggle the contradictory pressures and the ordeal of a long period of conflict learn flexibility and resilience and adapt to the imperatives of wartime governance.

Collier and his colleagues have noted that a successful insurgency is simultaneously a political organization, a military organization, and a business organization and that this "triple feature" is essential to understanding protracted armed conflict.[25] Insurgent or "warlord politics" face essentially the same sets of challenges as everyday politics, except in a context where violence and predation are more pronounced. Insurgent groups, like political parties, must recruit and retain supporters. The close organizational kinship between militarized groups (militias, insurgents, military governments) and political parties may be seen in the number of organizations that began as one thing and then evolved into the other. This is not surprising because, as Michels states, the "modern party is a fighting organization in the political sense of the term."[26] Like other social movements, wartime organizations may use selective incentives (such as jobs or land that benefit only those who participate), collective incentives (solidarity on the basis of an ethnic or other identity), or a combination of both to overcome the collective action problem. In this formulation, civil war is a form of contentious politics that requires a particular type of social movement and political organization.[27]

The institutions that thrive during wartime mobilize in and respond to the incentives of a context where identities have been shaped (or distorted) by war and fear. As Tarrow suggests, "widespread contention brings about uncertainty and fear; the breakdown of functional transactions that this produces increases the salience of preexisting ties like ethnicity, religion, or other forms of mutual recognition, trust, and cooperation."[28] In the context of fear and insecurity, identities are also more polarized. Violence may facilitate the process of ethnic outbidding or outflanking. Intraparty dynamics reward those hard-line leaders and factions that push the group's agenda the furthest and frame the conflict in the most categorical, least compromising way. Competition, therefore, is largely within rather than between parties.[29] In some cases, political entrepreneurs promote polarization so that their leadership is not challenged on the basis of nonethnic interests.[30] As Fearon and Laitin conclude, "Newly constructed (or reconstructed) ethnic identities serve to increase support for the elites who provoked the violence while favoring the continuation or escalation of violence."[31] Fear increases the consequences of identity as insecurity, and the breakdown of larger networks leads people to seek protection in narrower family, clan, ethnic, and religious networks. Militarized institutions therefore mobilize constituencies in part by offering collective incentives and appeals to solidarity in a manner similar to political parties and other social movements.

Militarized organizations also use patronage to construct selective incentives to mobilize key constituencies. Selective incentives are specific rewards available only to those who participate in the conflict, such as payment to soldiers or land or other goods distributed to communities that support one or another side. Governments also use resource incentives to hold onto the support of groups in campaigns to "win the hearts and minds" of segments of the population. To access resources for patronage, parties to a conflict often seek control over humanitarian aid flows or black market networks. Military organizations sometimes seek to capture high-value commodities (diamonds and other gems, tropical hardwoods, looted goods) or engage in drug trafficking, kidnapping, and other criminal activities to accumulate wealth and, hence, the patronage for selective incentives. In other cases, insurgents and governments rely upon support from neighbors, external powers, and diaspora groups with an interest in the outcome of the struggle in order to gain access to resources that then may be used as selective incentives to reward loyal supporters and sustain their organization.[32] Resources provide the means by which certain types of organizations thrive during wartime.

The National Patriotic Front for Liberia, for example, recruited supporters in part through patronage gained through commercial alliances and international trade in diamonds, gold, rubber, and timber. Military groups in Bosnia-Herzegovina similarly constructed complex economic networks and sustained themselves during the war in part through smuggling, protection rackets, and direct seizures of property. In Angola, Jonas Savimbi's National Union for the Total Independence of Angola (UNITA) insurgency and the ruling Movimento Popular de Libertação de Angola (MPLA) shifted from Cold War patronage in the 1980s to the exploitation of natural resources to sustain the war in the 1990s. The Khmer Rouge in Cambodia controlled the gems and hardwood markets while the incumbent government of the Communist Party of Cambodia channeled official aid flows to benefit its constituents. Similarly in Mozambique, the incumbent Frelimo government benefited from high levels of external aid during the war. In Tajikistan, multiple parties engaged in drug trafficking and gunrunning, thereby gaining access to considerable resources. In El Salvador, the Farabundo Marti National Liberation Front (FMLN) delivered highly valued services to the peasants by organizing cooperatives and other development projects. Most insurgencies use a combination of collective and selective incentives.

While the political party and social movement literature focuses on mobilization through collective incentives such as appeals to solidarity and selective incentives such as patronage, actors in a civil war also mobilize by promising security or threatening violence. Fear and violence are fundamental to wartime governance and play a particularly important—even critical—role with regard to mobilization in times of conflict. Militarized institutions differ from other institutions such as political parties in large part because they are organized in response to the incentives and opportunities presented by violence and wartime governance. Organizations that can mobilize effectively in a context characterized by fear and pervasive insecurity will become powerful during war.

There are two major variations of mobilization on the basis of fear—either credibly promise to protect a given constituency from a feared rival or threaten with violence if support is not forthcoming. Militia leaders may threaten a given population and thereby win at least acquiescence to their power as vulnerable groups try to appease the powerful leader by offering their support. In other cases, militarized groups offer to protect frightened groups from dreaded attacks by others. Call and Stanley argue that "public insecurity presents a political opportunity for any group that has sufficient organization and weaponry to present itself as a protector of a given community."[33] Those subject to pervasive insecurity often perceive such leaders, characterized as brutal warlords or war criminals by outside observers, as protectors and heroes.

Violence, rather than being an eruption of frustration and rage, may be understood in instrumental terms, as a calculated strategy to advance toward a goal. "Violence should be viewed as an instrumental act, aimed at furthering the purposes of the group that uses it when they have some reason to think it will help their cause," according to Gamson.[34] State-sanctioned violence in the form of death squads, for example, can be an instrumental strategy by a weak state to reduce active support for the opposition. Generating fear is often a cost-effective way to mobilize supporters.[35]

The use of violence to threaten and coerce support was a major (although not the only) means used by the Mozambican National Resistance (RENAMO) to establish and retain its base of support in the Mozambican countryside. RENAMO's violence against civilians was often horrific and terrifying—in fact, terror was the point of the violence and a critical component of RENAMO's strategy to control significant territory. In Angola, the National Union for the Total Independence of Angola (UNITA) had significant support among the southern Ovimbundu people but also used forced conscription and violence to force villagers to retreat with the soldiers into the bush in the late 1970s. In Bosnia-Herzegovina, militants used fear and violence to mobilize communities to engage collectively in ethnic cleansing. Many in the first wave of recruits to the National Patriotic Front for Liberia were Gios and Manos, groups targeted by Samuel Doe's military for reprisals, which then fled to areas controlled by the insurgent force for protection.

In some cases, support for a militarized organization is directly coerced. The inability of Zimbabwe's national liberation movements to offer selective, "utilitarian" appeals such as land compelled the organizations to rely on coercion along with nationalist and cultural appeals.[36] Conversely, Weinstein argues that the availability of selective incentives will reduce the insurgent need to build popular appeals through collective incentives.[37] The Revolutionary United Front in Sierra Leone and the Lord's Resistance Army in northern Uganda have used terror and the forced recruitment of child soldiers extensively. In any event, one critical set of decisions insurgents must make during the period of armed conflict is whether to elicit compliance through coercion or voluntary assent or inevitably a mixed strategy with elements of both.[38]

Conflicts have their origins in blocked political aspirations and are sustained through the creation of insurgent institutions and wartime systems of governance. The challenge of making peace and building security, therefore, is a challenge of transforming wartime governance based on violence, fear, and predation into peacetime governance based on security and nonviolent political competition. New systems of governance and the opportunities and incentives they foster may assist militias to become political parties.

GOVERNANCE AND THE POLITICS OF PEACEBUILDING

While sustaining civil war requires specific systems of governance that enable and reinforce violent actors and strategies, processes of peacebuilding are rooted in creating and sustaining alternative systems of governance that support and reward nonviolent actors and political behavior. One of the crucial challenges of civil war termination is the transformation of those militias, insurgencies, and militarized governments into institutions such as political parties and civil society that can sustain peace. Furthermore, in order for the peace to last, forms of governance that institutionalize conflict management are required. In the end, peace and security break down when structures of governance limit parties' ability to pursue their goals without resorting to violence. Therefore, the restoration of security requires a political system that can transform the institutions of war and shift contention from violence to "normal politics."

To have sustainable conflict management, political practices and institutions must develop robust yet flexible ways to manage conflicts constructively. One of the key ways to build security is to construct governance that allows for competition and contention within a secure framework. Some of the literature on transitions suggests that the best way to promote the shift from war to peace is to negotiate powersharing arrangements or political "pacts" to construct the broadest possible coalition in government.[39] Political pacts are a set of negotiated compromises among competing elites prior to elections that distribute power and thereby reduce uncertainty.[40] A number of transitions in Latin America, the Round Table talks in Poland, and the Convention for a Democratic South Africa process were organized around implicit or explicit agreements designed to provide powerful actors with sufficient guarantees so that they would accept the change.

Pacts, however, ultimately rely upon other mechanisms for enforcement and do not by themselves end uncertainty or resolve the difficulty in making credible commitments.[41] Pacts are more likely among elites with relatively clear and loyal constituencies, such as traditional political parties, labor unions, or other institutions in a corporatist setting. In the aftermath of a protracted civil war, such political and social organizations generally are absent, and the ability of military leaders to deliver the compliance of even their own fighters is often under question. In addition, the polarization and extreme distrust arising from the conflict will make such pacts more difficult if not impossible to negotiate. Finally, the ability to assess the political power of a military faction is difficult and the identity of the critical constituencies to include in a pact is unclear immediately following a conflict. Even if the military balance among factions is relatively clear (as indicated by a stalemate on the battlefield), the relative political power of these factions and the extent to which they are capable of representing significant civilian constituencies in peacetime may not be known.

If the focus is on rule by consensus and powersharing pacts, then governance becomes frozen in the polarized conditions of conflict. Shifting from conflict to peace entails moving from governance based on fear (where the main actors are military) to governance based on security (where the main actors should be civilian, if fear is diminished). A system of governance that takes a snapshot of the political topography and (mal)distribution of power at the moment of cease-fire and seeks to make this arrangement permanent will not work in the long run. Security depends upon vibrant and supple political processes rather than on security guarantees from external parties or power-sharing pacts. When seeking to build systems of governance that promote security, the goal should be to create structures that can facilitate change, allow dissent to be voiced, and emphasize flexibility. If security is sustained, then the population is likely to shift its support from militarized to civilian political organizations. Some organizations will make this transition along with their constituencies while others will fail and be replaced by new ones. The key to security is to manage conflicts in ways that allow for change, for new issues and actors to arise, without undermining the fundamental tenets of governance.

What often matters more than the formal rules of political competition or promises of power sharing is the degree to which governance attuned to the incentives and opportunities of war and violence is transformed into governance that can reinforce peacetime institutions. Much of the attention in the literature focuses on the transition of insurgent groups, but the transformation of military governments and ruling parties is often just as important.[42] Civilian-oriented political parties; open economies and rule of law; civil society; and diverse, multifarious identities based on security and trust are created by and support sustainable peace and democratization.

The organizations that enter into a peace process respond to incentives and rationally assess options with regard to which best promise to advance their interests. As Shugart has argued, "decisions by regime and rebel leaders alike to seek a democratic 'exit' from a conflict are based upon rational calculations of the possibilities and limitations inherent in playing the competitive electoral game versus continuing the armed conflict."[43] Strategies and behavior shift as calculations of the costs of war rise and the potential benefits of peace increase. Bermeo makes the point with regard to leaders, but the same challenges face organizations qua organizations: "Elites in emerging, post-war democracies face a double challenge. On the one hand, they must raise the costs of violent competition. On the other hand, they must lower the costs of electoral competition. The probability of stable democracy is a function of both these processes and the many variables that drive them."[44] Wartime governance must be demilitarized to provide opportunities sufficiently attractive to encourage militarized organizations to transform into political parties.

This transformation and the shift from military to political forms of struggle tend to generate intense intraparty debate and often result in schisms and breakaway factions.[45] It is common (perhaps inevitable) that one set of leaders will be ready to make the shift while others will not. Not every member of the leadership will assess opportunities in the same way, and every move toward peace strengthens some while weakening others. The fundamental shift from pursuing military strategies to pursuing electoral strategies may result from a divided leadership finally reaching a tipping point where a thin majority alters its assessments of the efficacy of the two options. Even if a majority accepts the need for a new direction, spoilers who are threatened by the transition often attempt to derail the process.[46]

These transitions require the demilitarization of politics, a process that entails building institutions capable of supporting electoral competition while weakening those best suited to engage in armed conflict.[47] Among the key institutions are effective, credible interim regimes (particularly electoral authorities), transformed militarized organizations and strong political parties, and joint decision-making bodies to manage the demobilization and security sector reform process. These processes and institutions increase and make more credible the rewards for participating in and accepting outcomes of electoral competition while simultaneously reducing the perceived rewards for engaging in violence. An electoral commission that is acceptable by all main parties as legitimate will reduce fears that the other party will cheat. The processes by which security sector reform is conducted also contribute to the demilitarization of politics. If done well, these processes of security sector reform decrease both the incentives and capacity to return to war. These two aspects are interlinked; progress on one encourages the demilitarization process in the other. For example, building effective political parties increases the prospects for demobilization as groups perceive that they can protect their interests through a political rather than a military means and therefore are ready to lay down their arms. Processes to demilitarize politics simultaneously increase both the incentives and the opportunities to play by the rules of nonviolent electoral competition, and decrease the incentives and opportunities to seek power by engaging in violence.

The manner by which interim institutions and new norms are established to manage the peace implementation period will create precedents, expectations, and patterns of behavior that will shape how politics after the election function. In some cases, institutions built around collaborative decision making, transparency, and confidence building managed the implementation process.[48] In Mozambique, for example, the two formerly warring sides engaged in joint decision-making processes on issues such as the electoral system and worked together to monitor the cease-fire and demobilization. Similar institutions operated in El Salvador and to a degree in Cambodia. In Angola, in contrast, the two parties rarely met during the interim and the transition was marked by suspicion and bad faith during the failed demobilization process. The interim administration during the implementation phase in Liberia similarly was stalemated due to the division of power among the warring factions. The manner by which interim institutions operate will influence whether postconflict elections move a war-torn state toward peace and democratization.

Demobilization and reform of the security sector similarly are at the heart of civil war settlements. Successful demobilization has a number of positive effects on postconflict peacebuilding, including the reallocation of public expenditures from the military to civilian use (the "peace dividend"), reducing the threat of violence and increasing personal security, and providing individual and collective incentives that reinforce the transition from war to peace. Such processes also shape the political process of shifting power and authority away from armed groups and violence and toward civil institutions and electoral politics. As Berdal argues, there is "interplay, a subtle interaction, between the dynamics of a peace process and the manner in which the disarmament, demobilization and reintegration provisions associated with that process are organized, funded and implemented."[49] As demobilization proceeds apace and as the dividends of peace deepen, actors may become trapped in a politics of moderation whereby the attractiveness of maintaining the peace rises, and the rewards for returning to war shrink, resulting in a higher probability of successful peace implementation. Financial support for well-designed demobilization programs is a valuable tactic of soft intervention. Demobilization encourages the demilitarization of politics both by decreasing the means and the likelihood of a return to warfare and by increasing confidence in—and, hence, the incentives to participate in—a political process.

The militarized organizations that sign peace agreements will almost inevitably remain the most powerful organizations in the immediate aftermath of civil war. In a postconflict election where voters are still worried about their security, a political party of civil society leaders will have difficulty making credible promises to provide protection. If the peace agreement holds, however, more diverse interests will likely rise in salience, and the overwhelming polarization of the conflict will recede. If security is maintained, however, over time the general population will have less and less of a need to rally behind militant leaders whose main attraction is their promise to protect. In a secure context, individuals will gradually join and create new, more diverse social networks organized around the agendas of peacetime rather than the polarization and security agendas of wartime. This means that the parties that dominated during the fighting will have to transform themselves in order to be relevant and retain power during peacetime.

Institutions endure and thrive in part by their capacity to adjust to changing contexts.[50] A change from violence to security will compel a transformation if the organization is to remain vital. This adaptation to a changing environment will be particularly challenging when the context moves from one set of incentives and opportunities, such as war, to another, such as electoral competition. The means by which organizations manage this challenge will be critical to processes to demilitarize politics and sustain security.

CONCLUSION

Conflict onset, prolongation, and resolution are fundamentally political processes in which parties engaged in contentious politics shift from nonviolent to violent and then back to nonviolent strategies in pursuit of their goals. There are distinct systems of governance associated with each of these phases of conflict. Governance that blocks the aspirations of significant constituencies is central to the escalation of conflict and the onset of civil war. Civil wars become protracted because alternative systems of governance are established that reward strategies of violence and predation as well as those militarized organizations that thrive in a context of fear and insecurity. The governance question is also at the core of the process of war termination and the creation of new institutions that can demilitarize politics and sustain long-term peacebuilding.

Notes

1. Mark Webber, Stuart Croft, Jolyon Howorth, Terry Terriff, and Elke Krahmann, "The Governance of European Security," *Review of International Studies* 30, no. 1 (2004), 3–26, at 25–26.
2. *The National Security Strategy of the United States of America* (Washington, DC: The White House, September 2002), 13–14.
3. Ibid., 1.
4. See, for example, Roland Paris and Timothy Sisk, eds., *The Dilemmas of Statebuilding* (Abingdon: Routledge, 2008).
5. See, for example, Michael E. Brown, Sean M. Lynn-Jones, and Steven E. Miller, eds., *Debating the Democratic Peace* (Harvard, MA: MIT Press, 1996).
6. See, for example, Karl Deutsch, Sidney A. Burrell, and Robert A. Kann, *Political Community and the North Atlantic Area: International Organization in the Light of Historical Experience* (Princeton, NJ: Princeton University Press, 1957); and Emmanuel Adler and Michael N. Barnett, eds., *Security Communities* (Cambridge: Cambridge University Press, 1998).
7. I. William Zartman, ed., *Governance as Conflict Management: Politics and Violence in West Africa* (Washington, DC: Brookings Institution Press, 1997), 1.
8. Donald Rothchild, "Management of Conflict in West Africa" in *Governance as Conflict Management: Politics and Violence in West Africa*, ed. I. William Zartman (Washington, DC: Brookings Institution Press, 1997), 197–98.
9. In this sense, "governance" as used here is similar to "regimes" as used in the international relations literature: it is recognized patterns of behavior or practice around which expectations converge. See Oran R. Young, "Regional Dynamics: The Rise and Fall of International Regimes"; and Stephen D. Krasner, "Structural Causes and Regime Consequences: Regimes as Intervening Variables," both in *International Organization* 36, no. 2 (1982).
10. Ken Menkhaus, "Governance without Government in Somalia: Spoilers, State Building, and the Politics of Coping," *International Security*, 31, no. 3 (2006–7): 74–106.
11. Christopher Clapham, "Introduction: Analysing African Insurgencies," in *African Guerrillas*, ed. Christopher Clapham (Oxford: James Currey, 1998), 5.
12. Feargal Cochrane, *Ending Wars* (Oxford: Polity, 2008), x.
13. James D. Fearon and David D. Laitin, "Ethnicity, Insurgency, and Civil War," *American Political Science Review*, 97, no. 1 (2003): 75–90. For a different look at the data, see Nicholas Sambanis, "What Is Civil War? Conceptual and Empirical Complexities of an Operational Definition," *Journal of Conflict Resolution* 48, no. 6 (2004): 814–58.
14. Lichbach, Davenport, and Armstrong argue that "civil wars are inherent in nature, influenced by lower-level dynamics of state repression and political dissent." Mark Lich-

bach, Christian Davenport, and David Armstrong, "Contingency, Inherency and the Onset of Civil War," (2004) unpublished paper available at www.yale.edu/macmillan/ocvprogram /Davenport.pdf. See also Patrick M. Regan and Daniel Norton, "Greed, Grievance, and Mobilization in Civil Wars," *Journal of Conflict Resolution* 49, no. 3 (2005): 319–36.

15. Mark Irving Lichbach, *The Rebel's Dilemma* (Ann Arbor: University of Michigan Press, 1998); 218–20; and Donald L. Horowitz, *The Deadly Ethnic Riot* (Berkeley: University of California Press, 2001).

16. Regan and Norton, "Greed, Grievance, and Mobilization," 322.

17. Edward E. Azar, "The Analysis and Management of Protracted Conflicts," in *The Psychodynamics of International Relationships*, ed. Vamik D. Volkan, Joseph Montville and Demetrios A. Julius (Lexington, MA: Lexington Books, 1991); and Louis Kriesberg, "Transforming Conflicts in the Middle East and Central Europe," in *Intractable Conflicts and Their Transformation*, ed. Louis Kriesberg, Terrell A. Northrup, and Stuart J. Thorson (Syracuse, NY: Syracuse University Press, 1989).

18. Trutz von Trotha, "Forms of Martial Power," in *Dynamics of Collective Violence*, ed. Georg Elwert, Stephan Feuchtwant and Dieter Neubert (Berlin: Duncker and Humblot, 1999), 39.

19. Mark Duffield, *Global Governance and the New Wars* (London: Zed Books, 2001), 136. See also Mary Kaldor, *New and Old Wars* (Oxford: Polity, 1999).

20. David Keen, "Incentives and Disincentives for Violence" in *Greed and Grievance: Economic Agendas in Civil Wars*, ed. Mats Berdal and David M. Malone (Boulder, CO: Lynne Rienner, 2000), 19.

21. Jeffrey Herbst, "African Militaries and Rebellion: The Political Economy of Threat and Combat Effectiveness," *Journal of Peace Research* 41, no. 3 (2004): 357–69.

22. Lichbach, *Rebel's Dilemma*, 261.

23. Morten Bøås and Kevin C. Dunn, "African Guerrilla Politics: Raging against the Machine?" in *African Guerrillas*, ed. Morten Bøås and Kevin C. Dunn (Boulder, CO: Lynne Rienner, 2007), 9–37.

24. Clapham, "Introduction," 9.

25. Paul Collier, V. L. Elliott, Havard Hegre, Anke Hoeffler, Marta Reynal-Querol, and Nicholas Sambinas, *Breaking the Conflict Trap: Civil War and Development Policy* (Oxford University Press and the World Bank, 2003), 56.

26. Robert Michels, *Political Parties: A Sociological Study of the Oligarchical Tendencies of Modern Democracy* (New York: Free Press, 1962).

27. Jeremy M. Weinstein, *Inside Rebellion: The Politics of Insurgent Violence* (Cambridge: Cambridge University Press, 2007); and Elisabeth Jean Wood, *Insurgent Collective Action and Civil War in El Salvador* (Cambridge: Cambridge University Press, 2003).

28. Sidney Tarrow, *Power in Movement: Social Movements and Contentious Politics*, 2nd ed. (Cambridge: Cambridge University Press, 1998), 145.

29. Donald Horowitz, *Ethnic Groups in Conflict* (Berkeley: University of California Press, 1985); and Stephen M. Saideman, "Is Pandora's Box Half Empty or Half Full? The Limited Virulence of Secessionism and the Domestic Sources of Disintegration," in *The International Spread of Ethnic Conflict*, ed. David A. Lake and Donald Rothchild (Princeton, NJ: Princeton University Press, 1998).

30. V. P. Gagnon Jr., "Ethnic Nationalism and International Conflict: The Case of Serbia," *International Security* 19, no. 3 (1994–95), 136–37.

31. James D. Fearon and David D. Laitin, "Violence and the Social Construction of Ethnic Identity," *International Organization* 54, no. 4 (2000), 846.

32. The recent surge of literature on this topic was sparked by Paul Collier and Anke Hoeffler, "Greed and Grievances in Civil War," World Bank Policy Research Working Paper 2355 (Washington, DC: World Bank, 2000). For some important treatments, see Mats Berdal and David M. Malone, eds., *Greed and Grievance: Economic Agendas in Civil Wars* (Boulder, CO:

Lynne Rienner, 2000). On diasporas and conflict, see Terrence Lyons, "Conflict-Generated Diasporas and Transnational Politics in Ethiopia," *Conflict, Security, and Development* 7, no. 4 (2007): 529–49.

33. Charles T. Call and William Stanley, "Civilian Security" in *Ending Civil Wars*, ed. Stephen John Stedman, Donald Rothchild, and Elizabeth M. Cousens (Boulder, CO: Lynne Rienner, 2002), 306–7.

34. William A. Gamson, *The Strategy of Social Protest* (Homewood, IL: Dorsey Press, 1975), 81.

35. T. David Mason and Dale A. Krane, "The Political Economy of Death Squads: Toward a Theory of the Impact of State-Sanctioned Terror," *International Studies Quarterly* 33, no. 2 (1989): 175–98; and Georg Elwert, "Markets of Violence," in *Dynamics of Collective Violence*, ed. Georg Elwert, Stephan Feuchtwant, and Dieter Neubert (Berlin: Duncker and Humblot, 1999), 90.

36. Norma Krieger, *Zimbabwe's Guerrilla War: Peasant Voices* (Cambridge: Cambridge University Press, 1992), 101–9, 152–57.

37. Weinstein, *Inside Rebellion*; and Wood, *Insurgent Collective Action*.

38. Nelson Kasfir, "Guerrilla and Civilian Participation: The National Resistance Army in Uganda, 1981–86," *Journal of Modern African Studies* 43, no. 2 (2005): 271–96.

39. Timothy D. Sisk, *Power Sharing and International Mediation in Ethnic Conflict* (Washington, DC: US Institute of Peace Press, 1996).

40. Terry Lynn Karl, "Dilemmas of Democratization in Latin America," *Comparative Politics* 23, no. 1 (1990): 1-21; Guillermo O'Donnell and Philippe Schmitter, *Transitions from Authoritarian Rule* (Baltimore: Johns Hopkins University Press, 1986), 37–47; and Frances Hagopian, "Democracy by Undemocratic Means? Elites, Political Pacts, and Regime Transition in Brazil," *Comparative Political Studies* 23, no. 2 (1990): 147–70.

41. David A. Lake and Donald Rothchild, "Containing Fear: The Origins and Management of Ethnic Conflict," *International Security* 21, no. 2 (1996): 41–75.

42. Camilla Orjuela, "Domesticating Tigers: The LTTE and Peacemaking in Sri Lanka," in *Conflict Transformation and Peacebuilding*, ed. Bruce Winfield Dayton and Louis Kriesberg (London: Routledge, 2009); and Tom Lodge, "Revolution Deferred: From Armed Struggle to Liberal Democracy; The African National Congress in South Africa," in *Conflict Transformation and Peacebuilding*, ed. Bruce Winfield Dayton and Louis Kriesberg (London: Routledge, 2009).

43. Matthew Soberg Shugart, "Guerrillas and Elections: An Institutionalist Perspective on the Costs of Conflict and Cooperation," *International Studies Quarterly* 36, no. 2 (1992): 121.

44. Nancy Bermeo, "What the Democratization Literature Says—or Doesn't Say—About Postwar Democratization," *Global Governance* 9, no. 2 (2003): 159–77.

45. Carrie Manning, *The Making of Democrats* (Basingstoke: Palgrave Macmillan, 2008).

46. Stephen John Stedman, "Spoiler Problems in Peace Processes," *International Security* 22, no. 2 (1997): 5–53.

47. This section draws on Terrence Lyons, *Demilitarizing Politics: Elections on the Uncertain Road to Peace* (Boulder, CO: Lynne Rienner, 2005).

48. Herbert C. Kelman, "Transforming the Relationship between Former Enemies," in *After the Peace*, ed. Robert L. Rothstein (Boulder, CO: Lynne Rienner, 1999), 203.

49. Mats R. Berdal, "Disarmament and Demobilisation after Civil Wars," IISS Adelphi Paper 303 (London: IISS, 1996), 73.

50. Tarrow, *Power in Movement*, 7.

Chapter 7

GOVERNANCE
A Development Perspective

Alasdair Bowie

Governance and development have been increasingly linked in development-assistance policymaking. This chapter focuses on how this causal connection is conceptualized and manifested by those in the development field, and on the implications of such causality for development policymaking and policy implementation. For the purposes of this chapter, "governance" refers to characteristics of the processes by which authoritative decision making regarding the allocation of public resources occurs. Such characteristics include transparency, participation, responsiveness, and accountability. "Development," as used here, refers to economic development and the improvement of material conditions, especially for the poor. This definition allows us to discern more easily the effects of development on governance, and vice versa. More comprehensive definitions of development are certainly available. For example, development may be seen to include not simply material gains but also what Amartya Sen refers to as "freedom." Development, Sen argues, includes social and political characteristics, such as process, participation, and voice, as well as processes that are responsive to the needs of individuals.[1] If freedom is a condition experienced by individuals who can attain redemption by seeing and participating in decision-making processes that are perceived to be responsive to individuals' needs, then development encompasses at least part of what we consider to be governance.

This problem of more expansive definitions of development that make it more difficult to attribute causality between governance and development will be discussed in more detail later. However, it must be recognized that more expansive definitions of both development and governance are widely used in the development field. This chapter will discuss both the definitions and their implications.

HOW GOVERNANCE IS DEFINED

"Governance" has been used in many ways, which has stimulated considerable disagreement. Of late, it has suffered from overuse among international development professionals. Some have argued that good governance has developed into nothing more than a buzzword.[2] Its "flavor of the month" currency—"governance" sounds more up-to-the-minute than does boring old "government," doesn't it?—and the wide range of referents attributed to it have given rise to considerable ambiguity.

In common usage today, governance is often indistinguishable from government or governing, or is linked in some unspecified hierarchy with these similar terms (e.g., governing as something governments do? government as one element of the governance process?). Less ambiguous—though still very general—definitions of governance include "the process through which citizens collectively solve their problems and meet society's needs, using 'government' as the instrument" and "the mechanisms and processes for citizens and groups to articulate their interests, mediate their differences and exercise their legal rights and obligations."[3] Note that in both cases the focus is on citizens and nonstate groups while the autonomous roles and interests of government institutions themselves or of the officials who occupy positions within them are overlooked. These institutions and officials are not neutral facilitating mechanisms. Rather, they seek to privilege particular dimensions of governance, for example, rule of law, political stability, and absence of violence. In patronage systems they may show favoritism toward certain ethnic or other groups. An early World Bank definition—"the manner in which power is exercised in the management of a country's economic and social resources for development"—implicitly points to the importance of managers and those who exercise power. When exploring how governance has been defined, we need to be aware of or take into account the agendas of these actors.[4]

Even among those who use a reliable, consistent, and more or less specific definition of governance and who draw a clear distinction between governance and its close synonyms, there are legitimate disagreements about what does—and does not—constitute governance. At their core, such differences stem from disagreements about the appropriate ultimate objective that improving governance serves and about how improving governance can best achieve this objective.

It is helpful at this point to consider how the principal objectives and means of governance improvement have changed in relation to development. From the late 1940s through the late 1980s, official development assistance (ODA) of the United States and of the Bretton Woods institutions focused on building government institutions (i.e., improved governance for state-building). The ODA's public administration focused on creating well-functioning civil services staffed by well-trained civil servants who embraced Weberian norms of professionalism and adhered to the rule of law.[5] Such civil services and executives would, it was hypothesized, pursue enlightened policies that would in turn result in more rapid development while discouraging a turn to socialist ideologies and ideologically motivated insurgencies of the disadvantaged and disaffected.

When state-building goals proved elusive—as demonstrated by the persistence of patron–client or patrimonial regimes in the 1970s—development assistance was reoriented toward strengthening checks and sanctions on constitutionally mandated authority structures.[6] In addition to improved public sector management, the goals included more accountability, greater transparency (more clarity as to what government is doing), and improvement of the legal system to provide a framework of rules for both public and private sectors.[7] Together these dimensions, once in place, sought both checks and sanctions on behaviors of policymakers that were prejudicial to development and, conversely, the encouragement of behaviors expected to result in more rapid development.

Multilateral development efforts for the past two decades by institutions such as the World Bank, the Organisation for Economic Co-operation and Development (OECD), the UN Development Programme (UNDP), and regional groupings such as the European Union (EU) have conceptualized improvement of governance as one component of their broader development-assistance strategies. "Good" governance first emerged explicitly as an issue in development policymaking in the late 1980s and the early 1990s.[8] While drawing attention to the importance of good governance, the institutions that were involved manifested different conclusions about the role of good governance, the ways to promote it, and to what developmental ends it should be promoted.

In a comprehensive 1989 report seeking the sources of weak economic performance in sub-Saharan Africa, the World Bank for the first time drew attention to a "governance crisis" that had to be overcome by focusing on "capacity building . . . through institutional reforms at every level of government and by measures to foster private sector and nongovernmental organizations."[9] Giving concrete attention to "good" governance, a term not yet used in the African report, a subsequent 1992 World Bank report defined it as "sound development management."[10] Improving governance, according to this report, required a focus on building capacity in the public sector, strengthening the accountability of public sector decision makers, improving the legal environment, and enhancing transparency.[11] However, acknowledging political accountability to be outside its mandate, the World Bank indicated that its focus would be in the area of the legal framework for development, concentrating on the procedural and institutional aspects that reflected the World Bank's "reputation for technical excellence and objectivity."[12] Nonetheless, the 1992 report mentioned that World Bank programs encouraged local "ownership" of development programs, decentralization, and participatory approaches in general, all of which clearly have the potential to redistribute political power.[13] While it saw programs explicitly designed to promote good governance as constrained by its mandate not to engage in politics, the World Bank saw some of its other programs—those involving decentralization or participatory budgeting processes, for example—as nevertheless being indirectly relevant to the goal of improving governance for development.

The OECD, often characterized as the "club" of rich countries, published its first report on governance in 1995.[14] Although the report defined governance "in accordance with a World Bank definition" as "the use of political authority and exercise of control in a society in relation to the management of its resources for social and economic development," it differed from the World Bank's approach to promoting good governance in that it explicitly recognized the links between good governance and political principles, such as those of participatory development, human rights, and democratization.[15] Thus, the OECD's approach, unhampered by mandates and unencumbered by a "reputation for technical excellence," has been to acknowledge the good governance agenda as including advancement of elements that are basic values in their own right, such as human rights and the principles of participation.[16] In practice, the promotion of good governance, from the OECD perspective, ought not be limited to the procedural and institutional aspects upon which the World Bank came to focus.

Several years later, in the late 1990s, the UNDP proposed a definition for governance that even more explicitly referred to the political aspects. It saw governance as "the exercise of economic, political and administrative authority to manage a country's affairs at all levels. It comprises the mechanisms, processes and institutions through which citizens and groups articulate their interests, exercise their legal rights, meet their obligations and mediate their differences."[17]

For the UNDP, the ultimate goal of development initiatives was sustainable human development, for which UNDP efforts would focus specifically on eliminating poverty; creating jobs and sustaining livelihoods; protecting and regenerating the environment; and promoting the advancement of women. Developing capacities for good governance underpinned the achievement of each of these dimensions of sustainable human development.[18] The UNDP conceived of good governance itself as an umbrella concept, encompassing not just the state but also interactions between the state, the private sector, and civil society organizations. In this sense the UNDP's approach to promotion of good governance was moving even further away than had the OECD's from the World Bank's emphasis on the procedural and institutional aspects of the state. This was made explicit in the UNDP administrator's foreword to the 2002 World Development Report when he used the term "democratic governance" to draw even more attention to the political dimension of good governance and to eclipse what he saw as an emphasis in debates on governance that had been placed "almost exclusively on economic processes and administrative efficiency."[19]

The EU was guilty in this regard. In fact, until the late 1980s, EU development cooperation dealt mainly with economic issues, particularly the granting of preferential trade agreements and financial aid to former colonies of member states.[20] In a series of resolutions in 1991, the EU responded to the earlier-mentioned international debates about governance by linking governance to development. Principles of good governance, such as democracy, human rights, the rule of law, transparent and accountable governance, and the fight against corruption, were cited by these resolutions as preconditions for development.[21]

While the EU approach to governance can be seen to have broadened through a series of international agreements and communications over the past two decades (such as the revised 1995 version of the Lome IV Convention; the 2000 Cotonou Agreement, which replaced the Lome Convention; and major European Commission communications on good governance and development in 2003 and 2006), the EU's notion of governance still emphasizes, to a much greater degree than is the case for the UNDP notion, the role of the state: "Governance concerns the state's ability to serve the citizen."[22] Also, whereas the OECD and the UNDP have conceived of good governance as including the advancement of elements that are basic values in their own right, such as human rights and the principles of participation and (in the case of the UNDP) democracy, the EU still conceptually differentiates governance from other issues such as human rights and democracy. Moreover, it sees improving governance as instrumental, a precondition for the ultimate goal of "proper delivery of public services and sustained economic growth."[23]

During the 2000s, certain preferred public policy outcomes under the "governance" rubric were privileged. This might be termed the improved-governance-for-economic-outcomes approach. Such outcomes included more secure property rights, less fettered markets, more favorable investment and tax rules for foreign multinationals, and stability, which might actually amount to favoring the powerful over the weak.[24] "Good" governance was associated with strengthening political institutions that secure and enforce individual and corporate property rights, establish regulatory regimes that prioritize and protect market competition, and embrace macroeconomic policies favoring stability, predictability, and the interests of existing market-dominating players over equity and the redistribution of economic power to the disadvantaged.[25]

The 2000s also saw the process aspects of governance come to the fore. Development assistance for improved governance targeted the participation in authoritative decision making of all stakeholders, not just officials (government), and not just organized interests (civil society), and had a broader conception of the kinds of policy decisions involved (governance characteristics were not limited to those related to economic decision making). This might be termed the improved-governance-for-political-inclusion approach.

To summarize, the earliest paradigms linking governance (although not by that name) and development focused on state-building as a way to strengthen state capacity to more effectively manage development. Improving governance was one way to make states stronger, and stronger states were more likely to achieve higher levels of development. When this approach did not yield the expected superior development outcomes, the paradigm expanded to encompass checks and sanctions on state policymakers. Improving governance now involved capacity-building and, simultaneously, constraints on rapacious government. The obvious tensions were manifest within country development-assistance programs broadly defined (i.e., including security assistance programs), pitting those who pursued a security agenda, those who sought to emphasize state capacity-building, against those who pursued a democratization, human rights, and rule of law agenda, those who sought to emphasize programs that balanced state power against societal interests, and those who asked: "improve capacity to what end?"[26] All too frequently in these struggles, the security agenda and pursuit of development goals easily measured in terms of macroeconomic indicators (e.g., per capita gross domestic product [GDP] growth rates) kept governance improvement centrally on the path of state capacity-building while relegating democracy assistance (particularly elections) and programs strengthening human rights protections and, more generally, rule of law (i.e., programs that constrained state actors) to second-tier concerns. In the international realm, the Paris Declaration of 2005 (on harmonization, alignment, and management of aid, signed by more than one hundred ministers) continued this endorsement of strengthening of state capacity at the center of donor development objectives.[27] However, the Declaration appears to have had little appreciable impact on country development-assistance programs.

By the early 1990s, when governance (and, later, good governance) came into common usage in development circles, the effective fostering of the private sector and nongovernmental organizations was explicitly part of the discussion of how governance could further development. But state actors were still in the driver's seat, and improving governance was seen as an instrumental means by which to achieve the ultimate goal of improving material conditions.

During the next decade, groups and organizations of developed countries and multilateral development-assistance organizations developed overlapping but far-from-identical conceptions of governance and its relationship to development. While World Bank governance programs—mindful of the Bank's mandate not to involve itself in the politics of member countries—continued to emphasize the procedural and institutional aspects of state management of development, numerous Bank programs promoted aspects of local "ownership" of development initiatives, decentralization, and participatory approaches in general, all of which clearly had political implications. The OECD embraced a good governance agenda that included advancement of elements that were declared to be basic values in their own right, such as human rights and the principles of participation. The UNDP challenged the scope of the ultimate development goal to be more holistic, and reformulated it as sustainable human development, for which the political aspects of governance became increasingly central. This was captured explicitly in the UNDP administrator's advocating "democratic governance," which emphasized the political over the procedural and institutional. While the EU saw good governance as a precondition for development, in contrast to the UNDP approach, it distinguished governance from other issues such as human rights and democracy. Moreover, it saw the ultimate development goal as the proper delivery of public services and sustained economic growth, and saw improving governance as instrumental, a precondition for achieving this goal.

We see from this that programs to improve governance have been associated with three ultimate development goals. For many programs, the goal is economic development (e.g., improving governance to more efficiently employ resources or, more generally, to improve material conditions). Such programs often conceive of governance in terms relating to corruption, transparency, and the establishment of a level playing field for economic players. For some, the goal is state-building, with governance improvement designed to achieve greater regularity, reliability, and predictability of regulatory and, more broadly, public policymaking processes and outcomes. These programs are concerned with enhancing the performance of government units linked in vertical hierarchies (e.g., national, provincial, and municipal) and arrayed in horizontal (executive-legislative-judicial) relation to one another. For a third group of programs designed to improve governance, the goal is achieving political inclusion or, more specifically, creating liberal polities (e.g., improved-governance-for-improved-"voice," or for enhanced individual freedoms). These programs seek to expand citizens' participation, rights, and oversight in the public policymaking process and to make policymakers more accountable to citizens. This approach to improving governance is principally aimed at establishing political conditions that ensure long-run support for liberal institutions.

The World Bank's definition of governance has evolved over the past decade in response to the governance approaches of others. It now recognizes the importance of those traditions and institutions in a country that are not necessarily those of the state. Governance is defined as "the traditions and institutions by which authority in a country is exercised. This includes the process by which governments are selected, monitored and replaced; the capacity of the government to effectively formulate and implement sound policies; and the respect of citizens and the state for the institutions that govern economic and social interactions among them."[28] By highlighting not only nonstate traditions and institutions but also process and respect, this approach now acknowledges the importance for good governance of the participation and affect of nonstate actors.

In keeping with this direction of evolution, I find governance best characterized as the process by which authoritative decision making occurs regarding the allocation of public resources. This definition encompasses, for example, the transparency of the process, the extent to which stakeholders participate, the responsiveness of this decision making to the concerns of stakeholders, and the extent to which those authorized to decide are responsive to stakeholder interests and can be held accountable for the outcomes of their decisions by those who are affected by them.

This approach, while consistent with aspects of the World Bank's approach, is closer to the OECD and UNDP approaches, which establish participation, human rights, and democratization as core values to be sought as part of the ultimate goal of development. The dimensions of this definition of governance—transparency, participation, responsiveness, and accountability—are consistent with approaches to governance that have as their ultimate goals economic development and poverty alleviation, state-building, and political inclusion.[29]

It seems reasonable at this point to ask whether the distinction between governance conceived as having to do with the constitutionally mandated authoritative institutions by which public policy is determined and enforced, on the one hand, and governance as more broadly conceived in terms of participation and accountability by nonstate stakeholders, on the other, is not so much descriptive as normative, namely Euro- or North America–centric. As with the case of allegations leveled at the "modernization" approach to development of the 1950s–1970s, challenges to these alternative conceptions of governance might focus on their status as mere proxies for Western European and North American descriptive characteristics that, under the World Bank's banner, have been assigned normative and prescriptive weight. Indeed, there has been a degree of non-European or non–North American pushback. For example, a number of African governments have endorsed the African peer-review mechanism, a voluntary mechanism whereby participating governments subject themselves to governance-related scrutiny from African experts in order to receive an internationally recognized standard akin to the International Organization for Standardization's 9000/14000 standards for private sector management and environmental performance that donors should take notice of.[30]

There also arises the problem of aggregation. The multidimensional character of governance is a problem for establishing causation between governance and development. The World Bank identifies six dimensions of governance—voice and accountability; political stability and absence of violence; government effectiveness; regulatory quality; rule of law; and control of corruption—and combines summary indicators of each dimension into a single index value by which 212 countries and territories are ranked (by percentile) annually.[31] However, conceptually, it seems implausible that these dimensions cohere into a single factor—governance—with a single vector. The "grab bag" of dimensions has contents that appear to pull in different directions at the same time. To the extent that these are distinct and separable, we can envision these dimensions having potentially distinct causal impacts on development. For example, in the case of voice and accountability (transparency, responsibility), absent voice, authoritative allocation of resources may be inefficient because it may fail to take into account the expertise and input of important stakeholders. Conversely, the political stability and absence of violence dimension favors entrenched interests, perhaps ultimately to the detriment of development. Similar arguments can be made for the diverse impacts of other dimensions on development (government effectiveness, regulatory quality, rule of law, and control of corruption).

The issue of how the various dimensions of governance cohere was perhaps one of the reasons why the leaders of the African, Caribbean, and Pacific countries, in renegotiating the Lome IV Agreement in 1995, rejected a proposal from the EU that cooperation be conditional upon compliance with good governance. They saw the concept as too diffuse; consequently, it was not included in the list of essential elements of the agreement.[32]

To complicate matters, there is the interaction problem. Not only are the dimensions of governance not always independent of one another, in some cases their interaction may result in outcomes that appear contrary to general notions of what "good" governance should be. For example, efforts to enhance political stability, at least in the short run, could include the use of security forces to both stifle voices of dissent and shield those in authority from demands for their accountability for the results of their policy decisions. Government effectiveness (e.g., in provision of public services) could be seen as inextricably linked to regulatory quality. For example, the provision of fire and emergency services, on the one hand, and the regulatory function of policing and enforcing building codes for fire, on the other, are part and parcel of the same public policy goal: to reduce damage, injury, and death from fire.

CAUSALITY IN THE RELATIONSHIP BETWEEN GOVERNANCE AND DEVELOPMENT

Consider the heterodox nature of the dimensions of governance. By incorporating characteristics of both the outputs of decision-making processes (regulations, government effectiveness) and of the decision-making processes from which such outputs emerged (degree of corruption, transparency, participation), the holistic approach to governance makes it more difficult to clearly distinguish cause from effect, that is, governance from development. For example, more broadly conceived, development would certainly encompass some measure of predictability associated with political stability. But political stability is also simultaneously one of the dimensions of governance in the broader definition of the World Bank.

Unless governance and development can be shown to be conceptually distinct, there is little point in asserting a causal relationship. I will explain shortly how this conceptual distinction is challenged by existing definitions of governance. Even if we were confident that the two concepts are distinct *and* causally linked, there would still remain unresolved the questions of the direction of causality and of which changes in the dimensions of governance would be associated with higher levels of development and which with declining levels.

Conventionally, the principal direction of causality linking improved governance and development runs from improvement in governance to development.[33] But development can also be shown to have fostered conditions conducive to improving governance. Although in the minority, some have argued persuasively that the evidence for development causing improvements in governance, rather than the other way around, is in fact somewhat stronger.[34] To cite but one hypothesized mechanism to which we might attribute this, countries with higher per capita incomes and improved infrastructure have populations more regularly exposed to mass media. This facilitates citizen oversight of and demand for participation in the process by which decisions are made; that is, development (here, growth in income) results in improved governance. Conversely, low levels of material welfare create conditions in which poor governance is more likely, a low-level governance "trap."[35]

Multilateral and bilateral donor organizations within the Washington orbit typically see governance and development as causally linked, with the direction of causation going from governance to development.[36] However, there is a great deal of variation in what they mean by development. For example, the principal US official development-assistance agency, USAID, states that "'good governance' assumes a government's ability to maintain social peace, guarantee law and order, *promote or create conditions necessary for economic growth*, and ensure a minimum level of social security."[37] USAID's Office of Democracy and Governance's goals are "to encourage more transparent and accountable government institutions in five areas: anti-corruption, democratic decentralization, legislative strengthening, security sector reform, and effective policy implementation."[38] If one embraces the alternative view that the primary direction of causality flows from development to improved governance, then none of these initiatives will have any effect on development.

Many development scholars also see the principal direction of causation as running from governance to development. Africanist Pierre Englebert, for example, argues that because most African states lack legitimacy, their leaders respond to their states' existential character (lack of legitimacy) by resorting to "bad" governance as their only means to retain political power, and this in turn results in low levels of economic development. In contrast, "governance states," (e.g., Uganda, Tanzania, Mozambique)—those that manifest some of the dimensions of "good" governance—achieve economic development outcomes that are far better.[39] The implication is that improving governance may be employed as one of

many mechanisms by which to achieve the ultimate objective of economic development. But Englebert's principal thesis is that these favorable economic development outcomes and the governance characteristics that give rise to them in a small
number of African countries stem from the "legitimate" nature of their states.[40]
This suggests that the existential limitations of many developing country states
may proscribe improvement in governance in many cases.[41]

Quantitative longitudinal studies of the relationship between governance and
GDP per capita in more than one hundred countries over the past decade have
found "only tepid support for the notion that improvements in governance lead
directly to improvements in the short-run rate of growth."[42] Continued program
support for governance improvement by multilateral and bilateral (USAID, DFID)
donors can nevertheless be based upon a rejection of the ultimate goal as short-run
growth. Either long-term prosperity or broader conceptions of development may
be supported by improved governance.

Nevertheless, among other international development stakeholders, particularly recipient country governments, the causal link between improving governance and resources for development is apparent in a most direct
way: funding. Developing-country governments, seeking to maximize incom-
ing development-assistance funds and minimize external constraints on their
room for policy maneuver, tend to pay attention to governance because governance has increasingly become an explicit focus for both private and official
development-assistance programs.

Another concern with respect to the causal relationship between governance
and development is that it may vary as the level or unit of analysis varies. Does this
relationship prevail only at the country (national) level? Does it also operate on
the international or subnational levels? Multilateral and bilateral donor organizations as well as development scholars usually concern themselves with one unit of
analysis, the country. Comparing country by country at one moment of time or
tracing one country's experience over various points of time are the main ways in
which they generate conclusions as to the nature of the governance–development
relationship.

A conceivable alternative unit of analysis might be the universe of international development assistance (IDA)—the IDA "community" as a whole—rather
than the country or territory. What impact might using this unit of analysis have
on the relationship between governance and development? We might conceive
the participation dimension of governance in this case as encompassing the
broad range of global development-assistance stakeholders: donor and recipient
governments; multilateral and bilateral donor organizations; development professionals in donor and recipient countries; host governments and citizens of
development-assistance-recipient countries; and so on. Development here might
encompass the collective economic development of assistance-recipient countries
as a whole. To facilitate a study of governance and development at this (systemic)
level would require knowing the governance characteristics of IDA. While criticism
of IDA governance at the systemic level in the popular media often focuses on the
inefficiencies associated with "development by consultant," I am not aware of a

systematic attempt to measure governance at this level that is comparable with the World Bank's measures of the governance of individual countries and territories.

Going from the systemic to the micro, if we consider instead a unit of analysis that is subnational in jurisdiction—the province, municipality, or district, for example—rather than the country, the effects of governance improvements at this level upon economic development, whether conceived of nationally or at the subnational level, are more difficult to discern. In part, this arises from practical concerns about the quality of available data, including its reliability, validity, and comparability, on subnational governance and economic performance. In part, it arises from the fact that, even in the most decentralized government systems, aspects of the national macroeconomic environment in which the jurisdiction nests (e.g., the value of the currency, the interest rate, inflation) are determined by processes exogenous to the jurisdiction. Looking the other way, governance improvements at selected subnational units rarely scale up to the national level. The development benefits that might arise from governance improvements at the subnational level are inevitably skewed toward richer regions.

Returning to the central concern of this section with the direction of causality, my perspective is that while the principal causal link by which governance and development are connected runs from improvement in governance to development, there is also a secondary, reciprocal causality whereby development fosters conditions conducive to further improved governance. It is possible that this secondary causal flow becomes primary at a certain level of development, although I have not seen data that specifically address this possibility.

Before concluding this section, let us also consider causality "on the down side," namely, situations where governance is deteriorating and where "undevelopment" rather than development is the trending direction for material conditions in a country. Paul Collier's description of the "conflict trap" that afflicts countries beset by civil war describes war as a condition of undevelopment: "Once a war has begun, the economic damage undoes the growth achieved during peace."[43] The business of avoiding armed conflict when the conflict trap makes it more likely than not and the vast literature on conflict avoidance are also concerned with governance.[44] War makes good governance, as I have defined it here, extremely difficult to achieve. This is true not "merely" because of the condition of undevelopment but also because the process concerns of responsiveness, accountability, and inclusion are subsumed in the broader struggle. But deteriorating governance by itself may be neither a necessary nor a sufficient condition to spark the downward spiral of undevelopment that is armed conflict.

It is worth noting, by way of a conclusion, that while the unit of analysis for measuring governance and development used by development-assistance institutions is invariably the country or territory, an increasing proportion of efforts at promoting good governance are in fact being focused on the subnational level. As will be discussed in the following, decentralization has been widely adopted in many regions of the developing world—partly in response to donor pressure—and donor governance programs have emphasized maximizing the benefits for improved governance from decentralization. Implicitly, this reflects an assumption that has yet to be statistically supported, that governance improvements from programs targeted at the subnational level can be aggregated and will have national-level effects that can be measured using the dimensions of governance approach with the country or territory as the unit of analysis.

MEANS USED FOR IMPROVING GOVERNANCE

Development-assistance programs seek to improve governance primarily through three approaches. One is providing technical assistance. An example is programs to achieve legislative strengthening, for example, in budget preparation, and to improve oversight of executive branch activities by legislative committees and their staffs. Another approach is imposing conditionality linked to dimensions of governance. This approach parallels "performance-based" development-assistance programs, as in the Washington Consensus model, whereby "good" governance has been established as one of the prerequisites for receipt of some kinds of ODA.[45] This use of governance "conditionality" as a gatekeeping mechanism has seen declining effectiveness as rising donor powers such as China offer alternative, non-conditioned (at least in terms of governance) sources of development assistance. In addition, the desire of donor countries to achieve the UN's Millennium Development Goals by 2015 has discouraged donor country reductions in development assistance based upon poor governance.[46] A third approach is the selective allocation of development assistance to beneficiary countries based upon the extent to which they demonstrate progress toward improved governance. An example of the last of these is the role of governance indicators in the scorecard process used by the US Millennium Challenge Corporation to rank and accept countries to be eligible to sign Millennium Challenge Account compacts.[47]

The means available by which to improve governance can be loosely grouped—with significant overlap—into those that are cultural and sociological, economic, and institutional. The extent of participation of organized (i.e., "civil") society in exercising voice and demanding accountability is clearly rooted in cultural or sociological norms. But cultural and sociological norms and practices change slowly over time. Patterns of joining and supporting civil society organizations typically remain generationally or regionally bound.[48] Thus, seeking to improve governance using the levers of cultural and sociological change is a strategy for the long term, although institutional support for existing civil society organizations and other nongovernment organizations (e.g., including organizations representing economic interests such as labor unions and business organizations) can be effective (see institutional levers, following).

Economic levers for improving governance are associated with the reciprocal causation between governance and development mentioned in the previous section. Countries or regions hamstrung by low (and often highly variable) levels of development often are characterized by hierarchical, reciprocal patterns of obligation that provide a degree of risk insurance. The "corruption" that is an inherent part of the favorable allocation of resources by officials to those "clients" committed to them by hierarchical obligation can be alleviated only when levels of development (and their predictability) are such that risk is reduced. However, without improved governance and control of corruption, the prospects for a country to achieve such development advances in an increasingly globalized world are dim.

Institutional levers for improving governance initially comprised public management reform efforts associated with creation or modernization of national-level bureaucracies. Foreign technical experts sent to developing countries sought to flesh out organizational charts, strengthen the legal underpinnings of national government rule, and firm up the regulatory apparatuses by which the behavior of nonstate actors was overseen. More recently, outside donors have seen decentralizing government—from the national level to provincial, state, municipal, or local levels—as a potent lever of institutional reform to improve governance and accelerate development.

DECENTRALIZATION

Decentralization programs in the developing world are diverse with respect to both the actors who design and implement them and the ultimate goals they seek to achieve. A brief exploration of this particular area of development-assistance policymaking with some examples from a particular country setting illustrates how different considerations of governance and development goals play out in practice.

While decentralization programs have been initiated by governments and donor institutions in Latin America, Africa, and South and Southeast Asia since the 1980s for a variety of reasons, including national integration, external pressures, and national budgetary shortfalls, those involved with implementing such programs are often acutely aware of their potential impacts—both positive and negative—on both governance and development. Given optimal conditions, decentralization programs are capable of engendering improvements in many of the dimensions of governance. The OECD, for example, in its 2005 report, *Local Governance and the Drivers of Growth*, observed that decentralization in principle "can make it easier for national government to align their resources with local conditions and needs" and that "decentralized decision making promotes pragmatic solutions to local problems" and "may provide greater administrative flexibility."[49] In fact, decentralization has been identified as having the potential to effect improvements in increased voice and accountability; reduction in political violence and increasing political stability nationally; improved (local) government effectiveness; improved regulatory quality; rule of law (related to citizens' voice and accountability); and control of corruption. Yet the OECD report also emphasizes what many participants have observed in countries such as Iraq and Afghanistan in the 2000s, that transferring authority and responsibility from national to subnational authority by itself may in fact worsen governance and can by no means assure progress toward ultimate development goals. Drawing attention to the diversity of interests involved in decentralization where economic growth is the ultimate goal, the report concludes that "local challenges to growth cannot simply be tackled through shifting powers between levels of government, as this type of action requires the combined inputs of a wide range of organizations and actors."[50]

While this shifting of powers is intended to transfer decision-making authority to those with pragmatic knowledge of local conditions, ironically, the governance of decentralization is most often top-down.[51] Multinational and bilateral development-assistance institutions have tended to support top-down decentralization, with the design and implementation of programs that have implemented and supported decentralization being more or less exclusively the domain of donor representatives and national-level bureaucrats and politicians. This has had its limitations in that national-level officials have perceived few benefits coming their way from devolving powers and prerogatives to subnational jurisdictions.

In Indonesia, for example, implementation of sweeping regional autonomy laws adopted by the national assembly in 1999 and due to come into effect in 2001 was hampered by foot-dragging on the part of the principal national government agencies charged with their implementation, such as the Ministry of Home Affairs, which stood to lose considerable powers. Various regulations, circulars, and decrees issued by ministers and their ministries to interpret the intent of the new laws not only came late (some were still being newly issued in 2005) but also contradicted each other. The not unexpected result was that the officials of subnational jurisdictions chose the interpretations most likely to enhance their authority and ignored competing directives from above.

Even where decentralization programs are specifically organized around the principle of participation involving as wide a range of local stakeholders as possible (as was the case with the Kecamatan Development Program [KDP], a World Bank program in Indonesia that between 1998 and 2006 extended to thirty-four thousand, or 49 percent, of the poorest villages), the perception of participants that the program is top-down can lead them to participate in decision-making in a manner consistent with hierarchy. That is, they tended to look to higher authority for direction as to which decisions were "acceptable."[52] This was the case with KDP participatory decision making at the village level over small-scale, local projects for which the World Bank and national government (and later the government of Indonesia alone) were providing resources.

Despite considerable funding for decentralization programs, and notwithstanding the showcasing of particular governance successes (e.g., the poster child of participatory municipal budgeting in Porto Alegre, Brazil), it has been difficult to link decentralization per se with governance improvements.[53] Like the advent of peace after cessation of armed hostilities associated with civil war or external military interventions, which Terrence Lyons discusses in his chapter, decentralization changes the institutional terrain in which existing contestation for power takes place (e.g., over natural resources, politico-religious power bases). Subnational elites and political organizations that mobilized during periods of administrative and political centralization to lobby the national administration for resources may now turn their political entrepreneurship to issuing and policing threat versus protection messages to target populations in subnational jurisdictions. In this respect emphasizing participation as part of improving governance in some decentralization cases has exacerbated communal conflict. Where development processes already have engendered or made more acute broad social tensions, participatory programs such as KDP, even where they were explicitly designed to incorporate direct dispute resolution mechanisms, have sometimes not helped and perhaps have even worsened conflict.[54] This could be the result of several mechanisms. One is the crucible effect, whereby top-down demands for participation as a condition for the release of scarce resources provide an opportunity for the venting of communal disagreements that otherwise might have been kept by community norms below the surface. Another is the very provision of indivisible resources (e.g., a bridge, a school) that may be located in one hamlet or another but not both, which therefore exacerbates the have/have-not distinctions. A third is the opportunity for the entrepreneurial local politician to scare and threaten communities into pre-emptive violence over resources.

CONCLUSION

This chapter has focused on the causal connections between governance and development: how they have been conceptualized, assessed, and acted upon in the formulation and implementation of development-assistance policy. Although the principal causal link by which governance and development are connected runs from improvement in governance to development, there is also a secondary reciprocal causality whereby development fosters conditions conducive to further improved governance.

Governance has been defined in a variety of ways, and this chapter has laid out some of the major definitional approaches, showing how these have given rise to ways of using governance in development assistance to achieve differing ultimate development goals. Although the conception of governance has broadened over time, it still encompasses a number of distinct dimensions, including the transparency of the process, the extent to which stakeholders participate, and the responsiveness of decision making to the concerns of stakeholders. There is also disagreement about the extent to which governance embodies basic principles, such as participation, that should be valued in their own right. One of the challenges in wielding improved governance as a mechanism to achieve development outcomes has been gaining an understanding of how these various dimensions interact as they impact development. Depending upon the different levels or units of analysis upon which one focuses (international, national, or subnational), these dimensions might have different effects on development.

This chapter has shown how the links between (good) governance and development have been conceived from the perspective of multilateral institutions and country development-assistance programs. It has also laid out the means commonly used to improve governance, grouped loosely under the headings cultural and sociological, economic and institutional. Among the institutional mechanisms, the latter part of this chapter has singled out decentralization for closer attention, observing that the evidence for causal linkages between decentralization, improved governance, and development is mixed, and offering some conjectures as to why this might be, drawing upon the experience of decentralization in Indonesia.

Notes

1. Amartya Sen, *Development as Freedom* (New York: Alfred A. Knopf, 2000), 3–4.

2. Tanja A. Börzel, Yasemin Pamuk, and Andreas Stahn, "Good Governance in the European Union," Berlin Working Paper on European Integration #7, January 2008, 14. www .polsoz.fu-berlin.de/polwiss/forschung/international/europa/arbeitspapiere/2008-7_Boerzel _Pamuk_Stahn.pdf.

3. Organisation for Economic Co-operation and Development (OECD), *Cities for Citizens: Improving Metropolitan Governance* (Paris: OECD, 2001), 11; and UN Development Programme (UNDP), *Governance Indicators: A Users' Guide* (New York: UNDP, n.d.), at www.lulu.com/items /volume_64/5983000/5983409/1/print/undp_users_guide_online_version_print.pdf.

4. World Bank, *Governance and Development* (Washington, DC: World Bank, 1992), 3.

5. Max Weber argued that the development of capitalism depended in part on the existence of a bureaucracy whose civil servants adhered more to explicit institutional norms than to personal norms of behavior that embodied family or ethnic loyalties. Max Weber, *Economy and Society*, ed. Guenther Roth and Claus Wittich (Berkeley: University of California Press, 1978).

6. A later study of patrimonialism in Nigeria coined the term "prebendal politics" to capture this phenomenon. Richard A. Joseph, *Democracy and Prebendal Politics in Nigeria* (New York: Cambridge University Press, 1987).

7. World Bank, *Governance: The World Bank's Experience* (Washington, DC: World Bank, 1994), 4.

8. The following paragraphs on the historical evolution of concern for good governance in the late 1980s and 1990s drawn upon Börzel, "Good Governance," 11–20.

9. World Bank, *Sub-Saharan Africa: From Crisis to Sustainable Growth* (Washington, DC: World Bank, 1989), 15.

10. World Bank, *Governance and Development* (Washington, DC: World Bank, 1992), 3.

11. Ibid., 12.

12. Ibid., 39.

13. Ibid., 20, 39.

14. OECD, "Participatory Development and Good Governance," Development Co-operation Guidelines Series (Paris: OECD, 1995). This followed interim reports such as OECD, Development Assistance Committee, "Draft Orientation Paper on Participatory Development, Good Governance, Human Rights and Democratization" (Paris: OECD, 1993).

15. OECD, "Participatory Development," 14 and 6.

16. Ibid., 8–14.

17. UNDP, "Governance for Sustainable Human Development: A UNDP Policy Document," *UNDP.org*, January 1997, accessed December 17, 2009, http://mirror.undp.org /magnet/policy/.

18. Ibid.

19. UNDP, *Human Development Report 2002: Deepening Democracy in a Fragmented World* (New York: Oxford University Press, 2002), v–vi.

20. Börzel, "Good Governance," 15.

21. Ibid., 16.

22. European Commission, 2003, 3, cited in Börzel, "Good Governance," 18.

23. European Commission, 2006, 5, cited in Börzel, "Good Governance," 19.

24. Michael E. Bell, "Local Democratic Governance: What Is It and How Do We Measure It?" Working Paper #031 (Washington, DC: George Washington Institute for Public Policy, 2007), 5, accessed January 19, 2009, www.gwu.edu/~gwipp/papers/wp031.

25. World Bank, *World Development Report: Building Institutions for Markets* (Washington, DC: World Bank, 2002), 99–116.

26. For a discussion of intra-agency debates relating to these tensions within the US government, see Thomas Carothers, *Revitalizing US Democracy Assistance: The Challenge of USAID* (Washington, DC: Carnegie Endowment for International Peace, 2009).

27. Paris Declaration on Aid Effectiveness (March 2, 2005) and the Accra Agenda for Action (September 4, 2008).

28. "Governance and Anti-Corruption," *World Bank*, accessed November 8, 2008, www.worldbank.org/wbi/governance.

29. Ibid.

30. See International Organization for Standardization website, www.iso.org/iso/home.htm.

31. World Bank, "Governance Matters 2008: Worldwide Governance Indicators 1996–2007," (2008), accessed November 8, 2008, http://info.worldbank.org/governance/wgi/.

32. Börzel, "Good Governance," 16.

33. Daniel Kaufmann, "10 Myths about Governance and Corruption," *Finance and Development* 42 (2005): 41; and Marcus J. Kurtz and Andrew Schrank, "Growth and Governance: Models, Measures, and Mechanisms," *Journal of Politics* 69 (2007): 551.

34. Kurtz and Schrank, "Growth and Governance," 538.

35. Paul Collier, *The Bottom Billion* (New York: Oxford University Press, 2007), 64–75.

36. World Bank, "Governance Matters"; USAID, "Promoting Democracy and Good Governance" (2008), accessed November 8, 2008, www.usaid.gov/our_work/democracy_and_governance/; and US Millennium Challenge Corporation (USMCC), "Guide to the MCC Indicators and the Selection Process: Fiscal Year 2008," accessed November 8, 2008, www.mcc.gov/documents/mcc-fy08-guidetoindicatorsandtheselectionprocess.pdf.

37. USAID, "Promoting Democracy." Emphasis added.

38. Ibid.

39. Graham Harrison, *The World Bank and Africa* (New York: Routledge, 2004), 23–42; and Mark Duffield, *Development, Security and Unending War* (Cambridge, UK: Polity, 2007), 165–70.

40. Pierre Englebert, *State Legitimacy and Development in Africa* (Boulder, CO: Lynne Rienner, 2000), 105–18.

41. Paul Collier makes a similar case in *Bottom Billion*, 64–75.

42. Kurtz and Schrank, "Growth and Governance," 551.

43. Collier, *Bottom Billion*, 33.

44. Ibid., 17–37.

45. John Williamson, "A Short History of the Washington Consensus," in *The Washington Consensus Reconsidered*, ed. Narcis Serra and Joseph E. Stiglitz (New York: Oxford University Press, 2008), 14–30.

46. UN, "Millennium Development Goals" (2000), available at www.un.org/millenniumgoals. An example is the UK Department for International Development (DFID).

47. USMCC, "Guide to the MCC Indicators."

48. James C. Scott, *Weapons of the Weak: Everyday Forms of Peasant Resistance* (New Haven, CT: Yale University Press, 1985).

49. OECD, "Local Governance and the Drivers of Growth" (Paris: OECD, 2005), 28–32.

50. Ibid., 28.

51. Here I am using "governance" as per my definition as characteristic of the process of decision making.

52. "Indonesia Kecamatan Development Program" *World Bank*, 2006, http://go.worldbank.org/3THYNMRD00. Kecamatan refers to a subdistrict. The KDP extended to 5,400, or 37 percent, of the kecamatan in the country.

53. José Eduardo Utzig, "Participatory Budgeting of Porto Alegre: A Discussion in the Light of the Principle of Democratic Legitimacy and of the Criterion of Governance Per-

formance," n.d., http://siteresources.worldbank.org/INTPCENG/214578-1116506912206
/20553242/Utzigpaper.pdf.

54. Patrick Barron, Rachael Diprose, and Michael Woolcock, "Local Conflict and Development Projects in Indonesia," Working paper, April 2007, http://www-wds.worldbank.org
/servlet/WDSContentServer/WDSP/IB/2007/04/17/000016406_20070417121152/Rendered
/PDF/wps4212.pdf.

GOVERNANCE
Editors' Comments

Joanna Spear and Paul D. Williams

The two chapters on governance highlight the rather different approaches to the issue evident in the security and development arenas. Although governance is seen as a crucial concept for both security and development, it has spawned a wide variety of sometimes incompatible definitions, usually dependent on parochial institutional agendas, and different views of the goals governance is supposed to bring about (development, state-building, political inclusion, conflict management, etc.). Whereas the security arena has always viewed governance as inherently political, development specialists have often approached it as a technical management issue, largely because of the pervasive influence of liberal political theory on orthodox development thinking. Not surprisingly, therefore, the development perspective focuses on governance in terms of the processes by which public resource allocation is decided. Conversely, the security perspective sees governance as an inescapable feature of social life that specifically refers to political structures that incentivize certain types of behavior and are thus crucial for understanding patterns of order as well as the dynamics of how wars start, endure, and end.

For the security arena, the central policy challenge is how to devise durable but demilitarized systems of governance. In war-torn territories the short-term emphasis thus falls on how to shepherd the transition from war to peace in such a way as to turn militarized actors (insurgents, government soldiers, militias, etc.) into effective political parties, security services, civic associations, and citizens. For development practitioners, conversely, the central debate has revolved around the relationship between governance and economic growth and prosperity. In Bowie's view, while the principal causal link by which governance and development are connected runs from improvement in governance to development, there is also a secondary, reciprocal causality whereby development fosters conditions conducive to further improved governance. The main praxeological questions have thus revolved around the most effective means to improve governance, which Bowie classifies as cultural and sociological, economic and institutional. For each of these means, it is notable that the level of analysis adopted may have different impacts on the relationship between governance and development.

Three other areas of convergence between the two chapters are also worth noting. First, both arenas define governance in process rather than static terms; this puts a premium on managing change. Second, both emphasize the importance of building institutions that can depersonalize politics—elite pacts are never enough—and that embody effective mechanisms of conflict management. Third, both security and development have witnessed significant and prolonged debates over the appropriate relationship between liberal political theory and the governance structures under construction in the world's war-torn and least developed territories. While advocates of building liberal governance structures have clearly enjoyed the upper hand since the end of the Cold War, the US-led efforts to stabilize Iraq and Afghanistan in particular have highlighted the limits and potentially counterproductive effects of the liberal agenda as well as the boundaries beyond which outside actors cannot successfully push against the local political grain. When it comes to governance both perspectives agree that there are no magic bullets, only long, painstaking, incremental processes.

Part IV

HEALTH

Chapter 8

HEALTH
A Security Perspective

George C. Fidas

The conventional view among social scientists and health experts has long been that social and economic decay, political upheaval, and conflict are a major cause of poor health and infectious disease spread. Only recently have we begun to realize that poor health and diseases such as AIDS (acquired immune deficiency syndrome), TB (tuberculosis), and malaria can contribute to such destabilizing factors and pose significant threats to human, national, and global security. Yet history teaches us that battles and wars have been lost due to disease outbreaks, and soldiers stricken by disease consistently exceed those felled by weapons of war. AIDS alone has killed more people than soldiers lost in all of the wars of the twentieth century. Diseases, led by AIDS, are creating a demographic catastrophe in the hardest-hit states that is reducing life expectancy by up to thirty years and felling in large numbers the young adult to middle age cohort that typically is the social backbone of state capacity, experience, and productivity. They are also contributing to insecurity by constraining economic growth; intensifying the political struggle for power and resources in ways not conducive to democratic development; and hollowing out police and military forces that more directly contribute to domestic tranquility, national defense, and global security by way of international peacekeeping operations.[1]

There is rarely a smoking gun to prove all of this, but a growing body of literature is providing strong evidence that health is, indeed, a security issue as well as a health issue. This has prompted the mobilization of governments, intergovernmental organizations, and nongovernmental organizations (NGO) over the last decade to devote unprecedented attention, expertise, and funding to the problem; these efforts are beginning to achieve impressive results in slowing if not reversing the destructive impact of diseases. Much remains to be done, and stark choices and differences in emphasis on how to deal with diseases and the problem of development in general may complicate the effort, but the general trajectory remains positive. The challenge will be to sustain these efforts for the decades that will likely be required to declare victory over diseases after the World Health Organization's (WHO) premature declaration of victory in the latter part of the last century. This will call for continued generous funding and collaboration within and between the world's governments, international organizations, philanthropists, and hard-hit countries; multisectoral approaches that focus on prevention, treatment, and care; and equal emphasis on the wars against diseases and poverty.[2]

NEW AND REEMERGING DISEASES ON RISE

Despite earlier optimism in the health community, infectious diseases remain a leading cause of death, accounting for one-quarter to one-third of worldwide annual deaths of 62 million and for two-thirds of childhood deaths. The renewed threat from diseases is owed to environmental degradation and global warming that is intensifying and spreading water-borne and insect-borne diseases; changes in human demographics and behavior, such as accelerated urbanization and unsafe sex and drug injection practices; and high-tech medical procedures that also carry a higher risk of infection. It also results from changing land and water use patterns that increase contact with disease vectors; growing international travel and commerce that can spread microbes as fast as the speed of aircraft; and the inappropriate use of antibiotics that fosters microbial resistance and makes them increasingly ineffective.[3]

Twenty well-known diseases—including TB and malaria—have reemerged or spread geographically over the last three decades, often in more virulent and drug-resistant forms. More ominously, forty new diseases have been identified, including HIV, Ebola, hepatitis C, and, more recently, Severe Acute Respiratory Syndrome (SARS), for which no cures are yet available. Of the biggest killers worldwide, AIDS, TB, and malaria continue to surge, with AIDS and TB likely to account for the overwhelming majority of deaths from infectious diseases among adults in developing countries by 2020, and with diseases in general remaining the single biggest cause of infant deaths for the foreseeable future.[4]

Some 60 million people have been infected with HIV over the last three decades, and at least 33 million were living with the virus as of 2010. The disease has killed nearly 30 million people, and at least another 30 million will probably die of AIDS by 2020, most of them in sub-Saharan Africa, including as many as one-half or more of young adults in the hardest hit countries.[5] The threat from tuberculosis, especially drug-resistant TB, continues to grow, fueled by poverty, the AIDS pandemic, and immigration. Some 9 million people develop TB annually, and 1.6 million die each year. Drug resistance is a growing problem, with some five hundred thousand cases emerging annually with a cure rate of less than 50 percent.[6] Malaria is making a deadly comeback, killing more than 1.2 million people annually and afflicting another 300 to 500 million worldwide each year.[7] Annual acute respiratory infections and diarrheal diseases appear to have peaked at nearly 4 million and 2 million, respectively, and will continue to take a heavy toll among young and old alike. Epidemiologists continue to believe that it is only a matter of time before another killer flu or related disease emerges on the scale of the catastrophic flu pandemic of 1918–19, which took some 50 million lives.[8] The emergence of terrorism as a primary form of violence since the 9/11 attacks and the proliferation of terrorist groups increases the prospects for bioterrorist attacks similar to or more lethal than the anthrax attacks in the United States shortly after those on 9/11.[9]

Although a formal, fully integrated surveillance and response system does not yet exist at the global level to nip disease outbreaks in the bud, the WHO is working with more than two hundred collaborating centers and laboratories that monitor specific diseases to improve the warning time needed to institute control efforts. It must still contend with the tendency of many countries to deny or hide outbreaks for political and economic reasons, but WHO's widely praised performance during the SARS outbreak and its more assertive approach toward reporting disease outbreaks since then increases the prospects that more outbreaks will be contained in the future.

THE SECURITIZATION OF HEALTH: PROPONENTS AND OPPONENTS

The 2000 US National Intelligence Estimate (NIE), "The Global Infectious Disease Threat and Its Implications for the United States," opened the debate about a link between disease and security by warning that "new and emerging infectious diseases will pose a rising global health threat and will complicate US and global security over the next 20 years. These diseases will endanger US citizens at home and abroad, threaten US armed forces deployed overseas, and exacerbate social and political instability in key countries and regions in which the United States has significant interests."[10] The NIE contributed to a broader debate between those who emphasized traditional approaches to state security and a growing body of scholars and some in government who emphasized personal security.

The traditional state-centric model focuses on protection of a state's territory and population from external military, economic, and ideological threats emanating from another recognizable sovereign state or alliance. Its responses call for strong defense budgets, military counteralliances, and the projection of diplomatic, economic, and military power.

The increasingly accepted human security–centric model argues that states cannot be stable or secure if their citizens feel insecure and threatened by pestilence, crime, poverty, environmental degradation, and unresponsive or repressive governments. The human security perspective also assumes that many of these threats do not emanate from recognizable or intentional threateners and thus calls for global cooperation to confront them.

Since publication of the NIE on infectious diseases, several academicians and researchers have elaborated on its points and have given it more empirical content, but debate persists. Traditional security scholars argue that expanding the concept of security to health—except for the deliberate spread of diseases in the form of biological weapons—dilutes security imperatives, is often a mere pitch for resources, and takes attention away from legitimate health solutions to health problems.[11] Others focus on the ethics of securitization, arguing that it dilutes the moral imperative of dealing with health in its own right and draws in the government security and intelligence communities in ways that can stigmatize diseases and produce crassly realistic policies shorn of moral content.[12]

Proponents of health securitization counter that the assumptions and mindsets of traditional security scholars and approaches have for too long ignored the impact of diseases on issues such as demography, economics, and governance, and the impact on stability and security of nations in general. Disease-induced or -related breakdowns of family and other social structures, large orphan cohorts, uneven economic development and economic decay, and diminished government and military capacity contribute to downward spirals resulting in instability and conflict.[13] They contend as well that, if anything, traditional defense programs have been overfunded, and that the balance must necessarily shift to deal with contemporary nontraditional but highly destabilizing threats, a view expressed most recently even by the US secretary of defense.[14] They also note that successful and well-funded programs such as the US President's Emergency Plan for AIDS Relief, the Global Fund to Fight AIDS, Tuberculosis and Malaria, and others belie the charge from ethicists and some in the health profession that securitization overshadows the moral imperative of confronting global health threats.

The United Nations, key developed countries led by the United States, and even most developing states now acknowledge a link between HIV/AIDS in particular and security. Convincing skeptics in the health, academic, governing, and NGO communities that infectious diseases such as AIDS pose a security threat is a daunting task because there is rarely if ever a smoking gun that can tie them directly to national and global security. Instead, to paraphrase Thomas Hobbes, diseases will make life even more nasty, brutish, and short. It is the cumulative effects of this Hobbesian process that erodes national and global security as mass killers such as AIDS, TB, and malaria undermine social and economic growth and development, stymie political development, and intensify the struggle for scarce resources, thereby destabilizing already troubled polities. Disease-related global economic slowdowns and boycotts, Zimbabwe's lurch toward state failure, the ferocity of the recent civil war in Sierra Leone, growing street crime and corruption in South Africa, periodic famine in sub-Saharan Africa, weakening state capacity and legitimacy in many countries, and reduced national and global security appear to be manifestations to one degree or another of these cumulative Hobbesian effects.

DISEASE-RELATED DEMOGRAPHIC CHANGES CONTRIBUTING TO INSTABILITY

Many of the disease-ridden countries in sub-Saharan Africa and, to a lesser extent, in other regions will face a demographic catastrophe as AIDS and associated diseases reduce life expectancy dramatically and kill up to a quarter or more of their populations over the next ten to fifteen years, including up to half or more of their young adults.[15] Until three decades ago, economic development and improved health care had raised life expectancy in developing countries to sixty-four years, with prospects that it would go higher still. The growing number of deaths from AIDS, TB, and, in particular, malaria will slow or reverse this trend by as much as forty years or more within ten years, according to various estimates, back to levels not seen since 1900.[16]

High infant mortality—which is highly correlated with infectious disease and underdevelopment in general—has a particularly strong correlation with the likelihood of state failure in partial or transitioning states. A CIA-sponsored study on the causes of instability that followed 127 cases over a forty-year period ending in 1996 suggests that infant mortality is a powerful predictor of political instability.[17]

Another study by Richard Hotez found that states with the highest mortality were seventeen times more likely to experience armed conflicts.[18] Such findings are reinforced by other studies of terrorist and criminal groups, which indicate that a disproportionately large number of members come from broken and dysfunctional families and societies.[19]

In addition to high infant mortality, the growing list of emergent and drug-resistant reemergent diseases has introduced a new and worrisome demographic dimension. Those approaching middle age are increasingly being felled by such diseases, led by HIV/AIDS. This dramatic shortening of life expectancy at adulthood is introducing a new and not yet fully comprehended impact on affected societies and social structures because it deprives them of the most experienced individuals that form their social and economic backbone and, in the case of the military and police services, their security shield as well.

The dramatic reduction in life expectancy may bring unexpected and far-reaching consequences in attitudes and behavior as the stricken recalibrate whether and when, for example, to save or invest in education or businesses, marry and have children, or act in a lawful manner, according to Alex de Waal. Cadres of the vicious Revolutionary United Front in Sierra Leone, for example, reportedly justified their rapaciousness and violence by claiming that they were doomed to die of AIDS anyway, so why not.[20] Gwyn Prins posits even more dire consequences when entire infected elites in countries such as Zimbabwe adopt a "nothing to lose" attitude.[21] This recalibration at the individual level will have reverberations at the communal and state levels, reducing their capacity to meet the needs of their citizens precisely when it is most needed. Indeed, we know little about societies whose population chart looks like the Washington Monument atop a somewhat broader base because it is unprecedented, but the consequences are likely to be far reaching.

The surge in adult mortality and the related incapacity and instability are exacerbating the rise of large orphan youth bulges wherein these children lack even the basic necessities, acculturation, and discipline of nonorphan youths. This huge orphan cohort will be unable to cope and will remain vulnerable to exploitation, criminalization, and radicalization. There were more than 13 million AIDS orphans in Africa in 2000, and one-third of the children in the hardest hit countries, or some 20 million, were projected to comprise this lost orphaned generation by 2010, according to UNAIDS, a figure that could easily double to 40 million by 2020. Ten of these countries have orphan populations ranging from 0.5 to 1 million already, and some, such as South Africa, were projected to have 2 million by 2010, according to the Actuarial Society of South Africa.[22] Laurie Garrett notes that countries with large youth bulges typical of sub-Saharan Africa and parts of Asia are three times more likely to suffer civil wars, coups, or civil conflict.[23] In 2003 UNAIDS noted that of the seventeen African countries with substantial AIDS orphans, thirteen were in conflict or on the brink of conflict or were heavily indebted and poor.[24]

Such countries will be at risk of further economic decay, increased crime, and political instability as some of these young people become radicalized or are exploited by various political groups for their own ends. The pervasive child-soldier phenomenon in Sierra Leone and Uganda is one example of such exploitation; the street gangs and glue boys in Nairobi, Johannesburg, and Rio de Janeiro, and the angry young terrorists emerging from dysfunctional societies and failed states may be others. Combined with the fact that many sub-Saharan African countries have majority or plurality Muslim populations of which a segment is becoming increasingly radicalized, the orphan bulge is setting the stage for an increase in the pool of potential terrorist recruits in a region in which they have been largely absent.

THE ECONOMIC TOLL OF DISEASE AS IT FUELS INSTABILITY

Infectious diseases, led by AIDS, malaria, and TB, will take an increasingly heavy economic toll at the individual, state, and international levels, thereby adding to individual insecurity, reducing state capacity in the security area, and exacerbating domestic and international political tensions. Poor health clearly contributes to individual and family impoverishment, and while the evidence on the linkage between economic status and radicalization, including terrorism, is inconclusive, there are too many exceptions to dismiss it altogether. AIDS and other diseases are producing a substantial drop in individual and family income, often also short-circuiting the education of affected children as their parents can no longer afford to pay for it or because children must work to replace an ailing breadwinner's income. This almost ensures prolonged poverty and poor life prospects for both. This is not to suggest that we will see a massive resort to crime, terrorism, or the joining of insurgent groups by such individuals, but enough of these individuals do join such groups to warrant attention. The connection between AIDS, poverty, and crime is well established in sub-Saharan African countries such as South Africa, Zimbabwe, and Sierra Leone. Prolonged socioeconomic exclusion and poor mobility, including lack of access to decent health care, can lead to riots and sustained disturbances, as was the case historically with African Americans in the United States and with more recent disturbances by Muslim youth in France. And while members of radical and terrorist groups generally come from both lower- and middle-class origins, the motivation for many of them is the perceived inequality and poverty in their host societies, along with exclusion from the political class, which they tend to blame for their country's ills. Their foot soldiers, however, often do come from impoverished families in regions such as Southwest Asia and the Palestinian territories.[25]

Poor health is more closely correlated with reduced economic growth and productivity at the state level and in some cases can constrain defense spending and create tensions between favored and excluded regions and groups. Infectious diseases have a particularly pernicious economic impact at the state level and will take an even greater toll on productivity, profitability, and foreign investment, according to a variety of models and empirical data. World Bank models suggest that when national AIDS infection rates exceed 5 percent, economic growth slows considerably; at 10 percent, growth stops; and at 20 percent, growth is reversed and economies shrink by 1 percent or more of gross domestic product annually. A growing number of studies suggest that AIDS and malaria alone will have reduced gross domestic product growth by 20 percent or more in the hardest hit countries by 2020.[26] TB is estimated to reduce income in the poorest states by some $12 billion annually, according to the Global Fund to Fight AIDS, Tuberculosis and Malaria.[27] These trends will likely affect the "guns versus butter" debate and exert pressure on spending for defense and other security needs.

At the international level, the growing health divide between the global "North" and "South" is likely to increase tensions as well. This owes to the fact that developed states are experiencing growing life spans and full access to new medicines and view the South as a disease vector, while the South experiences reduced life spans, limited drug access, and the growth of noninfectious diseases associated with developed-country lifestyles as well as the growth of infectious diseases.

DISEASES HOLLOWING OUT GOVERNANCE AND PARTICIPATION

The corrosive impact of AIDS and other infectious diseases on the socioeconomic underpinnings and elites of hard-hit states threatens to complicate governance by reducing human resources and institutional capacity and slowing or reversing political participation and democratic development. Because AIDS and related diseases are socially neutral in developing countries, they are also making major inroads into the professional classes of teachers, civil servants, engineers, doctors, nurses, and police officers who have formed the social backbone of recent advances in both political and economic life—and among the political class as well.

Well over 1 million teachers in sub-Saharan Africa have died of AIDS and related diseases over the last decade, while HIV infection rates range from 35–40 percent in Zambia, South Africa, and Botswana to an astonishing 70 percent in Swaziland. Health care workers also are being ravaged by AIDS and are often dying faster than they can be replaced. Civil servants across the subcontinent are experiencing high infection rates as well, endangering the capacity of governments to deliver services and probably adding to already pervasive corruption as civil servants seek to secure funds for treatment and to provide for their families after they die prematurely. Political leaders are being felled in large numbers as well, with Zambia, for example, holding 102 by-elections between 1984 and 2003, 29 of them due to the incumbents' deaths, almost certainly from HIV/AIDS.[28]

The infiltration of AIDS into the ruling political classes is likely to intensify the struggle for political power to fill vacant posts and control scarce state and societal resources. It also reduces the capacity of governments to provide needed social services and thereby erodes their legitimacy. Simultaneously, the economic impact of HIV/AIDS provides a disincentive for those in power to give it up, even if it means resorting to extralegal means. In the African context, de Waal notes that "in such an environment of uncertainty and austerity, governments tend to centralize more power. The most probable scenario is that those in power rely more heavily on a smaller circle of loyal comrades, and use more ruthless or corrupt methods to co-opt or buy support."[29]

The human losses from AIDS also will hamper the development of civil society and other underpinnings of democracy and will increase pressure on democratic transitions by limiting new investment, encouraging emigration of the best and the brightest, and generally adding to economic misery and political decay. One of the most significant studies on the impact of HIV/AIDS on civil society organizations in KwaZulu-Natal, South Africa, found that the disease undermined the capacities of local grassroots organizations through loss of both staff and volunteers, which suggests that this may expand to other forms of public activities conducive to democratic development.[30]

DISEASES ARE THE BIGGEST THREAT TO MILITARIES

The nexus between health and security is most evident and direct in the world's militaries, both historically and contemporaneously. Diseases such as the plague, typhoid, cholera, smallpox, and malaria incapacitated entire armies during Europe's many wars over the centuries. US military forces have experienced far higher rates of hospitalization from infectious diseases than from battlefield and noncombat injuries in wartime, including in the Gulf War in 1991.[31] In many former communist and developing countries, HIV/AIDS, TB, and related diseases currently confront militaries with an unprecedented threat to their recruitment pools, organizational capacity, combat readiness, morale, and ability to defend their countries from external and internal threats. Militaries have the discipline and power to attenuate the AIDS threat by restricting recruitment to noninfected individuals and securing disproportionate access to antiretroviral drugs, but they will be hard-pressed to eliminate it.

The greatest impact in militaries is among hard-to-replace commissioned and noncommissioned officers, soldiers with specialized skills, and advanced militaries with sophisticated weaponry. HIV prevalence among militaries is often substantially higher than that of civilian populations, owing to risky lifestyles, deployment away from home, and higher salaries to buy sex. Commencement of testing in most militaries and exclusion of HIV-positive recruits in the militaries of some countries, such as Uganda and Thailand, are reducing HIV prevalence, but it remains pervasive in most militaries, especially among middle and senior level personnel, though countries are reluctant to provide specific data for security reasons. Angola and the Democratic Republic of Congo have estimated military infection rates as high as 60 percent; Nigeria, 10 to 20 percent; and Zimbabwe and Malawi, 70 to 75 percent.[32] According to Gwyn Prins, covert collection of blood samples by a Swedish hematologist from the Zimbabwean army revealed that 80 percent of the sample was HIV positive.[33] South African prevalence estimates range from 21 percent to as high as 40–60 percent, with some units as high as 90 percent.[34] Various studies confirm that AIDS is now the leading cause of death among military and police forces in sub-Saharan Africa, including 60 percent of those in the Southern African Development Community.[35] Infection rates are considerably lower outside of Africa, although Haiti and Thailand, at 10 percent, and Cambodia, at 6–17 percent, more closely approximate African militaries, and AIDS was the fifth leading cause of death in India in 2005.[36]

Combat readiness entails access to a sizeable and healthy recruitment pool, a reservoir of well-trained officers and enlisted men, and the ability to deploy and sustain them, all of which are severely constrained by the AIDS pandemic and related diseases. Militaries typically recruit among the fifteen to twenty-four age cohort of young people, who have high prevalence rates and, assuming a maximum ten-year incubation period before those with HIV acquire full-blown AIDS, they will have to find replacements for those that die. AIDS is eroding the force structure, morale, career development, and cohesiveness of such militaries as well as their effectiveness as more funds are diverted to deal with AIDS-related health, recruitment, training, and other personnel expenditures. One study of the South African military estimated that by 2010 it will have lost 25 percent of its middle-level officers to AIDS.[37] The loss of middle- and high-ranking officers is forcing some militaries to elevate inexperienced junior officers to senior positions, reducing overall fighting capability. Others are providing antiretroviral drugs to more senior officers while denying them to those below, creating resentment and distrust. Some militaries retain infected junior officers but exclude them from training opportunities on the assumption that they will die prematurely. In Russia during the 1990s, one in three draftees was rejected for health reasons, and the problem also appears to be serious in Ukraine and possibly Belarus and Moldova.[38]

HIV prevalence and AIDS-related deaths sap morale and interfere with the organizational need for stability, continuity, and predictability in areas such as career advancement, which creates anxieties and resentments as well as sudden opportunities. An air force squadron in one country had an 85 percent HIV infection prevalence, while only one of South Africa's brigade-size divisions is combat-ready largely due to AIDS, which accounts for seven out of ten deaths in the South African military.[39] According to Prins, reliance on the military increases as AIDS weakens the sinews of the state, and it stokes social unrest at a time when it is also weakening the military by hollowing out the officer corps, eroding discipline, and making soldiers lethargic, irresponsible, and thus unable or unwilling to quash such unrest.[40] Clinical evidence from HIV-related studies indicates that the disease can also cause depression, frustration, and stress, which can lead to insubordination, indiscipline, and reckless behavior such as looting and plunder.[41]

On another level, persistent conflict further militarizes societies whose militaries are already politicized and prone to direct or indirect interventions.[42] Mounting HIV infections and AIDS deaths also may contribute to the deprivation, insecurity, and political machinations that incline some to engage in unlawful behavior aimed, more often than not, at plundering state coffers. By the same token, weakened militaries may actually pose less of a threat to other domestic institutions or to neighboring states in some cases, a positive development considering the predatory nature of many developing world militaries.

Police and internal security forces also are being decimated by AIDS at a time when criminal and other types of antisocial behavior are surging because of poverty and the growth of street gangs populated by AIDS orphans as well as ethnic, communal, and sectarian differences. Southern African police forces are bracing for a surge in deaths in their ranks that could rival those already documented in Kenya and Zambia, where AIDS has caused three-quarters of the deaths in their police forces.[43]

DISEASES LIMIT SUPPLY OF INTERNATIONAL PEACEKEEPERS

The impact of poor health on global security is most directly reflected in international peacekeeping operations where the demand for peacekeepers is outpacing the supply. The negative impact of high HIV prevalence and deaths in militaries, in particular, is likely to be felt in peacekeeping operations, affecting both the availability of peacekeepers and reactions to them in countries in need of peacekeeping operations.

Although the UN officially requires that prospective peacekeeping troops be "disease free," it is difficult to enforce this rule. The UN is reluctant to test for AIDS given the repercussions of testing on individual privacy, the likely noncompliance of many contributing states, and the paucity of available troops. Contributing states are increasingly hard-pressed to make troops available because of already high mortality rates and well-founded fears that deployment will actually increase HIV prevalence among them. In attempting to meet a UN request for one hundred peacekeepers for the Democratic Republic of Congo mission in 2000, for example, South Africa, which excludes HIV-positive soldiers from such missions, found that nearly 90 percent of the eight hundred tested for deployment were infected. During a peacekeeping exercise in South Africa by the Southern African Development Community in 1999, nearly 50 percent of the participating troops were HIV-positive, according to the director of the South African Institute of International Affairs.[44] Although the stigma associated with HIV/AIDS in Muslim states has made it difficult to gauge the impact on major peacekeeping force contributors such as Pakistan and Bangladesh, the Indian Defense Minister's revelation that HIV/AIDS is the fifth-largest killer of Indian military forces suggests that India, another major force contributor, may eventually have to reduce its peacekeeping role.[45]

Studies have shown that HIV infection among deployed military peacekeepers can be several times higher than for civilians, and a soldier's risk of infection doubles for each year of deployment.[46] Infection rates for Nigerian peacekeepers in Sierra Leone, Liberia, and Côte d'Ivoire are up to three times higher than for Nigeria's home-based military.[47] At the same time, a growing number of countries in need of peacekeepers may be reluctant to accept them from high-prevalence countries and militaries, as were Croatia and Eritrea when they had such a need some years ago.[48] Since nearly 40 percent of peacekeepers come from high-prevalence countries, these concerns may dramatically reduce the recruitment pool for the growing number of peacekeeping missions around the world that in January 2009 added up to some 90,000 uniformed personnel from nearly 120 countries in sixteen missions. It is noteworthy that in anticipation of such shortages, the United States in 2005 launched the five-year, $700 million Global Peace Operations Initiative to train an additional 75,000 foreign troops for peacekeeping missions.

In sum, if national security is defined as protection against threats to a country's population, territory, and way of life, then AIDS and other infectious diseases present a clear and present danger to much of sub-Saharan Africa and the Caribbean countries, as well as a gathering threat to the vast populations of Asia and Eurasia, which have the world's steepest infection curves.

DISEASES THREATEN DEVELOPED STATES AS WELL

The contribution of diseases to social, economic, and political decay and instability in the developing world clearly affects the overall security as well as health of developing states, especially those with a global presence and interests. Globalization entails many things, including the globalization of fear itself. From the developed country perspective, one component of that fear is the spread of diseases and vectors from their traditional developing country wellsprings. The spread of HIV/AIDS from West Africa, the West Nile virus from East Africa, food-borne diseases from Latin America, SARS from China, and multidrug-resistant TB from the developing world in general along with the ever-present prospect of another influenza pandemic are but the latest manifestations of this concern. Diseases kill some two hundred thousand Americans annually, and the number is likely to be proportionately higher in Europe, taking into account its larger population. Tourists and business travelers in developed countries and deployed military forces in developing countries face even greater health threats. Developed countries are likely to continue to be drawn into developing countries facing social, economic, and political upheavals that threaten their interests and values. To the extent that diseases contribute to downward spirals that provoke such upheavals, they will pose at least an indirect security threat to developed states. And developed countries will remain concerned about the deliberate introduction of diseases by state and nonstate actors alike.

The fallout from the infectious disease threat will also increase political tensions among countries owing to embargoes, boycotts, and disputes over intellectual property rights regarding the issue of access to drugs that will determine who lives and who dies. In particular, tensions are rising over intellectual property rights between mainly Western drug firms and their host governments, on one hand, and developing countries and their firms, on the other, over access to and pricing for antiretroviral AIDS and other drugs. The appearance of SARS in the fall of 2003 caused a global panic that temporarily brought the vibrant Chinese economy to a near standstill and curbed travel and commerce throughout much of the world. The bird flu and mad cow disease outbreaks in 2004 initially caused similar concerns and exacted a heavy economic price in affected Asian countries, Canada, and the United Kingdom, and international embargoes further roiled relations between these countries and their trading partners. In Zimbabwe, it was the outbreak of cholera in November 2008 and fear of its spread to other countries that produced the most intense calls for the ouster of its long-serving tyrannical president. Such responses are likely to be typical as new disease outbreaks occur and stoke public fears even when they are not particularly contagious or deadly, as is the case with SARS and cholera, whose fatality rate is less than 10 percent.

RESPONSES TO THE INFECTIOUS DISEASE THREAT INTENSIFYING

There is also a silver lining to this otherwise depressing picture. Following decades of indifference or complacency in developed countries, and denial or incapacity in developing ones, infectious diseases are now a prominent feature of the health and political agenda of the world's governments and international organizations. The Clinton administration declared AIDS to be a national security threat and launched a major effort in Congress, the UN, and with US allies and international lending institutions to secure more funding for it and related diseases. The Bush administration followed suit, with Secretary of State Colin Powell reaffirming that AIDS was a national security threat, pledging support for the establishment of the Global Fund, and announcing a bold new initiative to triple the amount of funding for AIDS treatment and prevention programs to $15 billion over five years—subsequently tripled yet again to $50 billion in 2008. "I know of no enemy in war," declared Powell at the UN General Assembly Special Session on AIDS in June 2001, "more insidious than AIDS, an enemy that poses a clear and present danger to the world." And in the midst of the US-declared global war on terror in April 2004, Secretary Powell reiterated that AIDS—not terrorism—posed the greatest threat to the world. This enhanced effort enjoys broad support within the Obama administration as well as with Congress and the public and is converging with that of AIDS activist groups, philanthropists, and governments in other developed countries.

Developing country hesitancy also is abating. With the notable exception of Uganda, Senegal, Botswana, Thailand, and Brazil, most developing and former communist countries initially were ambivalent about this increased attention to AIDS. They welcomed the prospect of greater assistance but were still reluctant to admit to the scope of the problem for cultural reasons, national prestige, fear of its impact on tourism and foreign investment, and a focus on broader priorities such as socioeconomic development and defense. These attitudes have begun to change over the last five years as African leaders themselves began to experience the loss of close relatives and friends and both public and international pressure to confront the problem increased. The dramatic increase in funds from a range of international sources is beginning to provide them with the means.

In addition, grassroots political pressures are on the rise as AIDS activists and NGOs across the globe are serving notice that AIDS must be a priority in national agendas or governments will be punished at the polls or experience street unrest. And they are winning the support of national judiciaries, beginning in South Africa, where the courts have ruled that the government must provide HIV-infected pregnant women with drugs to reduce mother-to-child transmission. Similar democratic currents have been sparked by the AIDS and SARS epidemics in China, where public and press comments have called for political liberalization and greater openness and communication to deal with such crises. In an unprecedented move, the Chinese government sacked its health minister and the mayor of Beijing for their handling of the SARS crisis, and the government has haltingly allowed greater public and press commentary on the AIDS and SARS issues.

KEY CHALLENGES AND CHOICES

As the donor community and hard-hit countries contemplate their responses to AIDS, TB, malaria, and other diseases, they will face a variety of complex challenges and choices. First, policymakers must assess the salience of the issue, including its political salience, since this will influence the attention and resources it is likely to receive. The trend is toward highlighting both the health and security risks of diseases, but opinion will likely remain divided on this. Clearly, AIDS and other diseases will be far better funded if they are seen both as a serious health and security issue.

Second, policy choices need to be made along three dimensions: spending for health versus spending for other objectives such as education, infrastructure, and defense; treating AIDS versus treating other serious illnesses; and preventing HIV infection versus treating those with AIDS. The issue of who gets treated and who does not—meaning the choice between who lives and who dies—could dramatically widen the health divide between rich and poor nations and within poor nations, and could become one of the most contentious issues of the twenty-first century. Although virtually all North Americans and Europeans have access to both prevention and treatment programs for almost all infectious diseases, including AIDS, most people in developing countries have neither. Even with drug treatment costs dropping below $150 annually, UNAIDS reports that only about 5 million of the developing world's 15 million people who require treatment were receiving it at the end of 2009.[49] History suggests those with access to such treatment will be the well to do, the well connected, and the powerful, which will further widen the fissures in these countries.

Nonetheless, there must be a continued effort to deal with the most immediate and destabilizing impact of AIDS—its relentless inroads into the very elites upon whom these countries must depend. The needs of refugees and orphans who are potential recruits as child soldiers, criminals, and even terrorists must also be met. UNAIDS, in this regard, has developed a strategic action plan that includes education and training in prevention and provision of condoms, including among uniformed services in fifty countries. The US Department of Defense also has initiated efforts to raise AIDS awareness in military-to-military contacts with developing countries. Countries such as Nigeria and Botswana have begun treating their militaries while another fifteen countries are preparing to do so, according to the UN's Department of Peacekeeping Operations. And the US Congress has decided that 10 percent of US funding for AIDS programs must be directed at helping AIDS orphans.[50]

Third, the international coalition that aims to confront AIDS, TB, malaria, and other diseases will remain fragile even though it is off to a good start. It will remain particularly dependent on the commitment of the major developed countries, agreement on the allocation of aid, coordination of the various initiatives and programs, and the success of approved projects. It will also depend on proper handling of the intellectual property rights issue to ensure that the need of drug firms to protect the fruits of their research and earn at least some profits is balanced by the need to provide affordable access to the millions suffering from such diseases.

Fourth, even with plummeting drug prices and growing international commitment and assistance, no international aid effort will succeed unless the recipient countries show similar resolve and receptivity to its goals and make their best efforts to use their own resources to combat the threat from AIDS and other infectious diseases.

THE WAY FORWARD

Although the challenges ahead are formidable and potentially divisive, a number of sensible policy responses are already under way. They vary in the attention they focus on detection, prevention, treatment, and broader socioeconomic development. But all note the need for a multisectoral approach, a steady increase in funding, and an emphasis on capacity-building to use such funds effectively. The need to build up health infrastructures as well as focus on efforts to fight specific disease is especially noted since the latter efforts are likely to falter without such health infrastructures.[51]

As for funding, winning the war on AIDS and other infectious diseases will be expensive but pales in comparison to what the world's governments spend on defense and more superfluous items. Some $16 billion was spent on dealing with HIV/AIDS in 2009, $10 billion short of what was needed in 2010, according to UNAIDS.[52] WHO estimates that nearly $5 billion is needed annually for TB control.[53] The UN's Roll Back Malaria Partnership, which commenced in September 2008, plans to allocate $5 billion annually to save 4 million lives by 2015.[54]

As for how to conduct the war against infectious diseases, virtually all policy proposals underscore the need for partnerships to better marshal the requisite material and human resources. In Africa, for example, emerging national AIDS commissions typically include several ministries as well as representatives of civil society. NGOs and community action groups were instrumental in securing and implementing Brazil's prevention and treatment program and in pressing the South African government to commence mother-to-child prevention. The Global Fund itself is a unique public and private partnership that includes NGOs on its board and grants money to both governmental and nongovernmental proposals to curb AIDS, TB, and malaria.

Finally, the war against AIDS and other infectious diseases cannot be won without winning the war on poverty and underdevelopment. Tackling the social, economic, political, and cultural factors that make states vulnerable to diseases is essential in forging an effective response and sustainable response. This means policies aimed at reducing hunger, increasing education levels, particularly among women, and reducing child mortality. It means better governance, more democracy, respect for the environment, and more conflict prevention and amelioration efforts. It means that there must be greater collaboration and coordination between health- and development-focused NGOs, international organizations (IGO), and government agencies to ensure that development and anti-AIDS programs are complementary rather than competitive. And it means that governments, IGOs, and NGOs should resist the temptation to make tradeoffs between confronting diseases and confronting poverty. Both wars need to be won, and that means devoting more to both.

Notes

This chapter does not represent the official views or policy of the Department of Defense or the US government but rather the author's own views.

1. Stefan Elbe, *Strategic Implications of HIV/AIDS*, IISS Adelphi Paper 357 (London: IISS, 2003), 7.

2. For an elaboration of the proposition that the world has turned the corner in combating AIDS, see, in particular, WHO, *UNAIDS Report on the Global AIDS Epidemic 2010* (Geneva: WHO, 2010), 7–15.

3. National Intelligence Council (NIC), "The Global Infectious Disease Threat and Its Implications for the United States," NIE 99-17D (Washington, DC: NIC, January 2000), 13–24. www.fas.org/irp/threat/nie99-17d.htm.

4. WHO, *World Health Report 2007: A Safer Future* (Geneva: WHO, 2007), ix–xxiii. www.who.int/whr/2007/en/index.html.

5. WHO, *UNAIDS Annual Report 2007* (Geneva: WHO, 2008), 3; WHO, *UNAIDS Report 2010*, 7.

6. David Brown, "5% of TB cases Don't Respond to Some Drugs," *Washington Post*, February 27, 2008, A2.

7. David Brown, "Anti-Malaria Efforts Yield New Success," *Washington Post*, February 1, 2008, A11.

8. NIC, "Global Infectious Disease Threat," 6.

9. Jonathan Ban, *Health, Security, and US Global Leadership*, Special Report 2 (Washington, DC: Chemical, Biological and Arms Control Institute, 2001), 17–25.

10. NIC, "Global Infectious Disease Threat," 5.

11. For a general critique of the human security approach, see Roland Paris, "Human Security: Paradigm Shift or Hot Air?" *International Security* 26, no. 2 (2002): 87–102.

12. For an elaboration and critique of the securitization of health and diseases, in particular, see Stefan Elbe, "Should HIV/AIDS Be Securitized: The Ethical Dilemmas of Linking HIV/AIDS and Security," *International Studies Quarterly* 50, no. 1 (2006): 119–44; and Stefan Elbe, *Virus Alert: Security, Government and the AIDS Pandemic* (New York: Columbia University Press, 2009). See also Rebecca Katz and Daniel A. Singer, "Health and Security in Foreign Policy," *Bulletin of the World Health Organization* (March 2007): 233–34.

13. For an elaboration of the centrality of health to national and international security, see Andrew T. Price-Smith, *Contagion and Chaos: Disease, Ecology, and National Security in the Era of Globalization* (Cambridge, MA: MIT Press, 2009); and Laurie Garrett, "The Lessons of HIV/AIDS," *Foreign Affairs* 84, no. 4 (2005): 51–64.

14. See, for example, Robert M. Gates, Landon Lecture, Manhattan, Kansas, November 26, 2007, www.defenselink.mil/speeches/speech.aspx?speechid=1199; and Jennifer Brower and Peter Chalk, *The Global Threat of New and Reemerging Infectious Diseases* (Santa Monica: RAND, 2003).

15. Woodrow Wilson International Center for Scholars (WWICS), "AIDS Orphans in Africa: Building an Urban Response" (Washington, DC: WWICS, 2001), 71. Available at www.wilsoncenter.org/index.cfm?topic_id=1417&fuseaction=topics.publications&group_id=113350.

16. Nana K. Poku, "HIV/AIDS and Governance in Africa," *Report from Africa: Population, Health, Environment, Conflict*, no. 12: 29–35, www.wilsoncenter.org/topics/pubs/Poku12.pdf; and Garrett, "Lessons of HIV/AIDS," 6.

17. Daniel C. Esty, Jack A. Goldstone, Ted Robert Gurr, Barbara Harff, Marc Levy, Geoffrey D. Dabelko, Pamela T. Surko, and Alan N. Unger, "State Failure Task Force Report; Phase II Findings" (McLean, VA: Science Applications International Corporation, July 31, 1998), vii, 2–3. http://globalpolicy.gmu.edu/pitf/SFTF%20Phase%20II%20Report.pdf.

18. Carla Koppell with Anita Sherman, "Preventing the Next Wave of Conflict: Understanding Non-Traditional Threats to Global Stability," Report of the Non-Traditional Threats Working Group (Washington, DC: WWICS Conflict Prevention Project. 2003), 98.

19. See Mark Schneider and Michael Moodie, *The Destabilizing Impact of HIV/AIDS* (Washington, DC: Center for Strategic and International Studies, May 2002), 5; Martin Schonteich, *HIV/AIDS, Policing Orphans and Crime in South Africa* (Washington, DC: Center for Strategic and International Studies, February 2003).

20. Alex de Waal, "How Will HIV/AIDS Transform African Governance," *African Affairs*, 102 (2003): 4.

21. Gwyn Prins, "AIDS and Global Security," *International Affairs* 80, no. 5 (2004): 994–95.

22. Ibid., 945; and WWICS, "AIDS Orphans in Africa," 17–23.

23. Garrett, "Lessons of HIV/AIDS," 61.

24. "Fact Sheet: HIV/AIDS and Conflict," UNAIDS Fact Sheet No. 2, August 2003, http://data.unaids.org/Topics/Security/fs_conflict_en.pdf, 2.

25. See Alan B. Krueger, *What Makes a Terrorist: Economics and the Roots of Terrorism* (Princeton, NJ: Princeton University Press, 2007); and the chapter in this volume by Paul D. Williams. See also Marc Sageman, "Leaderless Jihad: Terrorists Proving Harder to Profile," *Washington Post*, March 12, 2007, A1.

26. Mark Schneider and Michael Moodie, *The Destabilizing Impacts of HIV/AIDS* (Washington, DC: CSIS HIV/AIDS Task Force, May 2002), 6.

27. Koppell, "Preventing the Next Wave," 96–97.

28. Garrett, "Lessons of HIV/AIDS," 59.

29. de Waal, "How Will HIV/AIDS Transform African Governance," 15.

30. Ibid., 13.

31. NIC, "Global Infectious Disease Threat," 58–59.

32. Ibid., 53.

33. Prins, "AIDS and Global Security," 943.

34. Elbe, *Strategic Implications of HIV/AIDS*, 19.

35. John Kemoli Sagala, "HIV/AIDS Prevention Strategies in the Armed Forces in Sub-Saharan Africa," *Armed Forces and Society* 34, no. 2 (2008): 297.

36. Elbe, *Strategic Implications of HIV/AIDS*, 19–20, 27; and Garrett, "Lessons of HIV/AIDS," 55.

37. Lindy Heinecken, "Facing a Merciless Enemy: HIV/AIDS and the South African Armed Forces," *Armed Forces and Society* 29, no. 2 (2003): 281–300.

38. NIC, "Global Infectious Disease Threat," 52; and Garrett, "Lessons of HIV/AIDS," 3.

39. Prins, "AIDS and Global Security," 944.

40. Ibid.

41. John Sagala, "HIV/AIDS and the Military in Sub-Saharan Africa: Impact on Organizational Effectiveness," *Africa Today*, Fall 2006, 64–65.

42. Prins, "AIDS and Global Security," 943.

43. Sagala, "HIV/AIDS Prevention Strategies," 297.

44. Sagala, "HIV/AIDS and the Military," 66; and Elbe, *Strategic Implications of HIV/AIDS*, 42.

45. See Happymon Jacob, *HIV/AIDS as a Security Threat to India* (New Delhi: Manohar Publishers, 2005).

46. Alan Whiteside, Alex de Waal, and Gebre-Tensae Tsadkan, "AIDS, Security and the Military in Africa: A Sober Appraisal," *African Affairs*, 105, no. 419 (2006): 206.

47. Garrett, "Lessons of HIV/AIDS," 56–57.

48. Sagala, "HIV/AIDS and the Military," 66.

49. WHO, *UNAIDS Report on the Global AIDS Epidemic 2010*, 8.

50. *Addressing the HIV/AIDS Pandemic: A US Global AIDS Strategy for the Longterm* (New York: Council on Foreign Relations, 2004), 6; and Brown, "5% of TB cases."

51. Laurie Garrett, "The Challenge of Global Health," *Foreign Affairs* 86, no. 1 (2007): 14–38.

52. WHO, *UNAIDS Report on the Global AIDS Epidemic 2010*, 145.

53. Brown, "5% of TB Cases."

54. David Grushkin, "The End of Malaria," *National Geographic Adventure*, February, 2009, 28–29.

Chapter 9

HEALTH
A Development Perspective

Julie E. Fischer

The global burden of disease does not weigh evenly on the world's population. Even a cursory survey of population health indicators—measurements such as life expectancy and child mortality, which capture average outcomes across communities—reveals a sharp contrast between the health status of the poor and the wealthy, within as well as between countries.

To illustrate, average life expectancies at birth in the more developed European, North American, and Asia-Pacific regions rose from sixty-six years in 1950 to more than seventy-seven years by 2005. Average life expectancies at birth among least-developed countries also climbed during this period but reached only fifty-six years in 2005. In some cases, governance failures, economic stagnation, and the dual health and development catastrophe of HIV/AIDS erased even these gains. For example, life expectancies at birth in the heavily indebted, highly HIV/AIDS-burdened states of Zambia and Zimbabwe climbed between 1950 and 1980s only to fall back to their baselines of around forty-five years by 2005.[1] Worldwide, 10.4 million children under five years of age died in 2004. More than 70 percent of these deaths occurred in the low-income states of sub-Saharan Africa and South and Southeast Asia. On average, a child born in a low-income country in 2004 faced a fourteenfold higher risk of dying before age five than a child born in a high-income country.[2]

Working-age adults in these regions also face a significantly higher risk of premature death from communicable diseases, injuries, and complications of pregnancy than do their counterparts in developed countries. An increasing number engage in high-risk behaviors associated with urbanization and globalization (such as tobacco use, unhealthy diets, and sedentary lifestyles) that increase their susceptibility to cardiovascular conditions, diabetes, and other noncommunicable chronic diseases. Chronic illnesses tend to take a more severe toll at a younger age in developing countries, where health systems still contend with unresolved maternal–child health and infectious disease challenges. Without significant changes, this "dual disease" burden will erode household incomes and economic productivity over coming decades, costing emerging economies billions of dollars in lost growth.[3]

The association between national income levels and national health status has become widely accepted. International organizations increasingly include health indicators in metrics of sustainable development not just as a measurement of the capacity for economic growth but as one of its central objectives. The increasingly mainstream perception of the health–wealth link as a mutually reinforcing virtuous circle (or, conversely, a vicious cycle) underpinned a dramatic increase in development assistance for health at the turn of the twenty-first century.

The integration of global health and development strategies followed a century in which concerns about the deleterious effects of disease outbreaks on trade, trust, and human capital came full circle. By the beginning of the twentieth century, urban reform movements had spurred investments in basic public services such as safe water and sanitation in the growing cities of industrialized Europe and North America. Mortality from the epidemics that once routinely raced through crowded communities plummeted, and life expectancies began to rise steadily.[4] Self-interest drove wealthy governments to seek international agreements aimed at preventing the cross-border spread of disease without unduly impeding trade and travel. Their negotiations acknowledged that the disease burden in underdeveloped regions concerned all as people and health risks moved easily among expanded trade networks but focused on protecting those networks rather than improving health status in poor countries. These utilitarian motives persisted but were tempered by humanitarianism in the creation of the World Health Organization (WHO) in 1948, with a mission articulated in its constitution as "the attainment by all peoples of the highest possible level of health." The WHO and other UN agencies began to coordinate mass campaigns that saved millions of lives from infectious diseases but did little to address the root causes of morbidity and mortality.

Two key trends emerged in the 1970s: a period of economic turmoil throughout developing regions, and the maturation of multilateral agreements on human rights under the UN and regional organizations. The latter collectively obligated state parties to recognize the right to health—an important normative framework but one that has proved difficult to interpret and implement evenly. The former prompted national officials and international finance institutions to support profound economic liberalization strategies in heavily indebted countries. By the 1990s, concerns that policies to promote free markets might have undermined health and other social programs created momentum to address the equitable distribution of health resources and capabilities. The emergence of infectious diseases from HIV to SARS reinforced these arguments for a new focus on global health equity not just as a moral imperative but as a strategy to eliminate "mutual vulnerabilities" created where the health risks of poverty might give rise to crises with the potential to spill across borders, whether directly in the form of outbreaks or indirectly by undermining trade and trust, in an era of accelerated globalization.[5] This chapter will focus on these trends and on the evidence base for public health as an element and an outcome of sustainable development.

DEVELOPMENT AS BRIDGE TO HEALTH

For most of recorded history, diseases such as tuberculosis, measles, typhoid fever, and smallpox flourished wherever populations grew large enough to sustain disease transmission among vulnerable groups. By the late nineteenth century, political will and an improved understanding of sanitation and hygiene converged in rapidly urbanizing North America and Europe. The rising professional classes demanded that decision makers use the growing dividends of development to institute sanitary reforms. Investments in basic public services quickly reduced deaths from once-routine disease outbreaks. Later, technological interventions such as antibiotics, vaccines, and pesticides curtailed disease and deaths even further.[6]

Such efforts addressed the most basic of the underlying determinants of disease, those cumulative exposures to social, cultural, political, behavioral, environmental, and clinical risks that ultimately affect the distribution of the disease burden across populations. The poor generally enjoy fewer protections against such exposures than their more affluent counterparts. For example, most of the nearly 1 billion people in the world with no reliable source of clean water and the more than 2 billion who lack access to improved sanitation live in developing countries. Households forced to rely on untreated water sources for drinking and food preparation face an increased risk of exposures to water-borne bacteria, viruses, or parasites that cause acute diarrheal diseases. These infections can lead to life-threatening dehydration in the short term; chronic or repeated episodes can exacerbate malnutrition. Effective interventions that can be managed at the household level, from point-of-use water treatments to oral rehydration therapy that can avert deaths from acute diarrheal disease at a cost of pennies per course, currently reach only a fraction of target populations.[7] In the absence of improved sanitation, infected human wastes can contaminate surface and ground waters, creating a cycle of infection. Poor access to water also discourages hand-washing and other hygiene practices that can limit the spread of infectious diseases. Boiling drinking water appropriately can reduce the risks of waterborne disease, but this poses its own concerns. Among less-developed countries, many households burn solid fuels such as wood or charcoal for cooking, heat, and disinfecting water. Smoke from the indoor burning of solid fuels increases susceptibility to acute respiratory infections (the leading communicable cause of deaths worldwide) and chronic cardiovascular and respiratory conditions.[8]

Some risks (such as alcohol and tobacco use, high blood pressure, and high blood glucose levels) account for a significant share of the disease burden in developed and developing countries alike. In contrast, developing regions carry the vast majority of the global disease burden linked to unsafe water, poor sanitation and hygiene, indoor air pollution from solid fuels, and undernutrition.[9]

Household and community food insecurity is a major health risk in low-income countries. Maternal and child undernutrition underlie an estimated 3.5 million annual deaths, or 11 percent of the total global disease burden. Chronic undernutrition during pregnancy and early childhood (leading to underweight and micronutrient deficiencies) can increase susceptibility to infectious diseases and can exert lifelong effects on physical and cognitive development. Women affected by chronic undernutrition face greater risks of serious complications during pregnancy and childbirth that endanger mother and child.[10] The effects of poor underlying health status on maternal mortality are exacerbated where women also lack access to comprehensive health services. The estimated lifetime risk of maternal death in 2005 ranged from 1 in 47,600 in Ireland to 1 in 7 in Niger. Women in Western and Central Africa face an average 1 in 17 lifetime risk of maternal death.[11]

Conditions that primarily affect low- and low- to middle-income states are often characterized as "diseases of poverty." These include a cluster of water-, soil-, and vector-borne parasitic and bacterial infections termed "neglected tropical diseases" that affect more than 1 billion people, virtually all in the world's poorest countries. These diseases cause significant disfigurement and disability and could be controlled worldwide at an estimated cost of forty to fifty cents per person per year given adequate management and delivery infrastructures.[12] Infectious diseases such as HIV/AIDS and tuberculosis affect populations across income ranges but still disproportionately burden the developing world. Malaria offers a modern example of a disease transformed rapidly from worldwide scourge to affliction of poverty. The United States and other industrialized states redoubled their domestic malaria eradication efforts in the wake of World War II, investing in public health interventions to detect and treat human cases and control the *Anopheles* mosquito vector that transmits the disease. Urbanization and changing land use reduced mosquito exposures, augmented by development projects that drained swamps and other mosquito breeding sites. In only a few years, integrated public health and vector-control efforts had eliminated malaria from the previously endemic regions of the United States and Southern Europe. In contrast, malaria still infects hundreds of millions of people annually in developing countries, killing about 1 million each year—mostly young children in sub-Saharan Africa, where households lack access even to simple barrier protections such as bed nets.[13] The infectious disease burden depends on a complex web of social, cultural, economic, and political factors that influence household resources and government capacity and will to ameliorate environmental health risks.[14]

HEALTH AND DEVELOPMENT ON THE INTERNATIONAL AGENDA

The foundation of international public health cooperation evolved in the nineteenth century as a matter of mutual self-interest. The collapsing costs of international shipping and sudden trade liberalization by key Asian economies had sparked a transport revolution and the integration of markets around the world.[15] The easy movement of goods and people closed the distance between suddenly interdependent economies. In the 1830s, shipping introduced cholera—a deadly diarrheal disease endemic in South Asia—to Europe and the United States. Cholera spread in terrifying waves that killed tens of thousands and sparked civil unrest. Governments imposed variously stringent quarantine and isolation measures on ships and their passengers without any understanding of disease transmission.[16] These transboundary epidemics necessitated new domestic public health measures and created momentum for international cooperation to control the cross-border spread of health threats without hampering trade and travel.[17]

Concerns about epidemic-prone diseases such as cholera also spurred new scientific and epidemiological investigations. In the early twentieth century, the

Rockefeller Foundation launched a long-running program that combined labora-
tory and field approaches with a social agenda, supporting cross-border campaigns
to eradicate hookworm, yellow fever, and malaria in poor regions and establishing
operational precedents for international health efforts.[18] Public and private sector
institutions used the growing body of knowledge that such approaches produced
to guide increasingly successful cooperative programs in disease control.[19] The creation of WHO as a specialized agency of the UN integrated many of these activities
and provided a focal point for identifying cost-effective public health interventions available to national and international decision makers.

By the 1950s, public health leaders were well aware that infant and childhood mortality among the least developed countries of sub-Saharan Africa,
Southeast Asia, and South Asia greatly exceeded rates in wealthier regions—even
taking into account the resurgence of infectious diseases in war-ravaged European states.[20] Member states tasked WHO and the newly launched UN Children's
Fund (UNICEF) to meet the health and nutrition needs of vulnerable European
children as part of postwar development, and then expanded these child survival
efforts to less-developed regions.[21] Technologies such as antibiotics, vaccines,
and pesticides offered tools for limiting disease spread in developing countries
even without the sanitary reforms that had proved successful in industrialized
states. WHO launched ambitious mass campaigns to control or eradicate infectious diseases such as yaws, malaria, and smallpox deemed high priorities by
member states—generally those with resources and expertise to share. The successful eradication of smallpox saved millions of lives annually, mostly in developing countries where vaccination had not previously become routine, and
removed the mutual vulnerability of cross-border outbreaks. (In contrast, the
global malaria eradication campaign of the late 1950s bogged down in technical,
logistical, and political difficulties and ultimately succeeded only in developed
regions.[22])

The new UN structure also provided a platform for the inclusion of health
within the emerging international human rights framework. The Universal Declaration of Human Rights and multiple international and regional accords recognized health among human rights to be respected, protected, and facilitated
by national governments and international organizations. The International Covenant on Economic, Social and Cultural Rights (1976) obligated state parties to
take concrete steps toward the realization of "the right to the enjoyment of the
highest attainable standard of physical and mental health," the formulation included in the WHO Constitution. The 1978 Declaration of Alma-Ata under the
aegis of WHO created specific principles for achieving health equity and called
upon governments to guarantee a minimum standard of primary health care for
all as "an integral part . . . of the overall social and economic development of the
community."[23] Although some countries, including the United States, have resisted
fully endorsing the legal right to health, the normative content has powerfully
influenced expectations about the obligations of governmental and nongovernmental actors to mitigate preventable health hazards, and thus to use development
as a tool to achieve better health.[24]

Unfortunately, these norms began to take root just as a mounting debt crisis crippled many developing economies, particularly in sub-Saharan Africa and Latin America. By that time, economists had observed that the populations in fully industrialized countries generally enjoyed longer and healthier lives than those in poor countries, but they could not identify a formula equating incremental progress in economic growth to concomitant advances in health status. Theories that became popular in the 1970s asserted that industrialization itself provides the resources and will to improve nutrition and sanitation, driving improved health status regardless of state investments in health systems or services (and disregarding the disruptive effects of rapid urbanization and industrialization on population health).[25] Influential studies concluded that the process of industrialization naturally propels states through a linear transition: a period of predevelopment "pestilence and famine" preceding a phase of rising living standards, followed by a drop in mortality rates, then falling fertility rates as life expectancies lengthen (a trend extrapolated from Western European historical records).[26]

This model appealed to proponents of neoliberal economic policies focused on free trade and market growth as pathways to development. Accordingly, health received little attention as international finance institutions sought to shore up economies staggering under foreign debts and buffeted by a worldwide recession. Starting in the early 1980s, the World Bank and International Monetary Fund required debtor countries to adopt structural adjustment policies—measures to accelerate macroeconomic recovery through market liberalization—among conditions for securing or refinancing loans. UNICEF field officers in regions where adjustment policies dominated economic planning soon observed ominously rising levels of child malnutrition and mortality, especially among the poorest populations. UNICEF assembled a series of country-level case studies on the "human face" of adjustment policies: in the absence of specific policies to preserve basic public services, many governments cut public spending by slashing health and education budgets. Households faced high out-of-pocket costs for health care services of wildly uneven quality, with the poor—less insulated against health risks and economic shocks—the least able to cope.[27] Objective evidence that such policies undermined national health status over the long term remains scarce. However, whether an unintended consequence of adjustment policies or a direct result of collapsing purchasing power, many developing countries cut funding to operate, staff, and equip government health systems that were in effect the only game in town throughout the 1980s. Any progress toward strengthening health systems stalled or reversed.[28]

Given this evidence, economists began to reexamine drivers of national and international support for social programs. The World Bank published a strategy for health and development in 1993 that endorsed the "Health for All" agenda: promoting pro-poor health sector reforms to finance essential health services and reduce environmental health risks where the need is greatest. In contrast to the Declaration of Alma-Ata, which encouraged governments to promote worldwide health equity "in the spirit of social justice," the World Bank strategy emphasized the savings potential in redirecting health funds from expensive curative medicine to more cost-effective prevention programs.[29] This prosaic goal nonetheless provided a practical framework for harmonizing public health, poverty reduction, and social justice strategies.

By the late 1990s, prominent economists such as Joseph Stiglitz and Amartya Sen began to advocate for more comprehensive definitions of sustainable development that included human capital, environmental health, and health equity.[30] The increasingly evident impact of HIV/AIDS in sub-Saharan Africa emphasized the vulnerability of fragile economies to health crises, catapulting health issues to the top of an international development agenda increasingly focused on poverty reduction rather than economic growth alone (see Sud's chapter in this volume). In 1999, then-WHO director-general Gro Harlem Brundtland articulated a health and development platform: "Poverty breeds infections; infections breed poverty. The road out of this vicious cycle begins with efforts that contribute to a person's ability to meet basic needs."[31]

Three of the eight Millennium Development Goals (MDG) crafted by the world's development institutions as a blueprint to reduce global poverty focused on child mortality, maternal health, and HIV/AIDS and other infectious diseases. Several other MDG priorities addressed population health status, including sanitation, adequate nutrition, and access to clean water and affordable pharmaceuticals.[32] Analysis undertaken to support target-setting under the MDGs concluded that aid donors and recipients consistently underestimated the economic benefits of investing in health, endorsing the concept that reducing disease burdens in developing states might spur social and economic development—health as a means to development.[33]

ESTIMATING THE COSTS OF POOR HEALTH

Relatively crude "cost of illness" calculations first described in the 1960s allowed the public health community to express the economic burden of disease as a fraction of gross domestic product (GDP), but technical shortcomings rendered these models inconsistent and static. By the early 1990s, concerns about the economic consequences of HIV/AIDS drove researchers to refine these models. More sophisticated macroeconomic analyses arose that take into account not just lost work days but also altered consumption patterns, the loss of human and financial capital accumulation, and changes in the workforce structure, all of which may be aggravated by feedback loops in which disease patterns alter social and economic transactions. These new methodologies do not eliminate uncertainty but do allow comparisons of the national economic burdens of disease past and future. For example, studies estimate that endemic malaria costs high-transmission countries somewhere between 0.66 percent and 1.3 percent in annual per capita income growth—a significant cumulative drain on the highly burdened countries of sub-Saharan Africa over decades.[34]

The 1990s also brought a new focus on the microeconomic impacts of poor health. Disease and premature mortality tend to reduce household earnings. In the absence of public or private insurance or other means of pooling risk, households may face overwhelming out-of-pocket costs for health care services (e.g., the direct costs of medicines, clinical and hospital fees, and travel). Poorer households tend to spend a greater proportion of their income on health costs and are more likely to exhaust savings and liquidate assets to cope with even a single hospitalization. Surveys undertaken between 1990 and 2003 suggest that catastrophic medical spending drives more than 100 million people into poverty each year, 90 percent of them in low-income nations.[35] This spiraling debt can trap generations in poverty.

The enormous HIV/AIDS burden in many sub-Saharan African countries has particularly corrosive effects on household productivity, consumption, and savings. HIV-related illnesses and stigma often rob infected adults of the ability to participate fully in the workforce, including in the agricultural sector, erasing income and perpetuating household food insecurity. Children (particularly girls) are more likely to forego health care and educational opportunities, either due to the lack of resources for school materials or because of the need for additional household labor. Studies show that households are not likely to rebound to previous income levels following the death of the head of household from HIV/AIDS.[36]

The microeconomic impact of HIV/AIDS also affects businesses. Lost labor productivity, worker absenteeism, employee benefits, and turnover of skilled personnel due to HIV/AIDS add an estimated 0.4–5.9 percent to annual salaries and wage bills for businesses in affected sub-Saharan African countries, erasing any competitive advantages of low labor costs. Reduced productivity also reduces potential export earnings. Cumulatively, studies have estimated the loss to GDP per capita in the most heavily HIV-burdened nations at 0.6–4 percent, with the impact roughly proportionate to adult prevalence.[37]

The impact of HIV/AIDS, malaria, and other diseases of poverty varies among countries, ameliorated or exaggerated by national health policies and social insurance mechanisms. Because populations often suffer from comorbidities, or multiple simultaneous conditions, estimates of income lost to each specific condition cannot be simply added to reach a total national economic burden of disease. However, more sophisticated estimates of the micro- and macroeconomic effects of poor health—backed by empirical observation—give health advocates a pragmatic approach. If decision makers are not moved to seek "the attainment of the highest possible level of health" as a "worldwide social goal," as articulated at Alma-Ata, they might be convinced to support interventions that free human and financial capital and alleviate expenditures that offer populations little marginal utility.

ACCELERATING DEVELOPMENT THROUGH HEALTH—COUNTRY CASE STUDIES

Thailand and China offer examples of countries that pursued contrasting capacity-building strategies, accomplishing health and development objectives simultaneously.

Thailand's commitment to health systems strengthening began in the 1920s when Prince Mahidol, known as the "Father of Modern Medicine and Public Health of Thailand," became convinced that improved population health could catalyze national socioeconomic development. This required the transition to a modern health system built on the foundation of a skilled health workforce, which Thailand lacked entirely. While earning his own degrees in public health and medicine in the United States, Prince Mahidol negotiated an agreement with the Rockefeller Foundation on behalf of the Royal Thai government to provide technical and financial assistance for health education.[38] After a number of disease control projects, the Thai–Rockefeller partnership settled into a two-phase strategy: provide fellowships to allow superlative Thai students to pursue advanced education at US or European institutions, and support expatriate professors to lead the development of university life sciences departments until their Thai successors could assume their places. By 1978, the program at Mahidol University showcased Rockefeller's "University Development" efforts: the now entirely Thai faculty had produced dozens of doctorate and hundreds of master's degree graduates in life sciences, most of whom chose to remain within Thailand as productive researchers, teachers, and practitioners, embraced by academic and public health systems that offered rewarding professional development opportunities.[39]

The growing public health and clinical workforce staffed Thailand's expanding network of provincial and district hospitals and community health centers that made skilled medical care accessible even in poor rural areas, ensured by mandatory three-year periods of postgraduate rural service and augmented by more than eight hundred thousand village health volunteers. Starting in the 1970s, the government offered essential maternal, newborn, and child health services without charge, and by the 1990s had accomplished near universal childhood immunization rates and skilled birth attendance. Community access to effective contraceptives helped reduce total fertility rates to population replacement levels by 1990. Between 1990 and 2006, Thailand reduced child mortality by an average rate of 8.5 percent per year, the steepest reduction among low- and middle-income countries.[40] Successive national socioeconomic plans and constitutions defined health as an element of economic development and a basic right, supporting reforms that culminated in universal health coverage in 2001.[41]

Although imperfect, Thailand ultimately achieved equitable health care financing backed by high-quality essential health services and a strong knowledge base. Despite regional and global financial crises, gross national income per capita rose and poverty rates fell between 1990 and 2009, and Thailand met its MDG targets ahead of time.[42] At the microeconomic level, the incidence of impoverishment due to catastrophic medical spending declined among poor Thai households, even as their use of health services climbed steadily.[43]

China also partnered with the Rockefeller Foundation in the 1920s to build institutions for medical training, most notably the Peking Union Medical College, which produced a generation of medical leaders before succumbing to institutional and political stresses. By the 1960s public health leaders worldwide had begun to debate whether health workforce training in less-developed countries should emulate developed country models, producing a corps of trained professionals capable of delivering specialized care, or whether larger numbers of paramedical health workers should be trained to deliver less sophisticated community care.[44]

Upon taking power in 1949 the Chinese Communist Party (CCP) instituted universal health coverage and a series of public health campaigns to reduce staggering infectious disease and infant mortality rates. Mass campaigns engaged the public in efforts to control disease vectors and improve access to safe water, sanitation, and adequate nutrition. The CCP also centralized management of all health facilities, from urban hospitals to the rural cooperative medical system of village and township health centers.[45]

Despite policies that compulsorily relocated most medical graduates to rural areas, Mao Zedong remained unsatisfied with the resources available to China's 500 million rural peasants. In 1968, the CCP announced a national program that would send "barefoot doctors" with three to six months' training to serve at the village level. The barefoot doctor program added cost-effective interventions such as immunizations, skilled birth attendance, sanitation measures, and simple medical and surgical treatments to the panoply of traditional medicines, bringing modern health services to previously underserved communities.[46]

Aside from the famine caused by China's Great Leap Forward, this combination of concerted public health campaigns and expanded health care coverage steadily reduced infant mortality rates from more than two hundred to just thirty-four deaths per one thousand live births between the 1950s and early 1980s. Life expectancies nearly doubled, from thirty-five to sixty-eight years. At the same time, China's economy expanded rapidly, with average annual GDP growth of more than 8 percent. The story in China becomes more clouded with the 1978 decision to include the health system in transformational economic reforms. The CCP abruptly decentralized its health care and public health systems, devolving most responsibilities to the provincial and local levels while cutting central government health spending. To cushion the microeconomic effects of sudden privatization, strict government regulations allowed profits only on new drugs and technologies, encouraging barefoot doctors to peddle unnecessary treatments with little training. With the simultaneous dismantlement of the commune system, 900 million rural citizens lost guaranteed access to health care at once. Wealthy urban and coastal provinces continued to offer a relatively high level of services while the quality of care in poor rural areas became wildly uneven and out-of-pocket expenses rose. By 1999, only 7 percent of Chinese in rural areas had health insurance, compared to nearly 50 percent in urban areas. Although national life expectancies continued to lengthen at a more modest rate, infant mortality actually increased in rural areas between 1999 and 2005 as it fell in urban areas.[47]

Other countries successfully reduced mortality rates by more than 80 percent between 1976 and 2005, most notably Oman, Malaysia, and Chile. All of these cases share features: political leaders embraced health as a means to development *and* an entitlement. They committed resources to training health workers, who in turn supported equitable access to essential health services. Population health indicators improved, and households and incomes saw productivity rise and costs of health care fall. Economic growth created the resources to improve health systems still further and to ameliorate environmental health risks through public health interventions and rising living standards.[48]

Successes in improving child survival over the last decade demonstrate that public health interventions can ameliorate risks in developing regions without profound changes in relative wealth. However, one subset of low-income states has proved a stubborn exception to even incremental progress in life expectancies: those plagued by stagnant economic growth, a lack of legitimate political authorities, violence and conflict, corruption, and weak social and governmental institutions. Defined variously as "weak," "fragile," or "failing states," or as "low-income countries under stress," these countries account for about 10 percent of the world's population but a much larger share of its disease burden.[49]

ACCELERATING DEVELOPMENT THROUGH HEALTH: INTERNATIONAL ASSISTANCE STRATEGIES

In the 1970s, demographer Samuel Preston evaluated the association between income and health status, offering an alternative interpretation of the health–wealth link. His work tracked national per capita income levels and total life expectancy at birth for many countries over the first half of the twentieth century. Although life expectancies remained higher among developed than developing countries at any given point, life spans in each group rose consistently over time. The "Preston curve," which continues to hold true through the twenty-first century, suggested that some factor beyond income growth alone accounted for decreased mortality. Preston proposed that global diffusion of knowledge and health technologies might account for the steep worldwide increase in life expectancies.[50]

This logic underpins global health initiatives: if passively transferred public health advances developed in high-income states can reduce premature mortality in low- and middle-income countries, active technical assistance backed by resources should accelerate the same trends. Technological advances such as vaccination campaigns offer one of the most cost-effective examples. Vaccines, generally developed by the private sector in high-income states, can significantly improve child survival but may be excluded from developing country health plans because of cost. Donors can immunize populations directly or subsidize vaccine purchase for national immunization programs.[51] For example, an aggressive global vaccination campaign jointly supported by WHO, UNICEF, the American Red Cross, and the US Centers for Disease Control and Prevention helped reduce worldwide measles deaths by 74 percent between 2000 and 2007, from an estimated 750,000 annual preventable deaths to 197,000 (primarily in South and Southeast Asia).[52] The reduction of childhood illness presumably decreases the household costs of medical treatment and lost productivity for caretakers, although data to back this assumption remain frustratingly incomplete for the countries where the information is needed most. Technical interventions need not be expensive to be effective. Oral rehydration therapy, a formula of clean water, salt, and sugar developed through careful research, is estimated to avert up to 1 million child deaths each year from diarrheal diseases, requiring only common household ingredients and public health education.[53]

Concerns about the development impact of HIV/AIDS helped catalyze unprecedented increases in health assistance between 1990 and 2007 to accelerate this diffusion of knowledge and technologies. Worldwide, annual official development assistance for health more than doubled between 2001 and 2007, reaching $22.1 billion. Spending on HIV/AIDS accounted for about one-third of all global health assistance in 2007, driven by the massive US President's Emergency Plan for AIDS Relief—the largest single-disease campaign in history with a ten-year commitment of $63 billion.[54]

Governments, multilateral organizations, civil society, and private sector actors formed dozens of new public–private partnerships, including the Global Fund to Fight AIDS, Tuberculosis and Malaria and the Global Alliance for Vaccines and Immunization, in the hopes of using this massive infusion of resources innovatively. "Philanthrocapitalists," including the Bill and Melinda Gates Foundation, suddenly wielded significant influence in developing regions. Between 2000 and 2006, the Gates Foundation pledged about $6.2 billion to combat diseases that primarily affect the developing world—an amount roughly equivalent to the entire working budget of WHO during the same period.[55] Estimated annual overseas expenditures of privately contributed resources by US-based nongovernmental organizations increased to more than $3 billion by 2006 (although this number may exaggerate the value of in-kind contributions by corporate donors).[56]

Most debates about health assistance focus not on the question of whether these global health initiatives support broader development strategies, but on how to improve aid effectiveness (see Morrow's chapter in this volume). With sustained political and financial support, good management and strong training, appropriate tools, appropriate interventions and delivery systems, and good information management, public health initiatives can control conditions known to reduce household and macroeconomic productivity.[57]

Arguments that such interventions have propelled socioeconomic progress by alleviating disease burdens depend very much on context. Logically, greater investments in global health initiatives should yield concomitant improvements in health status. However, this is not necessarily the case. First, countries with the most significant disease burdens often started with the most fragmented health systems and lack capacity to absorb health assistance effectively at the community level. Disease-focused global health initiatives can address challenges, such as rapid increases in HIV/AIDS incidence that might otherwise overwhelm fragile health systems, freeing recipient countries to pursue their own development strategies.[58] However, these initiatives can also tax local resources, particularly given the estimated deficit of 2.4 million doctors, nurses and midwives in fifty-seven countries (mostly African) identified as having a critical shortage of health workers.[59] Faced with a lack of human resources, donors may either recruit scarce skilled health workers into programs that serve only a fraction of the population or may turn to international organizations to implement full-scale health initiatives quickly, doing little to build local capacities or ownership sustainably.

Second, although donors can now turn to a growing evidence base on the impact of specific diseases and the cost-effectiveness of interventions, they often target health assistance based on other priorities.[60] For example, although HIV/AIDS is undeniably a serious and preventable problem, donors earmarked funding for

HIV/AIDS that exceeded the "fair share" of the total disease burden from 1996–2003. In contrast, donors allocated only 2 percent of spending directly to acute respiratory infections, which accounted for about 25 percent of the calculated disease burden during the same general period.[61] Donors often target diseases or conditions that most concern their constituents, and shower aid on "donor darlings" perceived as particularly capable, transparent, or compliant. The influx of resources from multiple sources can leave developing countries with the attractive prospect of choosing among projects that best meet their own development priorities. In practice, the logistical demands of coordinating the plurality of stakeholders on the ground may overwhelm local planning and management capacities, diverting local resources from meeting patient needs to meeting administrative demands.[62]

HEALTH AND DEVELOPMENT: THE UNFINISHED AGENDA

Public health interventions that can reduce deaths and disabilities in developing countries are often well understood but fail to reach the most vulnerable populations, particularly women and children.[63] As many as 2.5 million children died of vaccine-preventable diseases in 2002, a problem of service delivery rather than technology. For example, almost two-thirds of the 23.3 million infants who missed their recommended measles immunization in 2007 lived in eight densely populated countries: the emerging economies of Indonesia, China, India, and Nigeria as well as Ethiopia, Pakistan, the Democratic Republic of the Congo, and Bangladesh.[64] Barriers include underdeveloped roads and transit infrastructures as well as the inability to maintain the "cold chain" needed to preserve the efficacy of some vaccines. Societal issues also play a significant role. Low levels of maternal education translate into decreased demand for vaccinations or other cost-effective prevention strategies, particularly where informal or poorly educated health care providers do not advocate such interventions.[65]

The health and development impacts of complex emergencies can persist for decades. Damage to infrastructure and the threat of violence often prevent public and private sector heath actors from reaching vulnerable populations with essential health services. In Sierra Leone, Angola, and Afghanistan, the risk that a child will die before the age of five is more than 250 per 1,000 live births; an estimated 1,800 women died of complications from pregnancy per every 100,000 live births in Afghanistan in 2005, contributing to a 1 in 8 lifetime risk of maternal death.[66] Unstable or repressive regimes rarely possess the capabilities and political will to integrate high-priority health interventions into integrated and equitable health systems, and donors face perennial challenges in making a transition from humanitarian assistance to sufficient, predictable, and coordinated health aid.[67]

Although overall under-five child mortality rates have declined worldwide over the last three decades, serious inequities remain. Of all health indicators, infant mortality tends to track most closely with wealth. Infant mortality rates serve as a reasonable proxy measurement of overall population health because they reflect environmental health risks and access to essential health services.[68] The divergence between average life expectancies at birth in more developed and least developed countries narrowed between 1950 and 2005 as life expectancies lengthened by thirteen and twenty years, respectively. During the same period, the least developed countries cut average infant mortality rates (deaths before one year of age per one thousand live births) in half, to around eighty deaths per one thousand live births. In contrast, infant mortality rates in more developed regions fell from about sixty to six deaths per one thousand live births between 1950 and 2005.[69] This means that the gap between average infant mortality rates in more and least developed countries actually grew during the late twentieth century, from about threefold to a thirteenfold difference.

This unfinished agenda persists even as the global health landscape is changing dramatically. Chronic noncommunicable diseases already cause a greater share of deaths and disabilities throughout the developing world than communicable diseases.[70] Climate change will affect disease distribution and increase stresses on already scarce fresh drinking water. In 2008 the world's urban population exceeded its rural population for the first time. An estimated one-third of the world's urban population—1 billion people—lived in slums, primarily in low- and middle-income countries. The very criteria used to define slums (lack of water, lack of sanitation, overcrowding, and nondurable housing structures) constitute environmental health risks.[71] These problems might once have been considered local challenges. Now, the implications of failures go far beyond immediate impact: the "international cities" of the developing world are often crossroads for the movement of people, animals, and goods (and the health risks that they carry) as well as drivers of national or even regional economic development.

As during the nineteenth century, the rapid international movement of people, animals, and information associated with intensified globalization has heightened both the risks for major health crises and general public awareness of their human impact. The SARS outbreak of 2003 helped catalyze adoption of the revised International Health Regulations (IHR, 2005) by WHO member states. The IHR legally requires all state parties to develop the capacity to detect, report, and respond to public health emergencies of international concern in a timely way, a profound shift from prior international agreements that focused on controlling specific diseases at borders and ports.[72] Although the IHR framework emphasizes the mutual responsibilities of all states to prevent international health crises, the demands may also be perceived as an enormous obligation for developing states assumed primarily for the benefit of wealthy states.[73] The securitization of global health interests has engendered tension among advocates who fear that the global health agenda has become conflated with US national interests, as reflected by the threat logic that values emerging disease control over pro-poor policies addressed at reducing health inequities.[74]

Such concerns are part of larger debates about the development–continuum gap, equity, the purposes and utility of aid, and the roles of health and development institutions. The past three decades have witnessed increasingly pervasive, if tacit, acceptance of health promotion as an ethical obligation and logical outcome of development. Conversely, arguments that a relatively small investment in the health of the world's poorest citizens could yield a rich harvest of economic and political stability helped catapult health issues onto foreign policy and security agendas for middle- and high-income nations, securing unprecedented resources. The question of whether development should be viewed as a means to health, or health as a means to development, is unlikely to be resolved in the near future. In part, this reflects the very pragmatic outlook of the global health community. At the practical level, a rights-based approach can help strengthen institutions that sustain equitable, acceptable, and effective health systems and health actions. Investments in public health predicated on building human capital and offsetting the most disruptive impacts of industrialization can accomplish the same ends, ultimately increasing the resources available to invest in even more comprehensive health services. In the long run, the two approaches mutually reinforce better alignment of health priorities with the greatest needs—and a movement toward health initiatives as building blocks of human security rather than weapons in a war against disease.

Notes

1. UN, "World Population Prospects: The 2008 Revision Highlights," Working Paper No. ESA/P/WP.210 (New York: United Nations, 2009). www.un.org/esa/population/publications /wpp2008/wpp2008_highlights.pdf.

2. WHO, *The Global Burden of Disease: 2004 Update* (Geneva: WHO, 2008).

3. Rachel Nugent, "Chronic Diseases in Developing Countries: Health and Economic Burdens," *Annals of the New York Academy of Sciences* 1136 (2008): 70–79.

4. Simon Szreter, "The Population Health Approach in Historical Perspective," *American Journal of Public Health* 93 (2003): 421–31.

5. Obijifor Aginam, *Global Health Governance* (Toronto: University of Toronto Press, 2005), 46–59.

6. Simon Szreter, "Industrialization and Health," *British Medical Bulletin* 69 (2004): 75–86.

7. Gareth Jones, Richard W. Steketee, Zulfiqar A. Bhutta, and Saul S. Morris, "How Many Child Deaths Can We Prevent This Year?" *Lancet* 362 (2003): 65–71.

8. Annette Prüss-Üstün and Carlos Corvalán, *Preventing Disease through Healthy Environments: Towards an Estimate of the Environmental Burden of Disease* (Geneva: WHO, 2006). www .who.int/quantifying_ehimpacts/publications/preventingdisease.pdf.

9. Majid Ezzati, Alan D. Lopez, Anthony Rodgers, Stephen Vander Hoorn, Christopher J. L. Murray, and the Comparative Risk Assessment Collaborating Group, "Selected Major Risk Factors and Global and Regional Burden of Disease," *Lancet* 360 (2002): 1347–60.

10. Robert E. Black, Lindsay H. Allen, Zulfiqar A. Bhutta, Laura E. Caulfield, Mercedes de Onis, Majid Ezzati, Colin Mathers, and Juan Rivera, "Maternal and Child Undernutrition: Global and Regional Exposures and Health Consequences," *Lancet* 371 (2008): 243–60.

11. UNICEF, *State of the World's Children 2009: Maternal and Newborn Health?* (New York: UNICEF, 2009), 8.

12. Peter J. Hotez, Alan Fenwick, Lorenzo Savioli, and David H. Molyneux, "Rescuing the Bottom Billion through Control of Neglected Tropical Diseases," *Lancet* 373 (2009): 1570–75.

13. Amar Hamoudi and Jeffrey D. Sachs, *The Changing Global Distribution of Malaria: A Review* (Cambridge, MA: Harvard Center for International Development, 1999).

14. D. A. Walton, P. Farmer, and R. Dillingham, "Social and Cultural Factors in Tropical Medicine" in *Tropical Infectious Diseases*, ed. Richard L. Guerrant, David H. Walker, and Peter F. Weller (New York: Elsevier Press, 2005), 26–35.

15. Kevin H. O'Rourke and Jeffrey G. Williamson, *When Did Globalisation Begin?* (Cambridge, MA: National Bureau of Economic Research, 2000).

16. Richard J. Evans, "Epidemics and Revolutions: Cholera in Nineteenth-Century Europe," *Past and Present* 120 (1988): 123–46.

17. David P. Fidler, "The Globalization of Public Health: The First 100 Years of International Health Diplomacy," *Bulletin of the World Health Organization* 79 (2001): 842–49.

18. John Farley, *To Cast out Disease* (New York: Oxford University Press, 2004).

19. Charles-Edward A. Winslow, "International Health," *American Journal of Public Health* 41, no. 12 (1951): 1455–59.

20. WHO, *The First Ten Years of the World Health Organization* (Geneva: WHO, 1958).

21. WHO, *The State of the World's Children* (New York: UNICEF, 1996).

22. Donald A. Henderson, "Eradication: Lessons from the Past," *Morbidity and Mortality Weekly Report* 48, no. SU01 (1999): 16–22.

23. "Declaration of Alma-Ata" (Alma-Ata, USSR: WHO International Conference on Primary Health Care, 1978).

24. Lawrence O. Gostin, *Public Health Law, Power, Duty, and Restraint*, 2nd ed. (Berkeley: University of California Press, 2008), 270–83.

25. Szreter, "Industrialization and Health."

26. Abdel R. Omran, "The Epidemiological Transition: A Theory of the Epidemiology of Population Change," *Millbank Memorial Fund Quarterly* 49 (1971): 509–38.

27. Richard Jolly, "Adjustment with a Human Face: A UNICEF Record and Perspective on the 1980s," *World Development* 19 (1991): 1807–21.

28. WHO, *World Health Report 2008: Primary Health Care—Now More than Ever* (Geneva: WHO, 2008).

29. World Bank, *World Development Report 1993: Investing in Health* (New York: Oxford University Press, 1993).

30. Joseph E. Stiglitz, "More Instruments and Broader Goals: Moving toward the Post-Washington Consensus," UN University-WIDER Annual Lecture, March 1998, available at www.wider.unu.edu/publications/annual-lectures/en_GB/AL2/; and Amartya Sen, "Why Health Equity?" in *Public Health, Ethics, and Equity*, ed. Sudhir Anand, Fabienne Peter and Amartya Sen (Oxford: Clarendon Press, 2004).

31. WHO, "A Call for Healthy Development" in *WHO Report on Infectious Diseases* (Geneva: WHO, 1999).

32. UN General Assembly Resolution 55/2, September 18, 2000.

33. WHO, *Macroeconomics and Health: Investing in Health for Economic Development*, Report of the Commission on Macroeconomics and Health (Geneva: WHO, 2001).

34. Department of Health Systems Financing, *WHO Guide to Identifying the Economic Consequences of Disease and Injury* (Geneva: WHO, 2009).

35. Ke Xu, David B. Evans, Guido Carrin, Ana Mylena Aguilar-Rivera, Philip Musgrove, and Timothy Evans, "Protecting Households from Catastrophic Health Spending," *Health Affairs* 26 (2007): 972–83.

36. Marisa Casale and Alan Whiteside, "The Impact of HIV/AIDS on Poverty, Inequality and Economic Growth," IDRC Working Papers on Globalization, Growth and Poverty Working Paper Number 3 (Ottawa: International Development Research Centre, March 2006).

37. Simon Dixon, Scott McDonald, and Jennifer Roberts, "The Impact of HIV and AIDS on Africa's Economic Development," *British Medical Journal* 324 (2002): 232–34; and Casale and Whiteside, "Impact of HIV/AIDS."

38. "A Complete Biography of His Royal Highness Prince Mahidol of Songkla," *Prince Mahidol Award Foundation* (2006), www.princemahidolaward.org/complete-biography.en.php.

39. James S. Coleman, "Professorial Training and Institution Building in the Third World: Two Rockefeller Foundation Experiences," *Comparative Education Review* 28 (1984): 180–202.

40. Jon Rohde, Simon Cousens, Mickey Chopra, Viroj Tangcharoensathien, Robert Black, Zulfiqar A. Bhutta, and Joy E. Lawn, "30 Years after Alma-Ata: Has Primary Health Care Worked in Countries?" *Lancet* 372 (2008): 950–61.

41. Thaworn Sakunphanit, "Universal Health Care Coverage through Pluralistic Approaches: Experience from Thailand," Social Security Extension Initiatives in East Asia series (Bangkok: ILO Subregional Office for East Asia, 2008). www.ilo.org/public /english/region/asro/bangkok/events/sis/download/paper31.pdf.

42. World Development Indicators database, World Bank, accessed January 30, 2011, http://data.worldbank.org/data-catalog/world-development-indicators.

43. Tewarit Somkotra and Leizel P. Lagrada, "Payments for Health Care and Its Effect on Catastrophe and Impoverishment: Experience from the Transition to Universal Coverage in Thailand," *Social Science & Medicine* 67 (2008): 2027–35.

44. Coleman, "Professorial Training."

45. Therese Hesketh and Wei Xing Zhu, "Health in China: From Mao to Market Reform," *British Medical Journal* 314 (1997): 1543–45.

46. Daqing Zhang and Paul U. Unschuld, "China's Barefoot Doctor: Past, Present, and Future," *Lancet* 372 (2008): 1865–67.

47. David Blumenthal and William Hsiao, "Privatization and Its Discontents: The Evolving Chinese Health Care System," *New England Journal of Medicine* 252 (2005): 1165–70.

48. WHO, *World Health Report 2008.*

49. Ibid.

50. Samuel H. Preston, "The Changing Relation between Mortality and Level of Economic Development," *Population Studies* 34 (1975): 231–48.

51. Tore Godal, "Viewpoint: Immunization against Poverty," *Tropical Medicine and International Health* 5 (2000): 160–66.

52. "Progress in Global Measles Control and Mortality Reduction, 2000–2007," *Morbidity and Mortality Weekly Report* 57, no. 48 (2008): 1303–6.

53. Joshua Nalibow Ruxin, "Magic Bullet: The History of Oral Hydration Therapy," *Medical History* 38 (1994): 363–97.

54. Jennifer Kates, Eric Lief, and Jonathan Pearson, *Donor Funding for Health in Low- & Middle-Income Countries, 2001–2007* (Washington, DC: Kaiser Family Foundation, 2009).

55. Jon Cohen, "The New World of Global Health," *Science* 311 (2006): 162–67.

56. Nirmala Ravishankar, Paul Gubbins, Rebecca J. Cooley, Katherine Leach-Kemon, Catherine M. Michaud, Dean T. Jamison, and Christopher J. L. Murray, "Financing of Global Health: Tracking Development Assistance for Health from 1990 to 2007," *Lancet* 373 (2009): 2113–24.

57. Ruth Levine, ed., *Millions Saved: Proven Success in Global Health* (Washington, DC: Center for Global Development, 2006).

58. WHO Maximizing Positive Synergies Collaborative Group, "An Assessment of Interactions between Global Health Initiatives and Country Health Systems," *Lancet* 373 (2009): 2137–69.

59. WHO, *World Health Report 2006: Working Together for Health* (Geneva: WHO, 2006).

60. Eeva Ollila, "Global Health Priorities: Priorities of the Wealthy?" *Globalization and Health* 1, no. 6 (2005).

61. Jeremy Shiffman, "Donor Funding Priorities for Communicable Disease Control in the Developing World," *Health Policy and Planning* 21, no. 6 (2006): 411–20.

62. Denis Drechsler and Felix Zimmermann, *New Actors in Health Financing: Implications for a Donor Darling* (Paris: OECD Development Centre, 2006).

63. Jones et al., "How Many Child Deaths."

64. "Progress in Global Measles Control and Mortality Reduction, 2000-2007," *Morbidity and Mortality Weekly Report* 57, no. 48 (2008): 1303–6.

65. "Vaccine Preventable Deaths and the Global Immunization Vision and Strategy, 2006–2015," *Mortality and Morbidity Weekly Report* 55 (2006): 511–15.

66. *The State of the World's Children 2008* (New York: UNICEF, December 2007).

67. WHO and World Bank, "Health in Fragile States: An Overview Note," High-Level Forum on Health MDGs, Paris, November 14–15, 2005, accessed January 30, 2011, www.hlf healthmdgs.org/Documents/HealthFragileStates.pdf.

68. D. D. Reidpath and P. Allotey, "Infant Mortality Rate as an Indicator of Population Health," *Journal of Epidemiology and Community Health* 57 (2003): 344–46.

69. UN, "World Population Prospects."

70. Nugent, "Chronic Diseases."

71. UN-HABITAT, *The State of the World's Cities Report 2006/7* (London: Earthscan, 2006).

72. WHO, *International Health Regulations (2005)*, 2nd ed. (Geneva: WHO, 2008).

73. Sara E. Davies, "Securitizing Infectious Disease," *International Affairs*, 84, no. 2 (2008): 295.

74. Ollila, "Global Health Priorities."

HEALTH
Editors' Comments

Joanna Spear and Paul D. Williams

Unlike some other issue areas, both the security and the development perspectives agree on the definition and nature of the major contemporary health challenges, namely, the effects of existing and newly emerging infectious diseases. They also agree that the disease burden is spread hugely unevenly across the planet and that the lack of respect that health challenges show for political boundaries means they deserve the greater attention that they have received in recent decades. From the security arena, the increased attention has been largely stimulated by the impact of the HIV/AIDS pandemic but also by concerns about bird flu and bioterrorism. In the case of development, the new focus on global health equity was stimulated in large part by the speed with which diseases were able to straddle the globe and by the impact this could have on undermining trade and trust between states.

Both arenas also agree on some of the central problems and limitations of current responses. For example, both call for greater effort to be devoted to building effective health infrastructures. There are also shared concerns about the need for more effective coordination between the diverse agendas and philosophies of a bewildering range of state and nonstate actors and public–private instruments engaged in health care provision. There are also shared concerns over prioritization as well as how to weigh the relative salience of issues, both how health issues should relate to other development and security priorities and which health challenges are the most pressing. To date, most of the policy debate has concerned the appropriate degree of attention and resources that should go to combating HIV/AIDS, but this has sometimes come at the neglect of other health challenges. Moreover, Fidas's chapter is an appeal for the security arena to take more seriously the ways in which health challenges not only affect human security but also pose significant challenges for systems of governance and military effectiveness.

The most prominent area of divergence concerns the impact of "securitization" in the health sector. Not surprisingly, Fidas is comfortable that framing health challenges as security threats is not only a necessary reflection of their potency but it is also more likely to deliver high-level attention and help reform the traditional defense sector. He suggests that it has already worked to good effect through initiatives such as the US President's Emergency Plan for AIDS Relief. Fischer, in contrast, is worried about the way securitization has prompted a shift in focus from the individual to protecting national and regional interests. This has generated concerns among development specialists who fear that the global health agenda has become conflated with US national interests, as reflected by the threat logic that values emerging disease control over pro-poor policies addressed at reducing health inequities.

In terms of policy processes and effectiveness, the traditional view in development circles was that advances in development would lead to better health for populations. More recent research, however, suggests that reducing disease burdens may actually be a prerequisite for development. In particular, more needs to be done to reduce infant mortality. For development, therefore, the major problems and elements of success in health care projects are reasonably well known. The problem is how to ensure that these lessons are practiced.

Both perspectives acknowledge the need for the sustained political will and leadership from the great powers. Finally, both see health as an issue that cuts across all levels of analysis: from building effective local health infrastructures to designing global surveillance capabilities. The major obstacle is how this can be done in a world of sovereign states sensitive about parochial politics.

Part V

POVERTY

Chapter 10

POVERTY

A Security Perspective

Paul D. Williams

Poverty is considered an important subject for political analysis for several reasons. For some, it is morally reprehensible and thus its alleviation should be the central target of development policies. Objective number 1 of the Millennium Development Goals, for instance, is to halve, between 1990 and 2015, the proportion of people whose income is less than one dollar a day. For others, poverty is thought of as a sickness. The World Health Organization's International Classification of Diseases, for example, classifies extreme poverty as disease Z59.5 (under problems relating to housing and economic circumstances).

But is poverty a security threat? For most of the Cold War, mainstream security studies relegated poverty to the category of low politics.[1] During this period security studies remained preoccupied with military threats to the world's most powerful states; particularly questions of nuclear strategy and crisis management. More recently, however, poverty became an important part of debates within security studies at a variety of levels. Poverty has clearly always been important for those who suffer from it, but with the end of the Cold War, poverty started to receive greater attention from the world's most powerful actors. By the turn of the twenty-first century, poverty was firmly established as part of the security studies agenda. British prime minister Tony Blair aptly summarized much of the official thinking on this issue in the foreword to his government's second white paper on international development. Here Blair highlighted the links between underdevelopment, injustice, and the United Kingdom's security, arguing that "many of the problems which affect us—war and conflict, international crime and the trade in illicit drugs, and the spread of health pandemics like HIV/AIDS—are caused or exacerbated by poverty."[2] This line of thinking also had powerful supporters elsewhere within the United Nations (UN) system, especially after the publication of the report of the Secretary-General's High Level Panel, *A More Secure World*. This identified economic and social threats, including poverty, as one of the six clusters of serious threats to international security.[3]

Statements such as these raise at least as many questions as they answer. Perhaps above all, they assume that we know what poverty is and what its political effects are. Unfortunately, this is not the case, not least because there is no universally accepted definition of poverty. As a consequence, there is no uncontested sense of which people fall into this category let alone agreement about how it affects their psychology and behavior. Instead, there exists a variety of competing approaches to thinking about poverty. For the purposes of this chapter, these can be divided into four main approaches: monetary, capability, social exclusion, and participatory.[4]

The monetary approach defines poverty as a shortfall in consumption (or income) from some previously identified poverty line. In contrast, the capabilities approach views poverty as deprivation in or failure to achieve certain "basic capabilities" defined as "the ability to satisfy certain crucially important functionings up to certain minimally adequate levels."[5] This approach places a heavy emphasis on the concept of human freedom as developed in the work of Amartya Sen. A third approach defines poverty as a form of social exclusion. According to a widely used definition adopted by the European Union, social exclusion is the "process through which individuals or groups are wholly or partially excluded from full participation in the society in which they live."[6] Here emphasis is placed on the potentially suffocating consequences social structures may exert upon certain individuals and groups. Finally, the participatory approach looks at the issue from the standpoint of those who are thought to be suffering from poverty; it gets these people to participate in decisions about what it means to be poor and the magnitude of poverty. The problems here, of course, are that this technique assumes we know which people to ask, and that it does not always provide a satisfactory means of adjudicating between competing accounts.

All four approaches suffer from huge problems concerning data availability and collection. All the approaches agree, however, that it is useful to try to define a category of "poverty" and that there is "some form of discontinuity between the poor and the non-poor that can be reflected in the poverty line."[7] There is therefore thought to be some form of qualitative inequality between the categories of poor/nonpoor that matters socially. Whereas the monetary approach draws our attention to economic inequality, the capabilities and social exclusion approaches focus more on issues of political and social inequality. I submit that while the absolute poverty associated with the monetary approach is clearly a huge security threat to many individual human beings, at the state and global levels the relationship between poverty and security is more significant if one adopts the capabilities or social exclusion approaches than if one thinks of poverty in monetary terms.

To substantiate this claim, I explore how the category of "the poor" might be considered threatening, and to whom. I do so by analyzing three different levels of the security equation: human security, state security, and global security. At the human level, I briefly discuss how poverty is arguably the primary security threat for a significant proportion of the planet's inhabitants because it can hugely reduce the life chances and choices of these individuals, their families, and other dependents. At the state level, I address three of the most pertinent questions on the contemporary international security agenda: Is there a causal relationship between poverty and armed conflict? Is poverty alleviation an important part of the "war on terror"? And is poverty related to state failure? In each case, the strength of the local state's capabilities and its level of legitimacy with the local population are important factors in deciding the answer. Finally, at the global level, I focus on the issue of inequality and the extent to which the growing divide between the rich and poor is a source of insecurity, especially in a context of large-scale demographic change and rapid urbanization.

Overall, the existence of widespread poverty is a telling sign that a political order is deficient morally, politically, or economically. Poverty can therefore be understood as a signifier of injustice. And to the extent that security is unavoidably about the ethics of how different groups should coexist, poverty should always be an important part of the security agenda.[8]

POVERTY AND HUMAN SECURITY

At the level of individual human beings, poverty is an enormous source of insecurity. If one adopts the monetary approach, estimates suggest that some 1.3 billion people exist on less than one dollar a day and perhaps as many as 3 billion survive on less than two dollars a day. From the perspective of the capabilities and social exclusion approaches, the numbers that fall into the broad category of poverty are even higher. As a condition that dramatically diminishes people's life chances and choices, poverty is thus a major source of insecurity.[9] Indeed, Gary King and Christopher Murray concluded that one potentially measurable definition of human security would be to define it as "the number of years spent outside a state of 'generalized poverty.'"[10] From this perspective, to be poor is to be insecure. As Caroline Thomas has put it, "poverty and human insecurity are in many respects synonymous. Both refer to a human condition characterized by the lack of fulfillment of a range of human entitlements such as adequate food, healthcare, education, shelter, employment and voice."[11]

Poverty renders people insecure in at least two main ways. First, in its extreme form it can dramatically reduce the prospects for longevity. To take just one comparison, a girl born in Japan in the early twenty-first century can look forward to a life expectancy of approximately eighty-five years.[12] A girl born in Zimbabwe during the same period will be lucky to reach her thirty-fifth birthday.[13] Whether it is because they lack steady income or access to basic services, the main contributory factors to this kind of statistic are the challenges poor people face in gaining access to the levels of nutrition, health care, and education that support reasonably high levels of longevity. The second way in which poverty renders people insecure relates to the consequences for family members, the relevant household unit, and other dependents on individuals who fall into poverty. One sole provider losing his or her employment or falling ill could thus jeopardize the human security of wider circle of relatives and other dependents.

POVERTY AND STATE SECURITY

While the threat agendas of the world's states are far from uniform, poverty has featured prominently in three areas of debate relating to armed conflict, terrorism, and state failure. The rest of this section discusses each of these issues in turn.

Armed Conflict

A survey of the relevant academic literature quickly reveals that there is no single or straightforward answer to the question of whether poverty causes armed conflict. In academic international relations, this issue has traditionally been framed as a debate about the relationship between economic inequality and political conflict. Mark Lichbach reflected the general mood in academia at the end of the Cold War when he concluded that the available "evidence supports the view that, in general, economic inequality is neither necessary, sufficient, nor clearly probabilistically related to dissent."[14] In sum, economic inequality may have a positive or negative impact on political dissent, or may have no impact at all. The key analytical issue was therefore to discern under what conditions economic inequality dampens or stimulates conflict among contending groups. This ambiguous conclusion was echoed by analysts who investigated the relationship between armed conflict within states and their Gini coefficient—a measure of statistical dispersion to measure inequality of income distribution. While some found it was related to such conflict, others found it to be insignificant.[15]

These conclusions may be frustrating, but they are all perfectly reasonable if we are content to conclude that there is more than one route to war and that economic inequality may sometimes play a role but not always. If so, the historian's approach of exploring the origins of particular wars might be more appropriate than the political scientist's search for the causes of warfare in general. This conclusion is not very useful, however, for those evaluating whether and when poverty alleviation should be seen as a form of deliberate conflict prevention.

In recent decades things have become a little clearer. It is now commonly accepted that the search for the general causes of warfare is less fruitful than an examination of the risk factors that increase the likelihood of political instability and conflict in particular contexts.[16] From this perspective it has become clear that poverty is a more important risk factor in some types of armed conflict than in others. Using the Uppsala Conflict Data Program's (UCDP) categories of interstate, intrastate, and nonstate armed conflicts, several general conclusions are apparent.[17] Poverty is not an important factor in the outbreak of interstate armed conflicts, especially as the utility of richer states conquering poorer states has declined.

More important for contemporary security studies, however, is the complex relationship between poverty and intrastate armed conflicts. Not only is the historical evidence mixed here, but it is also a more pressing topic for policymakers because the vast majority of contemporary armed conflicts are of the intrastate variety (although a significant proportion of them are internationalized). With regard to intrastate armed conflict, the relevant statistical evidence provides strong support for the idea that high-income countries are less likely to experience civil wars than low-income countries.[18] But as recent cases as diverse as Russia, the Balkans, the United Kingdom, and Spain attest, this does not mean that even relatively rich states are immune from intrastate armed conflicts. Thus while most contemporary examples occur in the poorest parts of the world, this is not necessarily the case. During 2006, for example, the UCDP recorded thirty-two state-based armed conflicts that took place in twenty-three countries.[19] According to the UN Development Program's Human Development Index (2007–8), four of these conflicts occurred in countries with high levels of human development, twenty took place in countries with medium levels of human development, and only eight (or 25 percent) took place in countries categorized as having low levels of human development (Afghanistan, Burundi, Central African Republic, Chad, Ethiopia [two conflicts], Iraq, and Somalia).[20]

The third broad category of armed conflict is nonstate—where organized groups fight without involving government forces.[21] Although research institutions have only recently started to collect systematic data about these conflicts, the UCDP's new database identified 361 such conflicts worldwide between 1989 and 2008. The vast majority of them (267, or 74 percent) have occurred on the world's poorest continent, Africa. These took place in twenty-four different African states and resulted in an estimated combined total of nearly sixty thousand fatalities. Somalia experienced the most nonstate armed conflicts, with nearly sixty identifiable dyads, while overall more than 80 percent of Africa's nonstate conflicts occurred in just seven states (the Democratic Republic of Congo, Ethiopia, Kenya, Nigeria, Somalia, Sudan, and Uganda), all of which were in the Human Development Index category of low human development for 2010.

Given the central importance of intrastate armed conflicts to the current debates about international security, I will focus on them. For some analysts, widespread poverty is not a powerful predictor of civil wars. In an influential set of publications, World Bank and Oxford University economist Paul Collier argued that it was "underlying economic conditions," not political grievances, that "create the risk of conflict." Specifically, he concluded that countries with many primary commodities and many uneducated young men (fifteen- to twenty-four-year-olds) are at the greatest risk. In his approach, the existence of poverty was much less important than these other conditions that permitted some greedy and well-organized individuals to profit from warfare and insurgency. Poverty (in either absolute or relative terms) appears only tangentially in Collier's theory as one factor among several encouraging young men to join a rebellion and thus sustain a conflict.[22] Other forms of economic analysis have stressed the importance of negative shocks in already fragile societies.[23]

Poverty has been considered more important in the sociological and political literature, where it has been given a more prominent place as both an underlying and a proximate factor in the outbreak of intrastate armed conflict. In the former case, poverty is considered one of the central factors—along with inequality and exclusion—which encourage grievances, "particularly when poverty coincides with ethnic, religious, language or regional boundaries."[24] In the latter case, growing economic inequities have been identified as one proximate cause of internal conflict.[25]

In more specific terms, poverty has been linked to the outbreak of particular forms of armed conflict. David Keen, for example, has argued that the lack of economic alternatives may drive poor people to engage in "bottom up" violence.[26] In Keen's view, the war in Sierra Leone (1991–2002) provides a good example of a conflict caused primarily by grievances among the poor and marginalized, particularly those who felt they had been humiliated by representatives of the existing political order and were so desperate that they could see no way forward other than turning to violence. Although supported by a range of actors outside Sierra Leone, the Revolutionary United Front emerged from a pool of poor youth and often articulated its demands in terms of poverty alleviation (in both the monetary and exclusionary senses). For these people, violence offered an opportunity to restore a sense of power and status and invert the existing social hierarchies. Their erstwhile opponents in the form of Sierra Leone's armed forces and the local self-defense forces (the Kamajors) were also mainly drawn from the ranks of the poor.[27]

In a similar vein, Paul Rogers has suggested that increased levels of socioeconomic polarization combined with developments that lead the marginalized to become increasingly aware of their marginalization may lead to a "revolution of unfulfilled expectations." This, he claims, has been evident in many contemporary insurgencies including the Zapatistas, Hamas, and the Islamic Salvation Front in Algeria.[28] Grievances related to social and political exclusion have also been identified as the underlying factor in Liberia's traumatic experience of war recurrence during the 1990s and early 2000s.[29]

A third line of argument has been developed by Frances Stewart and her emphasis on "horizontal inequalities." For Stewart, inequality combined with social and political exclusion, rather than absolute monetary poverty, often lies at the root of the world's protracted conflicts. Inequalities between groups rather than absolute levels of poverty are crucial because protracted wars are based on group mobilization; as such, groups need to be mobilized against other groups in the initial stages of these wars. Inequality is a crucial ingredient because it allows grievances to be directed against another specific group.[30]

In all these accounts, the outbreak of violence is related to occasions when poverty breeds a sense of injustice among the poor. This occurs when a significant gap develops between the expectations of the poor and their existing (and envisaged future) social conditions. Such claims are reminiscent of Ted Gurr's earlier work on the concept of "relative deprivation"—that is, the discrepancy between what people think they deserve and what they actually think they can get. From this perspective, people become frustrated if they do not enjoy what they think they are rightfully entitled to. If such frustration is felt for prolonged periods or intensely enough, it generates anger that may be expressed violently. Consequently, Gurr argued that "the potential for collective violence varies strongly with the intensity and scope of relative deprivation among members of a collectivity."[31]

Anecdotal evidence from a variety of recent conflicts appears to indicate that such feelings of injustice are most likely to occur when people lack access to health care and education, not necessarily when they fall below the (monetary) poverty line. It is also important to note that this sense of injustice is more likely to be held by people who have a degree of knowledge about how their situation compares to others both within and beyond their own society. This has led some analysts to conclude that it is the so-called transient poor (people who move in and out of poverty) who "are more likely to rebel" rather than the chronically poor (people who endure long periods in poverty) because the latter "tend to be the least organized and most passive group in society. Their limited social capital, both a cause and a consequence of their poverty, constrains their capacity for organized resistance. . . . The 'anxious classes' on the verge of poverty are more likely to turn to violence."[32] Put bluntly, the truly destitute have more pressing concerns of day-to-day survival than plotting insurrection.

As noted earlier, however, this does not mean these people will resist joining a significant rebellion once it has started, thus contributing to the sustainability of the conflict. This is important because, along with a sense of injustice, some form of political organization is required to actually start a war; grievances alone are not enough to establish an insurgency.[33] This is where the role of the state is crucial. If state authorities are able to exert control effectively, the voicelessness and powerlessness of the poor is more likely to translate into passivity than insurgency.[34] If, on the other hand, state authorities are weak and unable to control their territory, would-be insurgents are more likely to be able to attract supporters, organize the required resources, and exploit the strategic opportunities necessary to launch and sustain a rebellion. This means that on a priori grounds, "bottom up" violence is more likely within weak states than strong ones. Even so, it is important to remember that the relationships between poverty and internal armed conflict are probabilistic rather than deterministic and contingent upon particular historical conditions.

Terrorism

Like wars, terrorists come in different shapes and sizes, from powerful governments to tiny bands of true believers. Nevertheless, the literature on the relationship between poverty and terrorism has produced some relatively clear conclusions. First and foremost, policymakers and scholars alike agree that there is no clear causal relationship between monetary poverty and terrorism. As US president George W. Bush put it, "Poverty does not transform poor people into terrorists and murderers."[35] Similarly, Alan Krueger has concluded that "at both the individual level and the societal level . . . poor economic conditions do not seem to motivate people to participate in terrorist activities."[36] But this does not mean that there is no connection between monetary poverty and organizations that use terror tactics. Nor does it refute the possibility that poverty understood as a lack of freedom or that social exclusion might be significantly connected to organizations that resort to terrorism. In particular, poverty alleviation is an important part of counterterrorism for three main reasons.

First, there is evidence that some poor people do directly participate in acts of terrorism. For example, in Pakistan and Afghanistan between 2001 and 2007, suicide bombers were largely drawn from the ranks of the poor.[37] Poor people are rarely leaders of terror networks, but they can often be found among the foot soldiers fighting for the cause.

Second, on a priori grounds, the circumstances of people in poverty render them more susceptible than the nonpoor to recruiting strategies employed by radical extremists. This is especially true if they do not receive alternatives to radically fundamentalist forms of education. As Karin von Hippel has argued in relation to

Islamic extremism, education is an important factor in this equation in two main senses. First, even if they do not actively support organizations such as al-Qaeda, less educated people in the Islamic world are more likely to see the worldviews they promote as legitimate.[38] Second, because it is through education that people usually become politicized, if poor people do not receive good education from their state or other sources, they may be educated in "a narrow and violent version of Islam."[39] Receiving certain types of education—that provided in some Pakistani madrassas, for instance—does seem to make individuals more likely to engage in militant behavior. And it is not just education that is significant here. If poor people do not receive adequate health care, nutrition, and shelter from alternative sources, they may be more likely to support movements that provide them with a variety of welfare and charitable services. Movements such as Hezbollah and Hamas have been particularly successful in developing this dimension of their activities.[40] It is also important to recall that the poor might be more susceptible to the financial rewards offered to the families of "martyrs" by certain associations linked to suicide terrorism.[41] In this sense, poverty alleviation and basic service provision might well make it harder for extremists to recruit followers.

A third way in which poverty is related to terrorism is that the very existence of a large pool of poor, marginalized people can make it easier for elites who claim to speak for them to justify why the existing order needs to be violently over-turned. This politicization of poverty is important because even organizations such as al-Qaeda that now have potentially global reach were initially built upon local foundations and hence had to be able to point to local grievances. Although al-Qaeda was forged in the crucible of Afghanistan's wars, it was first and foremost a movement that developed around Arab Sunni radicals with the primary purpose of assuming power in the Arab states, especially Saudi Arabia.[42] In this sense, it is important to recall that despite much of the rhetoric (from Western governments and the movements themselves) describing international terrorism as a global phe-nomenon, in many respects "Islamist movements were primarily caused by, and directed at, conditions *within* their own societies."[43] This is not to deny al-Qaeda's evident desire to kill infidels wherever they might be found but merely to point out the regionally specific origins and primary goals of America's principal enemy. It is in these last two ways that the existence of widespread poverty can help cre-ate what Louise Richardson has called an "enabling environment" for extremist organizations.[44]

State Failure

Although (monetary) poverty is more a symptom than a cause of state failure, it is commonly thought to be related and is therefore often framed as a problem for state security. Jeffrey Sachs summarized a commonly held view of this relationship in the following manner:

> Economic failure abroad raises the risk of state failure. . . . When foreign states malfunction . . . their societies are likely to experience steeply escalating problems that spill over to the rest of the world. . . . Failed states are seedbeds of violence,

terrorism, international criminality, mass migration and refugee movements, drug trafficking, and disease. . . . If poor countries had reliably stable and functional state institutions, global poverty would remain a powerful humanitarian concern but would probably not be a strategic priority for the United States.[45]

From this perspective, poverty in foreign countries is viewed as a security concern because of its part in eroding the ability of the world's governments to control their territories and therefore prevent security threats from seeping beyond their borders. In extreme cases, Sachs suggests that states can fall into a "poverty trap" wherein "a poor country is simply too poor to achieve sustained economic growth." In such circumstances, outside attempts to resuscitate the state are thought to be the only way out.[46]

Such failing states present a range of security challenges both to the people who live in them and to the governments concerned about what might incubate within them and spread out from them. However, it is important to note that the concept of "state failure" commonly obscures much more than it clarifies. As Charles Call has demonstrated, state failure encourages a tendency to aggregate diverse states and their problems, conflate peacefulness with a process of state-building, devise generic Western-approved prescriptions, distract attention from more fundamental questions about democracy and the nature of specific regimes, and obfuscate the West's role in the contemporary condition of these states.[47] In contrast, Call has called for analysts and practitioners to disaggregate the various capacity gaps, legitimacy gaps, and security gaps that states experience.[48]

Regarding the latter, criminal activity remains a major source of concern and is considered a significant security challenge by a growing number of states and international organizations.[49] Although the definition of legality—and, therefore, criminality—is context-specific, particular attention has focused on the illicit trafficking of weapons, narcotics, natural resources, and people. Although poverty can facilitate organized crime, arguably of greater importance are the existence of armed conflict and weak and illegitimate state institutions. For example, armed conflicts tend to dramatically retard the formal economy while providing new opportunities for the informal and clandestine economy. This was clearly the case in Bosnia, as several analysts have demonstrated.[50] But organized crime does not need armed conflict to flourish. In West Africa, for instance, Antonio Mazzitelli has shown how the susceptibility "of national institutions to corruption, the porosity of borders, the structural deficiencies in states' control of their territories and enforcement of the rule of law [help explain] the increased importance of West Africa in the map of transnational organized crime, and the rapid growth and development of West African transnational criminal networks."[51] Of course, crimes do not affect state security equally. Thus, while annoying on a personal level, the flood of Nigerian "419" email scams are not in remotely the same security league as the leverage exerted by drug cartels on political elites in Guinea-Bissau.

At one end of the spectrum are cases where organized crime exists in a symbiotic relationship with the state. This has occurred in several parts of Africa where analysts have long focused on the "criminalization of the state," but it has also been apparent in other parts of the world including the post-Soviet region and the Democratic People's Republic of Korea.[52] At the other end of the spectrum, complete state collapse can affect organized crime in different ways. On the one hand, conditions in a collapsed state such as Somalia do not offer an easy environment for transnational criminals to operate, not least because of the lack of infrastructure, the relatively small numbers of bribable state officials, and the difficulty for foreigners to operate with anonymity. On the other hand, certain well-placed individuals and groups may be able to exploit the lack of official authorities. This has clearly occurred in relation to the recent increase in piracy off the Somali coastline.[53]

In less extreme cases, weak state institutions provide opportunities for well-placed elites to benefit from criminal activities and for marginalized communities to turn to crime as a potential way out of poverty or as part of their survival strategies. In both "criminalized states" and "weak states," criminal activity will often be used to target opponents and to provide pay-offs to potential supporters. Once again, however, poverty understood in its monetary sense is less important than poverty understood as marginalization and exclusion. As with terrorism, the existence of large numbers of poor people can provide an enabling environment for organized criminals, especially where government authorities do not possess the capabilities necessary to stop them.

POVERTY AND GLOBAL SECURITY

At the global level, debates about the relationship between poverty and security have revolved around the issue of inequality and the extent to which an unequal world order is an unstable world order. In one sense, poverty—in either the monetary or exclusionary senses—does not seem to have much bearing on the grand scheme of global war and peace. After all, the short twentieth century, 1914–91, witnessed the greatest economic growth and most sustained advances in democratic governance the world has ever seen, yet it was also "the most murderous century of which we have record by the scale, frequency and length of the warfare which filled it."[54]

At issue here is the extent to which inequality—specifically, rising levels of inequality between states and people—poses a threat to the stability of the current global order. Traditionally, inequality of power between states has been at the heart of the security studies agenda. Such inequalities were said to spur political competition and fuel the security dilemma. But inequalities of various kinds and at various levels were also the very foundation of the capitalist system that Western states in particular have supported for centuries. As Andrew Hurrell has pointed out, these inequalities generated several traditions of thought that stressed the need for greater equality between states. This was to be achieved through various means, such as appeals to sovereign equality, self-determination, and international law. There were even organized calls for greater material equality, such as the New International Economic Order of the 1970s.[55]

Part of the problem is that international inequality can be viewed both as a force for security and as a source of insecurity. On the one hand, institutionalized

inequality lies at the core of contemporary international society: think, for example, of the five states that are the permanent members of the UN Security Council and the nuclear weapons states in the nuclear nonproliferation regime, or the
allocation of voting rights within the international financial institutions. If these
great powers act responsibly, their power can be harnessed in the service of upholding the legitimate collective purposes of international society and thus justify
their privileged position. For example, we still look to powerful states to provide
law and order and a range of basic services, as well as to protect foreign populations
from massacre.

On the other hand, there are those who see rising levels of inequality—
between states and between people—as a threat to global order and stability. From
this perspective, the institutionalized inequalities of the sort mentioned earlier are
increasingly eroding the legitimacy of the contemporary world order. In academia,
the issue of international inequality has been discussed in lengthy debates about
the pros and cons of American hegemony and the competing merits of unipolar as
opposed to multipolar systems. In particular, analysts have sought to understand
how state behavior is affected by being part of a particular polarity structure, and
understand what consequences are likely to result from changes from one type of
polarity to another.[56]

In terms of inequality between individuals, in 1960 the richest 20 percent
of the world's population accounted for 70 percent of income. This share had
increased to 85 percent by 1991. During the same period, the share of the bottom
20 percent declined from 2.3 percent to 1.4 percent.[57] In real terms, by 2009, while
half the planet existed on less than two dollars per day, the combined net wealth
of the world's approximately 10 million millionaires stood at $39 trillion.[58] Put
bluntly, humanity has never been as economically polarized. Building on the idea
that a sense of injustice among the poor combined with the capacity to organize
has played a significant role in the outbreak of some recent intrastate conflicts,
there has been much speculation about the extent to which a similar set of dynamics might play out at the global level: a sort of worldwide "revolt of the margins,"
to borrow Paul Rogers' phrase.

This sort of diagnosis has led some analysts to conclude that there exists
among the global "haves" "a pervasive fear that impoverished people will threaten
the institutions of neoliberal global governance." This is apparently because the
impoverished pose all sorts of challenges to these institutions: "they migrate, they
riot, they demand resources, they suffer illnesses and help spread diseases, they
are destructive of the environment as they farm marginal lands to the point of de-
sertification, they attempt to seize the things that they need in order to survive."[59]
In response, those in charge of such institutions are said to be pursuing "a policy
of containment and quarantine of the effects of global poverty."[60] It should be
noted, however, that many of the accusations commonly leveled at "the impoverished" are myths: the destitute are generally stuck without funds to facilitate
long-distance migration; they demand far less of the world's resources than people
used to wealthier lifestyles; they spread diseases far slower than the transnational
elites who crisscross the planet on jet airliners; they destroy far less of the planet's

biosphere than transnational corporations; and they are usually kept from seizing anything by (state or private) security forces.

Nevertheless, it is fair to say that, in one sense at least, global poverty is being quarantined, although more by accident than design. Whereas the world's poorest citizens traditionally lived in rural areas, today growing numbers of them live in urban areas (see Goldstone's chapter in this volume). One of the consequences is that more and more poor people are slum-dwellers living on the fringes of the world's cities. The more reliable estimates suggest that more than 1 billion people live in slums, squatter communities, and shantytowns characterized by poverty, poor infrastructure and services, and rampant insecurity.[61] This urbanized poverty poses the biggest immediate security challenge for the world's "haves," primarily because of its proximity to their own homes.

Such large-scale and rapid urbanization is placing enormous stress on the governance capacity of states while also providing new opportunities for violence and criminal activities. Many of these slums are difficult for authorities to govern and plagued by high levels of violence—in some cases, especially in Latin America, higher levels than in the world's war-zones.[62] For example, although by no means confined to slums, fighting between Mexican authorities and various criminal cartels, and fighting between the cartels themselves, has killed approximately thirty-five thousand people between 2007 and 2010—far more than most ongoing armed conflicts. In other parts of the Americas, high levels of violence have existed for much longer. In 2004, for instance, the Brazilian city of Rio de Janeiro was experiencing approximately the same level of violent deaths—roughly fifty homicides per one hundred thousand inhabitants per year—as the eastern parts of the Democratic Republic of Congo, a country suffering from one of Africa's largest and most brutal ongoing wars.[63] Indeed, in preparation for various international sporting events in 2010, Brazilian authorities launched military operations involving tanks and helicopter gunships against sections of these slums that were suspected of falling under the control of drug cartels.

The response of the nonpoor to these types of developments has been to try and transform the urban landscape to protect themselves from crime and violence. They have done this by building greater numbers of "gated communities," hiring increasing numbers of private security personnel, and avoiding certain no-go zones. In many cities this has produced something akin to economic apartheid. As Teresa Caldeira has observed, interaction between the poor and the nonpoor in the world's cities has become marked by "tension, separation, discrimination, and suspicion."[64]

CONCLUSIONS

This chapter examined three levels of debate about the relationship between poverty and security. At each level I have suggested that the existence of large-scale poverty indicates that the respective political order is not working morally, politically, or economically. Poverty should therefore always be a concern for those who seek stability and the preservation of the status quo because its very existence can be used as a justification to challenge the competence and/or strategy of the governing authorities.

At the level of human security, poverty is one of, if not *the*, greatest immediate security challenge to approximately half of humanity because it dramatically reduces people's ability to gain access to sufficient levels of education, health care, and nutrition. Although international society has recognized this through the Millennium Development Goals and the target of halving poverty by 2015, without some truly dramatic changes in world politics, even this minimal objective will not be achieved.

At the state level, the relationship between poverty and security has generated several important debates. In terms of armed conflict, terrorism, and state failure, poverty is a more significant security concern if we adopt a capabilities or social exclusion approach than if we think of the concept in monetary terms. This is because armed conflicts, terrorism, and the problems associated with state failure are more likely to occur in circumstances where people develop a sense of injustice and are able to organize themselves politically than when individuals fall below a certain level of consumption.

Finally, at the global level, the debates about poverty and security have revolved around the issue of inequality (between states and between people) and the extent to which this threatens the stability of the existing world order. While a certain degree of inequality is both inevitable and desirable at both the international and individual levels, the process of large-scale and rapid urbanization is bringing "first world" and "third world" conditions into close proximity with one another, exemplified by the growing number of gated communities bordering impoverished slums. If these trends continue, security analysts might well have to spend more time analyzing the politics of zip codes than their traditional fixation with nuclear codes.

Notes

For their helpful comments on earlier drafts of this chapter, I would like to thank Christopher Corpora, Stuart Croft, and Matt McDonald.

1. See Bill McSweeney, *Security, Identity and Interests* (Cambridge: Cambridge University Press, 1999), 23–78; and Barry Buzan and Lene Hansen, *The Evolution of International Security Studies* (Cambridge: Cambridge University Press, 2009), ch. 4–5.

2. UK Department for International Development, "Eliminating World Poverty: Making Globalisation Work for the Poor," White Paper on International Development (London, The Stationery Office: Cm 5006, December 2000), 6.

3. The other five clusters of threat were interstate conflict; internal conflict; nuclear, radiological, chemical, and biological weapons; terrorism; and transnational organized crime. The report defined a threat as "any event or process that leads to large-scale death or lessening of life chances and undermines States as the basic unit of the international system." See Report of the Secretary-General's High Level Panel on Threats, Challenges and Change, *A More Secure World: Our Shared Responsibility* (New York: UN, 2004), 2.

4. Caterina R. Laderchi, Ruth Saith, and Frances Stewart, "Does It Matter That We Do Not Agree on the Definition of Poverty? A Comparison of Four Approaches," *Oxford Development Studies* 31, no. 3 (2003): 243–74.

5. Amartya Sen quoted in ibid., 253.

6. Quoted in ibid., 257.

7. Ibid., 245. It is worth noting that there have also been moves to distinguish between different categories of poverty—that is, poverty/extreme poverty, relative/absolute poverty, or transient/chronic poverty.

8. On why it is imperative to free security studies from the ethical straightjacket of political realism, see Ken Booth, *Theory of World Security* (Cambridge: Cambridge University Press, 2007); and McSweeney, *Security, Identity and Interests*.

9. It can also be understood as an illustration of what Johan Galtung called "structural violence." See his "Violence, Peace and Peace Research," *Journal of Peace Research* 6, no. 3 (1969): 167–91.

10. Gary King and Christopher J. L. Murray, "Rethinking Human Security," *Political Science Quarterly* 116, no. 4 (2001–2): 585.

11. Caroline Thomas, "Poverty" in *Security Studies: An Introduction*, ed. Paul D. Williams (Abingdon, UK: Routledge, 2008), 248.

12. "Japanese Women, Icelandic Men World's Longest Lived," *Reuters*, July 26, 2007, http://in.reuters.com/article/2007/07/26/idININdia-28667620070726.

13. Christina Lamb, "Zimbabwe's Silent Genocide," *Sunday Times*, July 8, 2007, www .timesonline.co.uk/tol/news/world/africa/article2042133.ece.

14. Mark I. Lichbach, "An Evaluation of 'Does Economic Inequality Breed Political Conflict?' Studies," *World Politics* 41, no. 4 (1989): 464.

15. See Jonathan Goodhand, "Enduring Disorder and Persistent Poverty," *World Development* 31, no. 3 (2003): 631.

16. See, for example, Jack Goldstone, Robert H. Bates, Ted Robert Gurr, Michael Lustik, Monty G. Marshall, Jay Ulfelder, and Mark Woodward, "A Global Forecasting Model of Political Instability," *American Journal of Political Science* 54, no. 1 (2010): 190–208.

17. The Uppsala Conflict Data Program is available at www.pcr.uu.se/research/UCDP/.

18. Jeffrey Dixon, "What Causes Civil Wars? Integrating Quantitative Research Findings," *International Studies Review* 11 (2009): 714.

19. Lotta Harbom and Peter Wallensteen, "Armed Conflict, 1989–2006," *Journal of Peace Research* 44, no. 5 (2007): 623–34.

20. The index ranks approximately 170 countries and groups them into categories of very high human development, high human development, medium human development, and low human development. Although the 2007–8 index did not list Afghanistan, Iraq, or Somalia (presumably because of problems related to data collection), I have assumed that these countries would fall into the low human development category.

21. The UCDP defines nonstate armed conflict as the use of force between two organized groups, neither of which is the government of a state, that results in at least twenty-five battle-related deaths in a year. See Therese Pettersson, "Non-state Conflicts 1989–2008: Global and Regional Patterns" in *States in Armed Conflict 2009*, Research Report 92, ed. Therese Pettersson and Lotta Themner (Uppsala, Sweden: Uppsala University, Department of Peace and Conflict Research, 2010), 183–201.

22. Paul Collier, "Doing Well out of War: An Economic Perspective," in *Greed and Grievance: Economic Agendas in Civil Wars*, ed. Mats Berdal and David M. Malone (Boulder, CO: Lynne Rienner, 2000), 105 and 94.

23. For example, Edward Miguel, Shanker Satyanath, and Ernest Sergenti, "Economic Shocks and Civil Conflict," *Journal of Political Economy* 112, no. 4 (2004): 727.

24. Goodhand, "Enduring Disorder," 635.

25. Michael E. Brown, "The Causes and Regional Dimensions of Internal Conflict," in *The International Dimensions of Internal Conflict*, ed. Michael E. Brown (Boston: MIT Press, 1996), 577. Brown is clear that the most important proximate factor is the decisions of elites or "bad leaders."

26. David Keen, *The Economic Functions of Violence in Civil Wars*, Adelphi Paper 320 (London: Oxford University Press for the IISS, 1998).

27. David Keen, *Conflict and Collusion in Sierra Leone* (Oxford: James Currey, 2005). See also Paul Richards, *Fighting for the Rain Forest* (Oxford: James Currey, 1996).

28. Paul Rogers, *Losing Control: Global Security in the Twenty-First Century*, 2nd ed. (London: Pluto Press, 2002), 86–87.

29. Charles T. Call, "Liberia's War Recurrence: Grievance over Greed," *Civil Wars* 12, no. 4 (2010): 347–69.

30. Frances Stewart, "The Root Causes of Humanitarian Emergencies," in *War and Underdevelopment: The Economic and Social Consequences of Conflict*, ed. Frances Stewart and Valpy Fitzgerald (Oxford: Oxford University Press, 2000), 1–42; and Frances Stewart, "Horizontal Inequalities and Conflict" in *Horizontal Inequalities and Conflict*, ed. Frances Stewart (Basingstoke: Palgrave, 2008), 3–24.

31. Ted Gurr, *Why Men Rebel* (Princeton, NJ: Princeton University Press, 1970), 24.

32. Goodhand, "Enduring Disorder," 637.

33. See Daniel Byman, *Keeping the Peace* (Baltimore: Johns Hopkins University Press, 2002), ch. 2.

34. Morris Miller, "Poverty as a Cause of Wars?" *Interdisciplinary Science Reviews* 25, no. 4 (2000): 275.

35. George W. Bush, "Securing Freedom's Triumph," *New York Times*, September 11, 2002.

36. Alan Krueger, *What Makes a Terrorist* (Princeton, NJ: Princeton University Press, 2007), 12.

37. Karin von Hippel, "The Role of Poverty in Radicalization and Terrorism," unpublished paper, October 2008, 7.

38. Ibid., 7.

39. Jessica Stern, quoted in Karin von Hippel, "The Roots of Terrorism: Probing the Myths," *Political Quarterly* 73, no. S1 (2002): 29.

40. For an overview, see J. Millard Burr and Robert O. Collins, *Alms for Jihad: Charity and Terrorism in the Islamic World* (Cambridge: Cambridge University Press, 2006).

41. von Hippel, "Roots of Terrorism," 27–28. In general, however, most people would rather donate money than family members to the cause.

42. Fred Halliday, *The Middle East in International Relations* (Cambridge: Cambridge University Press, 2005), 154–55.

43. Ibid., 158.

44. See Mary Robinson, "Foreword," in *The Roots of Terrorism*, ed. Louise Richardson (New York: Routledge, 2005), xii.

45. Jeffrey Sachs, "The Strategic Significance of Global Inequality," *Washington Quarterly* 24, no. 3 (2001): 187–88.

46. Ibid., 189.

47. Charles T. Call, "The Fallacy of the 'Failed State,'" *Third World Quarterly* 29, no. 8 (2008): 1491–1507.

48. Charles T. Call, "Beyond the 'Failed State': Towards Conceptual Alternatives," *European Journal of International Relations*, OnlineFirst, April 20, 2010.

49. See, for example, Mats Berdal and Monica Serrano, eds., *Transnational Organized Crime and International Security* (Boulder, CO: Lynne Rienner, 2002).

50. For example, Michael Pugh, "Postwar Political Economy in Bosnia and Herzegovina," *Global Governance* 8, no. 4 (2002): 467–82; and Peter Andreas, "The Clandestine Political Economy of War and Peace in Bosnia," *International Studies Quarterly* 48, no. 1 (2004): 29–51.

51. Antonio L. Mazzitelli, "Transnational Organized Crime in West Africa," *International Affairs* 83, no. 6 (2007): 1074.

52. See Jean-François Bayart, Stephen Ellis, and Béatrice Hibou, *The Criminalization of the State in Africa* (Oxford: James Currey, 1999).

53. Roger Middleton, "Piracy in Somalia: Threatening Global Trade, Feeding Local Wars," Chatham House Briefing Paper (London: Chatham House, October 2008), www.chatham house.org.uk/files/12203_1008piracysomalia.pdf.

54. Eric Hobsbawm, *The Age of Extremes* (London: Vintage, 1994), 13.

55. Andrew Hurrell, "Security and Inequality," in *Inequality, Globalization, and World Politics*, ed. Andrew Hurrell and Ngaire Woods (Oxford: Oxford University Press, 1999), 248–55.

56. For an overview, see Barry Buzan, *The United States and the Great Powers* (Oxford: Polity, 2004).

57. Alastair Greig, David Hulme, and Mark Turner, *Challenging Global Inequality* (Basingstoke: Palgrave-Macmillan, 2007), 4.

58. "World Wealth Report 2010," *Capgemini*, accessed January 15, 2011, www.capgemini .com/insights-and-resources/by-publication/world-wealth-report-2010/.

59. Peter Wilkin, "Global Poverty and Orthodox Security," *Third World Quarterly* 23, no. 4 (2002): 641.

60. Ibid., 634. See also Mark Duffield, *Global Governance and the New Wars* (London: Zed, 2000).

61. *Guns and the City: Small Arms Survey 2007* (Cambridge: Cambridge University Press, 2007), 161. www.smallarmssurvey.org/publications/by-type/yearbook/small-arms-survey -2007.html.

62. Ibid., 189.

63. See Julio Jacobo Waiselfisz, "Map of Violent Deaths," *Estudos Avançados* 21, no. 61 (2007): 120–38; and Benjamin Coghlan, R. J. Brennan, P. Ngoy, D. Dofara, B. Otto, M. Clements, and T. Stewart, "Mortality in the Democratic Republic of Congo," *Lancet* 367 (2006): 44–51.

64. Quoted in *Guns and the City*, 177.

Chapter 11

POVERTY
A Development Perspective

Inder Sud

Alleviation of poverty is at the core of development. Robert McNamara, at the time the president of the World Bank, was one of the first development leaders to draw attention to poverty reduction as the overarching goal of development. In his now-famous speech in Nairobi in 1973 on the plight of the rural poor, McNamara called "absolute poverty a condition of life so degraded by disease, illiteracy, malnutrition and squalor as to deny its victims basic human necessities and a condition of life so common as to be the lot of some 40% of the peoples of the developing countries."[1] McNamara described absolute poverty, in 1975 in another major speech focusing on the life of the urban poor, as "unspeakably grim." He went on to state that the "central task of development is the reduction and ultimately the elimination of absolute poverty."[2] More than three decades later, some 1 billion people in the developing world still live in the most degrading form of absolute poverty—not being able to afford even life's most basic necessities of food and shelter. The World Bank still proclaims itself "working for a world free of poverty." Development practitioners continue to debate whether this goal will ever be accomplished in the foreseeable future.

To be sure, there are many developing countries that have made enormous progress in eliminating poverty. The East Asian "tiger economies" were all poor when McNamara gave his Nairobi speech. Many countries in Latin America have recovered from the crises of the 1980s and 1990s and have virtually eliminated absolute poverty. More recently, China and India, the two largest developing countries, have made spectacular gains. Even in Africa, countries such as Botswana, Ghana, Kenya, and Senegal have succeeded in lowering the poverty levels. As a result, the share of developing world population living in absolute poverty has declined from 1.2 billion in 1980 to 1.0 billion in 2001, and is projected to decline further to 600 million by 2015—a particularly impressive achievement, considering that the population of developing countries would have increased by about 2 billion between 1980 and 2015.[3]

This chapter analyses development approaches that have underpinned these successes. While each country has its unique circumstances that require country-specific approaches, some common threads are discussed here.

WHAT IS POVERTY?

It is first important to understand how poverty is defined and measured in the context of development. It has evolved over time to encompass multiple facets.

Income Poverty

The most commonly understood and used definition of poverty is the obvious one: the lack of adequate income to meet even the very basic consumption needs of life, such as food and shelter. The basket of "essential consumption" has been calculated by the World Bank to cost $1 a day in 1985 purchasing power parity (PPP) terms (updated to $1.08 a day in 1993 PPP) and is widely referred to as the "$1 a day" line of poverty.

In 1990, some 28 percent of the population of developing countries was absolutely poor, with most concentrated in three regions: East Asia and the Pacific, South Asia, and sub-Saharan Africa. Poverty in East Asia and the Pacific declined steadily in the 1990s thanks to rapid growth in most major countries in the period, reaching 9 percent by 2004 (see table 11.1). South Asia also experienced declining poverty levels in this period, led by significant economic growth in India, although not at the same rapid pace initially as in East Asia, but the decline in poverty has accelerated in the last five years. Sub-Saharan Africa, however, is the one region that has lagged behind, with much slower progress. Overall, the world is well on its way to meet the Millennium Development Goal Target 1-A of halving, between 1990 and 2015, the proportion of people with incomes below $1 per day.[4]

Despite this global progress, however, the total number of poor has declined only marginally because of the still-growing population of developing countries. Current projections are for a declining but still significant number of absolute poor by 2015, the target year for achieving the Millennium Development Goals. Moreover, the number of absolute poor will have actually increased in sub-Saharan Africa (from 227 million in 1990 to 340 million by 2015) and South Asia would still have more than 200 million people in absolute poverty.[5]

Human Poverty

Many development practitioners, most notably Nobel laureate Amartya Sen, argue that income poverty alone does not capture the essence of human well-being, which is the capability of an individual to pursue their specific goals in life.[6] More specifically, Sen considers freedom as one of the most basic aspects of human life and suggests that well-being should be assessed not as much in terms of what people are or do but in terms of what they are able to be or do should they choose to. Inspired by Sen's work, the World Bank's *World Development Report 1990* broadened the definition of poverty to include not only material deprivation but also low achievements in health and education. Proxy indicators such as infant mortality, maternal mortality, life expectancy, primary and secondary school enrollment, adult literacy, and so on are commonly used to measure the level of human development. Although no particular benchmarks are established to define the human development poverty line, the indicators are used in measuring gaps in these areas that serve as guide to action.

The UN Development Programme (UNDP), starting with its 1997 annual human development report, introduced a human poverty index (HPI) as a single composite measure of the different features of deprivation in the quality of life to arrive at an aggregate judgment on the extent of poverty in a community. Rather

Table 11.1 Numbers and Proportions of Absolute Poor in Developing Countries

Region	No. Absolute Poor (million)			Absolute Poor as % of Total		
	1990	2001	2015 Projected	1990	2004	2015 Projected
East Asia and Pacific	472	271	19	29.8	9.0	2.8
Europe and Central Asia	2	17	2	0.5	0.9	0.2
Latin America and Caribbean	49	50	43	10.2	8.6	5.1
Middle East and North Africa	6	7	4	2.3	1.5	0.7
South Asia	462	431	216	43.0	30.8	21.5
Sub-Saharan Africa	227	313	340	46.7	41.1	31.4
Total developing countries	1,218	1,089	624	29	20	10

Data Source: World Bank, *Global Monitoring Report* (Oxford: Oxford University Press, 2005 and 2008).

than measure poverty by income, the HPI uses indicators of the most basic dimensions of deprivation: a short life, lack of basic education, and lack of access to adequate public health services measured by the percentage of the population with access to safe drinking water and the percentage of children underweight for age.[7]

In practice, there is considerable overlap between income and human poverty. For the most part, there is a strong correlation between income and the various elements of human well-being. Using cross-country and time series data, Goklany shows that all human indicators have steadily improved with rising incomes, very rapidly when starting at the low level and leveling off beyond certain levels of income.[8] This is indeed what one would expect: as incomes rise, both nations and households are able to increase expenditures on programs that affect human well-being. Nevertheless, as UNDP has pointed out consistently in the various human development reports, there is considerable variation among countries at the same level of income in their human development indicators, which highlights the importance of deliberate pro-poor public expenditure policies and choices of guns versus butter and other forms of spending, including on security.

CAUSES OF POVERTY

Like the multifaceted nature of poverty, there are multiple causes of poverty. The poor not only have fewer income earning opportunities, they are also much more vulnerable to falling into poverty from circumstances beyond their control, and they lack the ability to shape their destiny.

Lack of Income Opportunity

Formal, informal, or self-employment is central to improving the lives of the poor. The overall wealth of the country is an important influence on this: as a country grows richer, so (on average) do poor people in the country, with the main mechanism being greater employment opportunities and better-paying work. There is a strong correlation between economic growth and poverty reduction. Conversely, poverty rises with economic contraction. The spectacular decrease in poverty in East Asia in the 1980s and 1990s, and in India over the last fifteen years, was a direct result of sustained gross domestic product per capita growth rates of 4–5 percent per annum. The inability to make a dent in poverty in Africa in the same period is a direct consequence of economic stagnation or negative growth performance.

While economic growth is linked with poverty reduction, the rate at which growth translates into lower poverty varies. Growth derived largely from extractive industries may not create significant employment and thus may bypass the poor. Poor governance in such cases can result in neglect of the interests of the poor through inappropriate public expenditure policies. There is also evidence that a high initial level of inequality in the distribution of income can also temper the poverty reduction impact of growth. So, while growth is essential to poverty reduction, it is not sufficient. It needs to be accompanied by deliberate pro-poor policies to ensure the widest participation in the fruits of prosperity.

Vulnerability

Even with adequate current incomes and human development, households or individuals face the prospect of declines in income and general welfare because of their inability to face economic shocks, including natural disaster, catastrophic illness, crime, death, and so on, that lower earnings or force them into debt to meet the essential needs. In the era of globalization, the shocks can traverse national boundaries from the rich to the poor countries, as we have witnessed in the recent collapse of credit markets and economic downturn in the United States. Indeed, experience shows that poverty is not a static concept, and the risk of falling into poverty is real for many households.[9]

There are many different factors that can determine (or temper) vulnerability. If a household has assets that can be liquidated without a significant loss of current income, this might allow the household to weather short-term loss of income. Education may allow an individual to seek alternative employment opportunities when faced with loss of income in a particular vocation. Income diversification within the household also cushions against decline in one source of income. Access to credit can help in smoothing consumption during times of distress. Finally, links to social networks and the existence of an effective government safety net can provide a cushion. All these informal mechanisms are important but incomplete. It is important for public action to supplement these with insurance with appropriate attention to incentive effects.

Voicelessness

The poor often experience an acute lack of voice and power, and thus feel unable to influence decisions that affect them profoundly in their daily lives—getting their children quality basic education, accessing basic health services, getting remedies against injustice, protecting against violence, and so on. They regularly face inept and corrupt public institutions that fail to protect or promote their interests. The World Bank study *Voices of the Poor* presents perceptions of deprivation by the poor themselves from around the world.[10] "No one listens to us" is a recurring theme in many of the interviews reported in the study. The inability to influence decisions that the poor consider important (or voicelessness) feeds into the general despair felt by poor people and prevents their ability to gain fully from economic progress. Some have even suggested this as one of the root causes of radicalization.[11]

There are no ready measures that exist to measure voicelessness. In recent years, there have been some attempts to measure freedom as a proxy for voice, with the most notable index published by Freedom House.[12] However, this and similar indices tend to measure much more the political openness of the country rather than the extent to which people generally, and the poor specifically, have an adequate voice. Indeed, democratization should not be confused with giving voice to the poor. The poor can often have little voice in matters most important to them (e.g., responsiveness of local officials to development concerns) in countries considered as democratic; conversely, some authoritarian governments have shown much greater concern for the poor. Measuring voice or lack thereof, much less coming to grips with it, remains elusive in development thinking.

BEYOND POVERTY: INEQUALITY MATTERS

While the absolute level of income (and consumption) above the minimum is the priority of first order, there is still the issue of inequality. Besides income inequality between the rich and the poor, there is often inequality among specific groups. Women, indigenous people, ethnic minorities, and minority groups can often have both higher levels of income poverty and human poverty. There can also be location-specific regional differences within a country, between urban and rural, and between remote and the more accessible parts.

There are several measures of income inequality. The most commonly used is the Gini coefficient, which measures statistical dispersion of incomes by different percentiles of income groups. A low Gini coefficient denotes greater equality and a higher number, greater inequality. An alternative measure is the ratio of income of the top one or two deciles and the bottom one or two deciles. Across countries today, there is wide variation in inequality. Current estimates of Gini coefficient vary from a low of 0.247 for Denmark to a high of 0.743 for Namibia.[13] The income ratio of top and bottom deciles varies from a high of 168.1 for Bolivia to a low of 4.5 for Japan.

Why does inequality matter? There are two key arguments. First, there is a moral argument. While we all can accept inequality of outcomes that are determined by differences in preferences, talents, efforts, and luck, it is morally indefensible when unequal outcomes derive from inequality of opportunity arising purely from circumstances of birth. Disadvantaged children from families at the bottom of the wealth distribution do not have the same opportunity to receive quality education as children from the financially better-off families. So these disadvantaged children can expect to earn less as adults. They are less likely to be immunized from childhood diseases and have potential risk of loss of income from poor health. Because the poor have less voice in the political process, they will be less able to influence spending decisions to improve public schools or the delivery of public health services for their children. All this perpetuates what the World Bank refers to as the "inequality trap."[14]

Second, there is some evidence to suggest that a high level of inequality can be detrimental to sustained growth and thus to the overall welfare of society.[15] High levels of economic and political inequality tend to lead to institutions and social arrangements that systematically favor the interests of those with more influence. Such unequal institutions can generate economic costs by not harnessing fully the talents and potential of middle and poorer groups. Society as a whole is likely to be more inefficient and miss out on opportunities for innovation and investment.[16]

Reversing inequality, however, has not proven to be easy. Causes of inequality are complex and are rooted in historical and cultural traditions. Policies aimed at a significant redistribution of wealth have more often been ineffective and even counterproductive. The aim of policy should not be reversing inequality of outcomes. Rather, the aim should be creating a level playing field and eliminating barriers that inhibit the ability of the poor to share in the growing prosperity.

FRAMEWORK FOR POVERTY ALLEVIATION

Alleviation of poverty requires a multipronged approach that includes enhancement of overall wealth ("expanding the pie") while also ensuring that its benefits are distributed as widely as possible, particularly to the poor. Each of these objectives requires actions on multiple fronts.

Economic Growth

There is a strong correlation between economic growth and poverty alleviation.[17] Without exception, the countries mentioned earlier that have successfully reduced poverty to a significant extent had a record of sustained growth over several years. Conversely, no country has been successful in reducing poverty without economic growth.[18]

Increasing incomes from economic growth in turn translate into improvements in human development. All indicators of human development—life expectancy, maternal and child mortality, education attainment, nutrition—are strongly correlated with income.[19] Thus, developing countries that have experienced economic growth have also experienced a reduction in poverty in its various dimensions.

The link from income growth to poverty reduction, however, is not automatic. There is wide variation in poverty levels among countries and in human development across countries at the same levels of income. And, as discussed earlier, there are large inequalities in human development within a country. So growth needs to be accompanied by policies that help poor people share in the benefits of growth. This is discussed later.

What creates economic growth? Much of the debate centers on the policies underlying the so-called Washington Consensus—a term coined by the then–World Bank economist John Williamson in the context of the financial crisis in Latin America in the 1980s. Williamson postulated the following key policies—often described as neoliberal policies—to achieve growth following the crisis:

- A stable macroeconomic framework, particularly low levels of inflation.
- Greater openness to the world by promoting exports and encouraging foreign direct investment. Reduction and rationalization of tariffs was a key component of the export promotion, combined with a "competitive" exchange rate.
- Promotion of greater private investment in the economy through privatization, deregulation, and private property rights. This policy envisaged a shift from state-controlled to a much greater role for the private sector. Privatization was also seen as important for restoring fiscal balances since state-owned enterprise (SOE) losses typically represented a significant fiscal burden.
- A deepened financial sector through liberalization of interest rates, privatization of state-owned banks, and opening up of the capital account.[20]

The Washington Consensus policies have attracted much criticism over the years largely, with a few important exceptions, from noneconomists. The criticisms were initially fueled by the disappointing growth performance in Latin America in much of 1990s while the human costs were seen as high. Given that the financial crisis in Latin America was first and foremost a result of profligate expenditure policies and concomitant high inflation, significant fiscal contraction was at the heart of the adjustment process to achieve macroeconomic stability. This often entailed cutting public expenditures in virtually all areas, including the social sectors. Privatization of SOEs resulted in inevitable job losses. Absent a strong recovery of growth, these social costs were seen as an undesirable—perhaps even ill-advised—consequence of the Washington Consensus. Privatization of SOEs to foreigners also evoked protests about giving away the national treasures, even when previously the SOE concerned had been inefficient and a drain on the economy. The criticism of privatization became even louder when several countries of the former Soviet Union, notably Russia, decided to move rapidly with privatizing SOEs, which resulted in some distortions of its own (e.g., monopoly power, crony capitalism, and the emergence of oligarchs). Ironically, growth in Latin America has picked up since 2000, averaging more than 5 percent per annum. But the criticisms persist. Policy reversal in countries such as Bolivia are seen as proof of the failure of the Washington Consensus policies, notwithstanding the fact that other countries such as Brazil have continued with the policies even under socialist leadership.

It is unfortunate that Williamson chose to articulate the growth policies in the context of economic crisis in Latin America. In particular, the crisis sometimes required drastic actions, particularly on expenditure cuts. Some SOEs were probably privatized faster than they would have been under normal circumstances, but the crisis limited the degrees of freedom for action. One can only speculate what would have been the debate today had Williamson chosen to shape his consensus around the success stories of East Asia.

A second set of criticisms have been from respected economists such as Nobel laureate Joseph Stiglitz and noted Harvard economist Dani Rodrik. Some of
Stiglitz's criticisms, although often construed as criticisms of the Washington
Consensus policies, have been in reality criticisms of the International Monetary
Fund (IMF)–prescribed structural adjustment programs for East Asia following the
financial crisis in 1998.[21] He criticized the IMF for imposing too severe a fiscal contraction and causing recession and job losses, even though the East Asia crisis had
nothing to do with excessive public spending but was rather because of imprudent
private sector borrowing. But Stiglitz also had other concerns such as the need to
emphasize education, not privatizing monopolies, avoiding too hasty privatization, and so on. These are all valid points to consider in economic policymaking,
but there is nothing in the Washington Consensus policies that merits these concerns. Stiglitz's more pertinent criticism is what he sees as the "market fundamen-
talism" approach of the Washington Consensus policies, noting that they do not
give adequate recognition to the critical regulatory role of the government. The
recent global financial crisis gives credibility to Stiglitz's concerns.

Rodrik echoed some of Stiglitz's criticisms but also considered the Washington Consensus policies as too much of a straightjacket with an overemphasis on a
minimalist role for the state.[22] Citing examples from countries such as Korea, India,
China, and Mauritius, Rodrik suggested that there was much more room for a
proactive government role than implied by the Washington Consensus policies.

The implication of these various criticisms has been that the growth policies
of the Washington Consensus have cumulatively been caricatured by its critics as
a privatized economy with little or no role of the government; wanton cutting of
public expenditures; privatization of everything in sight; elimination of all tariffs,
the sooner the better; and complete deregulation of everything, even monopolies.
No single critic has articulated the criticisms exactly in these terms, but, cumulatively, this emerges as the implication. It cannot be, however, any further from the
policy prescription. There is unfortunately a lot of confusion and misunderstanding about growth policies.

The growth policies encompassed in the Washington Consensus were, and
continue to be, sound. But to interpret them as a rigid prescription without room
for any variations belies any understanding of policymaking in practice. As the
noted Yale economist T. N. Srinivasan points out, economic policymaking is as
much an art as a science.[23] The Washington Consensus policies provide the broad
directions within which policies in specific context must be shaped. The policy
agenda remains valid, but it is foolish to treat it as a "recipe" to be followed rig-
idly. Indeed, many of the deviations from these policies pointed out by Rodrik fall
well within the space of policymaking. But what should also be remembered is
that the lower the institutional capacity of the government, the less the ability to
design and implement interventions. Not surprisingly, most of Rodrik's examples
of policy variations either come from countries that have a higher institutional
capacity (e.g., Korea), or were large economies that have the ability to buck the
trend (e.g., India), or were simply examples from the 1970s and 1980s when the

international economy was far less integrated and there was more scope for adopting what Rodrik calls heterodox policies.

Having said this, it is also true that individual country circumstances at any given time should influence economic policy. This is one of the central messages, albeit unremarkable, to emerge from the recent report of the Growth Commission established by the World Bank and composed of eminent economists led by Nobel Laureate Michael Spence.[24] The challenge for policymakers is to ensure that "country circumstances" do not become an excuse for yet again falling back on the failed policies of excessive state intervention and direction of the economy, which often creates the illusion of action with negative consequences becoming apparent years after the fact.

One concern about a focus on growth is whether it exacerbates inequality. The theoretical literature suggests a trade-off between growth and inequality, based either on the Kuznet's effect or on the disproportionate increase in demand for skilled labor in the technologically driven growth.[25] However, these hypotheses are not supported by extensive empirical literature that is quite unanimous that growth has no impact, either positive or negative, on inequality.[26] Nevertheless, the popular perception continues to be of growing disparity between the rich and the poor. Globalization, which has produced spectacular growth in many countries, is seen as the culprit. Whatever the merits of the argument, the social and political aspects of inequality cannot be ignored. There is room for policy action that ensures that the poor adequately share in the overall improving overall prosperity.

Shared Growth: Investing in the Poor

While growth is fundamental to reducing poverty, its impact on reducing human poverty can vary. As discussed earlier, there is wide variation in human development among countries at the same income level, and the inequality of access hinders the ability of the poor to benefit equitably from the fruits of growth. Investing in basic education and health are obvious areas for public action. Educational attainment is an important path out of poverty. And poor health is one factor that lowers productivity and household incomes.

Unfortunately, both of these sectors are grossly mismanaged in many developing countries. Despite great strides in increasing enrollments, the quality of education remains poor. Public schools suffer from inefficiencies, waste, and neglect. Lack of sufficient operating funds, teacher absenteeism, poor pedagogy, dilapidated facilities, and poor management generally are all too common. Although basic education is free, in theory, poor parents face many hidden and other charges making education unaffordable to many, in practice. The fact that the middle and upper income groups have increasingly abandoned public schools for private schools contributes to their neglect. Public expenditure policies are often regressive, with large subsidies provided for higher education while neglecting basic education. There is a need for fundamental reforms, including increasing the level of public expenditures while ensuring greater accountability in outcomes by empowering local communities to exercise greater control. There is also a need for alternative nonformal education to reach at-risk children.[27]

The health systems suffer from inappropriate priorities, shortage of funds, a lack of trained personnel willing to work in the poor communities, and general lack of accessibility.[28] The sector suffers from a high degree of corruption. Publicly supplied medicines and supplies often find their way onto the black market. Doctors and health workers give priority to their private practice while neglecting official duties. Studies in several countries have shown low utilization of the "free" public health facilities while at the same time the poor frequent private practitioners.[29]

There is also a need to reconsider the current public health model of public provision. Consideration needs to be given to public–private partnerships, with the public sector responsible for funding the private and the nonprofit sectors for the delivery of health services to improve efficiency and to make the services truly accessible by the poor. This model has shown promise in countries such as Afghanistan and Cambodia.[30]

Reducing Vulnerability: Building Assets of the Poor

As indicated earlier, poverty is not a static concept. Research shows that the poor include those who were at one time nonpoor but who fell into poverty because of some catastrophic event—a serious illness in the family; the loss of a job because of recession; crop failure because of a lack of rain, floods, or natural disasters; and so on. An important component of a poverty alleviation strategy should be to have an adequate safety net that helps the poor cope with unanticipated disasters.

There are many different forms of safety net programs that can be considered. An important consideration in the design of these programs is the limited institutional capacity in most poor developing countries. This calls for programs that are easy to implement and, as much as possible, can be self-targeting.

Education is one of the most obvious components of the safety net. A person with even a basic education is much more likely to be able to acquire skills needed for different jobs. Education allows a person to shift occupations when demand for particular skills and services declines. It also permits households to diversify their sources of income—in nonfarm employment for rural households and in alternative employment for urban households. Improving education at all levels, but first and foremost at the basic level, is important not only for poverty reduction but also to serve as a potential safety net.

Access to finance also helps poor people diversify incomes. Microfinance programs have assumed a growing role in this regard since most poor lack access to the traditional collateral-based institutional finance. Most successful programs are run by nongovernmental organizations but also adhere to rigorous financial discipline. Many, if not most, are supported by international donors, but a growing number are examining ways to mobilize resources from the markets. Government has an important role to support these programs, primarily through providing an enabling regulatory framework.[31]

Finally, labor-intensive public works can be a mechanism both to provide income during distress and to diversify household income. Sometimes, these have been run as "food for work" programs that pay below market wages in the form of food. However, these programs have often suffered from high administrative costs, poor targeting, and in many cases, corruption. When food is imported, as is often the case, it can also have negative consequences for domestic agriculture. Social funds are alternative ways to create employment through public works. Social funds are implemented by autonomous government organizations through normal contracting. Targeting the poor is ensured by the selection of the works that are inherently labor intensive, small in size, and focused on geographic areas that suffer from high levels of poverty. The social funds too have been criticized for their approach to building "parallel institutions" instead of relying on existing institutions. However, they remain highly popular because of their ability to reach the poor quickly.[32]

In recent years, there has been a growing interest in cash transfers to the poor, either outright or conditional upon the families undertaking certain social obligations such as sending their children to school and having them immunized.[33] Most countries in Latin America have implemented cash transfer programs of some form in the last few years; the Bolsa Familia program in Brazil and the Opportunidad program in Mexico are two of the most successful conditional cash transfer programs.[34] The concept of cash transfer is attractive in that it assumes that the household is in the best position to know its most pressing needs. Conditional cash transfers can simultaneously promote investments in improving capability. However, either type requires greater institutional capacity to target the transfers and to ensure that funds are not diverted. Nevertheless, the concept is attractive and deserves further consideration.

Toward Equity in Access to Land

Improving access to land by the poor can have a significant impact on their lives. Much has been written on the importance of land reforms in rural areas, but land redistribution has proven to be difficult in most countries. Improving the functioning of land markets through clear titles and reduced transaction costs are measures that can also be effective. In urban areas, slums are a direct consequence of misguided land use planning and development that makes most urban land close to employment unaffordable by low-income groups and the poor. Illegal squatting is the only viable option left for them to meet their shelter needs. The municipal authorities are unwilling or unable to provide services because of the illegal land status, forcing the residents to live in conditions of squalor. Programs of slum upgrading accompanied by the regularization of titles have proven to be successful in many countries to integrate the poor into the fabric of the city, thus enhancing their opportunities and reducing vulnerability.

Integrate Rural with Urban Economies

Although rural development was at the heart of development efforts in the 1960s and 1970s, the effort trailed off in subsequent years as attention shifted much more to industrialization as the engine of growth. This was in part because the "green revolution" had already yielded spectacular results to the point that global food shortages stopped being a major concern. It was suggested that food insecurity is ultimately a matter of having adequate purchasing power rather than the availability of food per se. The financial crisis of the 1980s further constrained government action; rural investments took more than their share of cuts, justified in part by what was seen as generally poor performance of government programs for rural development. A consequence was a relative neglect of the rural economy.

Experience of successful developing countries indicates that a healthy rural economy also underpins industrialization. This point is best illustrated by Indonesia, where the opening of the economy proceeded concurrently with strong government policies in support of agriculture. The most notable were price support for rice, development of rural infrastructure, particularly irrigation and roads, and widening access to education.[35]

Unfortunately, experience with rural development programs in many countries has not been positive. There has been poor experience with public sector–led extension, inputs, and marketing support services.[36] Similarly, infrastructure services have suffered from a lack of maintenance. Weak institutional capacity, particularly in the context of implementation in rural areas, explains most of these failures. It is useful in these circumstances to think in terms of a minimum package that is within the capacity of the public sector to implement. This should include basic infrastructure (roads, irrigation, and water management) and education. In addition, experience indicates that these services are much more likely to be sustained if there is strong community involvement in the design, implementation, and subsequent maintenance.

Leadership Matters, Not the Nature of the Government

The experience of successful countries indicates that strong, committed, and sustained leadership is critical to promoting development and to reducing poverty. Strong leaders were behind virtually all successful development examples of the 1980s and 1990s—Singapore, Taiwan, Korea, Indonesia, Malaysia, Chile, and, more recently, China. Some development practitioners, most notably Amartya Sen, have emphasized the importance of democracy as a fundamental pillar of development. The reality is that there is little observed relationship between democracy and development. All of the examples cited earlier were led by strongmen. At the same time, it does not follow that dictatorship is the route to development; witness the dismal record of many dictators in Africa. More recently, some have suggested that development would be more durable under a democratic system than an authoritarian regime. This argument fails to recognize that development itself is a possible path toward democratization, as has happened in many countries mentioned earlier.

The important role of leaders who are committed to development is undisputed, whether in a democratic system or an authoritarian one. Experience also shows that effective leaders are homegrown. No amount of external aid can substitute for them.

CONCLUDING REMARKS

Despite enormous progress in the last fifty years, alleviating global poverty remains an unfinished agenda. Many developing countries have been successful in reducing absolute poverty. But many others, most notably in sub-Saharan Africa, remain very poor. Much can be learned from the experience of the successful countries and applied to those still struggling. Economic growth with an emphasis on distribution of benefits to the poor is the path forward. Equally important, investments in improving the capabilities of the poor and providing them with insurance against catastrophic events are needed to unleash the potential of the poor to improve their own well-being.

Notes

1. Robert S. McNamara, "Address to the Board of Governors," Nairobi, Kenya, September 24, 1973. International Bank for Reconstruction and Development, http://siteresources .worldbank.org/EXTARCHIVES/Resources/Robert_McNamara_Address_Nairobi_1973.pdf.

2. Robert S. McNamara, "Address to the Board of Governors of the World Bank," Washington, DC, September 1, 1975.

3. World Bank, *Global Monitoring Report 2005* (Oxford: Oxford University Press, 2005).

4. See "We Can End Poverty: 2015 Millennium Development Goals," *UN.org*, www.un. org/millenniumgoals/poverty.shtml.

5. In September 2008 the World Bank revised the definition of absolute poverty from $1 per day to $1.25 per day based on new surveys and revised estimates of purchasing power parity in some countries. This revision, which is disputed by some, increases the estimates of the absolute poor by about 20 percent; however, it does not alter the overall picture of progress on poverty alleviation.

6. Amartya K. Sen, *Commodities and Capabilities* (Amsterdam: North-Holland, 1985); Amartya K. Sen, "Well-Being Agency and Freedom: The Dewey Lectures 1984," *Journal of Philosophy* 82, no. 4 (1985): 169–221; Amartya K. Sen, "Capability and Well-Being," in *The Quality of Life*, ed. M. Nussbaum and A. Sen (Oxford: Clarendon Press, 1993), 30–53; and Amartya K. Sen, *Development as Freedom* (Oxford: Oxford University Press, 1999).

7. UNDP, "Human Development Report 2007/2008," available at http://hdr.undp.org /en/reports/.

8. Indur M. Goklany, *The Improving State of the World* (Washington, DC: Cato Institute, 2007).

9. Anirudh Krishna, "Reversal of Fortune: Why Preventing Poverty Beats Curing It," *Foreign Policy*, no. 154 (May–June 2006), 74–75.

10. Deepa Narayan, Raj Patel, Kai Schafft, Anne Rademacher, and Sarah Koch-Schulte, *Voices of the Poor: Can Anyone Hear Us?* (Oxford: Oxford University Press, for the World Bank, 2000).

11. Mohammed M. Hafez, *Why Muslims Rebel: Repression and Resistance in the Islamic World* (Boulder, CO: Lynne Reinner, 2003).

12. See www.freedomhouse.org.

13. UNDP, *Human Development Report 2007/8: Fighting Climate Change: Human Solidarity in a Divided World*, http://hdr.undp.org/en/reports/global/hdr2007-8/.

14. World Bank, *World Development Report 2006: Equity and Development* (Oxford: Oxford University Press, 2006).

15. Alberto Alsena and Dani Rodrik, "Distributive Policies and Economic Growth," *Quarterly Journal of Economics* 109 (1994): 465–90; and Roberto Perotti, "Growth, Income Distribution and Democracy," *Journal of Economic Growth* 1 (1996): 149–87.

16. World Bank, *World Development Report 2006*.

17. Francois Bourguignon, "The Growth Elasticity of Poverty Reduction: Explaining Heterogeneity across Countries and Time Periods," in *Inequality and Growth*, ed. T. Eicher and S. Turnovsky (Cambridge, MA: MIT Press, 2003); K. Deninger and L. Squire, "New Ways of Looking at Old Issues: Asset Inequality and Growth," *Journal of Development Economics* 57 (1998): 259–87; D. Dollar and A. Kraay, "Growth Is Good for the Poor," *Journal of Economic Growth* 7, no. 3 (2002): 195–225; James E. Foster and Miguel Székely, "Is Economic Growth Good for the Poor? Tracking Low Incomes Using General Means" (June 2001), IDB Working Paper No. 380. Available at SSRN: http://ssrn.com/abstract=1817251; and M. Ravallion, *Pro-Poor Growth: A Primer* (Washington, DC: World Bank, Policy Research Working Paper No.3242, 2004).

18. Socialist countries such as Cuba, Sri Lanka, Vietnam, China, and the state of Kerala in India succeeded to some extent in reducing poverty through redistributive means, but they were by and large not able to sustain the efforts and all have moved toward progrowth policies.

19. Goklany, *Improving State of the World*.

20. John Williamson, "The Washington Consensus Revisited" in *Economic and Social Development into the XXI Century*, ed. Louis Emmerij (Washington, DC: Inter-American Development Bank, 1997), 48–61.

21. Joseph Stiglitz, *More Instruments and Broader Goals: Moving toward the Post-Washington Consensus*, 1998 WIDER Lecture, Helsinki, Finland, January27, 1998(New York: W. W. Norton, 2002). Available at www.wider.unu.edu/; and Joseph Stiglitz, *Globalization and Its Malcontents* (New York: W. W. Norton, 2002).

22. Dani Rodrik, *One Economics, Many Recipes: Globalization, Institutions, and Economic Growth* (Princeton, NJ: Princeton University Press, 2007).

23. T. N. Srinivasan, "The Washington Consensus a Decade Later," *The World Bank Research Observer* 15, no. 2 (2000): 265–70.

24. World Bank, *The Growth Report: Strategies for Sustained Growth and Inclusive Development*, Report of the Commission on Growth and Development (Washington, DC: World Bank, 2008).

25. The Kuznets hypothesis suggests that, at low levels of per capita income, inequality increases with rising per capita income and decreases only in the later stages of development—resulting in an inverted U-shaped relationship between per capita income and income inequality.

26. Deninger and Squire, "New Ways of Looking"; Dollar and Kraay, "Growth Is Good"; S. Chen and M. Ravallion, "What Can New Survey Data Tell Us about Recent Changes in Distribution and Poerty?" *World Bank Economic Review* 11, no. 2 (1997): 357–82; and William Easterly, "Life during Growth," *Journal of Economic Growth* 4 (1999): 239–76.

27. Paul Glewwe and Michel Kremer, "Schools, Teachers, and Education Outcomes in Developing Countries," in *Handbook of the Economics of Education*, vol. 2, ed. E. Hanushek and F. Welsh (Oxford: Elsevier, 2006); and Lant Pritchett, "Where Has All the Education Gone?" *World Bank Economic Review* 15, no. 3 (2001): 367–91.

28. Deon Filmer, Jeffrey S. Hammer, and Lant H. Pritchett, "Weak Links in the Chain: A Diagnosis of Health Policy in Poor Countries," *World Bank Research Observer* 15, no. 2 (2000), 199–224.

29. A. K. Nandakumar, M. Chawla, and M. Khan, "Utilization of Outpatient Care in Egypt and Its Implications for the Role of Government in Health Care Provision," *World Development* 28, no. 1 (2000): 187–96.

30. Valery Ridde, "Performance-based Partnership Agreements for the Reconstruction of Health System in Afghanistan," *Development in Practice* 15, no. 1 (2005): 4–15.

31. In the last two years, microfinance institutions in some countries (e.g., India) have come under criticism for the high interest rates they charge and for pushing loans on custom-

ers who could not afford them. The issue of interest rates is largely a political issue since the very success of microfinance rests on the concept of beneficiaries paying the full cost of the loan, which tends to be high for very small loans. But the issue of excessive lending is real because of too rapid an expansion of microfinance in some countries that produced an excess of supply, resulting in bank officers sometimes pushing unviable lending. This highlights the importance of government ensuring an adequate regulatory structure to oversee microfinance institutions as any other financial institution.

32. Howard White, "Social Funds: A Review of the Issues," *Journal of International Development* 14, no. 5 (2002): 605–10.

33. Francois Bourguignon, Francisco Ferreira, and Phillippe Leite, *Conditional Cash Transfers, Schooling and Child Labor: Micro-Simulating Bolsa Escola* (Washington, DC: The World Bank, 2003); Elisabeth Sadoulet, Frederico Finan, Alain de Janvry, and Renos Vakis, *Can Conditional Cash Transfer Programs Improve Social Risk Management?* SP Discussion Paper No. 0420 (Washington, DC: World Bank, 2004); and Laura B. Rawlings and Gloria M. Rubio, "Evaluating the Impact of Conditional Cash Transfer Programs," *World Bank Research Observer* 20, no. 1 (2005), 29–55.

34. International Labour Organization, "Bolsa Familia in Brazil: Context, Concept and Impacts," Geneva, March 2009, www.ilo.org/public/libdoc/jobcrisis/download/109B09_28_engl.pdf; and Santiago Levy, *Progress against Poverty: Sustaining Mexico's Progresa-Oportunidades Program* (Washington, DC: Brookings Institution Press, 2006).

35. Peter C. Timmer, *The Road to Pro-Poor Growth: The Indonesian Experience in Regional Perspective*, Working Paper No. 38 (Washington, DC: Center for Global Development, April, 2004), http://cgdev.org/content/publications/detail/2753/.

36. Frank Ellis and Stephen Biggs, "Evolving Themes in Rural Development 1950s–2000s," *Development Policy Review* 19, no. 4 (2001): 437–48.

POVERTY
Editors' Comments

Joanna Spear and Paul D. Williams

This pair of chapters displays both convergence and divergence in the way poverty is addressed in the security and development arenas. Both chapters showed that poverty was a legitimate and important concern for security and development agendas alike, although within security studies it had assumed this position only recently. In addition, both perspectives acknowledged the difficulties involved in defining poverty and the related category of "the poor." Whereas the development perspective worked primarily with a monetary approach to define poverty and design programs to alleviate it, the security perspective focused on poverty as a variety of social exclusion and a marker of potentially unstable political orders.

These different emphases had consequences for the policy instruments each perspective discussed in order to alleviate the problem of poverty. Although the need to stimulate economic growth while simultaneously ensuring a degree of equity was the central policy challenge from the development perspective, the security chapter highlighted the need to build more inclusive systems of governance as a means to address the problem, whether at the national level or in the international realm. In terms of development policy, this has produced a long-standing set of debates about the pros and cons of the Washington Consensus, a reformed version of which remains dominant within official development circles. From the security perspective, however, the emphasis is on preventing people from becoming marginalized from society, as this would create an "enabling environment" for actors who wish to overturn the established political order through violent means. While there is no evidence to suggest that poverty is related to interstate warfare, the picture is more complex with regard to intrastate conflicts. Here, although the truly destitute rarely start rebellions, they can be persuaded (or forced) to join insurgencies, particularly in weak states. In urban areas and slums, poverty is more likely to be connected with the threats posed by criminality than by armed conflict and terrorism.

With regard to the levels of analysis, both perspectives share a focus on the individual as the ultimate referent object but shift to the national and international levels when devising appropriate policy solutions. For the development field the international level is clearly dominated by the constraints imposed by global capitalism and liberal conceptions of political economy. The state level has been the site of major debates about what type of government policies best promote equitable economic growth. At the substate level the development perspective highlights the need to address various issues relating to regional disparities, urban–rural divides, and equitable access to land. At the individual level Sud emphasizes the need for strong leaders who are willing to actively push pro-poor policies. In the security arena the challenge of poverty has also generated debates at a variety of levels. While poverty represents a major part of the human insecurity equation, widespread poverty can be linked to the onset of armed conflict, terrorism, and state failure. At the international level, the focus has been the double-edged nature of inequality between and among states and peoples.

Part VI

TRADE AND RESOURCES

Chapter 12

TRADE AND RESOURCES
A Security Perspective

Joanna Spear

For many decades security studies scholars thought they knew all they needed to about trade and resource issues and therefore paid scant attention to them. For the realists, resources and trade were key elements of national power and important components of balance of power calculations. For liberals, trade was a route to improved relationships between states; the more trade there was, the less war there would be. For structuralists, trade and resources were important tools of power that were used by the powerful (states and elites) to maintain control over the powerless (other states and the masses at home and abroad). Hence, unlike some other issue areas covered in this book, this topic had received attention from security studies scholars, albeit attention that was not consistent or high level.

Many security practitioners took a more active interest in trade and resource issues. Following liberal precepts, practitioners moved these ideas into reality with the transformation of postwar Europe into a powerful economic block. The European Union is a liberal success story; due to successful integration, it is able to focus security planning solely on responses to attacks from states beyond its borders. Another example of liberalism in practice was the détente era, when increased trade was seen as a way to link the Soviet block to the West and to give them incentives to behave well in order to keep the economic benefits that resulted.

Such practical successes allowed the security studies field to benignly neglect issues of trade and resources. The belief in the positive effects of trade was powerfully endorsed by the end of the Cold War and the worldwide embrace of capitalism. With more states joining the free trade system and deregulating their markets, the expectation—which to an extent has been realized—was that interstate peace would be extended.

The end of that ideological conflict led to former communist countries adopting neoliberal economic practices, many at breakneck speed.[1] Similarly, countries emerging from civil wars have also rapidly moved toward free market practices.[2] The subsequent deregulation and decentralization of trade has added to the tremendous velocity of globalization. There are now more actors—and more types of actors—in more places and involved in more types of business and trade than ever before. The sheer volume, transnational nature, and complexity of trade transactions mean that the system can mask many illicit and semi-illicit deals that have security implications.

This chapter charts how the security arena has now begun to pay more sustained attention to issues concerning trade and resources in light of recent developments. It discusses three types of security challenges that were facilitated by the transformation of the international marketplace: combatants who fund their activities through trade in resources (that is, trade causing or sustaining conflict), malevolent transnational actors who profit from the trade system, and US concerns with the new geostrategic role of China in the international marketplace.

ECONOMIC EXPLANATIONS OF CIVIL WAR

War has increasingly become the continuation of economics by other means.
        —David Keen, *The Economic Functions of Violence in Civil Wars*

During the 1990s, although major interstate war was no longer an imminent danger, some complex intrastate wars were initiated and others persisted (although the absolute number of armed conflicts declined by 35 percent in the 1990s, thanks in part to UN efforts to broker peace).[3] Security studies scholarship has sought to understand these intrastate conflicts and their duration through examining ethnicity, inadequate state making, and the role of bad leadership, among other explanations.[4] In the 1990s some scholars began to focus their attention on economic aspects of civil war, including Mark Duffield, Alex de Waal, William Reno, Mats Berdal, and David Keen.[5] This inevitably brought attention to the role of illicit trade in causing or sustaining intrastate conflict.

Security practitioners actively engaged in trying to end civil wars, for example, UN peacemakers, faced the practical consequences of economies distorted by conflict. The characteristics that define a state (and potentially a region) as having a "war economy" were elaborated by Karen Ballentine and Heiko Nitzschke:

- The formal economy shrinks while informal and black markets grow, and the lines between the formal, informal, and criminal sectors and activities are effectively blurred.
- Combatants use pillage, predation, extortion, and deliberate violence against civilians to acquire control over lucrative assets, trade networks, and diaspora remittances, and to exploit labor.
- War economies are highly decentralized and privatized, both in the means of coercion and in the means of production and exchange.
- Combatants increasingly rely on licit or illicit exploitation of or trade in lucrative natural resources where these assets obtain.
- Combatants thrive on cross-border trading networks, regional kin, ethnic groups, arms traffickers, and mercenaries, as well as legally operating commercial entities, each of which have a vested interest in the continuation of conflict and instability.[6]

War economies have particular consequences both for efforts at peacemaking—spoilers with access to resources have greater abilities and incentives to avoid settlements—and for postconflict reconstruction where the economic distortions of the war and ongoing corruption corrode efforts at peacebuilding and development.[7]

As Christopher Cramer notes, in the 1990s economists also began to show an interest in violent conflict, engaging with power and conflict issues that the discipline had traditionally shied away from because they were "political."[8] This shift led to the work on resource conflicts that has garnered the most scholarly and policy attention, both positive and negative, the work produced by a team working with economist Paul Collier of Oxford University and the World Bank. The work of Collier et al. uses the foundations of methodological individualism to explain the outbreak of conflict. Drawing on neoclassical economic models, Collier asks the question "what makes internal conflict probable?" The answer is derived using statistics that act as proxy measurements to create a rational choice model of violent conflict.

The team's work made them early proponents of the "greed" thesis as an explanation of civil wars.[9] They conclude that, based on statistical analysis, there is a formula that appears in cases of civil war: a reliance upon primary commodities, an oversupply of young men who were unemployed and undereducated, a diaspora to provide funding, and a sharply declining economy. This toxic cocktail is likely to produce civil war.[10] The analysis is supported by a slew of statistical evidence that seems to show that the "greed" thesis is unassailable.

It is indeed ironic that the ideas that have most stimulated the security arena in its thinking about the causes of internal conflict (and the role of trade in that) have come from outside the arena, from the field of economics. Much energy has subsequently gone into debating the roles of "greed and grievance" in intrastate war, and the tenor of that debate is revealing of how the security arena is thinking about resources and conflict. Certainly, these World Bank studies had an energizing effect on the security studies field, particularly among those who had fine-grained knowledge about the countries and conflicts reduced to statistics in their reports. Responses identified different problems with the World Bank's work, noting issues of methodology, causality, and focus.

Methodology

As Cramer shows, many of the traditional problems of neoclassical economics are transposed into these new analyses of conflict.[11] In the case of Collier et al.'s work, what looks to noneconomists to be unassailable statistical certainty is anything but that. Cramer concludes that "orthodox economic models of conflict begin with a set of arbitrary assumptions; efforts to test them empirically have so far foundered on misleading use of proxies; and these models have not succeeded in incorporating the irreducibly social on which they depend."[12] There are a number of examples of the problem of proxies. As Keen notes, in Collier's work, low levels of literacy are taken as a proxy for "greed," whereas they could equally be a signal of "grievance."[13] Kandeh critiques Collier's assumption that high rates of male unemployment are a proxy for "greed" rather than "grievance."[14] Similarly, Humphreys has pointed out that large diasporas could be a consequence of conflict rather than a cause of it.[15]

In a 2006 evaluation of the World Bank's two-volume publication *Understanding Civil War*, economist Daron Acemoglu concluded that "the regression evidence does not test any well-specified hypothesis, and the correlations that are interpreted as causal effects are really no more than correlations. . . . It is too early to jump to policy conclusions."[16]

Interestingly, the Collier team's finding of a positive correlation between primary commodity dependence and the risk of armed conflict is directly contradicted by the work of James Fearon and David Laitin, who—using a different data set—found "slight or no evidence" for such a causal relationship.[17]

Causality

While the data set that the World Bank team used for its analysis has remained essentially the same, the causality assumed and the conclusions that they have drawn from it have shifted significantly over time. This raises questions about the credibility and robustness of the causal analysis and the conclusions that can be drawn from it.

For example, in initial formulations of their thesis, Collier and Hoeffler put great emphasis on rebel calculations of the probability of victory. Rebels were said to calculate what the gains of victory would be against the resources that the government could mobilize for defense (i.e., defense spending) while considering how easy it would be to mobilize public support.[18] However, later iterations of their work play down the role of probability of victory in rebel calculations and instead highlight the availability of lootable primary commodities and the employment opportunities available (or not) to young men, that is, the greed variables.[19] Ballentine and Sherman noted a subsequent shift in analysis:

> In their initial strong formulation of the "greed theory" of rebellion, Collier and his team offered a rational actor account that focused on the *motives* of rebel actors, arguing that greed or loot-seeking rather than grievance or justice-seeking was the key factor in the onset of violent rebellion. This suggested that economic resources are not simply pursued to sustain war, but rather that war is pursued in order to capture resources. More recently, Collier's team has offered a weaker formulation of the greed thesis that places increased emphasis on the *opportunity* for organized violence.[20]

Many critics highlighted the extent to which politics is missing from Collier's work. For example, Charles Cater points out that although the statistical analysis has predictive value, Collier's causal argument is flawed because "his a priori assumption that all societies have grievances and would therefore erupt into civil war if given the right mix of opportunities ignores a crucial variable: governance."[21] The concern about the absence of politics from Collier et al.'s work has only mounted as the team has "refined" their analysis away from considering motivations to focusing solely on opportunity.

In a further shift—and possibly in response to Cater's criticisms—Collier's recent iteration of the arguments that support his data rebuts the charge of neglecting governance as now one of the "traps" that poor states fall into is the "trap of bad governance in a small country."[22] Again referring back to causality and proxies, this is regarded as enhancing rebel greed and playing no role in building grievance.

Collier's 2007 book *The Bottom Billion* builds on his team's previous outputs, presenting the arguments and findings without the data that they are derived from. Interestingly, while the first three sections of the book are careful elaborations of previous statistical work, the fourth and fifth parts are completely different; anecdotes are the major support for policy recommendations (raising new methodological issues). In particular, Collier is robust in his recommendation that there are circumstances in which a military intervention and international presence for a decade would be a positive and economical means to break states out of the traps that keep people in the "bottom billion."[23]

While in some ways this evolution of causal analysis is a good thing (they are obviously taking seriously the points made by critics) and has been praised by some commentators, it also strongly suggests that this is a data set in search of a theory as opposed to being the "natural" outcome of the data that they imply.[24] Just as Collier has accused his critics of political bias, the same can therefore be said of his work.

Focus

A number of critiques of Collier et al.'s work stem from concerns about what they *do not* focus on. In particular, their work on greed and opportunity focuses exclusively on rebel greed and opportunity, neglecting the role that a greedy or opportunistic government may play in causing and sustaining civil war. That some governments are a core part of the problem is obvious as soon as you look at individual cases (though this is not Collier et al.'s chosen level of analysis). This insight is helpful as it explains what are otherwise puzzling features of civil wars: the longevity of conflict and the evidence of collusion between rebels and governments.[25]

In Collier et al.'s work, the causality is focused on rebel greed or, in later iterations, opportunity, with no role for grievance except as a rhetorical device for legitimating greedy activities. This has led to questions of the applicability of this to specific conflicts.[26] These critiques are dismissed wholesale by Collier as being a manifestation of academic bias and ideology.[27] However, the insistence on an either–or causality means that the Collier team—led by the liberal idea of a clear division between economic and political activity—miss the various ways in which greed and grievance interact. For example, Keen discusses the case of Aceh, where the military were deeply involved in illicit economic activities including illegal logging, drug trading, seizing plantation land, and paying too little for goods with the result that "the military's economic activities have themselves deepened grievances in the region, a case of greed leading to grievance."[28]

Considering greedy and opportunistic governments also brings into focus the interventions of neighboring and more distant states. As the work of Michael Pugh, Neil Cooper, and Jonathan Goodhand shows, without examining war economies in their regional context, much of the dynamism of economic, military, political and social networks is missed and understanding of the conflict—and how to undertake effective peacebuilding—is thus denuded.[29] Considering greedy and opportunistic neighboring governments brings to mind the Democratic Republic of Congo as the preeminent example of this problem.[30]

In addition, the sole focus on rebels averts attention from the role of other nonstate actors of various kinds; the greedy or opportunistic national and international firms intent on acquiring resources are let off the analytical hook. More radically, Mark Duffield would assert that the negative role of international institutions and the development industry is ignored.[31]

Collier et al. focus on the question of what causes civil war, but equally important is the follow-on question of what sustains it. It is here that connections into a globalized economic system play a vital role. Commodities can be traded into the global economy with the ignorance—or collusion—of participants in the supply chain. Additionally, once international attention has begun to focus on a conflict, making it too difficult for the firms and states in the "normal" supply chain to deny the provenance of commodities, illicit trading networks become more vital—both for rebel groups and for governments—enabling all combatants to avoid defeat or settlement for long periods of time.

Regardless of the academic criticisms of their analysis, as Ballentine and Nitzschke noted, the apparent economic certitude of Collier et al's work made the greed thesis very attractive to policymakers trying to end civil wars. Moreover, the simplicity of the explanation suggested some straightforward policy responses: deny the greedy and opportunistic access to resources and the conflicts will end. Consequently, from the late 1990s within the UN system policies were specifically designed to weaken the financial resources available to rebel groups operating in West Africa.[32]

The "greed and grievance" debate and the role of conflict trade have been central issues for the security arena over the last twenty years. The ways in which greedy rebels access the global trade system also connects to another core concern in the security arena to which we now turn: transnational trade networks that are accessed by a range of nefarious groups.

TRANSNATIONAL NETWORKS AND SECURITY THREATS

Many of the issues that are now described as transnational security threats existed during the Cold War but were relegated to the category of domestic policing problems (human trafficking, drug distribution, organized crime, etc.). With the post–Cold War transformation of the economic and information systems, these problems have gone global.[33] This is often termed "the dark side of globalization." Importantly, transnational crime is a well-established part of the global economy. As John Picarelli makes clear, "Such criminal activities are frequently estimated to consume between 5 and 20 percent of [gross domestic product] per annum, making the illicit political economy a significant source of global revenues. While forced labour, small arms and illicit drugs are the three largest illicit markets globally, they reside within a plethora of other criminal activities. Such criminal markets are closely associated with increasing levels of money laundering and the spread of political corruption."[34] The global illicit economy includes more than just resources, encompassing services (such as protection rackets and prostitution), fraud, intellectual property theft, and counterfeiting. The latter two have direct impacts on global trade. In 1998 the Organisation for Economic Co-operation and Development estimated that 5–7 percent of global trade involved counterfeit products.[35]

All trade routes are essentially "dual-use" networks; what can carry legally logged timber from sustainable sources can just as easily carry illicit timber. There are many goods that are licit if transferred by a state or legitimate company but illicit if transferred by other actors. The key problem is that it is difficult to tell what is legal and what is not (particularly as groups can have different conceptions of what is legal and illegal). Given the volume of trade, the task of establishing provenance is enormous and has the potential to derail the normal flow of commerce, which means it is ordinarily not done.

Many contemporary transnational security issues are viewed not as threats in themselves but as having the potential to combine with terrorism and thus threaten state security.[36] From this perspective, the dilemma is that networks that can be used for ordinary crime (human trafficking, drug smuggling, money laundering, etc.) can also be a conduit for terrorists to enter a country, move money, or make money, and this is why they are problems. There is an ongoing debate in the security literature over the likelihood that a gang or organized crime group would collaborate with a terrorist cell.[37]

Another strand of security studies sees transnational security issues as threats in their own right, connecting particularly to human security (human trafficking, illicit drugs, etc.) but also for their potential to weaken the state.[38] It is near impossible to control the illegal transnational flows of money, drugs, people, resources, and other goods in a globalized economic system. The market is dynamic and groups will trade whatever is profitable—from caviar to "bushmeat."[39]

A new transnational threat to trade and security is actually an old threat retooled: piracy. It is on the rise in the Straits of Malacca, most visibly off the Horn of Africa.[40] Thus far international reactions have been ad hoc; various countries have sent naval vessels to the areas and a number of shipping companies are now employing private security contractors to protect their ships or sending them via different routes.

In a globalized system, closing off one route to illicit trade generally means that illicit trade merely finds a new route. This problem, familiar from arms control, is called the "balloon effect." Inevitably, national and international law enforcement is one step behind these illicit actors, who are über capitalists, lithe and unconstrained by sovereignty and the national rules that hamper enforcement and interdiction efforts. The balance to be struck between security and facilitating trade is a tricky one. To check every container entering a country might do more economic harm than withstanding a terrorist attack, making it worth taking the risk and only checking a small percentage of container traffic.

CHINA'S APPROACH TO TRADE AND RESOURCES

The third issue getting increased attention—especially from the US security studies community—is China's foreign trade relations. Over the last few years the US political and economic community has been deepening its relationships and increasing its interdependence with the rising economic power. By contrast, the US military community has been focused on China's increasingly sophisticated military capabilities and its policies in Latin America and Africa.[41] Consequently, US policies toward China have looked schizophrenic.

China is increasingly active in Latin America and is revitalizing old relationships with African countries. In building relationships with developing countries, China employs a number of common elements.

Solidarity

China reminds these potential economic allies that they have a common past; both were subject to imperial control and both—as part of the global South—are subject to political pressure from the Western states running the economic system. China also positions itself as a friend of the South in such economic forums as the World Trade Organization. Moreover, China presents itself as a powerful example of successful state-controlled economic development, and an alternative to the neoliberal model. China presents economic relations with a developing world country as a "win–win" situation; the developing country gets assistance without any aid conditionality or domestic interference while China gets the resources and new markets that it needs.[42]

Multilateralism

China works through multilateral political and economic institutions, for example, the Forum on China-Africa Cooperation,[43] the African Union (China is building the new African Union headquarters for an estimated $150 million[44]), the Asia Pacific Economic Cooperation forum, the Inter-American Development Bank (China is a donor), and the Organization of American States (as an observer). According to Joshua Kurlantzick, China is joining multilateral organizations to reassure states about its likely behavior.[45] Moreover, China's recent constructive role in UN peacekeeping has also assuaged some concerns about its behavior.

Economic Assistance

China provides debt relief or debt forgiveness, cheaper loans, and new aid or credits. The aid is sometimes hard to differentiate from foreign direct investment (FDI) because it is often for infrastructure development (forms of aid that the West ceased to use decades ago but that are very popular with recipients). Aid can also include providing doctors, building hospitals and clinics, and providing medical training in China.[46] There are also other forms of FDI provided to economic allies. In 1999–2000 the Ministry of Foreign Trade and Economic Cooperation selected thirty top Chinese companies to invest overseas. With access to low-interest loans from Chinese banks, these companies have played this role with gusto, developing joint ventures and investing in commodities production. "China takes the kind of risks that would be inconceivable for any major Western company."[47] Interestingly, their trade and investment is not as coordinated as might have been expected—sometimes these companies have even competed against each other for oil deals in Africa—and they seem to have considerable flexibility.

Military Assistance

China often provides military equipment to its economic allies. However, whereas "during the Cold War, Chinese arms transfers were motivated by ideology, now profit is the main objective."[48] Among the African countries getting weapons since 2003 are Burundi, Equatorial Guinea, Ethiopia, Eritrea, Sudan, Tanzania, and Zimbabwe.[49] Military cooperation is another important element of China's strategy.[50] China has significantly increased the number of military attachés it posts around the world. Moreover, it is increasingly using military exchanges to strengthen ties with its economic partners. For example, in 2009 it had at least thirty-four active military exchanges with African countries.[51]

Public Diplomacy

China has gone to great lengths to be seen to be treating its allies in positive and respectful ways. In particular, since Hu Jintao became president, he has traveled quite extensively to Africa and Latin America and has publicly hosted developing world leaders in Beijing with a level of pomp and circumstance they are rarely accorded elsewhere. Investment strategies are accompanied by public diplomacy to showcase Chinese culture and language. Since the first one opened in Seoul in 2004, Confucius Institutes have been springing up around the world. Ten exist in Africa with an additional 11 planned for the continent, and there are 17 in eight Latin American countries.[52] By November 2008 there were 307 institutes in seventy-eight countries.[53] China has a number of reasons for courting relations with a wide range of developing countries. These may be summarized as falling into economic, political, and (possibly) military categories.

The first priority is economic and concerns China's need for commodities such as oil, gas, minerals, and food staples. The Chinese leadership faces a major task in satisfying rising consumer demand. Energy is a priority for Beijing, and over the last fifteen years the leadership has been building relationships around the world to ensure China's access to sources of energy. "China is currently the world's second-largest oil importer and the second-largest consumer of African resources. Indeed, the abundance of natural resources in Africa has led Beijing to seek long-term deals with African governments that ensure continued access to all its raw materials and sources of energy. As China's national oil companies are excluded from the majority of Middle Eastern oil supplies, Beijing—determined to limit its vulnerability to the international oil market—encourages investment in Africa, courting states that the West has overlooked."[54] A similar strategy is being employed in Latin America, with deals signed with Peru, Colombia, Ecuador, and Venezuela. Deals involve purchasing existing oil and gas supplies and investing to develop new sources. This strategy has been dubbed a resource-based foreign policy.

Chinese investments in Africa include minerals such as platinum from Zimbabwe, copper from Zambia, and raw materials from Latin America: iron ore, oil, copper, tin, tungsten, molybdenum, aluminum, and nickel. It also purchases agricultural goods on both continents. In its dealings with the Mugabe regime in Zimbabwe, "tobacco goes directly to China's million smokers, as payment in kind for loans and investments from Chinese banks to Zimbabwe's bankrupt state-run companies. As Zimbabwe's agricultural sector collapses, the Chinese are taking over land the Zimbabwean government confiscated from white farmers, and cultivating the crops they need."[55] The Zimbabwean economy is in such poor shape that it barters with China using chrome, copper, platinum, and beef.[56] China also trades in timber with Gabon and has fishing businesses in Gabon and Namibia. It buys sugar as well as nickel in Cuba. "Chinese corporations[s] have vigorously pursued the political and business elite in Africa, often sweetening the deals they make with incentives provided by the central government."[57] This is equally true in Latin America.

Trade is not one-way, although it is not usually balanced. China is interested in developing markets for its manufactured goods. In return for raw materials, China exports goods such as computers, telecommunications equipment, tractors, fertilizer, clothing, shoes, and so on.[58] Trade with Latin America has grown significantly in the last decade, from $12.6 billion in 2000 to an estimated $150 billion in 2008.[59] Trade with Africa leapt from S10.6 billion in 2000 to $73.3 billion in 2007.[60]

In terms of politics, one of China's prime aims in Latin America and the Caribbean is to deny diplomatic recognition to Taiwan.[61] China has used trade and aid agreements to win countries away from Taiwan (and countries in the region are increasingly skilled at playing the two off against each other).[62] Whereas this is still a large part of diplomacy to Latin America, it has a much lesser role in relations with Africa than it used to, due to Chinese successes.[63] More broadly, in terms of politics, "China clearly has a strategy designed to increase its influence in developing regions—Southeast Asia, Central Asia, Africa, and Latin America—because Beijing believes it can wield greater influence there than in developed nations in Northeast Asia, Europe and the United States."[64]

In terms of military interests, China has given little indication that it has strategic ambitions for these relationships. Nevertheless, these are being extrapolated by China-watchers in the US strategic studies community. US concerns include China's relations with individual states, its inroads into Latin America (traditionally part of Washington's sphere of interest), its burgeoning relations with Africa (which the United States sees as increasingly strategically important), and China's effects on US energy security.

Some of the Latin American alliances that China has developed are of concern to Washington, in particular, support for the Castro regime in Cuba and for Hugo Chavez in Venezuela. Despite Chavez's activism, as Daniel Erikson notes, "China has shown little enthusiasm in becoming entangled in Chavez's larger goal of counter-balancing US influence in the hemisphere."[65] Nevertheless, China has attempted to sell weapons to Venezuela, raising concerns in Washington.[66] China is interested in further oil deals with Venezuela and is investing in oil and gas exploration there. China's trade with Cuba increased about 25 percent in 2007, and there are worries that the People's Republic of China is using Cuba as a listening post to eavesdrop on the United States.[67] Nevertheless, "one suspects that China is disappointed by Cuba's resistance to undertaking more robust economic reforms, while the hard-nosed approach of Chinese investors has chastened Cuban officials who seek 'socialist solidarity' from a China that is primarily driven by capitalist motivations."[68] Previously there were also concerns about Hutchison Whampoa, a Chinese company with ties to the military that had economic interests in two ports along the Panama Canal. Given the geostrategic importance of the canal, there was concern about China's likely behavior; however, so benign and trade-oriented has the company been that US and Japanese companies have now formed a consortium with it to bid for a role in the expansion of the Panama Canal.[69]

Although China has had official relationships with Africa for more than fifty years, it is Beijing's behavior since the China–Africa Forum of 2000 and the subsequent leap in the level of trade and investment that is of interest to the United States. China's engagement with Sudan has been of particular concern, given the state involvement in the genocide taking place in the Darfur region of the country.[70] The United States is also worried about China's funding of the Mugabe regime in Zimbabwe and the human rights records of other Chinese allies such as Chad.[71] However, China has begun to play a more constructive role in politics over Darfur and is beginning to distance itself from Robert Mugabe, perhaps evidence that China realizes that it cannot stick to its mantra of noninterference if it harms more important relationships with the West.[72]

China has been—relatively speaking—quite open about its plans to improve relations with African countries, even publishing a white paper that set out its intentions.[73] For Kurlantzick, China's trade behavior has a strategic motivation: "Chinese leaders fear that, in a conflict with the United States, Washington might be able to cut off international supply lanes or pressure American allies not to supply China. Consequently, Chinese firms search for equity stakes in oil overseas and try to 'secure the entire supply chain in critical industries.'"[74] China's trade policies are regarded by some around Washington as a form of geostrategic positioning, with negative impacts for US foreign and defense policy interests: "Certainly there is concern that Beijing's procurement of energy supplies will pose a challenge to the global dominance of Washington at a time when levels of cooperation between the two governments on matters of energy are at best weak."[75] Kurlantzick has suggested that Beijing distrusts the ability of global energy markets to always deliver what China needs.[76] This may be so, but, like the United States, Beijing is dependent on them for the foreseeable future. As Jennifer Cooke has noted, although around half of China's equity oil production comes from Africa, it is not shipped to China but is sold in the global market. Moreover, China's investments in upstream oil exploration and production also benefit the whole world by adding to global supply.[77]

There is a spirited debate going on—which crosses disciplinary lines—about how to understand China's economic behavior.[78] There are many who regard China as now playing pretty much by the rules of the free trade system, as a status quo player. There are others who point to China's behavior on currency valuation, the dumping of goods into developing world markets, Beijing's evasion of World Trade Organization restrictions (e.g., on textiles) and see a player challenging the system, not fully participating in it. There are still others who point to the puzzling contrast between China's disruptive behavior and its interests in the free trade system given its dependence on global markets.[79] Whereas many experts on trade and economics are prepared to regard China's behavior as "good enough" though not perfect, some in the security community have lingering concerns about Beijing's strategy.

China is also a threat as an alternative to the favored neoliberal model. It has been suggested that China's policy of noninterference and acceptance of authoritarian regimes nullifies Western attempts to apply aid conditionality and improve the human rights of African citizens. However, this is met with resistance by African scholars who point out that "many Africans nowadays question why human rights should suddenly occupy centre stage in the Europe–Africa discourse while Africa's own priority is development."[80]

The development of China's navy has attracted the attention of other countries, but particularly the United States.[81] As David Shinn notes, there is debate over China's intentions (does it want a blue water navy?) but naval power is linked to China's reliance on imported strategic resources and thus the freedom of the sea-lanes.[82] That China deployed a warship to the Horn of Africa in 2008—with US blessing—as part of a multilateral effort to deal with Somali piracy suggests that this is a good basis for further cooperation.[83]

While much of the attention of the security studies field toward China has focused on traditional realist geostrategic concerns about enhanced Chinese power and influence, the security threat manifesting from China's involvement in Africa is actually connected to weak states. China is investing in states that lack control over their own territories and lack true legitimacy. State making has been incomplete, and, as Taylor has pointed out, with Chinese investment, elites are insulated from having to make necessary economic and political reforms.[84] Thus the states remain weak and the benefits of new levels of trade are not necessarily shared equally—or shared at all—so there are persistent human security and transnational security issues.

Nevertheless, Africa was able to achieve a 5.8 percent growth rate in 2007 (its highest ever) thanks in large part to trade with China. Latin America also made gains. Even if all the conditions are not ideal, this seems to be bringing more to both continents than previous interactions with the West. Moreover, "the China equation in Africa has opened new avenues of flexibility and maneuverability for African states."[85] That said, there was evidence during the global recession that China pulled back from investments in Africa, with more than 160 companies abandoning mines in Congo and Zambia as commodity prices sank.[86] This seems to suggest that economics trumps politics and military issues in China's current engagement with Africa—and probably Latin America. Given the effects of the global recession on African and Latin American countries dependent on exporting commodities, this does not auger well.[87]

CONCLUSIONS

The three trade and resource issues discussed in this chapter, self-financing combatants (including rogue governments), transnational security threats, and China's trade policies, have all received significant attention from the security arena in recent years. None can be defined solely in traditional security terms—however hard some have tried in the case of China—so we need to look beyond interstate conflict to understand their importance. This is best done by looking at three distinct levels of analysis. First, all three of them in some senses challenge the norms of the international system, particularly the norms and institutions of the trading system. Second, all three can be seen as adding to the problem of weak states, either by failing to help strengthen them (China is happy to shore up authoritarian regimes with minimal legitimacy), by subverting income that should be channeled through governments (self-financing combatants and transnational smuggling both take trade and tax revenues away from states), or by facilitating opposition to them (the illegal trade in light weapons, the behavior of self-financed combatants against the state). Finally, both self-financing combatants and the activities of transnational crime can be seen as threatening human security in a variety of ways. On balance, China's trade and resource activities, by contrast, can be seen as enhancing human security for millions around the developing world and in Asia.

Notes

The author would like to thank Beth Cole of USIP and other participants in the Security and Development Nexus Workshop, for their comments on an early draft of this chapter.

1. Through explicit strategies such as "shock therapy" in the former Soviet Union, for example.

2. Roland Paris, *At War's End* (Cambridge: Cambridge University Press, 2004).

3. Andrew Mack, "Civil War," *Journal of Peace Research* 39, no. 5 (2002): 518.

4. Michael E. Brown, ed., *The International Dimensions of Internal Conflict* (Cambridge, MA: MIT Press, 1996).

5. Mark Duffield, "The Political Economy of Internal War," in *War and Hunger*, ed. Joanna Macrae and Anthony Zwi (London: Zed, 1994); Alex de Waal, "Some Comments on Militias in Contemporary Sudan" in *Civil War in the Sudan*, ed. Martin W. Daly and A. A. Sikainga (London: I. B. Tauris, 1994); William Reno, *Corruption and State Politics in Sierra Leone* (Cambridge: Cambridge University Press, 1995); Mats Berdal and David Keen, "Economic Agendas in War: Some Policy Implications," *Millennium* 26, no. 3 (1997): 795–818; and David Keen, *The Economic Functions of Violence in Civil Wars*, Adelphi Paper No. 320 (London: IISS & Oxford University Press, 1998).

6. Karen Ballentine and Heiko Nitzschke, "The Political Economy of Civil War and Conflict Transformation," in *Transforming War Economies*, Martina Fischer and Beartrix Schmelzme (Berlin: Berghof Research Center, 2005), 12.

7. Stephen John Stedman, "Spoiler Problems in Peace Processes" in *International Conflict Resolution After the Cold War*, ed. Paul C. Stern and Daniel Druckman, 178–224 (Washington, DC: National Academies Press, 2000); David M. Malone and Jake Sherman, "Economic Factors in Civil Wars" in *Leashing the Dogs of War*, ed. Chester A. Crocker, Fen Osler Hampson, and Pamela Aall (Washington, DC: USIP Press, 2007), 639; Philippe Le Billon, "Overcoming Corruption in the Wake of Conflict," Transparency International, *Global Corruption Report 2005* (London: Pluto Press, 2005), 74.

8. As Cramer notes, this move by economists into new areas of the social sciences has not been universally welcomed and has been termed a process of "economic imperialism" by Ben Fine. See Ben Fine, "A Question of Economics: Is It Colonising the Social Sciences?" *Economy and Society* 28, no. 3 (1999): 403–25. See also Christopher Cramer, *"Homo Economicus* Goes to War: Methodological Individualism, Rational Choice and the Political Economy of War," *World Development* 30, no. 11 (2002): 1846.

9. Paul Collier, "Doing Well Out of War," in *Greed and Grievance: Economic Agendas in Civil Wars,* ed. Mats Berdal and David Malone (Boulder, CO: Lynne Rienner, 2000), 91–111.

10. Paul Collier, "Economic Causes of Civil Conflict and Their Implications for Policy," in *Leashing the Dogs of War,* ed. Chester A. Crocker, Fen Osler Hampson, and Pamela Aall (Washington, DC: USIP Press, 2007), 197–217.

11. Cramer, *"Homo Economicus,"* 1855, 1857.

12. Ibid., 1856.

13. David Keen, *Complex Emergencies* (Cambridge: Polity, 2008), 28.

14. J. Kandeh, "The Criminalization of the RUF Insurgency in Sierra Leone," in *Rethinking the Economics of War,* ed. C. Arnson and I. W. Zartman (Baltimore: Johns Hopkins University Press, 2005), 96.

15. Macartan Humphreys, "Economics and Violent Conflict," Harvard University, August 2002, 12.

16. William Easterly, "Foreign Aid Goes Military," *New York Review of Books* 55, no. 19 (December 4, 2008). See also Abhijit Banerjee, Angus Deaton, Nora Lustig, and Ken Rogoff with Edward Hsu, *An Evaluation of World Bank Research 1998–2005,* September 24, 2006, 64, http://siteresources.worldbank.org/DEC/Resources/84797-1109362238001/726454 -1164121166494/RESEARCH-EVALUATION-2006-Main-Report.pdf; and Paul Collier and Nicholas Sambanis, *Understanding Civil War* (Washington, DC: World Bank, 2003).

17. Mack, "Civil War," 520, citing James Fearon, "The Political Economy of Civil Wars: Implications for Mediation, Peacebuilding and Prevention," unpublished memo (Stanford, CA, 2001).

18. Paul Collier and Anke Hoeffler, "On the Economic Causes of Civil Wars," mimeo (Oxford: Centre for the Study of African Economies, 1996); and Paul Collier and Anke Hoeffler, "On the Economic Causes of Civil War," *Oxford Economic Papers* 50, no. 4 (1998): 563–73.

19. Paul Collier and Anke Hoeffler, "Justice-seeking and Loot-seeking in Civil War," Working Paper 28151 (Washington, DC: World Bank, 1999); and Paul Collier and Anke Hoeffler, "Greed and Grievance in Civil War," Policy Research Working Paper WPS2355 (Washington, DC: World Bank, 2001).

20. Karen Ballentine and Jake Sherman, "Introduction" in *The Political Economy of Armed Conflict,* ed. Karen Ballentine and Jake Sherman (Boulder, CO: Lynne Rienner, 2003), 4. This logic was subsequently laid out in Collier and Hoeffler, "On the Economic Causes," 199.

21. Charles Cater, "The Political Economy of Conflict and UN Intervention: Rethinking the Critical Cases of Africa," in *The Political Economy of Armed Conflict,* ed. Karen Ballentine and Jake Sherman (Boulder, CO: Lynne Rienner, 2003).

22. Paul Collier, *The Bottom Billion: Why the Poorest Countries Are Failing and What Can Be Done about It* (Oxford: Oxford University Press, 2007), 5, 64–75.

23. Ibid., parts 4 and 5. Collier's case for interventions is largely based on the success of the British role in Sierra Leone. However, none of the differences between types of civil conflict, opposition, terrain, weaponry, and so on are considered. His recommendations are therefore capricious. Moreover, Sierra Leone had both the military intervention and a decade of support from Britain and other actors that he advocates. Nevertheless, its people have not broken out of the bottom billion, and in 2008 the country ranked in last place on the UNDP Human Development Index.

24. See Malone and Sherman, "Economic Factors in Civil Wars," 22ff, 650–51.

25. Keen, *Complex Emergencies*, 31–40.

26. See, for example, David Keen, *Conflict and Collusion in Sierra Leone* (Oxford: James Currey/Palgrave-Macmillan, 2005); and Michael Pugh, Neil Cooper, and Jonathan Goodhand, *War Economies in a Regional Context* (Boulder, CO: Lynne Rienner, 2003).

27. Collier, *Bottom Billion*, 18–19, 22.

28. Keen, *Complex Emergencies*, 36, citing Lesley McCulloch, "Greed: The Silent Force in the Conflict in Aceh," mimeo (Melbourne: University of Deakin, 2003).

29. Pugh, Cooper, and Goodhand, *War Economies*, 25–35.

30. John F. Clark, ed., *The African Stakes of the Congo War* (Basingstoke: Palgrave-Macmillan, 2002).

31. Mark Duffield, *Global Governance and the New Wars* (London: Zed, 2001); and Mark Duffield, *Development, Security and Unending War* (Cambridge: Polity, 2007).

32. Karen Ballentine and Heiko Nitzschke, "Beyond Greed and Grievance: Policy Lessons from Studies in the Political Economy of Armed Conflict," International Peace Academy Policy Report (New York: IPA, October 2003).

33. Misha Glenny, *McMafia* (New York: Alfred A. Knopf, 2008); and Moises Naim, *Illicit* (New York: Doubleday, 2005).

34. John T. Picarelli, "Transnational Organized Crime," in *Security Studies: An Introduction*, ed. Paul D. Williams (London: Routledge, 2008), 456.

35. Ibid., 459.

36. John Arquilla and David Ronfeldt, eds., *Networks and Netwars: The Future of Terror, Crime, and Militancy* (Santa Monica, CA: RAND, 2001).

37. Phil Williams, "Terrorism, Organized Crime, and WMD Smuggling: Challenge and Response," *Strategic Insights* 6, no. 5 (2007); and Andrew Blum, "Non-State Actors, Terrorists and Weapons of Mass Destruction," *International Studies Review* 7 (2005): 133–70.

38. Dejan Anastasijevic, "Crime Wave Clouds Croatia's Future," *Time Magazine*, October 29, 2008.

39. Glenny, *McMafia*, 48–52; Sharon Begley, "Extinction Trade," *Newsweek*, March 1, 2008; and Cathy Scott-Clarke, "Poaching for Bin Laden," *Guardian Weekend Magazine*, March 5, 2007, 18–23.

40. Graham Gerard Ong-Webb, ed., *Piracy, Maritime Terrorism and Securing the Malacca Straits* (Leiden, Netherlands: International Institute for Asian Studies, 2006); and Martin N. Murphy, "Contemporary Piracy and Maritime Terrorism," Adelphi Paper No. 338 (London: International Institute for Strategic Studies, 2007).

41. Office of the Secretary of Defense, "Military Power of the People's Republic of China 2009," Annual Report to Congress, www.defense.gov/pubs/pdfs/China_Military_Power_Report_2009.pdf.

42. Joshua Kurlantzick, "China's Latin Leap Forward," *World Policy Journal* (Fall 2006), 35.

43. For information on the Forum on China-Africa Cooperation, see the Ministry of Foreign Affairs, The People's Republic of China website, www.focac.org/eng/.

44. Kwesi Aning and Delphine Lecoutre, "China's Ventures in Africa," *African Security Review* 17, no. 1 (2008): 45.

45. Kurlantzick, "China's Latin Leap Forward," 36.

46. Jennifer Cooke, "Introduction," in "US and Chinese Engagement in Africa," ed. Jennifer Cooke, Report of a December 5–6, 2007, conference cosponsored by the Center for Strategic and International Studies, China Institute for International Studies, and Stockholm International Peace Research Institute (Washington, DC: CSIS, 2008), 7–8.

47. Aning and Lecoutre, "China's Ventures in Africa," 46.

48. Ibid., 44.

49. Stephanie Hanson, "China, Africa, and Oil," *Council on Foreign Relations Backgrounder*, June 6, 2008.

50. David H. Shinn, "Military and Security Relations: China, Africa, and the Rest of the World," in *China into Africa*, ed. Robert I. Rotberg, 164–75 (Washington, DC: Brookings Institution, 2008).

51. Jennifer Parenti, "China–Africa Relations in the 21st Century," *Joint Forces Quarterly*, 52 (January 2009): 120.

52. "Confucius Institutes Help Promote Exchange, Co-op between China and African Countries, Educators," *Xinhua*, October 8, 2008, accessed February 21, 2009, http://news .xinhuanet.com/english/2008-10/07/content_10160650.htm.

53. "Costa Rica Gets Confucius Institute," *China Daily*, November 19, 2008, accessed February 21, 2009, www.china.org.cn/culture/2008-11/19/content_16788915.htm.

54. Ian Taylor, *China's New Role in Africa* (Boulder, CO: Lynne Rienner, 2009), 19.

55. Lindsey Hilsum, "We Love China," *Granta*, no. 92 (Winter 2005).

56. Lloyd Sachikonye, "Crouching Tiger, Hidden Agenda? Zimbabwe–China Relations," in *Crouching Tiger, Hidden Dragon? Africa and China*, ed. Kweku Ampiah and Sanusha Naidu (Cape Town: University of KwaZulu-Natal Press, 2008), 131.

57. Taylor, *China's New Role in Africa*, 19.

58. David Shambaugh, "China's New Foray into Latin America," *YaleGlobal Online*, November 17, 2008, accessed July 11, 2011, http://yaleglobal.yale.edu/content/china%E2%80 %99s-new-foray-latin-america.

59. Ibid.

60. Hany Besada, Yang Wang, and John Whalley, "China's Growing Economic Presence in Africa," *CIGI Policy Brief No. 6*, Center for International Governance Innovation (Ontario: CIGI, 2008), 1.

61. Daniel P. Erickson and Janice Chen, "China, Taiwan, and the Battle for Latin America," *Fletcher Forum of World Affairs* 31, no. 2 (2007): 69–89.

62. Daniel P. Erikson, "The New Challenge: China and the Western Hemisphere," Testimony before the House Committee on Foreign Affairs, Subcommittee on the Western Hemisphere, June 11, 2008.

63. Aning and Lecoutre, "China's Ventures in Africa," 43.

64. Kurlantzick, "China's Latin Leap Forward," 33.

65. Erikson, "New Challenge."

66. Erickson and Chen, "China, Taiwan, and the Battle for Latin America," 82.

67. Ibid.

68. Erikson, "New Challenge."

69. Ibid.

70. Sharath Srinivasan, "A Marriage Less Convenient: China, Sudan and Darfur" in *Crouching Tiger, Hidden Dragon? Africa and China*, ed. Kweku Ampiah and Sanusha Naidu, 55–85 (Cape Town: University of KwaZulu-Natal Press, 2008); and Human Rights First, *Investing in Tragedy: China's Money, Arms, and Politics in Sudan* (New York: Human Rights First, March 2008), www .humanrightsfirst.org/wp-content/uploads/pdf/080311-cah-investing-in-tragedy-report.pdf.

71. Sachikonye, "Crouching Tiger, Hidden Agenda?" 124–37.

72. Joshua Kurlantzick, "China Is Making Friends and Influencing People: Why Beijing's Rising Power Is Good—and Bad—for America," *US News and World Report*, July 29, 2007, accessed July 11, 2011, www.usnews.com/usnews/news/articles/070729/6china.htm.

73. Aning and Lecoutre, "China's Ventures in Africa," 42.

74. Kurlantzick, "China's Latin Leap Forward," 35, citing R. Evan Ellis, "US National Security Implications of Chinese Involvement in Latin America," *Strategic Studies Institute Report*, US Army War College, June 2005, 5.

75. Taylor, *China's New Role in Africa*, 37.

76. Kurlantzick, "China's Latin Leap Forward," 35.

77. Cooke, "Introduction," 6.

78. Lawrence Summers, "The Global Consensus on Trade Is Unravelling," *Financial Times*, August 25, 2008, 9.

79. C. Fred Bergsten, Charles Freeman, Nicholas R. Lardy, and Derek J. Mitchell, "China's Challenge to the Global Economic Order," chap. 1 in *China's Rise: Challenges and Opportunities* (Washington, DC: Peterson Institute, 2008), 15.

80. Aning and Lecoutre, "China's Ventures in Africa," 47.

81. Office of the Secretary of Defense, "Military Power," 3–4.

82. Shinn, "Military and Security Relations," 179–83.

83. "Somalia: Piracy and Much Worse," *Economist*, October 4, 2008, 14–16.

84. Taylor, *China's New Role in Africa*, 19.

85. Aning and Lecoutre, "China's Ventures in Africa," 41.

86. Jeffrey Herbst and Greg Mills, "Commodities, Africa and China," *RSIS Commentaries* (Singapore: S. Rajaratnam School of International Studies, 2009), 2.

87. Jeffrey Herbst and Greg Mills, "Commodity Flux and China's Africa Strategy," *China Brief* 9, no. 2 (2009): 4–6.

Chapter 13

TRADE AND RESOURCES
A Development Perspective

Raymond Gilpin

Poverty and insecurity persist in most of the developing world, with an estimated 1.4 billion people subsisting in fragile environments on less than $1.25 a day. Decades of humanitarian and development assistance have done little to improve the lot of the chronically poor. In some cases, this assistance has worsened their plight and contributed to resource-rich countries becoming less self-reliant and more aid-dependent. Trade has the potential to be a viable path away from grinding poverty and insecurity. Trade offers an opportunity for a country's natural resources to become true national resources by creating avenues for the transfer of critical skills and technology and promoting economic growth. This would only materialize if trade is equitable, trading partners are fair, and trading arrangements are free from distortions. If these conditions are not met, perverse trading relationships could trigger violent competition, engender social and environmental degradation, jeopardize development prospects, and unleash rampant corruption. While the choice of trade policies and trading partners is important in fostering economic development, steps should also be taken to ensure that trade benefits the poorest in developing countries.

The relationship between commerce and development has occupied scholars, political leaders, and practitioners for centuries. Thinking has evolved from the fifteenth century when some early proponents of mercantilism viewed trade as fundamental for state-building and economic growth, through the nineteenth century when British economist David Ricardo popularized the theory of comparative advantage, to twenty-first century apprehensions about globalization and its pervasive effects. Understanding the relationship between commerce and economic well-being could help explain why global trade and productivity have risen significantly since the 1980s while poverty has persisted and underdevelopment appears to be entrenched. Proponents of trade as a vehicle for private sector–led growth point to its apparent ability to increase incomes, fuel growth, and create jobs. They argue that countries that adopt protrade policies are more likely to enjoy enhanced living standards. Opponents argue that inequities in the global trading system disadvantage the poor and point to enduring and pervasive poverty in many parts of Africa and Latin America where protrade policies were tried in the 1990s.

Underdevelopment and weak economic governance in countries that are home to the group Collier calls "the bottom billion" present a growing human security challenge and remain a scar on the conscience of the rest of the world.[1]

The apparent limited effectiveness of decades of aid-led economic reform programs has contributed to a resurgence of the debate concerning the relationship between trade and economic development. Analysts and practitioners are taking a second look at trade as a potential engine of economic growth and broad-based development and conclude that many developing countries could be put on the path to sustained economic progress through welfare-enhancing trade if they are provided the right incentives, robust institutions, and pro-poor economic policies.[2] However, while some research has been conducted into linkages between trade and economic growth (i.e., increases in national output), relatively little attention has been paid to understanding how trade gains could have a more positive and lasting impact on the development process.

This chapter starts by providing working definitions of economic growth and economic development. While trade could impact exports directly, economic development and poverty reduction require more broad-based initiatives over time. The following discussion of trade theory provides a framework for distinguishing increases in output from welfare and distributional issues. It explains how commerce creates winners and losers in the international arena. Countries implement trade policies to respond to market inefficiencies and promote national strategies. An examination of the pros and cons of trade policy choices is followed by an overview of strategies that could enable fairer trade to provide an engine for sustained economic development.

ECONOMIC GROWTH AND ECONOMIC DEVELOPMENT

Economic growth refers to changes in the production of goods and services in a country between time periods. The monetary value of goods and services produced could be measured by the gross domestic product (GDP). When the change (which is expressed in percentage terms) is positive, the economy is said to have grown. When negative, the economy experienced contraction. Comparing GDP over time usually requires adjustments to be made for the effects of inflation. This is done by dividing data by a measure of inflation called the GDP deflator to derive real GDP. Cross-country comparisons are also standardized for differences in population by dividing the value of national output with total population to give the share of GDP per citizen, or GDP per capita. Adjusting for exchange rate differences among countries provides another level of standardization in purchasing power parity (PPP) data. Although GDP data provide a reasonable assessment of the size of an economy and a useful indicator of economic growth, it must be noted that GDP is not a perfect statistic because it does not accurately measure all economic activity, particularly in the nonmonetized sector (for example, economic activity performed in the informal sector or in homes).

Economic growth as measured by the GDP only reflects the size of the economy and not how the wealth is distributed or the quality of life for citizens in a country. Generally, the more a country produces and trades, the more favorable the impact on productivity. The fastest-growing economies are those that trade the most. However, upon closer examination, it is clear that what a country trades also matters. Countries trading in manufactured goods and services grow faster than those trading in unprocessed or partly processed agricultural produce or minerals (generally referred to as primary products). These products are at the front end of the value chain for production and generally account for a small share of price of eventually traded goods. For example, cocoa and coffee producers account for less than 5 percent of the value of final manufactured outputs.[3] While processing, marketing, and distribution costs for coffee and chocolate have risen, the price paid to producers has fallen. This is partly because there are few large buyers of primary products. These buyers are able to dictate the world market price for these products, and the sellers are "price takers" who have little or no control over the prices they receive. Over time they receive less even if they produce more primary products. The only way to increase the value of their exports is to climb higher up the value chain because continued trade in primary products is clearly disadvantageous.[4]

While economic growth reveals a lot about the value of what is produced, it provides no insights into the distribution of output or living standards in a country. This is the realm of economic development. Quantifying the individual or group well-being is a complex endeavor that requires a range of indices such as poverty indicators, income distribution indices, social welfare statistics (especially health and education), measures of governance, infrastructure data, crime statistics, and environmental assessments. The most widely used composite is the Human Development Index, which was developed by the UN Development Programme (UNDP) in 1990.[5] A brief overview of trade theory will elucidate links between commerce and economic development.

AN OVERVIEW OF TRADE THEORY

Ricardo's theory of comparative advantage provides a useful starting point for a discussion of how trade works and why trade does not always have positive welfare implications.[6] Let us assume that the world is made up of two countries (Carland and Fruitopia) and automobiles and bananas are the only commodities produced by both countries. If there is no trade between the countries and all production is for domestic markets, the amount of automobiles and bananas produced by each country will be determined by the relative price of each good at any given point in time. If Carland produces automobiles more efficiently than bananas, more people will work in the car industry and more investment will flow into that sector. The proportions of automobiles and bananas produced will vary over time, ranging from zero cars and one hundred crates of bananas to zero crates of bananas and one hundred cars. This relationship represents the "production possibility frontier" for the economy, which indicates relative output of commodities produced in the country. An economy that does not trade is a "closed economy."

Economic actors eventually specialize in the production of one or more goods or services, which it trades for those commodities it does not produce efficiently. This specialization is based on the economy's comparative advantage. In our example, automobile production in Carland is more efficient relative to Fruitopia, and manufactured units have a lower unit cost. Carland has a comparative advantage in cars. The converse is true in Fruitopia, which has a comparative advantage in banana production. Differing labor and technology endowments explain this arrangement. Over time, Fruitopia could decide to sell its bananas to Carland in exchange for automobiles. Both countries would become trading partners with "open economies," with each country exporting goods they produce relatively cheaply and importing goods they find relatively more costly to produce. (To keep it simple we will assume that neither country has a comparative advantage in both goods).

Ricardo's work was subsequently revisited, notably by two Swedish economists in what became known as the Heckscher-Ohlin theorem.[7] Heckscher and Ohlin introduced the role of capital in the determination of comparative advantage and concluded that capital-intensive economies (such as Carland) will conduct most trade with labor-intensive economies (such as Fruitopia). In their view, trade patterns will be determined by differences in factor endowment (i.e., capital and labor), with such trade being the most beneficial. This simple illustration of trade between Carland and Fruitopia exposes a number of downsides to comparative advantage and free trade based solely on market forces. It is clear that automobile makers in Fruitopia and banana producers in Carland would eventually be priced out of their jobs as capital and labor flow out of those sectors. Furthermore, if the world price for bananas falls more sharply than the price of cars, Fruitopia would experience a worsening in its "terms of trade," meaning that earnings from its main export will be progressively less than the cost of its imports. This scenario plays out globally in trading relationships between exporters of manufactured goods and exporters of agricultural products. The value of exports from nonindustrial economies grows much more slowly, partly because their exports account for a small proportion of the value of end products and partly because there are very few buyers for their exports. This is true of diamonds in the jewelry industry, cocoa in the chocolate industry, and cotton in the textile industry. This makes countries that produce primary products "price takers" and less likely to grow consistently.

Just after World War II, economists observed that countries that export primary commodities would progressively earn less and not be able to afford the manufactured imports or technology required for development. Prebisch and Singer, whose work became collectively known as the Prebisch-Singer hypothesis, noted that the postwar global trading environment did not provide a level playing field. In their view such trade arrangements would progressively widen the gap between richer and poorer countries. Such relationships were entrenched in colonial arrangements, with the colonized countries in Africa, Asia, and Latin America providing minerals and agricultural products and the colonizing powers (primarily in Europe) exporting manufactured end products. By the 1960s, the Prebisch-Singer hypothesis had led to the development of "dependency theory," which called for new global trading arrangements to level the playing field.[8]

As countries became independent they adopted what came to be known as "import substituting industrialization" in a bid to redress the predicted deteriorating terms of trade. This entailed the creation of domestic manufacturing industries (often subsidized by the state) and the imposition of tariffs on imports to make the infant industries competitive in domestic markets. This effort did not succeed because the states had neither the skills nor the technology to run the industries profitably, the cost of subsidies became onerous, and domestic regional markets were small and fragmented. Coupled with these challenges were the oil shocks and debt crisis of the early 1970s, which forced the abandonment of this strategy. The Soviet Union attempted to increase trade and improve economic prospects by a combination of state-directed investment, extensive subsidies, and closed regional trade. This strategy was also abandoned because the subsidies became untenable and their exports proved to be uncompetitive, particularly after the Berlin Wall was toppled in 1989.

Dissatisfied with the perceived imbalance in global trade, countries sought to break out of what was viewed as a vicious cycle of underdevelopment and poverty. A number of countries sought to diversify their economies. India diversified by investing in information technology, Mauritius has become a garment manufacturer, and Indonesia manufactures electronic goods. This shift makes them less vulnerable to deteriorating terms of trade, less susceptible to commodity price fluctuations, and more likely to compete internationally. The global economy has changed since the dependency theory was advanced in the immediate post–World War II years. Intraindustry specialization has increased significantly. For example, an automobile produced in the United States needs technology from Europe, electronics from Asia, and paneling from Latin America. Trade within the value chain of manufactured goods is growing in importance.[9] This is another reason why trade among industrialized and industrializing nations is increasing, often at the expense of primary commodity exporters.

TRADE AND ECONOMIC DEVELOPMENT

There are many reasons why a country could trade and grow but fail to experience appreciable economic development. First, economic development requires sustained investments and multiple interventions that need time to take full effect. Petroleum-producing countries illustrate this in what has been described as the "paradox of plenty," where high oil prices result in high rates of economic growth but this fails to translate into economic development.[10] Studies of Nigeria conclude that antipoverty measures in the 1980s and early 1990s had a weak impact on overall poverty rates and economic development because they were piecemeal, lacked full political commitment, and required more time to make a significant impact on development.[11] China's impressive economic growth performance between 2000 and 2008 has nevertheless had a limited impact in most of rural China, where millions live in poverty. It will take a while for investments in health, education, and infrastructure to yield desired outcomes because economic development lags growth. This point was echoed in the "Economic Report on Africa 2008" produced by the UN Economic Commission for Africa.[12]

Weak governance is a second reason why trade-led growth may not lead to economic development. In Sudan real GDP grew by an astounding 10 percent in 2007 and almost 7 percent in 2008 (in spite of the global financial crisis), yet most Sudanese live in abject poverty. Decades of neglect have resulted in very few investments in infrastructure, services, or human capacity outside the capital, Khartoum. Ironically, the adverse effects are most prominent in the country's oil-producing regions, particularly in the South. The formation of a relatively autonomous government of Southern Sudan between 2005 and mid-2011 does not appear to have addressed the problem. It remains to be seen if the new government of the Republic of South Sudan will fare any better. Development indicators are yet to improve appreciably. Questions have been raised about corruption in both the North and the South, and analysts point to millions of petro-dollars that could not be accounted for.[13]

A third reason is that economic production in many primary commodity exporting countries occurs in enclave sectors that are not fully integrated into the local and national economies. Large (often foreign) firms produce and export agricultural or mineral products without employing many local people, purchasing local goods and services, or (in some cases) paying their taxes.[14] This is true of extractive industries (petroleum in Gabon or copper in Zambia), agriculture (banana exports in the Caribbean), manufacturing (shoe factories in India), or services (pharmaceutical research in Eastern Europe). Enclave investors that generally import practically all their inputs are more interested in optimizing and repatriating profits than contributing to economic development in host countries. This situation is made worse when these enclave operators have negative environmental impacts that can undermine host economies. Environmental damage in parts of the Democratic Republic of the Congo's (DRC) copper belt has affected both the soil and groundwater, making it difficult for communities to make a living via agriculture or fisheries.[15] Pollution impacts these communities through the costs of cleanup and diminishes food production. Both contribute to reduced economic development.

Generally, trade has a more direct impact on economic growth than on economic development. What is traded, with whom a country trades, and what the trade policy is help determine whether the impact on growth will be positive or negative. The link with economic development is less direct and is contingent upon policies and programs that promote equity, provide services and infrastructure, and protect the environment. Countries with fewer trade restrictions trade a lot more and enjoy higher levels of economic development. While there is clearly some correlation between the two, it is unclear whether there is any causality. And if there is a causal relationship, in what direction does it flow: Do countries trade more because they have more open trade policies? Or are they able to implement more open trade policies because of their volume of trade? In the 1980s and early 1990s the export-oriented Southeast Asian tiger economies owed their phenomenal growth to expanding trade. This led to a spirited debate about the role of openness versus government intervention in boosting trade. A World Bank report pointed to openness, enabling public policy and strategic investments in human and physical capital.[16] Others, like Stiglitz, argued that active government intervention was a deciding factor.[17] Stiglitz explained that such intervention succeeded because it complemented rather than replaced market forces. In the wake of the 2008 global financial crisis, a number of countries sought to supplant, rather than

Table 13.1 Global Trade and Economic Growth (annual percentage change)

	2002	2003	2004	2005	2006	2007	2008	2009
World								
GDP growth	1.9	2.7	4.1	3.5	3.9	3.9	1.7	−1.9
Export growth	4.5	6.3	11.4	5.2	9.2	5.8	3.0	−13.7
Import growth	4.2	7.7	12.1	7.0	8.5	6.6	2.2	−13.1
Developed countries								
GDP growth	1.3	1.9	3.1	2.5	2.8	2.5	0.3	−3.4
Export growth	2.3	3.1	8.4	4.9	8.5	3.9	2.8	−14.8
Import growth	3.0	5.1	9.0	5.9	7.2	3.7	0.0	−14.2
Developing countries								
GDP growth	3.9	5.4	7.3	6.7	7.4	7.8	5.4	2.4
Export growth	8.8	12.9	16.7	6.3	10.8	8.7	4.2	−11.7
Import growth	6.6	12.9	18.4	8.5	10.2	10.6	5.3	−9.5

Data Sources: UNCTAD, *Trade and Development Report, 2010 (2004–2009)* and UNCTAD database (2002–2003).

complement, markets through varying degrees of protectionism.[18] It remains too early to tell whether this will have a fundamental impact on the functioning or security of the trade system.

RECENT TRENDS IN GLOBAL TRADE

After growing steadily between 2002 and 2007, peaking at an estimated $16 trillion in 2007, world trade contracted by almost 2 percent in 2009 because of the 2008–9 global financial crisis (see table 13.1). The negative effects were felt more severely in developing countries. The economic downturn led to the first truly global contraction since the end of World War II and to a reversal of development gains in some developing countries, even though they experienced relatively modest contractions. Economic hardships in the developed world had an adverse effect on demand for developing country exports and resulted in lower aid flows, a reduction in investment flows, and an increased cost of credit—all of which weakened economic progress in many developing countries. Although the effects of the twin crises (the food crisis of 2007–8 and the financial crisis of 2008–9) will continue to be felt over the medium term, both trade and output in the developing world are expected to remain relatively robust. Understanding the relationship between these trends and economic development requires a careful consideration of five important developments in recent years: the 2008–9 global financial crisis, the virtual collapse of Doha trade talks, increasing globalization, the impact of conflict-affected states, and the role of nonstate actors.

Precipitated by the US subprime crisis, the financial turmoil of 2008 unearthed failures in global regulatory systems and had a debilitating impact on world trade. The resultant meltdown has dampened demand in the major economies—principally the United States, Europe, and East Asia—and has adversely impacted suppliers of commodities, manufactured goods, and services worldwide. The effects on trade were immediate and pervasive because of the increasingly interconnected nature of global business. As discussed earlier, vertical integration now means that a downturn in the US car industry means that suppliers and service providers in Africa, Asia, and Latin America suffer. The negative impact on economic development is most pronounced in developing countries where social safety nets or compensating mechanisms are either ineffective or do not exist. The economic downturn precipitated by the crisis also led to a drop in commodity prices, which has affected developing economies by reducing export earnings and threatening to reverse recent trade gains.

The second factor is the lack of progress with the Doha Round of trade talks, which started in November 2001 and were designed to boost global trade by reducing tariff and nontariff barriers to trade. In addition to increasing global trade, the rounds were intended to address equity and procedural issues. Elliott explains that while US tariffs on imports from Bangladesh average fifteen cents per dollar, the comparable figure for countries in Western Europe is one cent per dollar.[19] The World Bank's "Doing Business" report lists a wide range of administrative hurdles that make developing countries less competitive. World Trade Organization (WTO) data suggest that global output could increase by $300–700 billion if provisions in the Doha Round are fully implemented. Global welfare gains from a 33 percent reduction in tariffs could exceed half a trillion dollars.[20] Eliminating cotton subsidies could increase real incomes in Africa's cotton-producing countries by $150 million annually. However, after eight rounds little progress has been made.[21] Industrialized countries find it difficult to sell tariff reductions and subsidy removal to powerful domestic constituencies. Developing countries are insisting on pro-poor strategies, and some have difficulties implementing existing trade agreements. The issue of special and differential treatment for developing countries has also been difficult to negotiate. The trade talks have pitted the industrial countries (primarily the United States and Western European states) against the developing world (led by China, India, Brazil, and South Africa). While these parties have been bogged down in protracted discussions, the poorest countries continue to experience adverse terms of trade and face seemingly insurmountable barriers to trade both domestically and globally.

The virtual collapse of the Doha Round signals a shift from multilateral rules-based trade relationships to preferential trade agreements (PTA) on a bilateral basis and regional trade arrangements (RTA). Available data reveal that RTAs have grown rapidly over the last fifteen years and have become "defining features of the modern economy."[22] PTAs account for an estimated one-third of global trade.[23] Marked shifts in the direction of trade have implications for the development prospects of trading partners. Questions have been raised about equity as well as whether trading blocs create or divert trade. Bhagwati laments a pandemic of PTAs, which he describes as a "pox on the world trading system."[24] He argues that they are inherently discriminatory and lead to protectionism. Robinson questions the development effectiveness of PTAs and concludes that they result in "beggar thy neighbor policies" that undermine competitiveness and reduce welfare benefits.[25]

Furthermore, the increase in the number of PTAs has resulted in countries belonging to multiple trading groups, some of which have duplicative or conflicting objectives. The gradual diminution of multilateralism under the WTO and concomitant expansion of PTAs could have dire and lasting consequences for economic growth if the negative impacts are not recognized and mitigated.

Regional trading blocs (RTB) are also growing in popularity as developing countries (mostly small states with small, nondiversified economies) seek to benefit from economies of scale when trading and collective bargaining power in trade negotiations. Lipsey opines that RTBs could be welfare-enhancing if effective customs unions are established.[26] Wonnacott notes that the economies of scale resulting from RTBs could have a positive development impact through market expansion and if steps are taken to promote complementarity among member states.[27] Bhagwati points out that "free trade and free trade areas are not synonymous" and argues that RTBs could end up shifting production to less efficient countries.[28] There is also a significant gap between the multilateral principles espoused by RTB members and actual practices within RTBs. European Union (EU) subsidies, apparent protectionism within the Association of South East Asian Nations, and potential trade diversion within the African Union are examples. Baldwin advocates a "multilaterization of regionalism." In his view, most of the negative impacts of RTBs could be mitigated if mechanisms are put in place to uphold and enforce multilateral commitments within RTBs.[29]

The third factor intervening between growth and development relates to the increased pace of globalization in recent decades, which has been driven by technological advances, improved transportation, and deliberate policy choices.[30] Less-developed countries are disadvantaged because they lag behind in the uptake of technology and the provision of requisite infrastructure. This has resulted in ever-widening gaps between rich and poor countries. For example, since 1970 sub-Saharan Africa's share of world trade has fallen from 4 percent to 2 percent. Over this period the region's trade grew at three-fourths the global average and half the rate of Asia.

The fourth point concerns the burgeoning conflict economies in fragile states, which have given prominence to the role of militia, smugglers, and facilitators in the trade of strategic commodities that Paul Collier describes as "lootable goods."[31] Prendergast and Lezhnev explain how gold and tin ores in the DRC are traded outside formal institutions because of the disruptive effects of war and the increasing role played by combatants in the supply chain. Consequently, neighboring Uganda officially produced less than $600 worth of gold in 2007, yet it exported more than $74 million worth of gold. Similarly, Rwanda produced $8 million worth of tin ore but officially exported at least $30 million of tin.[32] Such developments deprive governments of much-needed fiscal revenues and divert funds from productive domestic investments to prosecute wars or enrich key actors in the war economy. The DRC is a prime example of seriously lagging development in a resource-rich but war-torn state.

Finally, and more speculatively, we should consider how the role of nonstate actors in global trade influences development outcomes. Transnational entities account for a significant proportion of global trade and their activities (particularly in extractive industries and manufacturing) could have far-reaching ramifications. Sovereign wealth funds, now estimated at $2.5 trillion, are expected to double by 2010 and reach $12 trillion by 2012.[33] Mattoo and Subramanian discuss two possible side effects. First, their portfolio decisions could potentially destabilize financial markets. This was evident in the East Asian financial crisis of the late 1990s when large portfolio movements by nonstate actors worsened the effects of financial contagion. The second is their control of strategic industries, which could be economically or politically destabilizing.[34] The relationship between oil corporations and the ruling National Congress Party in Sudan has been blamed for protracted conflict in that country. Public opinion and advocacy groups forced Canadian Talisman Energy to divest in 2003, and the China National Petroleum Corporation has been linked to excesses of the al Bashir government since Sudan's 2005 Comprehensive Peace Agreement.

TRADE POLICY AND DEVELOPMENT

As discussed earlier, market forces are not always efficient or welfare-enhancing. Countries intervene to address market failings, reduce poverty, or advance export-promotion or import-substitution strategies. This is primarily done through tariffs, subsidies, and quotas. These interventions are intended to make domestic goods and services more competitive, available, and affordable. Following the Great Depression in the 1930s, the United States introduced a system of subsidies to stabilize farm incomes and boost agricultural output. A similar approach was taken in the aftermath of World War II, when most of Europe faced food deficits and a potential collapse of its agricultural sector. This is how the European Common market's (now the EU's) Common Agricultural Policy, a system of local and export subsidies, was born. Similar arrangements existed in the Soviet bloc. In all cases, domestic production was protected by a system of quotas. While these efforts generally led to increased output, they also had adverse effects including significant fiscal costs, skewed incentives in local economies, and depressed international commodity prices (when surpluses arose). In addition, tariffs, subsidies, and quotas are very expensive and onerous to administer and could be prone to abuse and corruption. This was particularly true of the Soviet bloc. These interventions also had pernicious effects on global trade and poverty.

In the 1960s and 1970s many nonindustrialized countries in Africa, Asia, and Latin America introduced tariffs, subsides, and quotas for similar reasons; they wanted to protect their economies and foster income stability. Tariffs were also used to redistribute wealth from agriculture to their fledgling industries. These countries found it difficult to compete in the global economy. A combination of global economic shocks (the oil and debt crises of the 1970s), commodity price volatility, and limited market access precipitated economic woes. Many governments responded by increasing tariffs to boost revenues, whereas quotas and subsidies became part of a growing patronage system. Not surprisingly, output suffered and imports became costlier, leading to a progressive worsening of terms of trade (particularly in Africa) for most of the 1980s and 1990s.

Even after achieving their intended goals of stabilizing rural incomes and boosting exports, both the United States and Europe maintained the tariffs and subsidies. Initially, this was largely dictated by cold war competition but more recently because the now-wealthy farmers have become a formidable political constituency. Countries in Latin America, Asia, and Africa have been adversely affected by trade policy choices in industrial countries. Subsidies have depressed world market prices for their main exports and tariffs and quotas limited access to lucrative markets. EU sugar subsidies depressed world prices by 17 percent in 2001, making it impossible for Mozambique's postwar sugar industry to get off the ground (even though production costs in the country compared favorably internationally).[35] Research by OXFAM suggests that dairy subsidies in Europe (equivalent to 60 percent of the global price for milk powder and 136 percent the price of butter) severely weakened the Indian dairy industry. Cotton subsidies in the United States have affected West African producers in Benin, Burkina Faso, and Mali.[36] They depressed global prices by 15 percent in the early 2000s, leading to an estimated 25 percent drop in farmers' income. According to analysts at the Geneva-based 3D, Mali received $37.7 million in development assistance from the US Agency for International Development in 2001 but lost $43 million because of cotton subsidies.[37]

In hopes of maximizing benefits from trade, many developing countries have improved their trade policies by reducing tariffs and subsidies while streamlining the overall administrative and regulatory environment. For example, average Most Favored Nation tariffs dropped from 14 percent during the second half of the 1990s to 9 percent in 2007 while import restrictions fell dramatically in countries like Egypt, India, and the Seychelles.[38] WTO analysts attribute improvements in output to measures aimed at improving trade environments by reducing tariff and nontariff barriers to trade in developing countries, and advocate increased trade as a vehicle for sustained economic development.[39] This approach assumes that the benefits of growth will eventually trigger development by trickling down to the poorer segments of society. However, evidence from the developing world suggests that this is seldom the case, and productivity gains do not automatically translate into development for all.

Most of the tariff reform between 1983 and 2003 was autonomous and was not part of international trade rounds. The notion that reform is mainly constrained by stalled multilateral trade discussions is not entirely accurate. As shown in figure 13.1, the least-developed countries have the highest tariff rates. This is partly because they rely heavily on tariffs for fiscal revenues and partly because they anticipate some gains from protectionism. However, the net result does not appear to have been positive as these countries still underperform and lag behind the rest of the world. Domestic trade reform in developing countries could initiate significant change, which could be buttressed by multilateral efforts.

In ideal circumstances, trade liberalization could improve economic prospects through export promotion for commodities or services in which countries have (or

Figure 13.1 Trade Tariff Restrictiveness Index

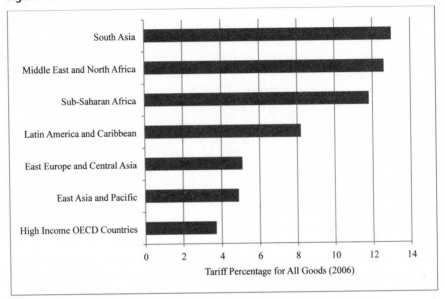

Data Source: World Bank, *World Trade Indicators 2008* (Washington, DC: World Bank, 2008), 6.

can develop) a comparative advantage. While some countries like the East Asian tigers were able to record sustained growth rates in the 1980s, most other developing countries have neither the resource endowment nor institutional framework to replicate the feat. Export-led growth has perpetuated single-commodity dependence in many cases, leaving the developing economies highly susceptible to the global price volatility. The trade liberalization argument assumes that developing countries would benefit from free trade in spite of their level of development, skills base, governance structure, and technology base. It also presumes perfect market information, access to market, and the ability of market participants to switch production in response to market information. Birdsall and Hamoudi have questioned research that suggests that trade openness fosters economic growth, highlighting the importance of structural and institutional reforms.[40]

Yusuf laments the apparent inability of empirical studies to fully understand what triggers and sustains growth.[41] In his view, "there is a dearth of thinking on [the complexities of growth] and a lack of preparedness, which is apparent from the disorganized and clumsy responses to recent crises and the absence of long-run efforts to strengthen global capacities."[42] Even less is known about the link between trade and economic development. While GDP rates have risen in recent years, the poorest countries are less integrated into the global economy, domestic income inequality is widening, and social indicators are lagging. Clearly, the positive macroeconomic effects of growing trade have not translated into improved economic development prospects for the vast majority of citizens in these countries.

TRADING EAST OR TRADING WEST

The choice of trading partners could also influence the prospects for sustained economic development. Most developing countries have been torn between the Western model (e.g., the United States), which emphasizes open markets and democratization, and an Eastern model (e.g., China), which is typified by state intervention, resource-based lending, and noninterference in domestic governance. Chinese trade with developing countries has grown significantly since the turn of the century. Between 2004 and 2009 China signed trade deals worth $14 billion with seven resource-rich African countries. The $3 billion copper deal with Afghanistan and trade expansion initiatives in Kazakhstan, Kyrgyzstan, Tajikistan, Turkmenistan, and Uzbekistan have raised eyebrows. China has been criticized for not doing more to encourage responsible and representative governance in developing countries, flouting labor and environmental laws, and turning a blind eye to corruption.

On closer examination, one can surmise that China's trade practices are guided by its own development experience and market conditions in developing countries. Brautigam explains how China used a combination of state intervention and resource-backed borrowing to kick-start its industrialization drive in the 1970s, when it had limited foreign reserves and questionable creditworthiness.[43] Operating in similarly constrained environments in Africa, Asia, and Central and Eastern Europe, China has opted to apply the same formula in its dealings with developing countries. Noninterference works for China because it affords a measure of predictability for longer-term investments. Questions have also been raised about the nature and fairness of these resource-based contracts.[44] China benefits by securing access to important resources and earning the gratitude of grateful leaders who support Chinese positions in international forums. Unfortunately, while the developing countries receive fees, taxes, and infrastructure projects, weak governance and corruption continue to undermine prospects for economic development.

Is trading with the West a better option for the developing world? Frankly, its record is not much better in the poorest regions of the world. Western companies hedge risk by generally focusing on short-term engagements, and governance conditions make negotiations slow and tortuous. Developing countries could go à la carte, judiciously selecting the best of both worlds and finding smarter ways to leverage their natural resources. In addition, the strong relationship between accountable governance and positive trade outcomes should encourage much-needed reforms to reduce distortions, minimize corruption, and ensure the equitable distribution of trade benefits.

ADDRESSING THE CHALLENGES

While we acknowledge that different trade regimes have merits and demerits, it is clear that trade can foster equitable economic progress if steps are taken to improve governance and remove bottlenecks in developing countries and if more developed trading partners do not adopt policies (e.g., subsidies) and practices (e.g., dumping) that disadvantage these countries. Significant and sustained efforts must be made to address tariff and nontariff barriers to trade, some of which are discussed in this section.

Freer and Fairer Trade

Paul Samuelson, widely considered one of the luminaries of international trade theory, cautioned against what he described as a "misinterpretation" of free trade. He pointed out that free trade is not necessarily optimal for all countries and added that "it is not possible to demonstrate rigorously that free trade is better for a country than all other kinds of trade."[45] As discussed earlier, free trade alone does not result in either growth or economic development. What is needed is "freer trade," which reduces or removes a broad range of domestic and global barriers to trade while compensating the losers. The barriers include price controls, excessive tariffs, developing country subsidies, inefficient institutions, protectionism, and overtaxation (actual and implicit). Studies indicate that the elimination of subsidies could expand global net trade by $40 billion annually and increase agricultural incomes in developing countries by some $24 billion.[46] Freer trade reduces distortions but provides a soft-landing while countries and communities adjust.

Fair trade gained popularity in advocacy circles as a strategy to redress the vulnerability of producers in developing countries and to ensure that they receive just prices, enjoy improved working conditions, and move toward self-sufficiency. Fair trade was introduced as a conscious attempt to connect trade and development. This is done by improving market access for producers (especially marginalized groups) and by establishing equitable trading relationships and awareness and advocacy campaigns. Fair trade aims to address market imperfections by negotiating market access as well as fair prices for exports. Some critics argue that negotiated prices are not market-determined and end up hurting the producers by lowering prices in the long run.[47] Producers respond to the artificially high prices by increasing supply. Lindsey described fair trade as "an interventionist scheme" that replaces one flawed pricing structure with another.[48] Bhagwati opined that fair trade can become "an exercise in insidious protectionism that few recognize as such."[49] Fairer trade will not seek to direct trade via intervention or protectionism. It will focus on the rights of workers, leveling the playing field and building institutions and capacity.

While freer and fairer trade would address distortions and help create an enabling environment for development-friendly trade, they are by no means sufficient to trigger and sustain economic growth. Key investments are required in infrastructure, technology, and skills in order to broaden and diversify both economic activity and trade. Improved governance and reduced corruption would result in investments that are more productive. Exports in the poorest countries are dominated by enclave economies (particularly in mining and commercial agriculture), which barely integrate other sectors of the economy. This means that while the economy might grow because of developments in one sector (usually extractive industries), the rest of the economy hardly benefits and remains underdeveloped.

Sustainable economic development demands sustained and concerted strategy involving both domestic and international actors.

Trade versus Aid

There is broad-based consensus that economic development in the world's poorest states would require consistently high rates of capital accumulation. As mentioned earlier, the poorest countries are not well integrated into the global economy and are very susceptible to commodity price fluctuation. Moreover, whatever gains are realized from trade might contribute to economic growth but not economic development. This suggests that trade alone is unlikely to help countries meet the Millennium Development Goals. Jeffery Sachs has suggested a significant increase in development assistance from $65 billion in 2002 to $195 billion a year by 2015 to help these countries meet their development goals.[50] As the figure on development assistance illustrates, scaling up to that extent would require aid to grow at unprecedented rates each year. This is more unlikely in the aftermath of the 2008–9 financial crisis. In addition, aid is regularly criticized as being wasteful and ineffective.[51]

Neither aid nor trade should be considered the panacea for the enduring problem of underdevelopment. They must complement each other. Targeted aid could help developing countries invest in the skills, technology, infrastructure, and institutions that would help them diversify their exports, become more integrated into the global economy, and ensure that trade contributes to increased living standards for all citizens.

Single-Commodity Dependence

The 2008 World Trade Report explains how single-commodity economies are more susceptible to global price volatility and, therefore, have lower GDP growth rates over the longer term. Diversification could help such economies mitigate the effects of price volatility. However, diversification is a long-term process that requires significant investment in physical and human capital as well as a focused strategy to make other sectors of the economy more competitive. The Export Concentration Index (see table 13.2) measures the extent to which economies rely on one or two commodities. Countries with the highest indices rely on a major primary export (oil or minerals) or are small island nations like Micronesia and Sao Tome. Medium- to long-term diversification would work best for the commodity exporters. Small island nations require more comprehensive support to initiate and sustain a range economic activity. In both cases, the issue of improved market access for new exports must be part of the strategy.

Growing demand for natural resources (unprocessed or semiprocessed petroleum, precious minerals, mineral ores, and agricultural products) over the past decade has provided windfall gains for many developing countries. This has been partly fueled by rapid industrialization in Asia, which now receives roughly 25 percent of Africa's exports, with China and India accounting for 10 percent.[52] These developments have reduced incentives to diversify as developing countries position themselves to make the most of growing demand.

Table 13.2   Export Concentration Index

	Ten Least Concentrated Economies		Ten Most Concentrated Economies	
		ECI (2006)		ECI (2006)
1	United States	7.6	Angola	95.5
2	South Korea	8.6	Iraq	92.4
3	Brazil	9.1	Micronesia	91.7
4	Thailand	9.5	Venezuela	91.1
5	Serbia	10.6	Equatorial Guinea	90.4
6	China	11	Sudan	87.2
7	Croatia	11.9	Sao Tome & Principe	86.9
8	Lebanon	12	Congo, Rep.	86.9
9	Canada	12.4	Yemen	85.2
10	Indonesia	12.9	Nigeria	85.1

Source: World Trade Indicators data (2008).

MOVING AHEAD

Trade could be a powerful catalyst for lasting economic development and global security if supported by welfare-enhancing trade policies, a progressive removal of trade distortions, and timely investments in human resources, technology, and infrastructure. More attention should be paid to programs that increase market access (without imposing onerous rules and restrictions) and initiatives that facilitate trade (without exacerbating income inequalities) and expand export capacity (without triggering the resource curse). Addressing these constraints discussed here could help make trade part of a more effective strategy for sustained growth and economic development. At the domestic level, efforts will focus on the distributive implications of trade, capacity constraints, tariff structures, and diversification. Important regional considerations will include the relative merits and demerits of regional trade integration while global efforts will seek to address the implications of globalization as well as growing need for freer and fairer trade.

Developing countries should make concerted efforts to provide policy environments that promote freer trade. Trade reform should also prioritize the removal of both tariff and nontariff barriers. Progress on tariff reduction must be deeper (providing more significant reductions) and broader (including more products). Nontariff barriers such as roadblocks, bureaucratic bottlenecks, and corruption must receive attention. Programs should also be introduced to facilitate cross-border trade, simplify and harmonize customs procedures, and improve trade-related services (such as credit, storage, communication, and transportation). Developing countries should consider steps to integrate more fully into the global economy. For example, regional or bilateral arrangements that are trade diverting could make the economies uncompetitive and less likely to grow. The costs of these programs would be offset by longer-term efficiency gains.

The industrialized countries could help boost trade and promote economic development by helping developing countries implement appropriate policies, bridge infrastructure gaps, build robust institutions, and acquire requisite skills and technology. This would enable them to compete more effectively and use trade as an integral part of a comprehensive strategy for economic development. This could be done by targeting increased aid flows, both financial and technical assistance. Assistance could be channeled via the Enhanced Integrated Framework, which is a multilateral initiative for the least-developed countries that aims to integrate trade into the national development plans of the poorest countries and to assist in the coordinated delivery of trade-related technical assistance.[53]

Trade could potentially contribute to economic development by raising incomes, generating employment, and bolstering economic growth. An appropriate policy environment could ensure that entrepreneurs have access to markets, obstacles to trade are removed, and the benefits of trade are equitably distributed. Freer, fairer trade also bodes well for sustained, country-owned progress because it has the capacity to wean fragile states off the dependency syndrome. However, trade must be part of a broader and sustained economic development if it is to be an effective engine for growth.

Notes

1. Paul Collier, *The Bottom Billion* (Oxford: Oxford University Press, 2007).

2. P. Messerlin, E. Zedillo, and J. Nielson. *Trade for Development: Achieving the Millennium Development Goals* (London: Earthscan, Report of the UN Millennium Task Force on Trade, 2005).

3. Christopher L. Gilbert, "Value Chain Analysis and Market Power in the Commodity Processing with Application to the Cocoa and Coffee Sectors," Discussion Paper No. 5 (University of Trento, Italy: Economics Department, 2006).

4. There are attempts to mitigate these problems through the fair trade movement (for example, in coffee, cocoa, etc.) This can be helpful when fair trade involves processing and manufacturing, as it allows exporters and traders to move up the value chain. However, the impact on actual farm-gate prices is patchy.

5. Details of the Human Development Index are available at http://hdr.undp.org/en/statistics/.

6. David Ricardo, *On the Principles of Political Economy and Taxation* (London: John Murray, 1821).

7. A. V. Deardorff, "The General Validity of the Heckscher-Ohlin Theorem," *American Economic Review* 72 (1982): 683–94.

8. Paul Baran, *The Political Economy of Growth* (New York: Monthly Review Press, 1968).

9. Work by Wassily Leontief in the mid-1950s observed that the United States (then the most capital-abundant country) exported labor-intensive commodities and imported capital-intensive commodities, in apparent contradiction with the Heckscher-Ohlin theorem. Leontief found that this was because labor was relatively cheaper than capital in the United States.

10. Terry Lynn Karl, *The Paradox of Plenty: Oil Booms and Petro-States*, Studies in International Political Economy (Berkeley: University of California Press, 1997).

11. T. Saji and S. Canagarajah, "Poverty in a Wealthy Economy: The Case of Nigeria," Working Paper No. 02/114 (Washington, DC: International Monetary Fund, 2002); and

S. Xavier and A. Subramanian, "Addressing the Natural Resource Curse: An Illustration from Nigeria," Working Paper No. 03/139 (Washington, DC: IMF 2003).

12. Economic Commission on Africa, "Economic Report on Africa 2008," www.uneca .org/era2008/.

13. See *2006 Global Integrity Report for Sudan,* http://back.globalintegrity.org/reports /2006/sudan/index.cfm; and "Corruption and Underdevelopment in Southern Sudan," *New Sudan Vision,* January 30, 2009, www.newsudanvision.com/index.php?option=com _content&view=article&id=1505:corruption-a-underdevelopment-in-southern-sudan&catid =11:letters&Itemid=49.

14. "Nigeria Demands $2bn in Tax Arrears," *BBC News Online,* May 21, 2008, http://news .bbc.co.uk/2/hi/africa/7412189.stm.

15. makeITfair, "Linking Extractives to Consumer Electronics: Responsibilities of Electronics Companies Down the Supply Chain." Summary Report of the International Roundtable, January 18, 2008, Brussels. http://makeitfair.org/companies/summary-round-table -brussels.

16. World Bank, *The East Asian Miracle* (New York: Oxford University Press, 1993).

17. Joseph E. Stiglitz, "Some Lessons from the East Asian Miracle," *World Bank Research Observer* 11, no. 2 (1996): 151–77.

18. A. Faiola, "'Buy American' Rider Sparks Trade Debate: Proviso Limits Steel, Iron from Abroad," *Washington Post,* January 29, 2009.

19. K. A. Elliot, "Opening Markets for Poor Countries: Are We there Yet?," Working Paper 184 (Washington, DC: Center for Global Development, 2009).

20. D. K. Brown, A. V. Deardorff, and R. M. Stern, "Computational Analysis of Multilateral Trade Liberalization in the Uruguay Round and Doha Development Round," Discussion Paper No. 489 (Ann Arbor: University of Michigan, School of Public Policy, 2002), http://ford school.umich.edu/rsie/workingpapers/Papers476-500/r489.pdf.

21. The trade rounds have been held in Doha (2001), Cancún (2003), Geneva (2004), Paris (2005), Hong Kong (2005), Geneva (2006), Potsdam (2007), and Geneva (2008).

22. Shaheen Rafi Khan, *Regional Trade Integration and Conflict Resolution* (London: Routledge, 2008).

23. D. Tussie and C. Quilliconi, "Market Access as Substitute for Development," Human Development Report Occasional Paper (New York: UN Development Programme, 2004).

24. Jagdish Bhagwati, *Termites in the Trading System* (New York: Oxford University Press, 2008).

25. Joan Robinson, "Review of *Money, Trade and Economic Growth* by J. G. Johnson," *Economic Journal* 72, no. 287 (1962): 690–92.

26. Richard Lipsey, "The Theory of Customs Unions: Trade Diversion and Welfare," *Economica* 24 (1957): 40–46.

27. R. Wonnacott, "Free Trade Agreements: For Better or Worse," *The American Economic Review* 86 (1996): 62–86.

28. Jagdish Bhagwati, "The World Trading System," *Journal of International Affairs* 48 (1994): 279–85.

29. Richard E. Baldwin, "Multilateralising Regionalism: Spaghetti Bowls as Building Blocs on the Path to Global Free Trade," *World Economy* 29, no. 11 (2006): 1451–1518.

30. D. Dollar, "Globalization, Poverty, and Inequality since 1980," *World Bank Research Observer* 20, no. 2 (2005): 145–75.

31. Paul Collier and Anke Hoeffler, "Greed and Grievance in Civil War," *Oxford Economic Papers* 54 (2004): 563–95.

32. John Prendergast and Sasha Lezhnev, "From Mine to Mobile Phone: The Conflict Minerals Supply Chain," *Enough: The Project to End Genocide and Crimes against Humanity,* November 10, 2009. www.enoughproject.org/files/publications/minetomobile.pdf.

33. Aaditya Mattoo and A. Subramanian, "Multilateralism beyond Doha," Working Paper No. 153 (Washington, DC: Center for Global Development, 2008).

34. Ibid.

35. "Stop the Dumping! How EU Agriculture Subsidies Are Damaging Livelihoods in the Developing World," Briefing Paper No. 31 (Washington, DC: OXFAM, 2006).

36. Elinor L. Heinisch, "West Africa versus the United States on Cotton Subsidies: How, Why and What Next?" *Journal of Modern African Studies* 44, no. 2 (2006): 251–74.

37. 3D, "US, and EU Cotton Production and Export Policies and Their Impact on West and Central Africa: Coming to Grips with International Human Rights Obligations," (Geneva: 3D, May 2004), www.3dthree.org/pdf_3D/1404-EGICottonBrief_FINAL.pdf.

38. Gianni Zanini and Roumeen Islam, *World Trade Indicators: Benchmarking Policy and Performance* (Washington, DC: World Bank, 2008).

39. World Trade Organization, *World Trade Report 2009: Trade Policy Commitments and Contingency Measures* (Geneva: WTO, 2009).

40. Nancy Birdsall and Amar Hamoudi, "Commodity Dependence, Trade, and Growth: When 'Openness' Is Not Enough," Working Paper 7 (Washington, DC: Center for Global Development, 2002).

41. Shahid Yusuf, *Development Economics through the Decades* (Washington, DC: World Bank, 2009).

42. Ibid., 117.

43. China leveraged its oil and coal reserves to attract a $10 billion loan from Japan for critical technology and infrastructure investments in the late 1970s. Deborah Brautigam, "Africa's Eastern Promise: What the West Can Learn from Chinese Investments in Africa," *Foreign Affairs*, January 5, 2010, www.foreignaffairs.com/articles/65916/deborah-brautigam /africa%E2%80%99s-eastern-promise.

44. John Reboul, of counsel at Ropes & Gray, which analyzed five of the major mining contracts in the Democratic Republic of the Congo for The Carter Center, described them as "some of the most one-sided agreements I have seen in 30 years of practice." See "Carter Center Urges International Community to Support Congo Mining Review Efforts," Press Release, *The Carter Center*, March 10, 2008, www.cartercenter.org/news/pr/drc_031008.html.

45. Paul Samuelson, "The Gains from International Trade," in *The Collected Scientific Papers of Paul A Samuelson*, ed. Paul A. Samuelson and Joseph E. Stiglitz, vol. 2 (Cambridge, MA: MIT Press, 1966), 781.

46. Eugenio Diaz-Bonilla, "Can WTO Agricultural Negotiations Help the Poor," *SAIS Review* 23, no. 1 (2003): 87–92.

47. Brink Lindsey, "Grounds for Complaint: 'Fair Trade' and the Coffee Crisis" (London: Adam Smith Institute, 2004). www.adamsmith.org/images/stories/groundsforcomplaint.pdf.

48. Ibid.

49. Jagdish Bhagwati, "Obama and Trade: An Alarm Sounds," *Financial Times*, January 9, 2009.

50. Jeffrey Sachs, *The End of Poverty* (New York: Penguin Press, 2005).

51. Dambisa Moyo, *Dead Aid: Why Aid Is Not Working and How There Is a Better Way for Africa* (New York: Farrar, Straus and Giroux, 2009).

52. Sanjeev Gupta and Yongzheng Yang, "Unblocking Trade," *Finance and Development* 43, no. 4 (2006).

53. For information on the Enhanced Integrated Framework, see www.enhancedif.org/.

TRADE AND RESOURCES
Editors' Comments

Joanna Spear and Paul D. Williams

Security and development experts are once again debating the causal relationships between trade and peace, and trade and economic development. In each arena this debate has taken place before, and the assumption had been that it was decisively solved: the security arena thought that trade would lead to more peace, and the development arena was agreed that trade would lead to economic development. Although this has broadly been the result of increasing levels of trade, the relationships have not been perfect. Thus, security specialists are struggling with the ways in which trade and resources have fueled intrastate conflict while development experts are grappling with the fact that increased growth as a result of trade has not always produced widespread economic development for the majority of citizens in developing countries. In both arenas scholars and practitioners are investigating why their assumptions about causality have proved faulty or insufficient.

More than any other factor, the complex processes of globalization have challenged these assumptions and stimulated another look at the consequences of trade. Specifically, globalization has intensified some challenges to security delivered via trade, including threats from malign transnational actors and self-financing combatants. On balance, however, Spear concludes that China's trade and resource activities can be seen as enhancing human security for millions around the developing world and in Asia. Globalization has also complicated the task of delivering economic development through trade even as it facilitates it, because winners win more and less developed countries are in a weak position to reap any benefits from the increased velocity of trade and demand for resources. Consequently, Gilpin concludes that governments and international organizations need to give economic development a chance by explicitly supporting welfare-enhancing trade policies, progressively removing trade distortions, and cultivating timely investments in human resources, technology, and infrastructure

Trade is also an area where states are not the only important actors. Although intergovernmental organizations have long played a role in trade, the World Trade Organization is the most powerful yet. While security experts have focused on two types of nonstate actors—self-financing combatants and transnational networks—development experts have increasingly considered the behavior of institutions such as sovereign wealth funds and private firms, whose investment choices can have a major impact on the relationship between trade and domestic levels of economic development within states.

While both security and development have traditionally viewed trade and resource issues from the state level of analysis, this not only misses some crucial actors, it also glosses over some of the vital effects of these issues. In development, the failure of economic growth to translate into broader and more equitable economic development is often hidden by a statist level of analysis. In the security realm the negative consequences for human security of the activities of self-financing combatants and malign transnational actors would also be obscured if analysis remained only at the level of the state.

Part VII

DEMOGRAPHY

Chapter 14

DEMOGRAPHY
A Security Perspective

Jack A. Goldstone

Since the end of the Cold War, the definition of "security" has expanded. Where once the main threats to Western nations were military attacks on themselves or allied governments, their security concerns now encompass a wide range of threats to a stable and secure world. These include failing states that create breeding grounds for terrorism, insurgencies, civil wars, and genocides; humanitarian disasters causing major refugee flows; issues of immigration and associated human, drug, and weapons trafficking; and fiscal and economic strains that threaten the capabilities of today's rich countries to respond to disorder.[1] While each of these threats has its own array of causes, the threats are linked in that each can be exacerbated, or even caused, by the consequences of local and global demographic change.[2]

This chapter examines five major trends in global population that are likely to pose significant security challenges in the coming decades:

- A major divergence in the global patterns of demographic growth, with most developed countries now stabilizing or shrinking in population while most of the developing countries continue to grow, some of them very rapidly. Thus, the demographic and economic weight of the advanced economies relative to the rest of the world will undergo a rapid decline.
- A concentration of large, youthful populations on the move in an "arc of instability" reaching from southern Africa through the Middle East and South and Southeast Asia.
- Rapid aging of European, North American, and East Asian societies.
- Increased immigration from Third World to First World countries.
- Increasing urbanization, especially in China and Africa.

For the most part, these trends cannot be altered by any reasonably practical means during the next two to three decades. The key to understanding the implications of these trends is that the security and conflict problems caused by population growth are not mainly due to shortages of resources. Rather, it is a problem of population distortions—in which populations grow too young or too fast, or are too urbanized or too mobile—for prevailing economic and administrative institutions to maintain stable socialization and labor-force absorption.[3]

A TILTING BALANCE IN THE GLOBAL POPULATION AND ECONOMY

Countries are growing today for two major reasons: high population growth rates and demographic momentum. In some countries, mainly in Africa and the Middle East, plus a few in Latin America and South Asia, birth rates remain much higher than death rates, so that growth rates are more than 2 percent per year. In these countries—including Guatemala, Iraq, Yemen, Ethiopia, Afghanistan, Democratic Republic of Congo, Pakistan, Angola, Chad, and Malawi, to name a few—populations are still doubling every generation, or roughly every thirty to thirty-five years.

In other countries, such as China, India, and Indonesia, population growth rates have recently dropped substantially, so that in percentage terms they are growing more slowly. However, because of past population growth, these countries have such a large cohort of women of childbearing age that their populations continue to add significant numbers each year. In China, for example, although most couples have fewer than two children, zero population growth is still several decades away. While current growth rates have sunk to around 0.6 percent per annum, that will still add more than 80 million people to China's population in the next decade. India, though not quite as large as China today, is still growing more than twice as fast, at 1.3 percent per annum, and will add roughly 150 million people in the next decade. Even with a continued decline in their birth rates, these two countries alone are expected to gain roughly 380 million people by 2030—that is more than the entire population of the United States and the United Kingdom today combined.[4]

Table 14.1 shows expected population growth in the twenty largest countries in the world over the next two decades. These are mainly countries with modest growth rates but large demographic momentum, and are thus the countries that will make the largest contributions to total world population growth in the next twenty years. Table 14.2 shows the current rate of growth in the fastest-growing countries with populations over 1 million; these are generally smaller countries but are facing the largest percentage burden of additional growth.

These tables show that global population growth for the next several decades is going to be concentrated in only a few regions and countries, mainly Islamic societies (almost the entire top half of table 14.2) and huge states with populations of 60 million or more. Most of the states that dominate tables 14.1 and 14.2 are also among the world's lower income countries.

By contrast, in Europe and Japan, population growth rates are already low and in some cases negative. This divergence means that the demographic weight of the advanced countries is going to be dropping dramatically in coming years, with great implications for both economic growth and the ability of these regions to take the lead in global affairs.

In 1950 all of Europe plus Japan, the United States, and Canada comprised roughly one-third of world population; by 2009 that had fallen to under one-fifth, and by 2050 that is projected to drop to under one-seventh. In the nearer term, to 2030, the population of the world outside of these regions is expected to increase

Table 14.1 The World's Largest Countries

2009 Population (millions)		2025 Estimated Population (millions)	
China*	1,345.8	China	1,453.1
India	1,198.0	India	1,431.3
United States	314.7	United States	358.7
Indonesia	230.0	Indonesia	263.3
Brazil	193.7	Pakistan	246.3
Pakistan	180.8	Brazil	213.8
Bangladesh	162.2	Nigeria	210.1
Nigeria	154.7	Bangladesh	193.8
Russia	140.9	Russia	132.3
Japan	127.2	Mexico	123.4
Mexico	109.6	Japan	120.8
Philippines	92.0	Ethiopia	119.8
Vietnam	88.1	Philippines	117.3
Egypt	83.0	Egypt	105.0
Ethiopia	82.8	Vietnam	102.1
Germany	82.2	Congo, DR	98.1
Turkey	74.8	Turkey	87.4
Iran	74.2	Iran	87.1
Thailand	67.8	Germany	79.3
Congo, DR	66.2	Thailand	72.6
France	62.3	Tanzania	67.4
United Kingdom	61.6	United Kingdom	66.6
Italy	59.9	France	65.8
South Africa	50.1	Italy	60.0
Myanmar	50.0	Myanmar	57.6

*Countries in bold have large Muslim populations.

by 1.5 billion people; while the population of these regions will increase by less than 40 million.

Economically, a similar fate awaits. The share of the world's total income obtained by the developed countries, with the richest billion people on the planet, will likely fall from roughly 60 percent in 2005 to less than 30 percent by 2050 (estimated using purchasing power parity–adjusted gross national income per capita in current US dollars). This is true despite rich countries keeping most of their huge disparities in per capita output. Even if the developed countries grow their incomes per capita at a robust 2.5 percent per annum for next forty-five years and the rest of world catches up only slightly, growing their per capita income at 4.5 percent per year, these results still follow. This is because while the total population of the developed countries is expected to stagnate, growing by only 3 percent to 2050, the population of the rest of the world is expected to grow by 50 percent, from 5.3 billion in 2005 to more than 8 billion people by 2050.[5]

Table 14.2 The Fastest Growing Countries, 2005–2010

	Annual Growth Rate (%)
Liberia*	4.1
Niger	3.9
Afghanistan, Burkina Faso	3.4
Syria, Timor-Leste, Uganda	3.3
Benin, **Palestine (occupied)**	3.2
Eritrea	3.1
Jordan	3.0
Burundi, **Tanzania, Yemen**	2.9
Chad, Congo (DR), **Gambia**, Malawi, **UAE**	2.8
Angola, Rwanda, Madagascar, **Sierra Leone**	2.7
Ethiopia, Kenya, **Senegal**	2.6
Guatemala, Togo	2.5
Kuwait, Mali, Mauritania, PNG, Zambia	2.4
Cameroon, Côte d'Ivoire, **Guinea**, Mozambique, **Nigeria, Somalia**	2.3
Guinea-Bissau, Iraq, Pakistan, Sudan	2.2
Ghana, **Oman, Saudi Arabia**	2.1
Honduras, **Libya**	2.0
Central African Republic, Congo, Namibia, Nepal	1.9
Bolivia, **Egypt**, Gabon, Ireland, Laos, Paraguay, Philippines	1.8
Israel, **Malaysia**, Venezuela	1.7
Cambodia, Haiti, Panama, **Tajikistan**	1.6
Algeria, Colombia	1.5

*Countries included here have at least 1 million people. Countries with 50 percent or more Muslim population are in bold.

The impact of the shrinking demographic weight of the richer countries puts them on the horns of a dilemma. If the economies of fast-growing developing countries do not start to close the gap with those of the richer countries, then the standard of life enjoyed by the West will seem more elite and unfair than ever, fueling resentment of developing country populations against the more developed world. Conversely, if economic growth in those countries does exceed that of the West, so that living standards in these countries starts to close the gap between rich and poor countries, then the combination of shrinking populations and lagging economies will render the currently developed countries more and more economically diminished relative to the world economy in the future.

These demographic and economic changes also imply that the military capacities of large developing countries will also increase as their populations and relative incomes rise. At the same time, the ability of the Group of Eight (G8, the United States, Russia, France, Germany, Canada, Italy, Japan, and the United Kingdom) and NATO nations—many of which will face drastically shrinking military-age populations in the near future—to put "boots on the ground" to actually control the sites of conflict will diminish. As noted in the following, the likely reduction of economic growth rates in these countries and the diversion of income to supporting retired and aging populations will also make funding tighter for new and techno-logically advanced weapons. The wealthy countries are having enormous problems today dealing with political instability, insurgency, and weak states in the devel-oping world. In the decades ahead, when the developing countries have far larger populations and more money for weapons while the rich countries have sharply diminished relative numbers and wealth, efforts to manage those conflicts will become far more difficult and more of a strain on their resources than before.

These trends require thinking about a major restructuring of international security and governance institutions. NATO, for example, will be composed almost entirely of countries with aging and stable or shrinking populations, and with slow-growing economies. If NATO is called upon (as it has been in Afghanistan) to contribute to efforts to stabilize countries in Africa, the Middle East, or South or Central Asia, it will be heading into countries with rapidly growing and youthful populations that will find it far easier to mobilize insurgents than NATO will to mobilize troops (a problem already apparent in Afghanistan today). Logistically and demographically, it would make much more sense, and be far more valuable, to have countries such as Brazil or Egypt enter NATO (as did Turkey for its size and strategic location) than countries such as Albania.

Making global economic policy will also no longer be a matter that makes sense to pursue in the context of the existing G8; those countries will be dramati-cally shrinking as portions of the global economy while countries such as China, India, Turkey, Brazil, Indonesia, and Mexico will become global economic powers. Admitting major regional powers into international governance bodies is vital if they are to retain legitimacy in the eyes of most of the world's population, and inclusion of the big emerging democratic economies of Brazil, India, and Indo-nesia into an expanded G-group is required if this group is truly going to grapple with the global economy. Dramatically increasing the importance of the Group of Twenty (G20) grouping relative to the G8 will become a foregone conclusion given the global shift in demographic and economic balances.

Naturally, all of these measures will provoke great opposition and controversy. However, there are no alternatives if global chaos is to be avoided. If the wealthier nations of the world do not encourage and welcome rapid economic growth out-side of Europe and North America, the results will be to fuel ever-greater resent-ment of that wealth, exacerbating the problems of terrorism, smuggling, and illegal trafficking as the only ways to "get ahead" and "get even." Moreover, because the developed countries will no longer be the prime engines of growth for the global economy, these countries will have no choice but to support and actively engage the fast-growing countries of the world, improve relations with their populations, and support and seek to share in their growth.

THE ARC OF INSTABILITY

If we look back at tables 14.1 and 14.2, it is striking that most of the fastest-growing and the large still-growing countries are either Muslim or have large Muslim minorities. This is because, in contrast to the societies of Latin America or East Asia, although Muslim countries have adopted the Western technologies that reduce their mortality, they have been more resistant to cultural changes that reduce birth rates and family size. The result is that deaths have fallen much faster than births, resulting in rapid population growth rates. There are exceptions; some Muslim countries—such as Indonesia and Iran—have had vigorous government-promoted programs of contraception, and their population growth rates have fallen sharply in recent years. However, they still bear substantial demographic momentum from earlier rapid growth and will continue to grow substantially for at least another one or two decades.

More generally, the regions with fast-growing populations also include central and Andean America and virtually all of Africa as well as the Middle East and most of South and Southeast Asia. These are all regions where traditional family patterns, with women bearing four to six children in their lives, persist even though better nutrition and medicine have significantly reduced death rates, particularly infant and childhood mortality.

These countries also have exceptionally youthful populations. With large numbers of children still being born and many more than before surviving to adulthood, the population is tilting toward having more and more youth in the total population. The dramatic increase in the number of workers entering the labor force produces a spike in un- and underemployment unless the economy grows extremely rapidly. Moreover, the older age groups in these societies are also benefiting from reduced mortality, so older cohorts continue to hold their jobs and positions in the economy longer, blocking the ascent of younger workers. As shown in figure 14.1, in the countries with large youth populations, the proportion of the population aged fifteen or younger is more than 30 percent, and in most cases is more than 40 percent; that is approximately twice the level found in the more developed countries.

A number of scholars have documented the greater incidence of civil violence and state breakdowns in countries with large youth bulges and several generations of rapid population growth.[6] A rapidly growing and exceptionally youthful population creates strains on systems of schooling and socialization; large unemployed and underemployed youth populations are vulnerable to radicalization and recruitment to criminal and insurgent movements. Growing populations frequently increase competition among elite groups for control of patronage resources, and force populations into encroaching on regions of poorer or already-claimed resources. Growing costs of administration, service provision, education, and security often arise before economic growth provides the resources to governments to meet those needs, leading to ineffective government. Population increase and rising demand can also push up the costs of items from basic foodstuffs and fuels (and increase the costs to government where such items are subsidized) to housing. Growing populations can also lead to the degradation of natural resources, including forests, grazing lands, fish and game stocks, and water supplies.

While a well-organized and effectively repressive regime can maintain order in such societies, it is a brittle order that can be overturned in the event of an

Figure 14.1 Percent of Population under Fifteen Years Old, 2009

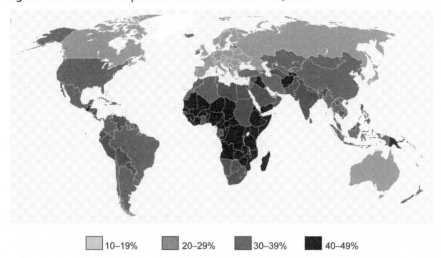

10–19%   20–29%   30–39%   40–49%

economic crisis or a failure of government leadership (as in a succession crisis). This is not merely a contemporary phenomenon, nor one characteristic of Asia and Africa. European countries also exhibited a much higher incidence of civil strife and state crises during periods of youth bulges and periods of high population increase.[7]

These demographic patterns mean that the instability in such places as the Democratic Republic of Congo, Iraq, Turkey, and Afghanistan is not just a result of disparate and specific conditions in those countries. Rather, the threat of chronic and intermittently acute instability will persist as long as there is a disjunction between the pattern of economic absorption of the economy and the growth rate and age structure of the population.

As has been seen in the last decade, international intervention by regional or global peacekeeping forces can help stabilize such conflicts.[8] However, as populations grow in this arc of instability, the difficulties of maintaining order will grow as well. Iraq has been difficult to stabilize with its current population of 31 million; in fifteen years, its population will be 44 million. Afghanistan and Pakistan currently have 28 million and 181 million people, respectively; in 2025 they will—on current trends—have 45 million and 246 million, respectively. In sum, the costs and difficulty of helping to stabilize crises in these and similar nations will escalate sharply.

The ways to respond to this situation to reduce future threats are well known: improve employment prospects for youth; improve the capacity of the governments in these nations to deliver services to the population; and reduce the provocations that focus grievances and discontent on governments and their allies—ranging from corruption and excessive or poorly directed repression to discrimination and exclusion of significant groups or elites from political and economic life. Unfortunately, while these objectives are easily stated and widely recognized, their attainment is exceedingly difficult and complex insofar as the tasks of promoting economic development, political inclusion, and better governance in the face of complex histories, social dynamics, limited institutional and administrative capacities, and cultural and social differences are immense. What we can say is that the resources that have been committed to these tasks by international development agencies over the last few years will likely need to be increased to cope going forward.

A BRAVE NEW WORLD: AGING AND WORK-FORCE REDUCTION IN EUROPE AND NORTH AMERICA

The excessively young population structures in the developing world face a mirror—what will soon be exceptionally aged populations in the developed world. In most of the richer countries, people over age sixty are expected to comprise one-third of the population by 2050.

Table 14.3 shows the projected population changes to 2050 in the major countries of Europe and several other countries. Many of the countries of Europe plus Japan and Korea will see their populations shrink, due mainly to a sharp decline in the number of children per couple. The average number of children born to women in most of these countries has recently fallen to well under 2.0, and in some cases under 1.5. Indeed the overall population of Europe is expected to shrink by 6 percent in the next forty years.

The change in total population, however, is not the most striking change evident in table 14.3. Because these countries are also rapidly aging, more of the remaining population is exiting their prime working years. The decline in working-age population in most countries in the coming decades is therefore expected to be many times greater than the decline in overall population. Most of the countries of Europe plus Japan and South Korea are expected to lose one-quarter to one-third of their prime labor force by 2050. Even China is likely to experience a decline in its prime labor force of 17 percent. Several countries that are expected to enjoy considerable population growth—such as France, Spain, and Switzerland, due in part to high rates of migration—will still have the aging of their populations overpower this growth, which will lead to a stagnation or decline in the population of prime working age.

At the same time that these countries are facing a startling decline in their labor forces, their older populations, age sixty or over, will rapidly increase. Most countries will see a roughly 50 percent increase in their over-sixty populations in the next four decades. Strikingly, this change is likely to be even more dramatic in those countries still enjoying the greatest growth in their overall populations as their larger, healthy populations age rapidly. Thus, as table 14.3 shows, Canada, the United States, and Spain face a doubling or more of their population over age sixty. Some countries that shifted rather recently and rapidly from high to low population growth—South Korea, China, and Ireland—are set to face staggering increases in their aged population. As a result, in Japan, South Korea, and most

Table 14.3 Aging and Labor Force Change in Major European and Other Countries, 2009–2050

	Projected Percentage Population Change		
	Total population	Population age 15–60	Population age 60+
Bulgaria	−29	−46	13
Belarus	−24	−42	46
Ukraine	−23	−40	21
Japan	−20	−37	19
Romania	−19	−38	50
Poland	−16	−38	70
Russia	−18	−36	47
Germany	−14	−32	32
Hungary	−11	−26	33
South Korea	−9	−36	146
Portugal	−6	−26	54
EUROPE	−6	−24	47
Italy	−5	−24	41
Greece	−2	−23	54
Czech Republic	−1	−23	57
Denmark	1	−6	29
Austria	2	−18	59
Finland	2	−10	36
China	5	−17	175
Netherlands	5	−9	53
Belgium	8	−7	52
France	9	−6	56
Switzerland	13	−4	56
Spain	14	−13	93
Sweden	14	4	40
United Kingdom	18	7	51
United States	28	15	97
Canada	32	9	116
Ireland	39	17	164

European countries, the proportion of the population over age sixty is expected to reach 35–40 percent of the total population by 2050. Even in the United States and Canada, the percentage of the population over sixty will grow substantially, from 16–17 percent today to 28–30 percent by mid-century.

This represents a highly novel and abnormal pattern. In the great sweep of history, there have been long periods in which population growth was stagnant, or even when major epidemics (such as the Black Death) substantially reduced populations in large areas. However, in these periods the cause of population stagnation or decline was high mortality, especially among the young. Birth rates remained high, and when conditions were more propitious to growth, population increase resumed. Populations thus remained predominantly young, as they have been throughout all of history, with relatively few older people. In modern Europe (and other high-income countries, such as the United States, Canada, and Japan), it is changing birth rates that have precipitated population decline, as people have chosen to have smaller and smaller families. Women are marrying later, if at all, and having fewer children.

This slowdown in population growth has major implications for overall economic growth.[9] Stimulus to the economy from growing numbers of consumers and growing demands for housing will simply be absent. The capital growth generated by larger generations of young people approaching their peak earning years and saving for retirement will cease as well. When the labor force of the developed countries was growing at 1 percent or 2 percent per year, as it did all the way up to 2005, even modest increases in real output per worker of 2 percent per year provided overall growth levels of 3–4 percent per year or better. With the labor force in the developed countries instead shrinking by 0.7–1 percent per year, the same 2 percent increase in real output per worker will yield only 1–1.3 percent in overall growth. In other words, even if Europe's productivity growth remains constant, its overall economic growth rate will likely be cut in half, from 3 percent to less than 1.5 percent per year, over the next forty years.

An overall growth rate this small allows few margins for accumulation to head off economic downturns, or to invest for the future. As Benjamin Friedman has argued, substantial growth rates allow more groups to share to some degree in growth, and provide social resources for a variety of services and investments.[10] Overall growth rates below 2 percent per year, by contrast, allow for little redistribution or investment and tend to heighten social conflicts over such issues as pensions, migration, and labor or employer relations.

This pattern will likely be exacerbated by a shrinking of the workforce that will be more dramatic than the overall slowdown in population. A declining birthrate plus increasing numbers in larger, older cohorts mean that the working age population is being reduced at both ends. The turning point in this process for Europe was in fact precisely in 2005. From 1950 to 2005 Europe's working age population (fifteen to fifty-nine) increased steadily from 330 to 480 million. But from 2005 to 2050 Europe's working-age population is projected to steadily decline and entirely reverse these gains. By 2050, the working-age population of Europe is projected to decline by 150 million workers, shrinking all the way back to its 1950 level.

This shift in the demographic pattern also raises major concerns about the recovery from the current (2008–) economic crisis. After the Great Depression, a vigorous baby boom in the United States and Europe helped fuel demand and overall growth, spurring the pace of recovery. Unless current demographic patterns change rapidly, this spur to growth will be missing in the coming decades. Recovery is thus likely to be much slower, with no sharp spike in demand for homes, major appliances, cars, or other items typically acquired by young families and workers as they enter the work force and then their prime earning years.

The combination of slowing economic growth and rapidly escalating obligations for pensions and health care for an aging population will place great fiscal strain on the richer economies. These strains bring risks of bankruptcies (which are on the horizon if health care costs cannot be brought under control), but even if bills are paid, the amount left over for spending on weapons and defense will contract sharply.[11]

It is often noted that older people today are healthier and more active. But they will then demand the hip and knee replacements, cornea replacements, heart transplants, diabetes treatments, blood pressure treatments, and other procedures and medications necessary to sustain an active and healthy life into older ages. Moreover, the most expensive year of life is the last, and this will be true whether people are living into their eighties and nineties instead of just their seventies. The relevant data for these costs in the future is that the number of people over age eighty in the United States, as in most other rich countries, will more than double. This will occur at a time when the supply of new doctors and nurses will likely decline.

There will be other problems for the economy that cannot be solved simply by keeping the elderly population at work. Older workers will generally not welcome entry-level work at entry-level wages, or physically demanding work. Those gaps in the labor force will have to be filled by younger workers. Moreover, while older workers excel in experience and judgment, they are less good at thinking outside the box. Path-breaking innovations in science and technology overwhelmingly come from those under age forty-five; countries with fewer and fewer younger workers will likely lose an edge in innovation as well. In short, the richer countries face major demographic obstacles to maintaining their defense spending in the future even as the incidence and scale of disorders in developing countries will likely increase.

There are four routes by which the developed nations can try to head off this impending growth slowdown. The first is to ramp up investment in productivity-increasing technology. An increase in productivity producing a 1 percent greater gain in output per capita per year would offset the change in population. Increased technological prowess would also help Europe, Japan, and the United States maintain their global economic leadership role because companies and countries in areas of rapid growth would turn to them for technology.

The second route is to increase immigration and seek as quickly as possible to raise immigrants' productivity and earnings to the average level in receiving countries. While there have been efforts in Europe to increase the flow of skilled workers, it may well be unskilled and entry-level labor that is required in the coming decades. This is not a short-term fix, however; integration and education of immigrants can take a generation or more. Moreover, if the children of unskilled migrants do not have the opportunities to find fulfilling roles in the receiving societies, their frustrations can create more problems than solutions. However, the United States, Australia, and Canada have enjoyed the benefits of making it easy for immigrants to start a business, acquire educations, and move into the mainstream of life such that the incomes of many immigrant groups exceeds the national norm.

Unfortunately, in Europe, Japan, and recently in the United States, debates on immigration have expressed the fear that immigration steals wealth from the countries that attract immigrants. This mistaken view is as pernicious as the idea that protecting trade through high tariffs or blocking foreign investment will preserve the prosperity of a country that builds such walls to global exchange around itself. Migrants tend to self-select for entrepreneurial talent, ambition, and energy, and make net gains for national economies that accept them.[12] A Europe, United States, or Japan that has lost much of its own demographic momentum and energy can ill afford to exclude new generations, even if they come from abroad, in place of the ones they are no longer producing themselves.

A third way would be to pursue pronatal policies that encourage larger families among the existing populations. Unfortunately, it is not clear what policies would produce this gain because the reasons for baby boomers are still not fully agreed upon by demographers. Unless a value shift occurs that places a higher value on larger families than on the endless expansion of consumer goods consumption, small families will continue to be preferred. It is striking that higher fertility is found in richer countries mainly among more religious families—this is one of the factors accounting for much higher population growth in the United States than in Europe.[13] Short of a religious revival in Europe, a major increase in fertility and family size seems the least likely solution to Europe's demographic decline. Still, vigorous pronatal policies in Sweden and France do seem to have had some effect in raising fertility in those countries relative to other European nations.

A fourth and more daring approach would be to encourage a "reverse flow" of older migrants from developed to developing countries; this could create great benefits for both. If older migrants take their retirement along the southern coast of the Mediterranean, or in Latin America or Africa, it can greatly reduce the costs of their retirement. Of course, it will be necessary to create and encourage the development of first-world quality residential and medical facilities in those countries to make them desirable medical destinations. Yet that may be far preferable to the constant drain of medical and nursing talent to rich developed countries that is taking place currently. Medical tourism to many developing countries has already begun as a way for developed-country residents to obtain optional medical procedures at a lower price. Investing in facilities that will make long-term retirement attractive in cheaper locales will reduce pension and medical cost burdens for developing countries while channeling needed jobs and investment to developing countries that have ample labor.

Care for the elderly and provision of retirement and leisure services are also labor-intensive activities. Relocating a portion of these activities to developing countries can help provide employment and training needed to address the needs of the elderly. Of course, precautions will have to be taken that such activities do not become local enclaves that exclude the indigenous population and cream talent away from local activities. Rather, such facilities should be regulated like other foreign direct investment to provide training and jobs to local populations as well as services to first-world migrants. Medical staff and facilities should provide parallel services for local populations, financed in part out of the proceeds of those services. In this way, both sending and local populations could benefit.

While Europe, the United States, and Japan by themselves will have pathologically older populations, and many nearby developing countries will have pathologically younger populations, the global population as a whole will nonetheless be heading for a relatively healthy age distribution of population. The most logical way to overcome the population distortions in varied regions will therefore be to ease the barriers to movement across borders to take advantage of the overall balance.

Yet we should recognize that one of the biggest obstacles to several of these solutions is the growing antagonism between the West and much of the Muslim world. While Europe and America draw immigrants from countries and cultures around the world, most of the largest and fastest-growing countries in the world have large Muslim populations. Many of these countries are also relatively close to Europe, in northern Africa and the Middle East. Thus, we can expect that pressures to correct the imbalance between high youth density and low youth density populations in close proximity will be realized through increased Muslim migration to Europe.

The way forward for the West lies in greater openness and integration, in greater investment in growth abroad, and greater integration of immigrant communities and ease of emigration to fast-growing but youthful societies. None of this is possible with high levels of fear, mistrust, and antagonism between the West and populations of many of the largest and fastest growing countries of the world. Stopping terrorism is an important but minor aspect of Muslim–Western relations. Of much more fundamental importance is realizing the degree of cooperation that is needed to respond to the global population trends already in place for the next half-century. Much more than terrorism, these trends will affect the long-term prosperity of the developed but stagnating and rapidly aging populations of the West, and the fast-growing and extremely youthful populations of the developing and largely Muslim nations.

INCREASED MIGRATION FROM THE DEVELOPING TO THE DEVELOPED WORLD: PROBLEM OR SOLUTION?

The obvious result of the growing imbalance between overly youthful countries with poor employment prospects and nearby aging populations with entry-level labor shortfalls is already taking place—a massive migration of young and working-age populations from the developing world to the developed world. The forces propelling this movement are like gravity, with populations being irresistibly drawn from high youth density regions to low youth density regions to take up entry-level and physically demanding jobs. Yet this immigration is increasingly contentious in the developed world, and one cannot help but wonder about a growing backlash as the number of potential migrants from developing countries rockets upward while the population and workforce of developed countries shrink.

Historically, Europe has been a net source of out-migration to other countries, principally North and South America and Oceana. Only in recent years have net inflows of immigration characterized European nations. However, they have now become an important component of Europe's demography. In 2002, the annual net migration rate into Europe was 0.28 percent, accounting for 85 percent of Europe's total growth (for EU-25).[14] The number of nonnationals living in the enlarged twenty-five-nation EU is 14.7 million people, around 3.3 percent of the total population.[15] In some countries with greater volumes of immigration, such as the United Kingdom, France, and the Netherlands, this figure is higher.

By comparison, in the United States from 2000 to 2005, the annual net migration rate averaged 0.42 percent per year, and this accounted for only about 40 percent of the United States' national growth rate. Moreover, since the United States has been experiencing a much higher rate of immigration than Europe for decades, the number of foreign-born individuals living in the United States has risen dramatically as well. The proportion of immigrants in the US adult population has roughly doubled from 1980 to 2000, from 9.6 to 20.6 percent. This ratio is higher than for all foreign-born residents because immigrants are concentrated in working ages. However, the percentage of all foreign-born residents in the United States in 2003 is estimated to be 12 percent, still almost four times greater than in Europe.[16]

Of course, Europe will not approach American rates of foreign-born population any time soon—the United States has been a nation of immigrants for a very long time. Even if the EU would increase its immigration rates to American levels, from 0.28 percent to 0.42 percent per year, this would not be enough to offset the decline in population growth and keep population constant, and not enough to have any impact on the aging of the population. Indeed, it would take immigration levels of almost 1 percent per year, or more than 4 million immigrants per year, to more than offset Europe's population decline and sustain even just under a 1 percent rate of positive population growth.

Nonetheless, there are good reasons for Europe to expect that it will gradually move toward a more "American" percentage of foreign born, probably doubling or tripling the current very low percentage of non-Europeans (3.3 percent) in the EU. Europe will have to learn to make this a positive experience for both natives and immigrants.

The first reason for admitting more immigrants is that they create net gains to economic growth.[17] Although there is considerable economic debate on how to calculate the net gains, and some economists still dispute the conclusion, much of this debate is about the role of unskilled labor. There is no doubt that the migration of skilled laborers boosts the economy—indeed, many of the leading companies of Silicon Valley resulted from the entrepreneurial efforts of skilled immigrants from South Asia. Unfortunately for Europe and the United States, many of the skilled Chinese, Indian, and Pakistani engineers who headed for the United States are now more likely to head home as economic growth in those regions will provide opportunities that they lacked two and three decades ago. However, it seems likely that even if African and Arab countries increase their supply of well-trained doctors, nurses, technicians, and scientists, their countries will not be able to provide them with competitive opportunities in the next generation, and many will seek to migrate to developed countries.

The second reason for admitting more immigrants is that they will be difficult to keep out. The fact that there will be an enormous surplus of young people in the countries of Africa and the Middle East along with a looming shortage of young workers in Europe means that the normal forces of supply and demand will impel workers to migrate to Europe and employers to hire them. Many of these jobs will be precisely the kind of low-skill service jobs—in retail, janitorial, in-home care, and domestic service—that an aging population in Europe will need, and that cannot be "outsourced" to labor overseas. The enormous pressure this market situation will create will make it difficult to hold off substantially increased migration in the future. These considerations suggest that designing ways to cope with an increase of immigrants should be a high priority, rather than seeking ways to reduce or reverse their movement.

Unfortunately, it is already clear that rising numbers of immigrants are creating problems of assimilation in Western Europe; the consequences range from petty violence to major acts of terrorism. This is not because Europe has large numbers of migrants; it has far less, in percentage terms, than the United States, Canada, or Australia. Rather, it is because large-scale immigration is relatively new to Europe. European countries do not have a centuries-long tradition of accepting immigrants, and even in the last few decades have tended to treat even their long-term migrants as if they were "guest workers" come for a temporary stay. The results, especially for second-generation immigrants who are native born but not identified as true members of their nations, are a growing sense of exclusion and alienation toward their countries of residence and a sometimes morbid flight into extremist versions of the ideology and culture of their parents' country of origin.

There are numerous mechanisms to help migrants and native populations adapt to increased numbers of foreign born and their descendants in their midst. At the least, politicians must be shamed and restrained from seeking to make political gains from denouncing immigration and foreign cultures. Sadly, taking advantage of people's normal fears of the unknown and anxieties about differences is an easy way for politicians to gain support—much easier than actually solving the unavoidable problems of adapting to the actual situation. The difference between diverse peoples living and working together and those people forming hostile groups aiming at conflict is most often whether politicians seek to overcome or inflame such hostility.[18]

Successful assimilation depends on both attitudes and opportunities. If migrants have opportunities to work, seek education, and open businesses, they will view migration positively; but natives also need to view and treat migrants as valuable members of the community. The problem is rarely so much for first-generation migrants, who are clear about their identities and have migrated mainly to work—and are usually grateful for it. The real problems arise chiefly with second-generation immigrants. These individuals are caught between cultures, native to their parent's land of immigration but not treated as native by the long-standing native population or, often, by the authorities. They often face problems of motivation and identity that lead them to do poorly in school; in addition, they often face subtle discrimination that makes it difficult for them to achieve up to their potential.

There are thus three major solutions to the immigration problem. The first is political—elites and authorities must recognize that increased migration is inevitable and desirable and must work to praise migrants and lead their populations in accepting them. The second is practical—extra effort must be given to the children of immigrants regarding education, counseling, job placement, and even recreation to help their integration into society. The third is to offer reassurance. There should be concrete programs to reassure long-standing natives that immigrants will not be "taking advantage" of them. This could mean that first-generation migrants should have to demonstrate they are working, and they should be ineligible for extended unemployment benefits until they have worked for a substantial number of years. It could mean that first-generation migrants should have to demonstrate that some family members are working so their children are eligible for placement in schools.

Migrants virtually all migrate for economic opportunity (putting asylum seekers aside). They want to work. Natives mainly fear that immigrants will either not work and thus take advantage of state benefits or the immigrants will take "their" jobs. Politicians thus need to take concrete steps to assure long-standing natives that immigrants will not qualify for state benefits unless they are working. Politicians must also demonstrate that, with the native labor force set to shrink rapidly, the only way to provide needed services and increase economic output to provide for everyone's benefit is to admit and use the work and success of immigrant workers.

Assimilation of immigrants is not easy, and differences in religion, language, and culture are probably greater today for migrants to Europe than they were for earlier European migrants to Canada and the United States. Thus, Europe will probably have an exceptionally difficult time assimilating migrants. Conversely, the advantage that Europe does have is that it already is composed of groups of diverse language, religion, and histories, so making room for a few more newcomers and added variety should not prove an overwhelming task (as opposed to the homogeneity of Japan, for example).

In this regard, the admission of Turkey to the EU could provide substantial advantages. Although many Europeans are concerned about admitting a large, young, and Muslim country to the Union, there is already a substantial population of young Muslim—especially Turkish—immigrants and their children within Europe. What matters most for Europe's future stability and success is whether those migrants and especially their descendants view themselves as outsiders or as fully contributing Europeans. Having a large secular Muslim country within the Union should provide a touchstone for all Muslim immigrants in the Union and provide a positive model for their behavior and integration into Europe.

The flow of reverse migration of older workers and retirees to the developing world can also help with the mutual understanding required for the populations of the developed and developing countries to work more closely together. Provided that enclaves of health and retirement migrants do not act as parasites on the resources of developing societies but instead act as centers to stimulate growth and to provide services to local populations, they can be a very positive force. For example, a new hospital that only serves wealthy foreigners and draws doctors and nurses away from treating a country's own population would be a focus of resentment and anger. However, if the new hospital also provided otherwise unavailable services to the local population, and if a portion of the nurses and doctors trained and employed in the new facility also provided some time at clinics to meet local needs, it would be a welcome addition to the community.

URBANIZATION: THE DEVELOPING WORLD CATCHES UP

A hallmark of higher-income countries and regions throughout history has been the rise of large cities, from Xi'an to Rome to Constantinople (Istanbul) to Edo to London. Most low- and middle-income countries are now going through a transition from a situation in which most families were rural farm-producing families to a condition in which most families are urban consuming families. This creates new pressures on education, sanitation, energy supply, transportation, food storage, and distribution, all of which are greater in cities. These demands fall chiefly on governments, which can face opposition and even violence in the absence of jobs and adequate food supplies. Today, it is not so much the number of people per se but the changing consumption and distribution pattern of populations (much of it linked to rising incomes and urbanization) that is putting pressure on global food and energy supplies.

For less-developed regions as a whole, the United Nations projects the percentage of urban population will increase from 42.7 percent in 2005 to 56 percent by 2030 and 67 percent by 2050. That is a 50 percent increase in the urban percentage, but because this is occurring in fast-growing countries, the total urban population is projected to more than double by mid-century. That projection entails the incredible figure of 3 billion additional urban residents in the less-developed countries, added to the 2.3 billion of 2005.

In sub-Saharan Africa, urbanization will be even more rapid, with the urban percentage expected to almost double, from 35 percent in 2005 to 67 percent in 2050, entailing a tripling in total urban population from roughly 300 million today to more than 1 billion by midcentury. In China and India, urban populations are also expected to grow explosively to 2050, increasing to 73 percent of total population in China (from roughly 40 percent today), and rising to 55 percent of total population in India (from under 30 percent today). Together, these two megapopulations are projected to increase their urban populations by over 1 billion people.[19]

Of course, these are projections and may not be realized. However, it is vital to recognize that the "normal" urban percentage for developed countries is about 75 percent today, and it is logical to expect low- and middle-income countries to move toward this figure as they develop. Because increasing employment and the efficiency of agriculture generally entails moving people off the land and into urban centers, it is reasonable to treat these projections as likely rather than as grim or abnormal.

Still, these levels of urbanization—at more than 60 percent—are likely to be reached at much lower levels of per capita income in most of the world than was the case for the developed nations today. Today's more developed regions did not attain urbanization levels of 65 percent until 1970, and the United States did not reach this level until 1950.[20] In fact, the rapid urbanization in today's developing world is most likely to occur in a manner similar to that of nineteenth-century Europe, when policing was inadequate; jobs were demanding, cyclical, and unregulated; and sanitation and education were limited. The result then was widespread labor strife and periodic urban rebellion and even revolutions (the 1820s, the 1830s, and in 1848). Given that the developing world is facing a very similar situation of high youth, rapid development, and high urbanization, yet has relatively weak and often undemocratic governance, it is likely that systemic disorders will also arise unless efforts at global integration and support for fragile states can blunt those tendencies.

However, a major concern, again, is the continuing hostility between Muslim and Western nations. Urban settings—even more than remote caves—offer excellent opportunities for recruitment and hiding of terrorist networks. The sheer proliferation of mosque and neighborhood networks, access to the Internet, and easy transportation links and concentration of targets mean that unless the proclivity of Jihadist groups to seek violence against the United States and regimes allied to the West is sharply reduced, we can expect rapid urbanization to create increased opportunities for terrorist acts.

In addition, migration from countryside to city is only one step in what tend to become growing migration networks, in which people move first from the countryside to regional urban centers; then a portion of those move to national metropoles, major ports, or industrial centers; and then have increased access to international migration networks. Increased urbanization in the developing world is thus likely to increase the flow of international migration from the developing to the developed world, again, just as the nineteenth-century European pattern showed increased international migration to the Americas.

ARE THERE SOLUTIONS?

The list of security threats and their demographic causes enumerated earlier may seem both tedious and discouraging. If these underlying trends are unavoidable and their consequences so extensive and so varied, is there anything that can be done? Or do we simply bemoan the fact that the peaceful and secure post–Cold War world we thought we would gain has instead turned out to be ridden with local conflicts, angry and frustrated youth, state failures, insurgencies, and terrorism—all amplified by the stresses of weaker economies among the richer states? The range and complexity of these problems certainly makes a single answer impossible. Yet that does not mean nothing can be done to reduce the impact of these threats—big problems just require longer-term and more extensive actions, and more creative thinking, than simple problems require.

In terms of security and management of global financial risks, the existing global institutional structures based on the G8 and NATO as the dominant multilateral economic and military features will soon be obsolete; revision or new structures will be needed for effective responses to the likely instability and power shifts that seem inevitable in the next half century. The development of multilateral alliances that can provide trained workers sufficient for the policing and peacekeeping operations likely needed to maintain stability in a developing world filled with youthful cities and weak governments is especially vital. Such alliances will need to combine the skills and experience of G8 and NATO countries with the economic growth and labor resources of large and fast-growing states such as India, China, Brazil, Mexico, and Turkey. New international frameworks that can integrate these nations to pursue shared goals must be created.

Any broader solutions to global demographic change will have to involve greater integration of developed and developing regions, because although each alone has an abnormally imbalanced population in terms of age distribution, together they complement each other and form a more balanced whole. Movement of young and unskilled labor from the developing to the developed world should be welcomed and the assimilation challenges met head on; meanwhile, reverse migration of skilled and older professionals from the developed world to the developing world for both late-career and retirement life stages would be mutually rewarding. Economically, Japan, Europe, and the United States will have to invest in and be involved in economic growth in Asia, Africa, and Latin America because the latter areas are where the majority of global economic growth is likely to take place.

We have not at any time since 1800 seen a world in which the majority of economic growth occurs outside of the United States and Europe, in which any countries had sixty-year-olds constitute 30–40 percent of their populations, and in which large countries at relatively modest levels of income per capita reached urbanization levels of 60 percent. Yet that is the world of the next half century. The economic, social, and development policies of the last century are thus obsolete, and it is imperative to find new ones.

Notes

1. Jessica Tuchman Matthews, "Redefining Security," *Foreign Affairs* 68 (Spring 1989): 162–77.

2. Population trends also factor into environmental issues, including climate change, which some analysts include in new views of security (see Norman Myers, *Ultimate Security: The Environmental Basis of Political Stability* (New York: Norton, 1993)). However, this chapter sets aside complex environmental concerns, however critical, to focus on how threats of violence, lawlessness, uncontrolled migration, and economic or fiscal strains are directly exacerbated by population change.

3. Jack A. Goldstone, "Population and Security: How Demographic Change Can Lead to Violent Conflict," *Columbia Journal of International Affairs* 56 (2002): 245–63; Richard Cincotta, Robert Engelman, and Daniele Anastasion, *The Security Demographic: Population and Civil Conflict after the Cold War* (Washington, DC: Population Action International, 2003); Elizabeth Leahy, with Robert Engelman, Carolyn Gibb Vogel, Sarah Haddock, and Tod Pres-

ton, *The Shape of Things to Come: Why Age Structure Matters to a Safer, More Equitable World* (Washington, DC: Population Action International, 2007); Henrik Urdal, "A Clash of Generations? Youth Bulges and Political Violence," *International Studies Quarterly* 50, no. 3 (2006): 607–30; and Henrik Urdal, "The Demographics of Political Violence: Youth Bulges, Insecurity and Conflict," in *Too Poor for Peace? Global Poverty, Conflict and Security in the 21st Century*, ed. Lael Brainard and Derek Chollet (Washington, DC: Brookings Institution Press, 2007), 90–100.

4. UN, *World Population Prospects: The 2008 Revision*, selected tables (New York: UN Secretariat, Population Division, 2009), www.un.org/esa/population/publications/wpp2008/wpp 2008_text_tables.pdf. All population data in this chapter are from the medium-growth projection variant detailed in this report.

5. Population and gross national income per capita data from Population Reference Bureau, *World Population Data Sheet* (2005), www.prb.org/pdf05/05WorldDataSheet_Eng.pdf.

6. Thomas Homer-Dixon, *Environment, Scarcity, and Violence* (Princeton, NJ: Princeton University Press, 1999); Goldstone, "Population and Security"; Colin C. Kahl, *States, Scarcity, and Civil Strife in the Developing World* (Princeton, NJ: Princeton University Press, 2006); Leahy et al., *Shape of Things to Come*.

7. Jack A. Goldstone, *Revolution and Rebellion in the Early Modern World* (Berkeley: University of California Press, 1991).

8. Human Security Center, *Human Security Report 2005: War and Peace in the 21st Century* (Oxford: Oxford University Press, 2005); and Virginia Page Fortna, *Does Peacekeeping Work? Shaping Belligerents' Choices after Civil War* (Princeton, NJ: Princeton University Press, 2008).

9. Nicholas Eberstadt, "The Population Implosion," *Foreign Policy* 123 (March–April 2001): 42–53.

10. Benjamin Friedman, *The Moral Consequences of Economic Growth* (New York: Alfred Knopf, 2005).

11. Richard Jackson and Neil Howe, *The Graying of the Great Powers* (Washington, DC: Center for Strategic and International Studies, 2008).

12. Julian L. Simon, *The Economic Consequences of Immigration*, 2nd ed. (Ann Arbor: University of Michigan Press, 1999); and Philippe Legrain, *Immigrants: Your Country Needs Them* (Princeton, NJ: Princeton University Press, 2007).

13. Philip Longman, "The Return of Patriarchy," *Foreign Policy* 153 (March–April, 2006): 56–65.

14. European Commission, "The Social Situation in the European Union: Overview," 2004, 25. http://ec.europa.eu/employment_social/social_situation/docs/ssr2004_en.pdf.

15. Ibid., 9.

16. *Foreign-born Population of the United States. American Community Survey 2003* (US Bureau of the Census, 2009), www.census.gov/population/www/socdemo/foreign/acst2.html.

17. Simon, *Economic Consequences of Immigration*; and LeGrain, *Immigrants*.

18. Michael S. Teitelbaum and Jay Winter, *A Question of Numbers: High Migration, Low Fertility, and the Politics of National Identity* (New York: Hill and Wang, 1998).

19. Data in the preceding two paragraphs are from *World Urbanization Prospects: The 2007 Revision Population Database* (UN Secretariat, Population Division, 2008), http://esa.un .org/unup.

20. Ibid.

Chapter 15

DEMOGRAPHY
A Development Perspective

Richard P. Cincotta

Turning the attention of policymakers to demography's role in development has never been easy. It is not surprising; the pace of demographic change is typically slower and its effects are less obvious than an upsurge in armed conflict or an abrupt political reversal, which are more commonly the subjects of televised interviews and ambassadorial démarches. That said, one cannot help but notice the increasing frequency at which articles on demographic topics have appeared lately in influential foreign policy journals and magazines.[1] Why has there been an upsurge in interest?

Perhaps the conclusions of the past two decades of research by economic and political demographers—which this chapter synthesizes—caught policymakers by surprise. As the world's states diverged demographically and as demographic data became increasingly detailed and accessible, researchers focused less on the effects of population-growth-driven depletion and scarcities of resources (associated with the neo-Malthusian paradigm) and more on looking for influences of the population's age structure (the distribution of residents by age) on a state's economic, social, and political ecology. This is a new development agenda concerned with states that are "demographically cresting" as well as with the effect of this "cresting" on those states' future growth and prosperity.

Three component assumptions are embodied in the neo-Malthusian paradigm. First, proponents assume that a rapid rate of population growth in states with underdeveloped institutions and insufficient infrastructure will outpace economic growth, job growth, and the development of vital services and infrastructure. Second, proponents assume that high population densities will translate into high aggregate demand for renewable and nonrenewable natural resources, leading to economically detrimental resource scarcities, including food insecurities and the overloading of natural "sinks" for waste absorption. These scarcities, proponents assert, slow development and encourage aid dependency in less-developed countries. And third, proponents of this paradigm assume that the developing world's renewable natural resource base (its stock of natural capital)—composed of forests and natural rangelands, agricultural soils, fisheries, watersheds, and endemic species—will be vastly depleted by overexploitation, overmanipulation, pollution, and land-use change, much of these due to the human population's growing aggregate requirements for basic levels of food, energy, and shelter and its expanding demand for productive livelihoods.

Proponents of the neo-Malthusian paradigm, many of whom were academics in the biological sciences, were criticized for their lack of understanding of the ability of markets and international trade to mediate resource distribution, their lack of faith in institutions, and their environmental sentimentality. The most vocal opponent, Julian Simon, took the diametrically opposite view of neo-Malthusians. For Simon, continued population growth drove ingenuity and produced a larger pool of creative individuals. Resource scarcities, he argued, would be mediated by the marketplace, by substitution, and by technological change.[2]

By the early 1980s, proponents of this paradigm—both in academia and in the development donor community—felt confident that developing economies were showing economic and social strains related to neo-Malthusian effects. In response, in 1982, the US Agency for International Development's (USAID) Office of Population commissioned the National Academy of Science's Committee on Population (a nongovernmental body in Washington, DC) to organize a study through the US National Research Council (NRC) to use available data to evaluate the extent of rapid population growth's effects on the economic development of less-developed countries.

Published in 1986, the NRC study considerably dampened academic support for the neo-Malthusian paradigm.[3] In the NRC panel's view, rapid population growth's net effect on developing economies, in aggregate, was ambiguous. Slowing population growth, the authors stated, would likely ease rates of degradation of certain renewable natural resources and make it easier to reduce income disparities between social classes. But the NRC report also recognized the mounting economic contributions of these countries' urban economies and improvements to their citizens' school enrollments and health status, despite high rates of population growth.

Would a fresh review of more recent economic research tell a different development story? Most economic demographers believe that it would because the review would dwell far less on population growth, density, and aggregate demand (the focus of neo-Malthusians) and would likely dedicate most of its pages to reviewing literature that assessed the dynamic influence of age structure (the focus of the Coalesian paradigm, named for demographer Ansley Coale) on economic, social, and political conditions (as this chapter does).[4] And it might be broader, covering not only the youthful age structures that persist in Africa and parts of Asia but also extending its discussion to population aging in the industrialized regions of the world.

This chapter reviews this ground by explaining what population age structures are, then illustrating the successional sequence through which they typically mature, and finally discussing their implication for development. The latter part of the chapter discusses the development implications of population density and growth. It introduces a nontraditional approach to dealing with this persistent quandary—the institutional perspective—and uses two critical population-growth-related development concerns as examples.

Figure 15.1 The Demographic Transition Showing Idealized Death Rate and Birth Rate Transitions and Relative Changes in Population That Result

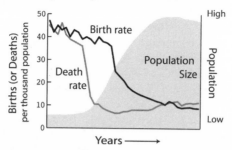

Source: Richard P. Cincotta and Laurel Hummel, "Africa's Youthful Age Structure and Its Security Implications," in *Africa's Strategic Geography*, edited by Amy Richmond Krackowa and Laurel Hummel, 257–82 (Carlisle, PA: US Army War College, 2009).

THE DEMOGRAPHIC TRANSITION

Two hundred and fifty years ago, the world's collection of states, ethnic federations, and empires probably looked very similar to each other in the way their populations were distributed by age. Reconstructed age structures from English records from the mid-sixteenth century until the mid-nineteenth century depict a series of moderately youthful societies in which, on average, 60 percent of the population was under thirty years of age and about 5 percent were over age sixty-five.[5] England's population age structure grew even more youthful during the early decades of the nineteenth century.[6]

Today, age structures range from extraordinarily youthful populations—more youthful than eighteenth or nineteenth century Europe ever experienced—to populations that are older and longer-lived than was ever thought possible by the actuaries and tax collectors of those times. In Niger, the Palestinian Territories, Afghanistan, and Uganda, people under thirty years of age make up more than 70 percent of all residents while those aged over sixty-five—the seniors—comprise between 2 percent and 4 percent of the populace. On the other side of today's age-structural spectrum are the populations of Japan and Italy, where under-thirties now comprise less than 30 percent of the population and 20 percent of all residents are seniors.

This is what is called the demographic transition. During this transition, death rates and birth rates are driven downward by three interrelated and sequential trends (figure 15.1). First, childhood death decreases, lowering the overall death rate (annual deaths per total population). Later—decades later, in some cases—the birth rate (annual births per total population) begins to decline.[7] The decline in childhood mortality (assumed by the mortality curve) and the decline in maternal mortality that typically accompany declining fertility boost average life expectancy throughout the middle of the transition. In late transition, death rates must rise as the elderly, who risk mortality from natural causes and chronic diseases of old age, assume a larger proportion of the population.

Historically, declines in the death rate have always preceded declines in the birth rate. However, the pace, timing, and length of these component transitions have varied. Some posttransition populations are already experiencing a death rate that exceeds their birth rate (as shown). The future of death and birth rate trends in post-transition populations remains uncertain.

Perhaps the most important point is that the timing and pace of the demographic transition vary enormously. Most European populations started much earlier than the rest of the world, and their transitions proceeded more slowly. For example, it took Sweden about ninety years to decline from a birth rate above thirty-five births per one thousand individuals in the population (ca. 1865) to a rate that settled under fifteen per one thousand (ca. 1955).[8] In South Korea, a similar decline took thirty years (1965 to 1995), a pace that Iran is likely to match as well.[9] By contrast, the birth rates of the populations of Niger and Afghanistan have only begun to descend from levels greater than fifty births per one thousand.

The principal sources of state-level population growth are the wide gaps between birth and death rates that normally occur during the early and middle stages of the demographic transition. Today the gap between birth and death rates are widest in sub-Saharan Africa and in parts of South and Central Asia. Although the gaps between these rates are narrowing elsewhere and have actually gone negative in Japan, Russia, and a few European states, UN demographers calculate that the global population of 6.9 billion individuals in 2010 is projected to grow to between 8 billion (the low-fertility variant projection) and 10.5 billion (high-fertility variant projection) by 2050.[10] In the low projection, world population will peak between 2040 and 2045 and then begin to decline.

Because of the current high variation in fertility, this growth increment will be distributed unevenly across the world's regions. Today's poorest regions are experiencing the most rapid growth. Of the additional population projected to accumulate between 2010 and 2050, 40 percent is expected to reside in sub-Saharan Africa and another third in South and Central Asia. Demographic changes are only adding to the development challenges that these regions face.

THE AGE-STRUCTURAL TRANSITION

The age-structural transition is a process driven by a state's progress through the demographic transition. In this secondary transition, age structures pass through a predictable successional sequence of distributions—from a high-fertility youthful distribution (a median age of fifteen to twenty-five years) to an intermediate distribution (twenty-five to thirty-five years) and then to a mature population (thirty-five to forty-five years). States that sustain below replacement levels of fertility over an extended period will most likely pass into a postmature age structure (forty-five years or higher).

Compared with changes in population growth, shifts in age structure move relatively quickly. The abrupt decline of Japanese fertility after World War II, coupled with that country's virtual absence of immigration, fueled a rapid age-structural transition (figure 15.2). Japan's population is projected to reach a median

Figure 15.2 The Successional Sequence of Population Age Structures Experienced by Japan, 1935–2025

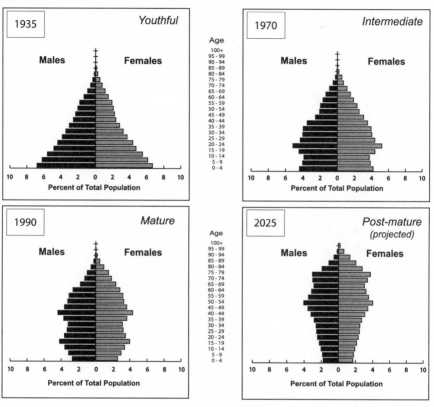

Japan's 2025 age structure depicts the UN medium fertility variant projection.

Sources: Naohiro Ogawa, *Japanese Population by Age and Sex, 1920–2000*, 1935 data set (Tokyo: Nihon University Population Research Institute, 2002); and UN Population Division, 2009.

age of forty-seven years by 2015, well into postmaturity. Iran's transition is moving at an even faster pace. Because average fertility in the Islamic Republic is below two children per woman, the country's youthful age structure is projected to reach the mature stage—a median age of thirty-five—by 2025. This age-structural transition also has implications for development, which are discussed below.

To help analysts visualize the relative progress of countries through the age-structural transition, the figure below graphs the current age structures of the world's countries in terms of the proportion of their population under thirty years of age and the proportion sixty-five years and older (figure 15.3). When graphed, most of the world's country-level populations line up fairly tightly along a smoothly sloping curve that ends in a cluster of three countries—Italy, Germany, and Japan—that are furthest advanced in the transition (although it is not clear why these three countries occupy this position). Those packed closely along this

Figure 15.3 The Positions of the Populations of the World's Countries along the Path of the Age-Structural Transition

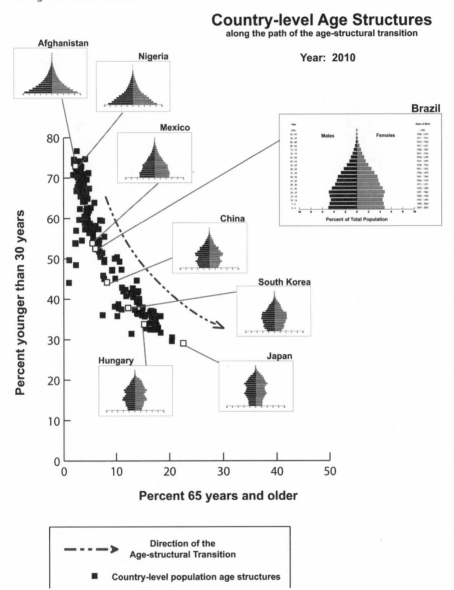

The countries that are positioned distinctly to the left of the thick swath of points have age structures that are substantially influenced by immigration.

Source: UN Population Division, 2009.

curving pathway (referred to as transitional age structures) have shapes that have been primarily determined over time by the dynamics of the demographic transition, that is, by changes in fertility, childhood mortality, and longevity. Outlying populations—that is, those along the margins of the transitional pathway—have age structures that have been strongly influenced by other demographic forces (referred to as extratransitional influences), particularly international migration (for example, the oil-rich Gulf States with their large proportions of temporary labor migrants) and premature adult mortality (AIDS-related mortality in southern Africa, and male middle-age mortality in Russia and the Ukraine).

HIGH- AND LOW-FERTILITY TRAPS

For development economists in the early 1960s, the "low-income, high-fertility trap" explained a great deal of the economic setbacks experienced by states in Asia, Africa, and Latin America. Poor couples in subsistence agricultural economies required children as farm laborers, to cushion risk as remittance generators, and ultimately as a source of old-age support. Under such conditions, their desire for large families, it was reasoned, created an educational and health burden that neither governments nor parents could afford. The failure to increase per capita investment in education—to build human capital—guaranteed the transmission of much of high levels of poverty into the next generation. Boosting income growth, most development economists agreed, provided the quickest and most actionable escape from this trap.[11]

Developments in East Asia, however, proved them wrong. In the late 1960s and early 1970s a handful of Asian governments decided to invest in programs to make modern contraception more widely available and affordable to low-income families.[12] The governments of South Korea, Taiwan, Thailand, Indonesia, and Singapore were the most successful at organizing these services and acquiring financial assistance, technical assistance, and training through programs supported by the USAID. By the time these family planning programs were first assessed, contraceptive use had begun to rise rapidly in the cities. More surprisingly, their use spread almost as fast when services were extended into the countryside. As a result, fertility in these East Asian states declined at unprecedented rates, leaving economic development to play catch-up.

Their economies did, in fact, catch up. Yet none of East Asia's economic tigers escaped from the World Bank's low-income category until their total fertility rate descended below 3.5 children per woman (figure 15.4). Thailand and Indonesia dropped below the three-child level before passing this development milestone, and China descended below two before it happened.[13]

However, not all developing countries followed East Asia's "fertility-first" income-fertility pattern. In Brazil and Mexico, and later in Botswana and South Africa, fertility and per capita income declined somewhat in tandem—a "tit-for-tat" pattern. And the tracks of other Latin American states, such as Chile and Colombia, fell between East Asia's "fertility-first" and Brazil and Mexico's "tit-for-tat" patterns. Interestingly, among the wave of recently developing states, the

Figure 15.4 The Income–Fertility Trajectories of Four East Asian and Four Latin American States

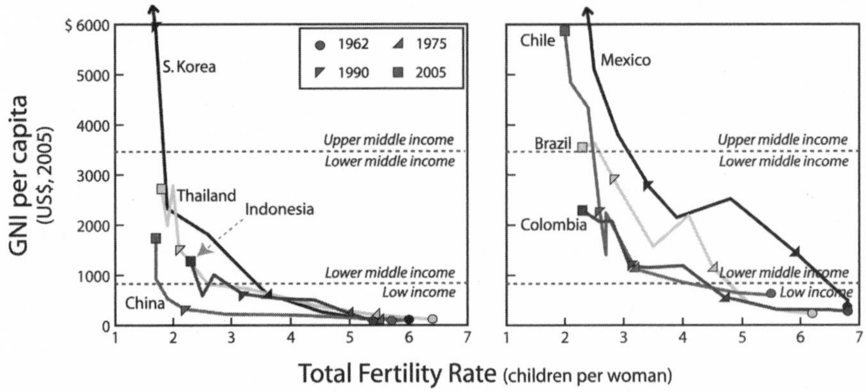

Total Fertility Rate (children per woman)

The trajectories of Chile and Colombia lie between East Asia's "fertility-first" income–fertility pattern and Mexico and Brazil's "tit-for-tat" pattern.

Sources: UN Population Division, 2009 (TFR); World Bank, 2008 (GNI per capita, World Bank Income Classes).

"income-first" income-fertility pattern, presupposed by many political scientists, was conspicuous for its absence.

By the 1980s, US population assistance programs had been joined by bilateral programs funded by the United Kingdom, the Netherlands, and the Scandinavian countries, and by efforts from the UN Population Fund. By the mid-1990s, fertility decline had taken root in North Africa, Iran, and Turkey, and in the southern states of India, leaving demographers confident that if a low-income, high-fertility trap did exist, it was weak. Development inertia, they were convinced, could be overcome with a mix of programs that provided increased access to, and information about, affordable contraception, broader maternal and child health care, and special efforts to increase the educational attainment of girls.[14] This paralleled the shift in development away from the focus on state-level poverty alleviation policies to an agenda that prioritized bottom-up projects focused on individuals.

During this decade, efforts to address persistent high fertility in sub-Saharan Africa became complicated by the spread of the human immunodeficiency virus (HIV), and by efforts to treat acquired immunodeficiency syndrome (AIDS) and to reduce HIV infection. Although the two public health efforts seemed complimentary, initial attempts to integrate services proved difficult. Nonetheless, demographers were encouraged by upticks in contraceptive use in South Africa, Botswana, Zimbabwe, Kenya, and Ghana, and many had become convinced that once fertility in these countries descended from very high levels, the trend would continue to descend smoothly until coming to rest at near-replacement levels (just above two children per woman).

By the early twenty-first century, however, health surveys were making it clear that the global transition was not going precisely as projected. In West, Central, and East Africa, in parts of West and Central Asia, and in a few scattered populations elsewhere—including Timor-Leste, Yemen, and Gaza—fertility remained high or had stalled after a short period of decline.[15] It appeared that the high-fertility trap was real, and stubborn, and that its sources could be traced to the traditionally low status of women and to a cycle of protracted and reemerging ethnic and civil conflicts. Meanwhile, the United States, even as its support for AIDS treatment and HIV prevention in Africa vigorously expanded, shied away from condom promotion and backtracked on its prior commitments to international family planning.[16]

In Europe, another demographic topic was causing a stir. Since the 1970s, almost every country in Europe had experienced a decline to a fertility level below replacement. In Germany, Italy, and Russia, fertility declined to unprecedented lows—below 1.5 children per woman. Japan experienced the same trend. And in South Korea, Singapore, Hong Kong, and Taiwan, fertility dropped lower still—nearly to the one-child level.

The unexpected depth and persistence of low fertility stimulated considerable discussion. Several demographers suggested that these countries may be stuck in a low-fertility trap, and have proposed a model of economic and social conditions that reinforce a one-child-family norm.[17] They could be right. Despite the ongoing scramble to encourage childbearing with nationalist rhetoric, financial and child-care incentives, and programs that promote a more child-friendly environment, few countries—perhaps with the exception of France—can yet document much, if any, success in coaxing fertility upward.[18]

AGE STRUCTURE AND DEVELOPMENT: THE STATUS OF THE STATE, IN FOUR STAGES

The scientific study of the economic implications of age structure has taken time to mature. The notion that fertility decline in low-income countries could stimulate economic growth was first posed in 1958 by demographer Ansley Coale and economist Edgar M. Hoover. Unlike prior analyses, and much that would follow (including most of the 1986 NRC report), their thesis—which would come to be known as the Coale-Hoover hypothesis—had little to say about population numbers or growth. Instead, for Coale and Hoover, the principal demographic engines of economic change were family size and age structure. Developing economies would be better off, they claimed, with a larger proportion in their adult working years and relatively fewer children.

Since Coale and Hoover's initial research, a considerable amount of theoretical modeling, observation, hypothesizing, and testing have extended the investigation of age structure from the youngest stage of the age-structural transition (a median age less than or equal to twenty-five years) to a stage that is more mature (median age greater than forty-five years) than the population of today's most mature countries (Japan, Italy, and Germany). This research has also extended investigations into a much broader realm of developmental effects, including (but not limited to) intrastate armed conflict and instability, regime type, aggregate savings, human capital accumulation, migration effects, and the solvency of pensions and old-age health care systems. These will be discussed in the following subsections as four distinct age-structural types: youthful, intermediate, mature, and postmature. While there are dramatic demographic differences between the average age structure in each type, the boundaries between types are artificially discrete. These boundaries are necessary for classification. However, the age-structural transition is continuous and the rates that influence it—fertility, age-specific mortality, and migration—produce a virtually endless array of possible structures.

The following discussion does not feature the commonly used term "youth bulge." This has been omitted because demographers and economists embrace one definition of the term and political scientists assume another. Economists typically follow demographers in defining a youth bulge by its appearance in a population profile (population pyramid). For them, a youth bulge is truly a bulge; it appears when young adults, typically in the early part of the working age (fifteen to thirty-four) in the total population, are more populous than either children (below them) or older adults (above them). In political scientists' definition, children are not counted. A youth bulge is defined as the proportion of young adults (fifteen to twenty-four years of age) in the adult population (fifteen and older), or the fifteen- to twenty-nine-year-olds as a proportion of the working-age population. In terms of the discrete age structures presented in the following subsections, the youth bulge of the political scientists occurs in the youthful type and is typically associated with political instability. The youth bulge of demographers and economists emerges in the intermediate type and is characteristically associated with economic and social opportunities for accelerating development.

Youthful Age Structures

Youthful age structures (median age less than or equal to twenty-five years) have been much more the focus of political scientists than of economists, and for good reasons. Burdened by large and rapidly growing infant and school-age cohorts, and by the demands for childhood and maternal health care, these states often fail to provide adequate services. In high-fertility extended-family systems, their high rates of workforce growth and unemployment promote systems of patronage that further exacerbate inequalities in the distribution of services and investments among ethnicities and regions.[19] For a significant proportion of states in the youthful category—including Afghanistan, Somalia, the Democratic Republic of the Congo, and Rwanda—political violence has proved to be the most daunting of all development constraints; its costs in human capital, infrastructure, and lost investment are economically debilitating.

Age structure appears to play a role in the complex relationship between regime type and development. Youthful countries that have attained high levels of liberal democracy—"free" in Freedom House's annual assessment[20]—appear more vulnerable to political violence than are more mature democracies.[21] Because most states require political stability to sustain economic and social progress, countries with youthful age structures tend to find political stability under a partial democracy (Freedom House's "partly free" assessment) or autocracy (their "not free" category). The swift economic rise of South Korea, Taiwan, Thailand, and Indonesia

between 1970 and 1990 is consistent with this hypothesis. Only after these countries entered their intermediate stage did their regimes strengthen civil liberties and
political rights until each was assessed as a liberal democracy.

Intermediate Age Structures

A substantial decline in fertility sends youthful age structures into the intermediate type (median age, greater than twenty-five to thirty-five years) and—at
least theoretically—should produce four effects. The first, and probably the most
difficult-to-refute effect of the four, is the production effect. With more people in
the working ages and fewer childhood and elderly dependents, one can generally
expect more production per capita than in youthful populations. The second effect
is arguably the most important, however—age structure's ability to boost savings
rates. Parents with small families save more than those with large families. With a
large proportion of workers, taxes collected on production and wages can exceed
public spending—so governments save too. The third is a human capital effect.
Small families allow parents to invest more in each child, both financially and in
care. Likewise, with fewer cohorts entering school, governments can invest more
educational resources in each student, and in their health. Ultimately, a fourth effect should emerge from slowing workforce growth. While relatively cheap labor
costs provide an advantage for export-oriented industrial development, wages are
likely to rise for small, better-educated cohorts entering the workforce.

While the parental responses to small families were never in doubt, economists stressed that the governmental contribution to this "demographic bonus," as
it came to be called, was conditional and limited to a "window of opportunity."[22]
Economic and social progress at the state level, they argued, depended on the
timely response of institutions to this collection of demographically generated
opportunities. Country comparisons suggested that it mattered whether savings
were wisely invested and those investments protected; whether the government
boosted investments in children; whether it provided an inviting environment for
investment, technology transfer, and scientific and technological development; or
whether the government squandered these opportunities.[23]

Nonetheless, there is a great deal of empirical support for this "demographic
bonus." As fertility declined across East Asia and the Caribbean, and then edged
more slowly downward in Latin America and North Africa, states that experienced
dramatic changes in age structure as a group experienced higher savings rates and
rapid human capital accumulation.[24] However, while recent research acknowledges
the role of age structure and small family size to gains in school enrollments and
per-pupil spending, not all of the recently demographically maturing states reacted
in a timely fashion to boost per capita educational investments or to increase
the quality of schooling broadly across society—particularly in Latin America and
India.[25]

Nevertheless, several economists credit a significant portion of economic
growth achieved among the newly industrialized economies of East Asia—in one
study, as much as one-third during the 1970s to early 1990s—to the effects of
age structure.[26] Similar upturns in savings rates, human capital accumulation, and

economic growth have been noted in other states as geographically distant and culturally distinct as Ireland, Tunisia, Vietnam, and Chile, which have passed through their intermediate age-structural period.[27] For most countries in their intermediate period, their export advantage from relatively cheap labor is likely to decline as they move toward the next period (the mature age-structural type) and as wages increase while their increasing political stability typically turns them into a more favorable site for investment.

Mature Age Structures

As the workforce's largest cohort ages into its late-thirties, a country's population shifts into the mature age-structural type (median age greater than thirty-five to forty-five years). In this demographic condition—that of almost all developed countries in 2010—the advantages bestowed by a demographic bonus are expected to dissipate markedly. However, because the largest cohorts are still in the prime working years (between age fifteen and forty-four years), providing needed services to dependent children and seniors should still remain a reasonable task even as the proportion of retirees increases to significant proportion (among European countries, the proportion ranged from 12 percent to 20 percent in 2010). Recent economic modeling suggests that, where governments sustain heavy investments in human capital, higher than average savings rates—though not as high as the bonus years—could be prolonged into more mature, less economically favorable age-structural stages as some middle-aged skilled workers and professionals save more intensely for an approaching retirement that they believe is unlikely to be supported by their children or to be sufficiently provided for by a state-supported system.[28] Despite the overall favorability of the mature period, slowed workforce growth, rising wages, and the rising number of retirees with demands for an increasingly secure social safety net can be expected to reduce industrial and service sector competitiveness, pushing some production and services overseas while pressuring both private and public sectors to be more efficient.

Postmature Age Structures

Many European and several Asian countries will likely pass beyond their mature stage into postmaturity (median age greater than forty-five years) over the next fifty years. The populations of Japan, Germany, and Italy will progress into the early portion of this range between 2015 and 2020. So far there is little opposition to the hypothesis that such an age structure will slow down or even retard state economic progress and increase social equality among the elderly. Postmature age structures will feature a large proportion of people over sixty-five years of age—an unprecedented "pensioner bulge" that promises to strain pay-as-you-go state-funded pension and medical programs.

Countries that are amassing a large proportion of seniors face the possibility of a decline in economic productivity and slower aggregate gross domestic product growth or stagnation. In the future, governments of postmature countries could be pressured to vastly restrain discretionary state spending and impose a higher tax burden. Some analysts expect aging societies to be risk averse and fiscally limited, and they contend that some European and East Asian states are likely to conclude that they cannot afford to maintain a sizable military or extend its power overseas.[29] For some low-fertility Western European countries that have poorly integrated Asian and African immigrants, the rapid growth of these minorities could erode social cohesion and promote reactionary politics.[30] Despite their logic, most of these impacts remain speculative. The magnitude of aging's effects and the ability of states with well-developed institutions to minimize aging's negative impacts are still unknown and may mitigate some of these expected problems.

In the United States and Russia, the advance of the median age and the accumulation of the proportion of seniors will proceed more slowly. For the United States the factors slowing age-structural change are a high rate of immigration (around 1 percent per year) and a fertility level that is near replacement. Russia's slow pace of aging is, somewhat ironically, the outcome of tobacco use, alcohol abuse, and related accidents. At age sixty, Russian men can expect to live, on average, another fourteen years, limiting the burden that they impose on state and family structures.

POPULATION, GROWTH, FOOD, AND DEVELOPMENT

Writing near the very end of the eighteenth century, Thomas Robert Malthus called attention to the possibility that exponentially growing aggregate demand for food would eventually outstrip the linearly growing food supply unless individual or social restraint or forms of natural or human-precipitated calamities intervened. However, the future of agricultural productivity did not turn out to be linear; Malthus had vastly underestimated the power, scope, and longevity of the scientific and technological revolutions that, even as he wrote and taught, were unfolding around him.

When Malthus's "An Essay on the Principle of Population" was first published, the article dramatically influenced European intellectual thought and public discussion.[31] That influence has since become global. However, Malthus' focus on the limits of population and population-driven aggregate demand distracts from a more nuanced appreciation of how states, through their institutions and international institutions, adapt to population density and growth (and, now, population decline in some European states and in Japan).

The following two subsections reflect an institutionalist perspective on two salient population growth and development issues. The institutional perspective has emerged from observations that the impacts of population growth have been minimized in states where there are well-developed, well-staffed, and well-funded state-sanctioned institutions—including water and resource management systems, schooling and health systems, housing and job markets, energy production and delivery systems, and credit and banking systems. In some industrial countries, these institutions have succeeded in turning much of the potential economic and social burden of population growth into benefits. Where institutions are weak, positive outcomes are less likely.

The perspective also embraces a portion of the economic literature that suggests that institutions are biased—that they favor the interests of the parties who create and fund them.[32] The observable outcomes of institutional bias are negative externalities. In other words, the positive contributions of population—such as affordable labor, needed skills, and additional consumers—generally go to the state and society's mainstream while the costs of mediating population growth and density are often shunted to local communities and interests that are underrepresented within the institution, unprotected by the state, and therefore bereft of recourse: for example, the politically marginalized, those beyond state boundaries, and future generations (and, some might argue, other species). In sum, this perspective expects the growth of population to be proportional to the flow of externalities from adaptive institutions. In its current form, the hypothesis seems difficult to test, but the process it attempts to capture is observable in the following two examples.

Grain Price Vulnerability

The dip in global grain supplies during 2007 and 2008 paved the way for heavy speculation in the international grain market, driving an unprecedented spike in food prices. While the various grains have declined from peak prices, agricultural economists remain worried. The global aggregate demand for grain in the coming decade (2010 to 2020) promises to be augmented by an additional ~700 million people in Asia, Africa, and Latin America; increasing dietary preferences for protein; and a high likelihood of a rise in the demand for grain-based biofuel. On the supply side, global warming trends are likely to depress agricultural productivity in some regions.

What is wrong with importing grain? Nothing, unless you are a low-income country with meager foreign currency reserves that are better spent on importing job-creating machinery and technology. Even some countries with substantial foreign currency reserves perceive their exposure to a volatile grain market as a national security risk. State-financed companies and sovereign wealth funds from Saudi Arabia, United Arab Emirates, India, South Korea, and China—countries that are either already experiencing low per capita cropland levels or are due for substantial population increases over the coming decades—have recently acquired rights to farmland in Africa.[33]

In 2010, twenty-one countries, accounting for about 600 million people, are assessed as either cropland or freshwater scarce, according to internationally accepted benchmarks.[34] Current technology and input costs put these countries well below the realm of food self-sufficiency. On the basis of population growth alone, another fifteen countries will join their ranks by 2025, discounting speculative changes in freshwater and cropland availability. By that year, 1.4 billion people are projected to live in the thirty-six countries that will experience either cropland or freshwater scarcity.[35]

From an institutional perspective—acknowledging the mediating power of institutions within states and of international institutions (UN organizations, World Bank, bilateral development donors, foundations)—the future growth of human population is an unlikely cause of either mass starvation or warfare. Rather, the most plausible scenarios feature major reforms in developing countries to ameliorate their food security by further developing regional grain markets, by improving their own agricultural output efficiency, and by increasing foreign reserves by developing export industries. The most plausible scenarios, however, feature the world's major grain producers bearing the bulk of the costs by intervening in international grain markets to guarantee an equitable global pattern of distribution of affordable grain.

Renewable Natural Resources and Associated Livelihoods

History has made it glaringly apparent that the geographical expansion of human populations, the advance of urbanization, and the growth of consumer demand—all of which are influenced in no small part by population growth—have extraordinarily positive effects on the economies of states, and ultimately on state power. There is another perspective, however. Ecological histories and studies of landscape and land-use change have made it just as apparent that these effects have had dramatic and largely deleterious effects upon the productivity of renewable natural resources, the functioning of ecosystems that support these resources, and, in most cases, those human communities whose livelihoods have depended on those resources' productivity. Many, if not most, of these hard-hit communities have included indigenous populations.

The world over, the pattern of production-system change is largely the same. And, although complex, the process features increasingly higher human densities and more intimate involvement in the global economy. Hunter-gatherers yield to swidden (i.e., slash and burn) agriculturists and pastoralists, who ultimately yield to farmers.[36] Where population growth leads to urban expansion into farming areas, the latter often loses out to urban housing and infrastructure.

How does the state fare in this tradeoff? The answer is it almost always does very well. Institutions that are controlled or promoted by the state are typically biased toward actors and their actions that increase economic activity and tax revenues, augment state power, and help maintain political stability. State institutions can therefore reinforce themselves—in the name of development—at the expense of local agricultural populations.

What was the net contribution to development in these cases? The answer to that question depends on who is responding. For example, the thousands of Indian subsistence farmers and herders displaced by the Sardar Sarovar Dam's reservoir on the Narmada River are much less likely to see the dam as a contributor to Indian development than will the farmers who receive the dam's irrigation water, or the urban dweller who receives its turbines' electric power and food from the cropland it irrigates.

DEMOGRAPHY-AWARE PUBLIC POLICIES

In considering public policy options that have as their objective a response to demographic conditions or a modification of demographic trends, it is appropriate to divide states into groups according to their age-structural characteristics. In this section the discussion returns to the three categories of countries discussed previously: youthful, intermediate and mature, and postmature. For each of these age-structural categories the policy objectives and options are very different.

Youthful Countries

Those countries in the early phases of their age-structural transition are the most politically volatile and conflict-prone as a group, and they currently pose the greatest challenges to the international system. However, as recent history has shown, their populations need not remain youthful. Of the 139 countries that began the 1970s with youthful populations—i.e., with a large youth bulge—59 have advanced beyond this category. Much of this change parallels gains in women's educational attainment. A significant portion of it was facilitated by international programs that helped governments make modern contraception and reproductive health care accessible where it was previously unavailable. That said, the task may be more demanding than it once was.

The most difficult cases remain—countries where women's social and legal status is low, where infrastructure is poor, where institutions are weak, and where political stability is lacking. Most of these remaining states are in the western, central, and eastern regions of sub-Saharan Africa, with others scattered in western, south, and central Asia. A broad range of government policies and types of donor assistance can be brought to bear to advance the age-structural transition in these remaining youthful countries. In the medium and long term, international development donors should scale up efforts to help governments improve girls' school enrollment and lengthen their educational attainment. Governments can improve women's access to family planning and maternal and infant health care, and can promote income-generating opportunities for women. Where external actors have the leverage, they should encourage a shift of family cases out of religious courts—which limit women's rights—and into secular judicial systems.

There are economic policies that may help encourage transition as well. International donors could reduce the financial risk to domestic and foreign investors who might introduce and expand labor-intensive industries and technologies capable of improving urban job markets for educated young adults, diversifying rural job markets, and stimulating a demand for schooling and job training.[37] It may also pay to improve opportunities for labor emigration from places where the growth of the young working-age population has far outstripped the national job market.

Intermediate and Mature Countries

The policy focus of countries that have reached an intermediate age structure should focus on capitalizing and sustaining their demographic bonus while preparing for the transition to even greater maturity. The wisest move that governments can make in this stage of age-structural maturity is to invest its revenue in education broadly, extending attainment among poorer regional groups and minorities. In this stage of maturity, governments should work to extend social safety nets and pension plans, as well as the taxation systems to support them, moving beyond government employees to private industry and rural communities. States in the intermediate and mature categories should be working to bring more women into the workplace as workforce growth slows. Governments can do this by promoting workplace conditions that allow women to achieve and compete even as they meet their childbearing intentions. They can focus on enhancing immigrant and minority women's opportunities to improve their educational status, access services, and integrate and succeed in the job market.

Postmature Countries

Where fertility has reached very low levels—as it has in parts of Europe and East Asia—the coming decades will bear witness to concerted efforts by policymakers in those states to reverse or slow the trend of demographic aging, to ultimately halt population declines to boost fertility, and, in some cases, to minimize the impact of immigration and ethnic shifts. While there are as yet no simple policies that boost fertility, it is a safe bet that governments of postmature countries will spend a great deal of money and effort attempting to make their society more child-friendly and more comfortable for women who are considering marriage and childbearing.

There can be little doubt that welfare states will be fiscally pressured to re-structure their systems funding old-age pension and health care plans, and that major reforms to the schedule and process of benefits loom in the future. Some governments could also be dragged into a political confrontation between pensioners (who need health care) and young families (who need education for their children) competing over limited funding. Someday demographers may decide in hindsight that the challenges of advanced aging were a small price to pay for the economic and social benefits that accrued during the intermediate and mature periods when age structures were more favorable to development. Then again, they may conclude that population aging was a destructive factor, wholly incompatible with the modern state and the extensive welfare promises it extended to its citizens in the mid-twentieth century.

CONCLUSIONS

Joseph Chamie, the former director of the UN Population Division, once told a Washington audience, "While demography may not be destiny, it's probably the next closest thing."[38] This chapter bears out this analysis. History, culture, governance, leadership, institutions, and international actors can mediate and modify demography's effects. They can influence, in some cases, the course of demographic change. Nonetheless, as recent research indicates, demography's role in development is extensive and profound, and its course over the medium term—at least over the next two decades—is largely predictable.

Many policymakers remain surprisingly underinformed about demographic trends, especially age structures, in their own countries. Many are unaware that these demographic conditions influence their government's efforts to employ young people, or that age structure affects savings, the cost of public programs, crime levels, and political stability. It is little wonder, then, that few policymakers understand how a shift in age distribution could influence a range of economic, development, and social indicators.

Hopefully, that will change. In Europe and Japan, where the challenges of population aging are palpable, it already has. As the evidence of demography's role in development grows stronger and its theories become more coherent, policymakers are likely to consider demographic conditions as a development priority rather than an incidental outcome.

Notes

1. See Jack Goldstone, "The New Population Bomb: The Four Megatrends That Will Shape the Global Future," *Foreign Affairs* 89, no. 1 (2010): 31–43; and "Go Forth and Multiply a Lot Less," *Economist*, October 31, 2009, 29–32.

2. Julian L. Simon, *The Ultimate Resource 2* (Princeton, NJ: Princeton University Press, 1996).

3. National Research Council, *Population Growth and Economic Development: Policy Questions* (Washington, DC: National Academies of Science, 1986).

4. The Coalesian paradigm is so named in recognition of Ansley Coale's research on the economic implications of age structure; see Ansley J. Coale and Edgar M. Hoover, *Population Growth and Economic Development in Low-Income Countries* (Princeton, NJ: Princeton University Press, 1958); and Ansley J. Coale, *The Growth and Structure of Human Populations* (Princeton, NJ: Princeton University Press, 1972).

5. See Edward A. Wrigley and Roger S. Schofield, *The Population History of England 1541–1871* (Cambridge: Cambridge University Press, 1987), ch. 8; and Jack A. Goldstone, "The Demographic Revolution in England: A Re-examination," *Population Studies* 49 (1986): 5–33.

6. This trend was reversed when fertility declined from about 5 children per woman to around 3.5 toward the end of the nineteenth century. By 1910, nearly all of Western Europe's populations were experiencing total fertility rates below 4.0 children per woman, with the exception of the populations of Portugal, Spain, Italy, and the Scandinavian states. And by 1980, nearly all of Europe, excepting the Balkan states, Ireland, and Iceland, had dropped below the 2-child-per-woman replacement level. For perspectives on the implications of changes in fertility and mortality in preindustrial Europe, see Jack A. Goldstone, *Revolution and Rebellion in Early Modern Europe* (Berkeley: University of California Press, 1991); Massimo Livi-Bacci, *The Population of Europe* (Oxford: Blackwell, 2000); and Edward A. Wrigley, *Poverty, Progress, and Population* (Cambridge: Cambridge University Press, 2004).

7. In this chapter, the measure of fertility cited is the total fertility rate (TFR), the number of children that a woman in the population is expected to bear, on average, during her lifetime. Unless otherwise stated, the source of estimates and projections of this measure, and all other demographic indicators, is the UN Population Division, *Population Prospects: The 2008 Revision* (New York: UN, 2009).

8. Jean-Claude Chesnais, *The Demographic Transition* (Oxford: Clarendon Press, 1992).

9. The forecast of Iran's transition relies on the medium variant fertility projection published by the UN Population Division, *World Population Prospects*, 2009.

10. Ibid.

11. For a historic discussion of this development perspective, see Nancy Birdsall, "Population Growth and Poverty in the Developing World," Working Paper 404 (Washington, DC: World Bank, 1980).

12. For a review of the history of this effort, see Phyllis T. Piotrow, *World Population Crisis: The United States Response* (New York: Praeger, 1973); Peter J. Donaldson, *Nature against Us: The United States and the World Population Crisis, 1965–1980* (Chapel Hill: University of North Carolina Press, 1990); and Oscar Harkavy, *Curbing Population Growth* (New York: Plenum Press, 1996).

13. The case of fertility leading economic development is statistically examined by Holger Strulik and Siddiqui Sikandar in "Tracing the Income–Fertility Nexus: Nonparametric Estimates for a Panel of Countries," *Economics Bulletin* 15, no. 5 (2002): 1–9.

14. Notably, this strategy was elucidated nearly two decades before in a classified national security study requested by the Nixon administration; see the now unclassified report: National Security Council, *Implications of Worldwide Population Growth for US Security and Overseas Interests* (Washington, DC: National Security Study Memorandum 200, 1974). Funding for USAID family planning assistance increased steadily thereafter until the 1996 Republican-dominated Congress dramatically reduced its budget. Because USAID's education assistance program was coeducational, girls' education received little attention until the second term of the Clinton administration.

15. John Bongaarts, "The Causes of Stalling Fertility Transitions," *Studies in Family Planning* 37, no. 1 (2006): 1–16.

16. David Brown, "Africa Gives ABC Mixed Grades," *Washington Post*, August 15, 2006; and Richard P. Cincotta and Barbara B. Crane, "The Mexico City Policy Restrictions and US Family Planning Assistance," *Science* 294, no. 5542 (2001): 525–26.

17. Wolfgang Lutz, Vegaard Skirbekk, and Maria Rita Testa, "The Low Fertility Trap Hypothesis: Forces that May Lead to Further Postponement and Fewer Births in Europe," *IR-06-017* (Laxenburg, Austria: Institute of Applied Systems Analysis, 2006).

18. Richard Jackson and Neil Howe, *The Graying of the Great Powers* (Washington, DC: Center for Strategic and International Studies, 2008).

19. Roel van der Veen, *What Went Wrong with Africa* (Amsterdam: Kit Publishers, 2004).

20. In political science literature, liberal democracy has been associated with the category "free" in Freedom House's annual assessment, or with values of +8 to +10 in Polity IV polity scores. See Freedom House, *Freedom in the World* (Washington, DC: Freedom House, 2009); and Montgomery G. Marshall and Keith Jaggers, *Polity IV Project, Political Regime Characteristics and Transitions, 1800-2007: Dataset Users' Manual* (Fairfax, VA: Center for Systemic Peace, George Mason University, 2009).

21. Richard P. Cincotta, "How Democracies Grow Up: Countries with Too Many Young People May Not Have a Fighting Chance for Freedom," *Foreign Policy* 165 (2008): 80–82; and Richard P. Cincotta, "Half a Chance: Youth Bulges and Transitions to Liberal Democracy," *Environmental Change and Security Project Report* 13 (2008–9): 10–18.

22. José Alberto de Carvalho and Laura Rodrigues Wong, "Demographic and Socioeconomic Implications of Rapid Fertility Decline in Brazil," in *Reproductive Change in India and Brazil*, ed. George Martine, Monica Das Gupta, and Lincoln C. Chen (Oxford: Oxford University Press, 1998), 208–40.

23. David E. Bloom, David Canning, and Jaypee Sevilla, *The Demographic Dividend* (Santa Monica, CA: Rand, 2002); and Nancy Birdsall, Barbara Bruns, and Richard H. Sabot, "Education in Brazil: Playing a Bad Hand Badly," in *Opportunity Foregone*, ed. Nancy Birdsall and Richard H. Sabot (Washington, DC: Inter-American Development Bank, 1996), 7–47.

24. Bloom, Canning, and Sevilla, *Demographic Dividend*; Ronald Lee and Andrew Mason, "What Is the Demographic Dividend?" *Finance and Development* 43, no. 3 (2006): 16–17; Matthew Higgins and Jeffrey G. Williamson, "Age Structure Dynamics in Asia and Dependence on Foreign Capital," *Population and Development Review* 23, no. 2 (1997): 261–93; and David E. Bloom and Jeffrey G. Williamson, "Demographic Transitions and Economic Miracles in Emerging Asia," *World Bank Economic Review* 12, no. 3 (1998): 419–35.

25. Dennis A. Ahlburg and Eric R. Jensen, "Education and the East Asian Miracle," in *Population Change and Economic Development in East Asia*, ed. Andrew Mason, 231–56 (Stanford, CA: Stanford University Press, 2005); Birdsall, Bruns, and Sabot, "Education in Brazil."

26. Jeffery G. Williamson, "Demographic Change, Economic Growth, and Inequality," in *Population Matters: Demographic Change, Economic Growth, and Poverty in the Developing*

World, ed. Nancy Birdsall, Allen C. Kelley, and Steven W. Sinding, 107–36 (Oxford: Oxford University Press, 2001).

27. David E. Bloom and David Canning, "Contraception and the Celtic Tiger," *The Economic and Social Review* 343 (2003): 229–47; Centro Latinoamericano y Caribeño de Demografía, CEPAL, "Proyección de Población: América Latina y el Caribe," *Observatorio Demográfico*, no. 3 (Santiago de Chile: United Nations, 2007), 17–23; UNFPA, "Golden Opportunity, Golden Pitfalls," March 17, 2010, accessed, February 7, 2011, www.un.org.vn/en/news-highlights-press-centre-submenu-254/1242-golden-opportunity-golden-pitfalls-.html.

28. Andrew Mason and Ronald Lee, "Reform and Support Systems for the Elderly in Developing Countries: Capturing the Second Demographic Dividend," *GENUS* 62, no. 2 (2006): 11–35.

29. Mark L. Haas, "A Geriatric Peace? The Future of US Power in a World of Aging Populations," *International Security* 32, no. 1 (2007): 112–47; and Jackson and Howe, *Graying of the Great Powers*.

30. Jackson and Howe, *Graying of the Great Powers*; and Eric Kaufmann, *Shall the Religious Inherit the Earth?* (London: Profile Books, 2010).

31. Thomas Malthus, *An Essay on the Principle of Population* (London: Printed for J. Johnson, In St. Paul's Church-Yard, 1798), accessed January 27, 2011, www.esp.org/books/malthus /population/malthus.pdf.

32. Douglass C. North, *Transaction Costs, Institutions, and Economic Performance* (Panama City, Panama: International Center for Economic Growth, 1992).

33. Andrew Rice, "Is There Such a Thing as Agro-Imperialism?" *New York Times*, November 22, 2009, MM46; Michael Kugelman and Susan L. Levenstein, eds., *Land Grab? The Race for the World's Farmland* (Washington, DC: Woodrow Wilson Center, 2009); and Michael Kugelman and Susan L. Levenstein, "Sacrificing the Environment for Food Security," *World Politics Review*, January 20, 2010, accessed January 27, 2011, www.worldpoliticsreview.com/article .aspx?id=4969.

34. The per capita renewable resource benchmarks are discussed in Richard P. Cincotta, Robert Engelman, and Daniele Anastasion, *The Security Demographic* (Washington, DC: Population Action International, 2003), 90. These benchmarks were developed from research by Malin Falkenmark and C. Widstrand, "Population and Water Resources: A Delicate Balance," *Population Bulletin* 47, no. 3 (Washington, DC: Population Reference Bureau, 1992); and by Vaclav Smil, *Global Ecology* (London: Routledge, 1993).

35. Calculation using data compiled by Population Action International, "People in the Balance Database," accessed February 4, 2011, http://209.68.15.158/Publications/Reports /People_in_the_Balance/Interactive/peopleinthebalance/pages/index.php.

36. See Richard P. Cincotta and Ganesh Pangare, "Population, Agricultural Change and Natural Resource Transition: Pastoralism amidst the Agricultural Economy of Gujarat," *Overseas Development Network Paper*, 36a (July 1994): 17–35; and Esther Boserup, *Population and Technological Change* (Chicago: University of Chicago Press, 1981).

37. UN Office for West Africa, *Youth Unemployment and Regional Insecurity in West Africa* (New York: UN, 2005).

38. Quoted with permission from a presentation given July 26, 2004, at the Center for Strategic and International Studies, Washington, DC.

DEMOGRAPHY
Editors' Comments

Joanna Spear and Paul D. Williams

There is significant agreement between the security and development arenas about demography and demographic effects. Both authors noted that demographic change can cause, catalyze, or exacerbate other security and development challenges. Nevertheless, the relatively slow-moving pace of demographic changes means that the challenges they pose have rarely achieved the top-level policy attention they merit in either the security or the development arena.

Although accurate cataloguing of populations is notoriously difficult, especially in war-torn territories, both authors are in broad agreement about the data, the causal analysis, and the meaning of the data. They both note that traditional Malthusian concern about levels of population increase have been replaced by greater focus on how the age structure of populations affect the political, economic, and social ecology of states. Thus, both chapters emphasize the importance of understanding the demographic challenges posed by states with youthful populations (generally developing countries) and states with graying populations (generally the advanced industrial economies).

Given their focus on populations, both perspectives naturally work across multiple levels of analysis to assess the implications of demographic data at the global, state, and individual levels. However, the levels at which they see the most important challenges and opportunities are different.

The security arena places greater emphasis on the consequences for weak states of the demographic challenges of youthful populations and is particularly concerned with the potential for youthful populations to exacerbate the risk of terrorism and armed conflict. Reflecting the concerns of security specialists, Goldstone makes particular mention of Muslim states with weak governments and youth bulges. His analysis therefore implies an agenda of shoring up such weak states through military and economic engagement while at the same time raising concerns about the ability of the traditional "interveners" (NATO, the G8) to deliver solutions because of their decreased power due to their graying populations. This top-down approach is geared toward dealing with the symptoms of demographic transitions, not their causes, because he is skeptical that developing countries will be able to implement the public policies that would be needed to really reverse these demographic trends.

By contrast, much of Cincotta's analysis focuses on what states should do in terms of public policy to try to ease the demographic challenges they currently— or will—face. This new development agenda is concerned with states that are "demographically cresting" and the affect of this cresting on their future growth and prosperity. In this sense, his ideas are focused at the individual level of analysis—for example, his focus on improving the status of women as a means to lower fertility rates in youthful societies. He therefore takes a more bottom-up approach to tackling some of these demographic problems.

Both chapters highlight a sobering reality for policymakers; the time it takes to make an impact on demographic changes is two to three decades. Given that most policymakers do not necessarily think two or three years into the future, this is a fundamental challenge. Finally, both authors focus the majority of their attention on states. However, demography is an issue where international organizations, particularly the UN system, play important roles. There are several advantages to working through international organizations on these issues, but the fact that they can think and operate in terms of long time horizons is particularly helpful.

Chapter 16

CONCLUSION

The Comparative Conversations between Security and Development

Joanna Spear and Paul D. Williams

This conclusion does three things. First, it briefly reviews the findings of our authors across the seven core issues covered in this book, focusing on how they conceive the relationship between security and development. Second, it considers the relationships between the statist paradigms traditionally used in both the security and development arenas. Third, it summarizes some of the benefits for both security and development of adopting paradigms that are not based on the state as the level of analysis and the referent object.

MAPPING THE RELATIONSHIP

This book's contributors each explain how their arena (either security or development) looks at a core issue area in international relations: aid, humanitarian assistance, governance, health, poverty, trade and resources, and demography. Each of these issues is examined both from a security and from a development perspective. The order of the issues is deliberate; it starts with those that deal with aspects of the "failed" or "failing" states and counterinsurgency problem (where many analysts and practitioners have claimed there is a "nexus" between security and development) but goes on to consider a wider range of issues where the relationship between security and development has not necessarily been systematically considered.

This material provides a rich canvas on which to draw out the relationship between security and development in a variety of contexts. In chapter 1, we note that the existing literature on the security–development relationship can be categorized as broadly falling into eight different categories. These are summarized in table 16.1. We now use these same categories to assess how our authors characterized the relationship and what overall conclusions might be drawn about the security–development relationship more broadly.

We did not ask our contributors to assess explicitly the relationship between security and development but instead asked them to report on how their arena handled an issue of concern. Nevertheless, all of the chapters have significant things to say about the relationship between the two arenas, some of which produce some interesting contrasts. For example, Morrow's chapter on aid from a development perspective depicts the relationship as hierarchical, with the framework of security threats determining the existence, levels, and focus of aid. The companion chapter

Table 16.1 Conceptualizing the Security–Development Relationship

Type of Relationship	Description
Zero-sum	Security and development are framed in either–or terms where allocating resources to one detracts from the potential to achieve the other; e.g., the guns versus butter debate.
Positive-sum	Security and development are understood as mutually reinforcing; the provision of one increases the likelihood of achieving the other.
Distinct	Security and development are both viewed as important goals but are understood as distinct enterprises best pursued using different methods.
Synonymous	Security and development are basically about the same thing: ensuring that the referent object can pursue its cherished values effectively.
Sequential	Security and development are conceived as preconditions for the other; e.g., development can only progress in a secure environment or genuine national security requires a certain level of economic development.
Hierarchical	Security priorities are said to structure the choice of development projects undertaken. For some, this has produced a situation where the development industry has become a project to support the peace and stability of the North.
Selectively co-constitutive	Security and development are interconnected but in complex and not necessarily similar ways; e.g., only in certain contexts or with respect to particular issues.
Sui generis	Security and development issues are always entirely context dependent; hence, it is impossible to draw meaningful conceptual generalizations across different times and places.

by Harborne, which looks at aid from the perspective of the security arena, sees the relationship as sequential but with the potential to be positive-sum. In the two chapters on humanitarian assistance there is some agreement that the security–development relationship is, in current practice, hierarchical, but whereas Maletta and Spear suggest this produced negative outcomes, Dewan considers how to improve the relationship to make it potentially positive-sum.

The two chapters focused on the core issue of governance might have been expected to exhibit the much-vaunted "nexus" between security and development given that they are centrally concerned with the problem of dealing with "failed" and "failing" states. Yet the chapters focus on completely different aspects of governance, and we can conclude that on this issue the security–development relationship is somewhat distinct.

The chapters concerned with poverty, on the other hand, indicate a positive-sum and synonymous relationship between security and development inasmuch as both chapters are focused on alleviating poverty, albeit for different reasons and with different operative definitions of "the poor." They are the only chapter pair to do so. Indeed, in a number of the book's chapters, although there is common agreement between the security and development arenas about the data and the broad problems to be addressed, big cleavages open up as these chapters move to consider what aspects of the issues matter, why and how, and the instruments and policies that should be used to deal with them. The chapters considering health and demography would fall into this category, showing the relationship to be selectively co-constitutive on these issues.

The chapters that focus on issues unconnected to the problems of "failed" and "failing" states illustrate how different the agendas of the security and development arenas can be. For example, the chapter by Gilpin on trade and resources focuses on the problem of how these can be used to facilitate economic development, whereas the chapter by Spear sees the security arena fixed on problems of self-financing rebels, transnational actors using the trade system to hide their crimes, and a rising China using trade (in some interpretations) to its geostrategic advantage. Clearly, for Gilpin and Spear looking at trade and resources, the security–development relationship is distinct, focused on completely different aspects of the issue.

Reflecting on the evidence about the seven core issue areas covered in this book, the relationship between security and development is selectively co-constitutive; there are points where the arenas come together and points where they are far apart. Where the two arenas are closer together tends to be where the paradigms being used are not the traditional statist ones but are focused on individuals (often scaled up in groups) as the referent objects. The next section examines the problems and possibilities of the statist paradigms before turning to consider the heterodox alternative.

PARADIGMS LOST?

As noted in chapter 1, traditionally both the security and the development arenas have worked with paradigms that focused on the sovereign state as both the referent object—the object to be developed and secured—and as the principal level of analysis for thinking about issues and delivering policies. One fundamental problem with such an approach is the sheer diversity of sovereign states: can a paradigm that conceptualizes the United States, Tuvalu, Sweden, Somalia, and North Korea as similar entities really provide an adequate basis for theorizing, let alone actually providing, security and development? A second problem is that states and other forms of political community represent the means to deliver security and development to the human beings within them; the continued survival of these entities is not an end in itself.

Moreover, even when both arenas continue to work with a statist paradigm, what they want to achieve is usually completely different. To illustrate, when the security and development arenas look at the problem of a "failed" or "failing" state (from a statist paradigm), the major security concern is about the potential for that state to become a safe haven for terrorism and insurgency—that is, the potential threat it poses to external actors. By contrast, even when working at the same level of analysis, the principal development problem is the state's inability to provide economic development for its citizens. These conceptions of the problem naturally demand rather different policy remedies. Although there is often common agreement on the need to strengthen the state and some other areas of compatibility (for example, over strengthening the levels of expertise within a government), there is often significant disagreement about the priorities, the best sequencing, and the appropriate time horizons for achieving these goals.[1] Thus, even here, using comparable statist paradigms, the security–development relationship is at best selectively co-constitutive. In reality, as discussed in several chapters in this volume, the relationship in these situations is more clearly hierarchical, where security issues inevitably trump development concerns.

In the security arena there have been a number of attempts to retool the statist paradigm to make it more applicable to dealing with contemporary real-world problems. One of these modifications has been the increasing acceptance of the need to pay attention to transnational actors, that is, nonstate actors with an ability to affect outcomes beyond the borders of the state. However, the manner in which transnational actors have been incorporated into the orthodox security paradigm has been to conceive of them as a threat to the state (which therefore remains the referent object) but not as a challenge to the paradigm as a whole.

In the development arena, a variety of different approaches have been tried to solve the problems of underdevelopment and uneven development. In pursuit of solutions some of these new approaches have moved away from the statist paradigm. They have done so, first, by challenging the idea that the state should be the main agent of development and focusing instead on markets as the most efficient way to deliver economic development. This can be seen, for example, in the approach of the US Millennium Challenge Corporation or International Monetary Fund policies. But they have also challenged the state's place as the central referent object by recognizing that governments are often impediments to development rather than an enabler. From this more market-based perspective the state apparatus should not be particularly large and governments have been encouraged to pare back their expenditures; to privatize and deregulate many functions to become attractive places to engage in transnational business. Nevertheless, even these more market-focused approaches need functioning states to ensure stability and provide a regulatory environment within which business can be conducted in a predictable manner. What are supposed to emerge are relatively lean state structures designed first and foremost to facilitate the operations of markets but not interfere with them unduly.

Where the development arena is working with a market-oriented paradigm but the security arena is working with a statist paradigm, there are obviously going to be tensions. Some of these tensions can be seen in situations where the development arena has been calling for certain types of aid conditionality or selectivity, or both, designed to facilitate markets (e.g., ending subsidies on basic foods such as grains), but where these policies might increase security problems by hollowing

out the state. For example, in the 1990s Egypt implemented these types of structural adjustment programs to facilitate market-stimulated economic development.
This was a massive change from the Nasserite policies of state provision of food,
welfare, and economic development. One direct consequence was that "in an important sense, the regime became hollow. It had effectively renounced the ideology
on which it was based and the principles that gave it legitimacy. Thus development
did not, in itself, constitute a threat to regime stability. . . . However, by abandoning any pretense of upholding the basic premises of statism, the regime created an
opportunity for alternative conceptions of the policy to develop and gain broader
support."[2] Interestingly it seems that the United States intervened in the early
1990s to ensure that laxer economic conditionality was applied to Egypt out of
concern for the stability of the Egyptian state at a time of regional turmoil.[3] This
is another example of the hierarchical relationship between security and development when the statist paradigm of security is combined with a market paradigm
of development.

PARADIGMS FOUND?

Clearly there are continuing—potentially insurmountable—challenges in trying to
improve the security–development relationship when the two arenas are working
with incompatible aims and paradigms. A potentially more fruitful paradigmatic
combination would involve security accepting the individual as its primary referent object and development working from an individual, bottom-up perspective.

Adopting a human security paradigm brings a larger number of topics into
the purview of the security arena, but many of these issues have been of concern
to the development arena for many years. Moreover, in such circumstances, there
would be a greater degree of alignment over what the arenas wanted to do about
the issue in question. For example, looking at the issue of poverty from a human
security perspective means that there are many more synergies with the development arena's approaches to poverty alleviation. This was why both Williams and
Sud could conceive of the approaches to poverty as being positive-sum and synonymous (see chapters 10 and 11).

Looking at security issues from a human security paradigm has several advantages in terms of creating synergies between security and development. One of
them is the greater compatibility of time horizons. As was noted in chapter 1, the
statist security paradigm works with radically shorter time horizons than (even the
statist) development paradigm. Another is that using a human security approach
effectively will actually have positive implications for state security and development, at least over the long term. Not only does the human security paradigm help
illuminate problems that were previously obscured by the statist perspective, but in
the long run it also provides the best route to stabilizing the state system. As this
book goes to press the mass protests taking place against regimes across northern
Africa demonstrate only too clearly what can happen if governments continue to
deny their people security and development. To pursue policies that simply try to

keep the lid on such outbursts is shortsighted and counterproductive to long-term stability. Ultimately, stable governments are those that work hard to give their people security and development.

Finally, we should address head-on one of the common problems leveled against the human security paradigm: how to prioritize issues among such a broad threat agenda. Our response is that this cannot and should not be settled at the abstract level alone. While theoretical discussion can identify generic categories of potential threats, it is only through analyzing real places and their unique challenges that analysts and practitioners can decide which issues deserve priority in any given situation. In other words, prioritization should be the result of a political process rather than conceptual adjudication. This means that even a long book such as this one should not be seen as providing all the answers—the comparative conversation needs to continue.

Notes

1. Of course, it is also important to note that, at least in the short term, attempts to increase state capacity may well increase the levels of conflict and insecurity as well as set back the development prospects of some segments of the population. This is especially likely to occur if the regime in question is widely perceived as illegitimate. There is no more compelling illustration of this problem than contemporary Somalia. See Ken Menkhaus, "Governance without Government in Somalia," *International Security* 31, no. 3 (2006–7): 74–106.

2. Bruce K. Rutherford, *Egypt after Mubarak: Liberalism, Islam, and Democracy in the Arab World* (Princeton, NJ: Princeton University Press, 2008), 140.

3. Tony Walker, "Baker in Pledge on Egypt Aid," *Financial Times*, March 12, 1991.

ABOUT THE CONTRIBUTORS

Alasdair Bowie is associate professor of political science and international affairs at the George Washington University and a policy research affiliate at the George Washington University Institute for Public Policy. A 2010–11 Fulbright research scholar and former Wilson Fellow, Dr. Bowie's research focuses on decentralizing government, democratization, and local economic governance in Indonesia and Vietnam. He has written *The Politics of Open Economies: Indonesia, Malaysia, the Philippines and Thailand* (with Danny Unger; Cambridge University Press, 1997) and *Crossing the Industrial Divide: State, Society and the Politics of Economic Transformation in Malaysia* (Columbia University Press, 1991). He holds a PhD from the University of California, Berkeley.

Richard P. Cincotta is the demographer-in-residence at the Henry L. Stimson Center in Washington, DC, and a consultant on political and environmental demography for the Woodrow Wilson Center's Environmental Change and Security Project. His research focuses on the demographic transition and human migration, and he has published on their relationships to ethnoreligious politics, to the onset of civil conflict, to regime type and political stability, to natural resource dynamics, to human health, and to population policies.

Sabina Dewan is the associate director of international economic policy at the Center for American Progress where she works on economic issues ranging from the role of globalization to that of trade, aid, and monetary policies in raising living standards around the globe. Sabina also directs the Just Jobs Program at the Center for American Progress, which explores ways to extend the benefits of economic integration and trade to all workers who power the global economy. Prior to joining the Center for American Progress, she was a research analyst at the International Labor Organization in Geneva, Switzerland. She holds masters degrees from the Catholic University of Brussels and from the University of California, Los Angeles. She has traveled widely and has lived in such countries as Afghanistan, Sierra Leone, and India.

George C. Fidas is an adjunct professor at The George Washington University's Elliott School of International Affairs and has served as visiting professor at the National Defense University and the National Defense Intelligence College. He also served tours in several government agencies, including the Department of State and the National Intelligence Council. He was the principal drafter of the National Intelligence Estimate, *The Global Infectious Disease Threat and Its Implications* *for the United States* (National Intelligence Council); authored the chapter "Health and National Security" in *Divided Diplomacy and the Next Administration*, edited by Henry R. Nau and David Shambaugh (George Washington University, 2004); and has presented several papers on health and security issues in European and US forums. He holds a master's degree from the University of Rhode Island and has done additional graduate work at the University of Maryland.

Julie E. Fischer leads the Henry L. Stimson Center's Global Health Security project, which explores the tools, policies, programs, and partnerships that strengthen global capabilities for disease detection and response. She previously worked as an International Affairs Fellow, AAAS Congressional Science and Technology Fellow, and professional staff with the Senate Committee on Veterans' Affairs. She served as a senior research fellow at the Seattle Biomedical Research Institute and as an independent consultant to a Thai–US collaboration aimed at strengthening capacities to identify and control emerging infections of regional and global significance. Dr. Fischer holds a PhD in microbiology and immunology from Vanderbilt University.

Raymond Gilpin directs the Sustainable Economies Centers of Innovation at the United States Institute of Peace in Washington, DC. He leads the institute's work on analyzing relationships among economic actors during all stages of conflict and designing appropriate capacity-building and tools for conflict environments. He also teaches the economics and conflict course at the USIP Academy and manages the Web-based International Network for Economics and Conflict. He holds a doctorate in development economics from Cambridge University in the United Kingdom.

Jack A. Goldstone (PhD Harvard) is Hazel Professor of Public Policy and a Fellow of the Mercatus Center of George Mason University. He has won prizes from the American Sociological Association and the Historical Society for his research on revolutions and social change, and has won grants from the MacArthur Foundation, the US Institute of Peace, and the National Science Foundation. He recently led a National Academy of Sciences study of USAID democracy assistance and worked with USAID, DFID, and the US State and Defense departments on developing their operations in fragile states. His latest books are *Why Europe? The Rise of the West 1500–1850* (McGraw-Hill, 2008) and *Political Demography: Identities, Change, and Conflict* (Paradigm, 2011).

Bernard Harborne is the lead conflict adviser for the Africa Region in the World Bank. He has been with the World Bank since 2004, advising on policy and operational aspects of the Bank's work in fragile and conflict-affected states. From 2007 to 2008 he was the country manager in Côte d'Ivoire. Before the World Bank, he worked and lived for a decade in various places: in Gaza in the Palestinian Territories and then Cambodia as a human rights lawyer, and for seven years in

Africa with the UN, with his last posting as head of the UN Coordination Office for Somalia. He then worked for two years with the British government in London as the senior conflict adviser for Africa, managing the Africa Conflict Prevention Fund. He started his career as a lawyer for five years in the United Kingdom with an international law master's degree from the London School of Economics.

Terrence Lyons is associate professor at the School for Conflict Analysis and Resolution and codirector of the Center for Global Studies at George Mason University. His publications include *Politics from Afar: Transnational Diasporas and Networks* (coedited with Peter Mandaville; Hurst/Columbia University Press, 2011); *Avoiding Conflict in the Horn of Africa: US Policy toward Ethiopia and Eritrea* (Council on Foreign Relations, 2006); and *Demilitarizing Politics: Elections on the Uncertain Road to Peace* (Lynne Rienner, 2005), as well as numerous articles in a range of journals and policy-oriented publications.

Robert Maletta was Oxfam's Senior Policy Adviser on Somalia during the most recent turbulent phase of that country's history. His Somalia experience goes back to the days before the collapse of the national government, and during and after the civil war. For more than twenty years he has lived, worked, and traveled throughout the Somali-inhabited areas of the Horn of Africa. His policy expertise is grounded in his operational management of aid agencies in complex environments and his involvement in emergency response activities in the Sudan, Somalia, Rwanda, Burundi, and Ethiopia. He is also a UK-registered photojournalist and for several years documented peacebuilding and conflict management activities in Somaliland, South Africa, Uganda, and northern Kenya for purposes of advocacy and raising awareness among policymakers.

Daniel Morrow taught courses related to aid effectiveness and economic policies toward developing countries at the Elliott School of International Affairs, George Washington University, from 2003 through 2009. His recent publications include "Adjusting Conditionality: Prescriptions for Policy-Based Lending," in *Conditionality Revisited: Concepts, Experiences, and Lessons*, edited by S. Koeberle et al. (World Bank, 2005). He worked at the World Bank as regular staff from 1979 through 2001, and as a consultant since that time, focusing most recently on poverty reduction strategies for low-income countries and aid effectiveness initiatives. He holds a PhD in public policy from Harvard University and a BA from Stanford University.

Joanna Spear is director of the Security Policy Studies Program and associate professor of international affairs in the Elliott School of International Affairs at the George Washington University. She was previously a senior lecturer in the Department of War Studies, King's College London. Her research interests include the global trade in weapons, disarming, demobilizing, and reintegrating military forces after conflict, and the role of the military as a development actor. She holds a PhD from the University of Southampton and completed her postdoctoral work at Harvard University.

Inder Sud is principal, Results for Development Institute in Washington, DC, and director of the international affairs MA program at the Elliott School of International Affairs, George Washington University. He also consults for a number of aid organizations and has advised several developing country governments. He holds a PhD from Stanford University.

Paul D. Williams is associate professor in the Elliott School of International Affairs at the George Washington University where he is associate director of the Security Policy Studies Program. His research interests lie in contemporary peace operations, Africa's international relations, and theories of international security. His books include *War and Conflict in Africa* (Polity, 2011); *British Foreign Policy under New Labour, 1997–2005* (Palgrave-Macmillan, 2005); *Understanding Peacekeeping*, 2nd ed. (Polity, 2010); and *Security Studies: An Introduction* (Routledge, 2nd ed. 2012). He holds a PhD from the University of Wales, Aberystwyth.

INDEX

3D (defense, diplomacy, development),
    42, 77
9/11 attacks, 8, 15, 18, 58, 87, 103, 115,
    154

access to land, 219, 226
Aceh, 81, 233
Adelman, Kenneth, 26
aerial bombing, 40
Afghanistan
    China's trade with, 259
    collapse of Najibullah government, 120
    demographics of, 183, 272, 274, 277,
        293–94, 300
    development assistance, 16, 18, 39,
        41–44, 58, 64, 83–84, 102, 104
    lessons learned from, 23, 25, 65, 67, 107,
        143, 150
    National Solidarity Program, 65
    NATO, 275
    Provincial Reconstruction Teams (PRTs),
        25, 48, 51
    public-private partnerships, 218
    refugees, 79
    terrorism (as a result of poverty), 199–
        200
    UNDP Human Development Index, 197
    US operations in, 9, 15, 22, 80, 83
Africa
    East, 163, 299
    North, 211, 298, 301
    South. See South Africa.
    Southern, 161–62, 271
    sub-Saharan
        age-structural transition, 294, 306
        "diseases of poverty" (HIV/AIDS,
            tuberculosis, and malaria), 154,
            156–60, 163, 171, 174–75, 177–78
        economic performance, 133, 176,
            210–11, 221
        globalization, 255
        urbanization, 287
    West, 79, 163, 201, 234, 257
African Peer Review Mechanism, 137
African Union, 7, 24, 236, 255

aging populations, 275, 278–85, 292,
    302–3, 307–8
agricultural development, 97–98, 102, 220,
    256, 260, 305
aid
    conditionality of, 60, 142, 236, 240,
        316–17
    coordination, attempts to improve, 40,
        43, 65, 85–86. See also whole-of-
        government approaches.
    delivery, privatization of, 80
    effectiveness, how to measure, 18, 59
    to fragile states, 23, 44–46, 49, 58,
        63–68, 74
    improving effectiveness of, 60–63, 68, 74
    multidonor trust funds (MDTF), 43
    multilateral versus bilateral, 44
    negative effects of large influxes, 45–
        46, 49
    problem of improving effectiveness of,
        46–47, 59–62
    or trade, 247–48, 261
    for transition economies, 57–58
    trends in foreign, 39–43, 45–49
    utilization by militaries for
        counterinsurgency, 41–42, 48, 83
Albania, 275
al-Qaeda, 41, 84, 86, 104, 200
al-Shabaab (Harakat al-Shabaab al-
    Mujahideen), 86, 89
American Red Cross, 181
Angola
    demographics of, 183, 272
    economy of, 262
    and HIV prevalence in military, 160
    and peacebuilding, 125–26
    UNITA and MPLA exploitation of
        resources, 121
    UNITA use of violence and conscription,
        122
Annan, Kofi, 7
Arab Sunni radicals, 200
armed conflict
    and aid, 39, 48, 111
    changing nature of, 15, 40, 230

armed conflict (*continued*)
  and demographic challenges, 157, 311
  and governance, 115–18, 120, 141,
      200–201
  and poverty, 102–3, 196–99
  and transitions to peace, 44–45, 124–26,
      205, 226
Asia
  Asia Pacific Economic Cooperation
      forum, 236
  Central
    and China, 238
    demographics of, 275, 294, 299, 306
    development aid to, 57
    poverty in, 211
  East
    IMF structural adjustment programs
        for, 216
    East Asian Tiger economies, 209, 252,
        258, 297
  South, 174–75, 210, 271–72, 276, 284
  Southeast, 143, 171, 175, 181, 238, 271
Association of Southeast Asian Nations,
    255
Australia, 281, 285
authoritative allocation of resources, 4,
    131, 137–38

"balloon effect," 235
Bangladesh, 79, 162, 254, 273
Barre, Siad, 85
Belarus, 161, 279
Benin, 257, 274
bird flu, 163, 189
Blair, Tony, 193
Bolivia, 213, 215, 274
Bono, 26
Bosnia-Herzegovina, 42, 79, 121, 122,
    201
Botswana, 159, 164–65, 209, 297–98
"bottom billion," 233, 247
Brahimi Report, 25
Brazil
  and AIDS, 164, 166
  cash transfer programs, 219
  decentralization programs, 144
  demographics of, 273, 297–98
  and development aid, 39
  in international institutions, 275, 289
  and trade, 254, 262
  urbanization of, 204
  and the Washington Consensus, 215

BRIC (Brazil, Russia, India, China)
    countries, 39, 50
Brundtland, Gro Harlem, 177
Burkina Faso, 257, 274
Burma/Myanmar, 11, 273
Burundi, 50, 197, 237, 274
Bush, George W., 199
Bush, George W. administration
  and counterinsurgency, 26
  response to AIDS, 164
  US President's Emergency Plan for AIDS
      relief (PEPFAR), 58, 156, 182, 189

Cambodia
  AIDS in, 160
  Khmer Rouge's control of resources in,
      121
  and peacebuilding, 125
  politically motivated aid to, 79
  population growth rate, 274
  and public-private partnerships, 218
Canada
  and bird flu, economic impact of, 163
  demographics of, 278–80
  immigration to, 281, 285–86
  in international institutions, 274
  and trade, 262
  whole-of-government approach, 42
cash transfer programs, 219
Central African Republic, 50, 197, 274
Chad
  and armed conflict, 197
  and China, 239
  collapse of Hissèn Habré's regime, 120
  demographics of, 272, 274
Chamie, Joseph, 307
Chavez, Hugo, 238
Cheney, Dick, 26
child soldiers, 122, 157–58, 165
Chile, 180, 220, 297–98, 302
China, People's Republic of
  alternative to the neoliberal
      development model, 216, 240, 259
  approach to trade and resources, 5, 230,
      235–41, 251, 254, 259, 261–62, 267,
      315
  China-Africa Forum, 239
  China National Petroleum Corporation,
      256
  Confucius Institutes, 237
  demographics of, 5, 183, 209, 271–73,
      278–79, 287, 297, 304

China, People's Republic of (*continued*)
  and effective leadership, 220
  as an emerging aid donor, 17, 39–40, 73,
    92, 142
  initiatives on health of, 179–181
  in international institutions, 275, 289
  and SARS, 163–64
cholera, 160, 163, 174
civil liberties, 8, 301
civil-military relations in hostile
  environments, 104
civil wars
  and aid, 106
  economic explanations of, 229–34,
    271
  and governance, 116–19, 127
  as international security threats, 1, 271
  and population demographics, 157
  poverty as an explanation of, 196–97
clientelism, 66
Clinton administration
  in contrast to post-9/11 military policy, 41
  on democratization as a security goal, 9
  response to AIDS, 164
Clooney, George, 26
Cold War
  mentality of, 12, 17, 39, 43, 57, 78–89,
    82, 111, 121, 193, 234
  end of and postwar trends, 8, 13, 20, 40,
    45, 57, 79–80, 150, 193, 196, 229,
    234, 237, 257, 271
Colombia, 11, 50, 237, 274, 298
combatants
  and excombatants, 48–49, 51
  FDLR (Forces Démocratiques pour la
    Libération du Rwanda), 47
  humanitarian aid to, 82
  self-financing by, 5, 230, 234, 241, 255,
    267–68
complex humanitarian emergencies, 80,
  107, 183
conditionality, 60, 142, 236, 240, 316–17
conflict assessments, 43, 46
conflict prevention, 20, 22, 44, 50, 196
conflict transformation, 101, 123–26
"conflict trap," 141
Côte d'Ivoire, 162, 274
Cotonou Agreement, 134
counterinsurgency (COIN)
  Counterinsurgency Field Manual, 27, 83
  and development aid, 42, 48, 51,
    111

and the security-development nexus, 1,
  4, 7, 313
  in Somalia, 89–90
  US military strategy, 26–27
counterterrorism measures, 47–48, 73, 90
Croatia, 162, 262
Cuba, 238–39
Cyclone Nargis, 11

Declaration of Alma-Ata (1978), 175–76,
  178
defense
  and AIDS awareness, 164–65
  impact of disease on, 153, 158–59
  relationship to development, 7, 15,
    38–39, 42, 47, 77, 108, 189
  spending on, 9, 41, 155–56, 166, 232,
    281
demilitarization of politics, 123–26
demobilization, 22, 25, 48–49, 73,
  125–26. *See also* disarmament,
  demobilization and reintegration
  (DDR) of excombatants.
democratic peace thesis, 9, 116
Democratic People's Republic of Korea
  (North Korea), 106, 202, 315
Democratic Republic of Congo (DRC)
  aid to, 44, 49, 51, 84, 102, 233
  and China, 44, 240
  conflict in, 37–38, 46–47, 197, 204
  demographics of, 272–74, 277, 300
  economy of, 252, 255, 262
  and health challenges, 183
  and HIV prevalence in the military, 160
  UN peacekeeping mission in, 162
demographics
  Coale-Hoover hypothesis, 299
  Coalesian paradigm, 292
  decline in working-age populations, 171,
    278–81
  demographic bonus, 301–2, 306
  demographic cresting, 5, 291, 312
  demographic shifts, 272–75, 294, 302,
    308
  impact of, 275–81
  demographic transition, 293–94, 311
  and age-structural transition, 294–97,
    299–300, 306
  disease-related shifts in, 156–58
  effects of HIV/AIDS, 153–54, 156–58
  effects on military capacities, 274–75
  impact of disease on, 160–62

demographics (*continued*)
exacerbating security threats, 156–58, 274–78, 288–89
global trends in, 5, 271–83
growth in Islamic societies, 272–76
immigration, 271, 281–87, 289
low and high fertility traps, 297–99
NATO effects on, 274–75, 289, 311
neo-Malthusian paradigm, 291–92, 311
"Preston curve," 181
reverse flow of older migrants, 282, 286–87, 289
youth bulge, 157–58, 271, 276–78, 300, 306
Department for International Development (UK), 140
Department of Defense (US), 9, 27, 99, 104, 106
dependency theory, 250–51
developmentalization of the military, 78, 83–84
development assistance. *See also* Official Development Assistance (ODA).
diversion after Cold War, 8–9, 39–40, 43–44, 57–69, 80, 86, 140, 142, 145, 247, 257, 261
during the Cold War, 57, 132
in relation to humanitarian assistance, 97–108
diamonds, 121, 250
diplomacy, 74, 81, 91, 111. *See also* disaster diplomacy.
and China, 237–38
as part of the 3D agenda, 7, 38, 42, 77
disarmament, demobilization, and reintegration (DDR) of excombatants, 22, 25, 48–49, 73, 125–26
disaster diplomacy, 78, 80–81, 91, 111
disease
costs of fighting, 166
deaths from, 154, 156–57, 171–72, 297
economic toll from, 158–59, 171–72, 174, 177–78
effects on supply of peacekeepers, 162–63
new and reemerging, 154–55
threat to militaries, 160–62
Djibouti, 48, 89
donors
BRIC, 39, 50

China's practices, 17, 39–40, 73, 142, 236–37
Gates Foundation, 17, 39, 182
new, 17, 39–40, 73, 80, 92, 142
preferences in health, 182–83
Rockefeller Foundation, 175, 179
traditional, 39–40, 42

East Timor/Timor-Leste, 43, 65, 274, 299
economic development
and demographics, 278, 292
market approach to, 236, 316–17
relationship to governance, 131, 133, 137, 139–41
relationship to health, 156, 164, 175, 177, 179, 184, 297
relationship to security, 7, 21, 57–58
relationship to trade, 5, 8, 247–49, 251–54, 257–58, 263, 267
economic growth
and poverty reduction, 201, 210–11, 214–17
relationship to demographics, 272, 274–76, 280, 284, 299, 302
relationship to development, 5, 12–13, 37, 58, 136, 139, 143, 149, 221, 225, 251, 268
relationship to health, 153, 156, 158, 171, 176–77, 180–81
relationship to security, 202, 289
relationship to trade, 247–49, 251–53, 258–61, 263
Ecuador, 237
Egypt, 257, 273–74, 275, 317
elections, 4, 22–23, 25, 46, 118, 123, 125–26, 135, 159
El Salvador, 121, 125
enclave investors, 252
Enhanced Integrated Framework, 263
Eritrea, 119, 162, 237, 274
Ethiopia, 48, 183, 197, 237
aid to, 44, 58, 79, 105
demographics of, 272–74
forces in Somalia, 86–87, 89
Europe
as aid donor, 40–41
and China, 238, 240
decline in working-age population, 271–72, 278–83, 302–3, 308
and disease, 163, 165, 172–75
Eastern, 57, 252, 259

Europe (*continued*)
  economy of, 9, 229, 250–51, 253, 256–57, 289
  immigration to, 284–86, 288
  low fertility rates, 294, 299, 307
  poverty in, 211
  securitization and, 14, 22
  Western, 137, 176, 254
European Union (EU), 24, 133–34, 136, 138, 194, 255, 257, 284, 286
  Common Agricultural Policy, 256
Export Concentration Index, 262

F-22 debate over funding, 9
failed states, 1–2, 4, 18, 20
  aid to, 41, 63–68
  correlation with high infant-mortality rates, 156
  poverty and, 194–95, 200–201, 205, 226
  security threats posed by, 15, 57, 115, 158, 200, 288
fair trade, 260
financial accountability, 66
Financial Action Task Force, 47
Finland, 279
food insecurity, 173, 178, 220, 304–5
foreign direct investment (FDI), 236, 282
fragile states, 23, 44, 49, 58, 63–68, 74, 101, 255, 263, 288
France, 158, 198, 273–74, 278–79, 282, 284, 299
Freedom House, 213, 300
free trade, 176, 229, 239–40, 250, 255, 258, 260

Gabon, 238, 252, 274
Gates, Robert, 24
Gates Foundation, 17, 39, 182
Geneva Conventions, 77
genocide, 14, 18, 41, 45, 101, 117, 239, 271
Germany, 22, 273–74, 279, 295, 299, 302
Ghana, 61–62, 198, 209, 274
Ghani, Ashraf, 64
Global Alliance for Vaccines and Immunization, 182
global financial crisis, 37, 216, 251–54, 261, 280
Global Fund to Fight AIDS, Tuberculosis and Malaria, 58, 61, 156, 159, 164, 182

globalization, 12, 163, 171–72, 184, 212, 217, 229, 234, 247, 253, 255, 262, 267
global war on terrorism (GWOT), 41, 80–81, 85, 88, 90, 92, 105
Goma peace engagement (Democratic Republic of Congo), 37
governance
  and civil war onset, 116–18
  and decentralization, 143–45
  definitions of, in development, 8, 131–38, 149
  during war, 118–23
  "good" governance, 6, 13, 40, 131–39, 141–43, 145
  impact of disease on, 155, 159–60, 166, 189
  measurement of, 44, 48, 249
  and peacebuilding, 123–26, 225
  and population growth, 288
  in relation to development, 63, 103, 138–42, 149, 212
  and trade, 251, 258–60
Great Depression, 256, 280
Greece, 80, 279
greed and grievance
  debate, 230–34
  driving conflict, 45, 118–19, 197–200, 231
gross domestic product (GDP), 37, 135, 158–59, 177, 212, 234, 248, 302
gross national income (GNI), 9, 179, 273
Group of Eight (G8), 274–75, 289, 311
Group of Twenty (G20), 275
GTZ (German development cooperation), 44
Guatemala, 272, 274
Guinea, 237, 262, 274
Guinea-Bissau, 50, 201, 274
Gulf States, 297

Haiti, 43, 51, 160, 274
  failures of aid to, 67
  Haitian Stabilization Initiative (HIS), 98–99
Hamas, 198, 200
health
  costs of poor health, 158–59, 177–78
  efforts to improve through aid, 89, 97–98, 104, 106, 181–83, 189–90, 298, 306

health (*continued*)
   and governance, 102–3, 159–60, 217–18,
      251, 303
   "Health for All" agenda, 176–78
   in Millennium Development Goals, 177
   and population age structures, 180–81,
      297, 300–301, 307
   in relation to poverty, 171–74, 183–85,
      193, 205, 210–14
   and the Rockefeller Foundation, 178–80
   and security, 2, 4–5, 7, 14, 19, 25, 27,
      58, 153–58, 160–67, 189, 195, 198,
      200
health workers global shortage, 182
Hezbollah, 18, 82, 200
HIV/AIDS
   Bush administration response, 164
   children orphaned by in Africa, 157
   Clinton administration response, 164
   costs of, 165–66, 177–78
   deaths from, 41, 153–54, 157, 159–60,
      171
   as a "disease of poverty," 174, 177, 189,
      193
   and fertility rates, 298–99
   and globalization, 163
   Joint United Nations Program on
      HIV/AIDs (UNAIDS), 157, 165–66
   as part of the Millennium Development
      Goals, 18, 177
   and security, 25, 153, 156, 158–60
   toll on militaries, 160–63
   US President's Emergency Plan for AIDS
      relief (PEPFAR), 58, 156, 182, 189
Hizbul Islam (Somalia), 86
Hobbes, Thomas, 156
household-level data analysis, 50
humanitarian assistance
   instrumentalization of, 16, 77–81, 90–
      92, 104, 111–12
   and rebels' use of, 81–83
   military delivery of, 83–84
   relationship to development assistance,
      16, 97–103, 105–8, 111–12
   in Somalia, 85–90
humanitarian disasters in Somalia, 85–90
humanitarianism, 77, 99–100, 172
human rights:
   abuse of, 41, 87–88, 117–18, 239
   in the development discourse, 7, 14,
      133–36, 240
   international framework, 175

human security, 1, 7, 19–20, 58, 62, 68, 79,
      111, 189, 194–95, 205, 235, 240–41,
      267–68, 317–18
   definitions of, 12–13, 23, 57, 155–56
Human Security Gateway, 25
Hutchison Whampoa, 239

immigration, 154, 271, 281–87
   assimilation, 285–86
   to Europe, 281–87, 307
   and Japan, 294
   to the US, 281–87, 303
India
   as an aid donor, 17, 39
   demographics of, 272–73, 287, 298, 301,
      304–5
   economy of, 210, 216, 251–52, 275, 284,
      289
   and HIV/AIDS, 160–62
   and poor health, 183
   and poverty, 209, 212
   and trade, 254, 257, 261
Indonesia, 105, 183, 220, 251, 262, 272–
      73, 275–76, 297, 300
   Kecanatan Development Program,
      144–45
inequality
   between groups, 194, 213
   between individuals, 158, 205, 212, 226
   between states, 23, 202–3, 205, 226
   consequences of, 195–98, 202–3, 205,
      213–14, 217

infant mortality rates, 166, 171, 175–76,
      183–84, 214, 276
   in China, 180
   correlated with state failure, 156–57
   and demographic transition, 293, 297
   as a Millennium Development Goal,
      177
   reductions in Thailand, 179
influenza (flu), 154, 163, 189
instrumentalization, 8, 20, 27
insurgencies, 27, 117, 119–21, 123, 198,
      225, 271, 288
InterAction, 104
Inter-American Development Bank, 236
International Committee of the Red Cross,
      100
International Covenant on Economic,
      Social and Cultural Rights (1976),
      175

International Crisis Group, 26
international financial institutions (IFIs), 24, 37, 47, 172, 176, 203. *See also* World Bank; International Monetary Fund.
International Health Regulations (IHR 2005), 184
International Monetary Fund (IMF), 61, 176, 216, 316
Iran, 82, 106, 273, 276, 294–95, 298
Iraq
  aid to, 18, 22–23, 39, 43–44, 51, 58, 64–66, 79
  conflict in, 9, 15–16, 26–27, 40–43, 58, 83–84, 150, 197
  and demographics, 274, 277
  and economy, 262, 272
  and governance, 143
  and Provincial Reconstruction Teams (PRTs), 25, 48
Ireland, 174, 274, 278–79, 302
Islamic Courts Union (Somalia), 86
Islamic Salvation Front (Algeria), 198
Israel, 11, 45, 82, 274
  Israeli-Lebanese War (2006), 18, 104
Italy, 273–74, 279, 293, 295, 299, 302

Japan
  aging population, 278–83, 293–95, 299, 302, 308
  aid from, 57
  demographics of, 272–74, 303
  immigration to, 281–82, 286
  and inequality, 195, 213
Jintao, Hu, 237
Johnson Sirleaf, Ellen, 103
Jolie, Angelina, 26

Kant, Immanuel, 9
Kashmir, 81–82, 84
Kazakhstan, 259
Kenya, 46, 84–85, 105, 162, 197, 209, 274, 298
Korea, Republic of, 202, 216, 220, 262, 278–79, 294, 297, 299–300, 304
Kosovo, 25, 41
Kuhn, Thomas, 12
Kyrgyzstan, 259

landmines, 17
Latin America, 50, 123, 143, 163, 176, 204, 282, 289

and demographics, 272, 276, 297–98, 301, 304
and poverty, 209, 211, 215, 219
and trade, 236–38, 240, 247, 250–51, 254, 256–57
Lebanon, 18, 82, 262. *See also* Israeli-Lebanese War (2006).
lessons learned, 25
levels of analysis, 12, 190, 225, 241, 311
liberal governance, 115–16, 150
  neoliberal economic policies, 13, 176, 215, 229
liberalization, 8, 13, 164, 172, 174, 176, 215, 257–58
liberal peace or liberal internationalism, 20
Liberation Tigers of Tamil Eelam (LTTE), 81–82
Liberia, 45, 48, 103, 118–19, 121–22, 126, 162, 198, 274
  National Patriotic Front for Liberia, 118, 121–22
life expectancies, 153, 156–57, 171–72, 176, 183–84, 195, 210, 293
  in China, 180–81
Lomé Convention, 134, 138
Lord's Resistance Army, 122

Madagascar, 274
mad cow disease, 163
Mahidol, Prince of Thailand, 178–79
malaria, 153–54, 158, 160, 165–66, 174–75, 177–78. *See also* Global Fund to Fight AIDS, Tuberculosis and Malaria.
Malawi, 160, 272, 274
Malaysia, 180, 220, 274
Mali, 257, 274
Malthus, Thomas Robert, 303
  neo-Malthusian paradigm, 291–92, 311
Marshall Plan, 9
Mauritius, 216, 251
McNamara, Robert, 209
measles, 84, 172, 181, 183
Médecins Sans Frontières, 84
methodology, 3, 231–32
Mexico, 11, 219, 273, 275, 289, 297
microfinance, 13, 18, 218
Micronesia, 261–62
migration, 8, 20, 201, 203, 278, 280, 283–89, 297, 299–300
  reverse flow of older migrants, 282, 286–87

militarized contractors, 15
military, 47, 83–84
　as aid donors, 78
　capacity of, 17, 156, 27
　in China, 237–40
　coups, 118
　delivering aid, 15, 18, 26–27, 41–42,
　　47, 49
　"developmentalization" of, 15
　and governance, 123–26, 233
　and humanitarian assistance, 78, 81,
　　83–84, 90–91, 97, 104, 106–7
　humanitarianism, 79–80, 101, 103–5
　and insurgencies, 120–21
　lessons learned, 25
　as part of traditional security paradigm,
　　13, 17, 193, 271
　spending, 39–40, 41, 50, 59, 155, 303
　thinking about development, 38
　threat of disease to, 153, 160–62, 165,
　　189
Millennium Challenge Corporation, 18,
　　61, 142, 316
Millennium Development Goals (MDGs),
　　18, 38, 40, 142, 177, 179, 193, 210
Mkapa, Benjamin, 37
Moldova, 161
Mozambique, 125, 139, 257, 274
　aid to Frelimo government, 121
　RENAMO (Mozambican National
　　Resistance) use of violence, 122

Nagl, Lt. Col. John, 27
Namibia, 213, 238, 274
national security, 7–9, 14, 38, 41–43, 49,
　　81, 99, 163–64, 304, 314
neoliberalism, 13
　China as an alternative to, 236, 240, 259
Nepal, 105, 274
Netherlands, 42, 279, 284, 298
New International Economic Order, 202
Niger, 174, 274, 293–94
Nigeria, 39, 79, 160, 162, 165, 183, 197,
　　251, 262, 273–74
Nkunda, Laurent, 37
nongovernmental organizations (NGOs),
　　3, 11, 17, 20, 22, 25–26, 46, 62–64,
　　133, 136, 142, 153, 156, 164, 166–
　　67, 182, 218
　and humanitarian assistance, 77–80, 83,
　　85–92, 98, 100, 102–4, 106–8, 112

North Atlantic Treaty Organization
　　(NATO), 40, 82, 311
　demographic effects on 274–75, 289
Northern Ireland, 42

Obama administration, 22–24, 164
Obasanjo, Olusegun, 37
Official Development Assistance (ODA),
　　8–9, 39–40, 43–44, 50, 57–58, 106,
　　142. See also aid.
oil, 37, 237–39, 251–52, 256, 261, 297
Oman, 180, 274
Operation Enduring Freedom
　　(Afghanistan), 104
oral rehydration therapy, 173, 181
organizational culture clashes, 24–25, 42,
　　99–101
Organization for Economic Co-operation
　　and Development (OECD), 9, 44,
　　63, 73, 133–34, 136–37, 143
OECD DAC (Development Assistance
　　Committee), 23, 39, 58, 60
OECD DAC Accra Declaration (2008),
　　40, 61–62
OECD DAC Paris Declaration on Aid
　　Effectiveness (2005), 40, 60–68, 74,
　　135
Organization of American States, 236
organized crime, 15, 201–2, 234, 235
organized violence, role of low national
　　income levels in exacerbating,
　　44–45
Ottawa Convention, 17
Ould-Abdallah, Ahmedou, 88
Oxfam, 26, 257

Pakistan, 11, 44, 58, 78, 84, 162, 183,
　　199–200, 272–74, 277, 284. See also
　　Kashmir.
　earthquake (2005), 81–82
Panama Canal, 239
paradigms
　Coalesian (demographic), 292
　neo-Malthusian, 291–92, 303, 311
　linking governance and development,
　　135, 317
　shifts in development, 12, 27
　shifts in security, 12–13, 27, 42, 49–50, 57
　statist, 12, 15, 17, 50, 57, 313, 315–16
peacebuilding, 7, 45, 49–50, 117, 123–27,
　　230, 233

peacekeeping, 24, 37–38, 41, 51, 98, 153, 277, 289
China and, 236
effects of disease on, 162–63
UN Department for Peacekeeping Operations, 165
US Global Peace Operations Initiative, 162
peacemaking, 230
Pentagon, 8, 24, 26, 39, 99, 102. *See also* Department of Defense (US).
Peru, 237
Petraeus, Gen. David, 27
Philippines, 237, 274
piracy, 85, 202, 235, 240
political pacts, 123–24
Post-Conflict Needs Assessment (UN System and World Bank), 43
postconflict reconstruction, 7, 18, 20, 23, 45, 49, 64–65, 83, 86, 103, 230
poverty
absolute, 11
in aid definition, 39, 73
and armed conflict, 103, 117, 196–99
causes of, 211–13
debate over definition, 194, 209–11
and disease, 154, 174, 178–79
framework for alleviation, 214–21
in the Millennium Development Goals, 18, 38–40
reduction imperative, 107
reduction, need for leadership, 220, 226
reduction as a response to terrorism, 41, 44
reduction strategies, 12–13, 40, 58, 61, 97, 99, 102–3, 107–8, 111, 166–67, 177, 198, 217–18
reduction strategy in Liberia, 103
safety nets, 218–19
as a security threat, 193, 195–200, 202–4
and state failure, 155, 200–202
and terrorism, 158, 199–200
and trade, 247–49, 251, 256
trap, 201
and UN Development Program (UNDP), 134
Poverty Reduction Strategy Initiative (World Bank and IMF), 61
Poverty Reduction Strategy Paper (PRSP), 40
Prebisch-Singer hypothesis, 250
preferential trade agreements, 254–55

Presidential Decision Directive 25 (US), 41
privatization, 13, 80, 180, 215–16
protracted emergencies, 84, 97–98, 101–3, 106–7
Provincial Reconstruction Teams (PRTs), 25, 48, 51
public-private partnerships, 166, 182, 218

regional trade arrangements, 254
regional trading blocs, 255
relief-to-development continuum, 4, 97–98, 105, 108
complicated by protracted emergencies, 101–3
remittances, 39, 230
Al-Barakat money transfer system, 47
resources
and aid, 57, 67, 77, 82, 105, 140
allocation of, 1–2, 8–9, 19, 21, 23–24, 27, 46, 58, 83, 102, 107–8, 131–33, 136–38, 142–45, 155, 165, 172, 189, 278, 314
and China, 235–37, 240, 259
and conflict onset, 81, 119, 199, 232
and demographics, 5, 271, 275, 276, 286–87, 289, 291–92, 301, 305
and health, 4, 153, 156, 159, 165–66, 172, 174–76, 178, 180–83, 185, 189
and poverty, 201, 203, 218
sustaining conflict, 73, 117, 119, 121, 199, 234, 267
and trade, 229, 235, 247, 261–62, 267
trade by combatants, 5, 230–32, 234, 255
Rice, Condoleezza, 15
Rockefeller Foundation, 175, 179
rogue states discourse, 115
rule of law, 7, 48, 124, 132, 134–35, 138, 143, 201
rural development programs, failure of, 199–220
Russian Federation, 39, 161, 196, 215, 273–74, 279, 294, 297, 299, 303
Rwanda, 25, 38, 41, 45, 47, 62, 82, 255, 274, 300

Sao Tome, 261–62
Save the Children, 26
securitization, 4–5, 14, 78, 90
of health, 155–56, 184, 189
security communities, 116

security sector reform, 8, 25, 43–44, 125, 139. *See also* disarmament, demobilization, and reintegration (DDR).

Senegal, 164, 209, 274

Serbia, 41, 262

Severe Acute Respiratory Syndrome (SARS), 154–55, 163–64, 172, 184

Seychelles, 257

Sierra Leone, 41, 48, 50, 156, 158, 162, 183, 197, 274

  Revolutionary United Front of, 119, 122, 157, 198

Singapore, 220, 297, 299

single-commodity dependence, 258, 261–62

slums, 98, 184, 204–5, 219, 225

smallpox, 160, 172, 175

soft power, humanitarian assistance as, 78

Solomon Islands, 48

Somalia, 4, 11, 41, 43, 45, 47, 78–80, 84–91, 101–2, 115

  Transitional Federal Government, 85–90

Somaliland, 45, 86, 89

South Africa, 123, 156–57, 159–62, 164, 166, 254, 273, 298

South Korea. *See* Korea, Republic of.

South Sudan, Republic of, 252

Soviet bloc, 229, 256

Spain, 196, 278–79

statebuilding, 4, 45

State Department (US), 24, 99

  Quadrennial Diplomacy and Development Review, 24

subsidies, tariffs, and quotas, 250, 256–58, 260, 282

  effects of elimination, 215–16, 254, 257, 262

Sudan, 20, 26, 43–44, 58, 102, 197, 237, 251, 262, 274

  Chinese engagement in, 40, 239

  relations with oil companies, 256

Swaziland, 159

Sweden, 279, 282, 294, 315

Switzerland, 278–79

Syria, 274

Taiwan, 220, 238, 297, 299–300

Tajikistan, 121, 259, 274

Taliban, 64, 84, 104, 120

Tanzania, 62, 87, 139, 237, 273–74

technology and development

  cash payments via mobile (cell) phones, 50–51

  and disease, 183

  in relation to military power, 41, 105

  as a solution to aging populations, 281

  and trade, 247, 250–51, 255, 258, 260–63, 267, 304

terrorism. *See also* global war on terrorism (GWOT).

  and bioterrorism, 189

  and failed states, 1, 16, 85, 200–202, 271, 315

  and immigration, 285

  in Muslim-Western relations, 283

  post-9/11, 38, 41, 105, 112, 154

  and poverty, 44, 158, 195, 199–200, 205, 225–26, 275

  and rogue states, 115

  and trade, 235

Thailand, 79, 160, 164, 178–79, 262, 273, 297, 300

trade. *See also* liberalization; preferential trade agreements; regional trade arrangements.

  and China, 235–41, 259, 267, 315

  and disease, 172, 174, 189

  during conflict, 121, 230–31, 234, 267, 315

  and economic development, 1, 5, 8, 18, 176, 247–48, 251–53, 256–63, 267–68, 282, 292, 315

  and economic growth, 248–49

  recent trends in, 253–56

  theory of, 249–51

  transnational nature of, 193, 229, 234–35, 267, 315

Transitional Results Matrices (UN and World Bank), 43

transnational actors, 202–3, 204, 230, 234–35, 255–56, 267–68, 315–16. *See also* organized crime.

transnational networks, 201, 234–35, 267

transnational threats, 5, 12, 15, 44, 85, 234–35, 241

Trans-Sahara Counterterrorism Partnership (2006), 47–48

tsunami, 81–82, 104

tuberculosis, 153–54, 172, 174. *See also* Global Fund to Fight AIDS, Tuberculosis, and Malaria.

Turkey, 80, 273, 275, 277, 286, 289, 298

Turkmenistan, 259

Uganda, 46, 139, 158, 160, 164, 197, 255, 274, 293
Lord's Resistance Army, 122
National Resistance Movement of Uganda, 119
Ukraine, 161, 279, 297
UN Children's Fund (UNICEF), 89, 175–76, 181
UN Department for Peacekeeping Operations, 165
UN Department of Political Affairs, 90
UN Development Program (UNDP), 13, 23, 85, 89, 91, 133–34, 136–37, 197, 210–11, 249
Human Development Index, 197, 249
Human Development Report (1994), 13, 23
human poverty index, 210
UN Economic Commission for Africa "Economic Report on Africa 2008," 251
UN High Commission for Refugees (UNHCR), 25–26, 89
United Kingdom, 7, 42, 163, 196, 272–74, 279, 284, 298
Department for International Development, 140
threats to exacerbated by poverty, 193
United Nations, 4, 7, 9, 79, 112, 156, 193, 287
United Nations Joint Program on HIV/AIDS (UNAIDS), 157, 165–66
United States
9/11 attacks on, 15, 41, 58, 80, 103–5, 115, 154
bombing of US embassies in Kenya and Tanzania, 87
Centers for Disease Control and Prevention, 181
Combined Joint Task Force for the Horn of Africa (CJTF HOA), 48
Commander's Emergency Response Program (CERP), 18, 83
concerns about China, 5, 230, 238–40
Congress, 164–65
demographics of, 272–73, 278–83, 288–89, 303
and economic recession, 212, 253
foreign aid, 9, 18, 22–23, 61, 66, 73, 99, 106–7, 165, 298–99, 317. *See also* United States Agency for International Development (USAID).

Global Peace Operations Initiative, 162
and immigration, 281–86
infectious diseases in, 155, 158, 160, 174
and the Iraq War (2003), 26, 64, 66, 83, 150
military and disaster response (humanitarian assistance), 25–26, 64, 77–79, 81–84, 98, 103–5
National Intelligence Estimate on infectious diseases, 155
National Security Strategy (2002), 115
National Security Strategy (2006), 7
National Security Strategy (2010), 7
and policy coordination, 24, 42, 47, 77
policymaking system of, 22–23
President's Emergency Plan for AIDS relief (PEPFAR), 58, 70, 156, 182, 189
and trade, 251, 253–54, 256–57, 259, 262
United States Agency for International Development (USAID), 18, 23–24, 42, 44, 63, 83, 99, 105–6, 139–40, 292, 297
Bureau for Democracy, Conflict, and Humanitarian Assistance, 106
Office of Democracy and Governance, 139
Office of Foreign Disaster Assistance, 106
United States Institute of Peace, 116
Universal Declaration of Human Rights (1948), 175
UN Office for the Coordination of Humanitarian Affairs, 85
UN Operation in Somalia II (UNOSOM II), 85
UN Peacebuilding Commission, 49
UN Political Office for Somalia, 89
UN Population Fund, 298
UN Secretary-General's High-Level Panel on Threats, Challenges and Change (2004), 24, 193
UN Security Council (UNSC), 41, 89
UNSC Resolution 1856 (DRC), 37
Uppsala Conflict Data Program, 196-97
urbanization, 154, 171, 174, 176, 195, 204–5, 271, 287–89, 305
Uzbekistan, 259

vaccines, 173, 175, 181, 183
Venezuela, 237–38, 262, 274
Vietnam, 42, 45, 47, 62, 273, 302

Vietnam Veterans of America, 17
violence, 11, 14, 37–38, 48–51, 100–102,
  104, 154, 230, 232, 300
  and governance, 15, 24, 116–27, 132,
    138, 143, 145, 204, 212, 276
  and health, 157, 181, 183
  and immigration, 285
  and poverty, 44, 46, 197–200, 204, 212
  and urbanization, 287–88

war economies, 73, 121, 230, 233, 255
warfare, 16, 116, 120, 126, 196–97, 202,
  225, 305
  fourth generation/networked warfare, 42
  third generation/maneuver warfare, 40
warlord politics, 86, 88–90, 119, 120
war zones, 2, 42, 74, 100
Washington Consensus, 142, 214, 225
  criticisms of, 214–16
weapons, conventional, 8–9, 17, 153, 185,
  201, 241, 271, 275, 281, 321
  China's supplies to allies, 237–38
weapons of mass destruction, 115
West Bank and Gaza, 45
whole-of-government approaches, 38, 42, 77
World Bank, 23–24, 38, 41, 43, 45–46, 65,
  158, 197, 209–10, 214, 252, 297
  Doing Business report, 254
  and governance, 132–34, 136–39, 141,
    144

Growth Commission, 217
"Health for All" agenda, 176
Independent Evaluation Group (IEG), 67
Poverty Reduction Strategy Initiative, 61
Task Force for Low-Income Countries, 63
Understanding Civil War, 231
Voices of the Poor study, 212
World Development Report (1990), 210
World Health Organization (WHO), 153–
  55, 166, 172, 175, 177, 181, 182,
  184, 193
World Trade Organization (WTO), 8, 236,
  254–55, 257
  Doha trade talks, 253–54
World Trade Report (2008), 261
World War II, 39, 45, 57, 174, 250, 253,
  256, 294

Yemen, 262, 272, 274, 299
youth bulges, 157, 271, 276–77, 283, 293,
  300–301, 306, 311

Zaire, 82, 120
Zambia, 159, 162, 171, 237, 140, 252, 274
Zapatistas, 198
Zedong, Mao, 180
Zimbabwe, 40, 156–58, 160, 163, 171, 195,
  238–39, 298
  rebel recruitment, 122
Zoellick, Robert, 23